Organizational Behavior in Sport Management

Christopher R. Barnhill
Natalie L. Smith · Brent D. Oja

Organizational Behavior in Sport Management

An Applied Approach
to Understanding People
and Groups

palgrave
macmillan

Christopher R. Barnhill
Georgia Southern University
Statesboro, GA, USA

Natalie L. Smith
East Tennessee State University
Johnson City, TN, USA

Brent D. Oja
University of Northern Colorado
Greeley, CO, USA

ISBN 978-3-030-67611-7   ISBN 978-3-030-67612-4   (eBook)
https://doi.org/10.1007/978-3-030-67612-4

This Palgrave Macmillan imprint is published by the registered company Springer Nature Switzerland AG.
The registered company address is: Gewerbestrasse 11, 6330 Cham, Switzerland

Contents

Christopher R. Barnhill, PhD Barnhill is Associate Professor of Sport Management at Georgia Southern University, where he also serves as Program Coordinator and Chair of the Sport Management Advisory Board. His primary research interests include topics related to employer-employee relations and sport management education. Before entering academia, Barnhill has held ticket sales and operations positions with the Florida (Miami) Marlins, East Tennessee State University Athletics, and Kansas State Athletics.

Barnhill has received a Bachelor's of Science in Sport Management from the University of Tennessee and a Master's of Business Administration from East Tennessee State University. He holds a PhD in Sport Management from Ohio State University. You can find him on Twitter at @DrBarnhill.

Natalie L. Smith, PhD Smith is Assistant Professor of Sport and Recreation Management at East Tennessee State University, where she coordinates the Esports Management certificate. Her primary research interests include creativity and innovation in sports, #LiveitTeachit. Before entering academia, Smith has worked in operations and business development for both Sky Blue FC and the league offices of Major League Soccer. She also has industry experience in college athletics and non-profit management.

Smith received her Bachelor's degree from Pomona College, where she was also a member of the Sagehens Women's soccer team. She holds a Master's degree with the FIFA Master Program and also a PhD in Recreation, Sport, and Tourism with an emphasis in Sport Management from the University of Illinois. Find her on Twitter at @NatalieLSmith.

Brent D. Oja, PhD Oja is Assistant Professor of Sport Administration at the University of Northern Colorado. His research focuses on sport employee professional growth and development and the link to organizational performance. Before entering academia, Oja worked in equipment operations for the athletics departments at Iowa State, the University of Virginia, and the University of Colorado.

Oja received dual Bachelor's degree in History and Sport Studies from the University of Minnesota. He holds a Master's degree in Sport Management from West Virginia University and a PhD in Education with an emphasis in Sport Management from the University of Kansas. You can find him on Twitter at @BrentOja.

List of Figures

List of Tables

The sports industry shares many characteristics with other industries; yet, it is also so unique that it demands its own academic discipline. Similarly, managing a sport organization shares many similarities with managing an organization outside of sport but simultaneously presents challenges that are unique to the sports industry. In this unit, we introduce the concept of organizational behavior, the unique characteristics of sport organizations, and how human behavior shapes the functioning of sport organizations. Within this section, you will learn how internal and external stakeholders, politics, resource limitations, and organizational size influence organizational decisions. The unit concludes by exploring how the diversity of sport organizations play an important role in the modern sports industry and explores the ethical, financial, legal, and customer aspects of diversity and inclusion. These are the building blocks for any manager to understand organizational behavior in the sports industry.

▷ **Learning Objectives** After reading this chapter, students should be able to:

- Explain the history of organizational behavior study in sport.
- Discuss the concept of positive organizational behavior.
- Explain why working in sports is unique.
- Discuss the concepts of legitimacy and isomorphism.

1.1 What Is Organizational Behavior?

Organizational behavior is a robust paradigm that has predominantly grown from the fields of psychology and sociology. Broadly, the study of organizational behavior seeks to inform scholars and practitioners about employees' thoughts, attitudes, and actions and their interpersonal relationships within a given organization. These areas represent essential facets of the daily lives of employees. Thoughts, or cognitions, encapsulate how one thinks and their various opinions and held beliefs. For example, the recognition of membership with a sport organization, a major component of social identity theory, is a critical thought for an employee who identifies with the organization. Suppose an employee does not believe they belong with an organization. In that case, it will be difficult for them to engage or even enjoy working for their employer fully.

Attitudes and emotions can determine the quality of sport employees' experiences. Suppose an employee is upset or in a foul mood. In that case, there are likely to be negative repercussions for the employee and their coworkers. For example, try to imagine a time when you had to work with someone who was consistently angry. Did any of those emotions impact your emotions? Conversely, employees who nearly always come to work with a positive attitude are likely to be well-received by others. Emotions are contagious, and having positive emotions in a workplace helps to create a constructive workplace environment. Behaviors (actions), as one might assume, are also critical to sport organizations. The sports industry is known for its constant change and movement; having employees with the desire and ability to react quickly and tend to a situation is vital to sport organizations' livelihood. Similar to the value of positive emotions, relationships with others can promote a promising organizational culture. Working with colleagues who are difficult to interact with makes for a difficult day at work. On the other hand, working with those you genuinely enjoy can help sport employees get through the long hours and ups and downs of life in the sports industry.

You might ask yourself, "Does this really matter… it's just work?" Consider your previous work experiences, whether or not they took place inside or outside the sport industry. Did you enjoy going to work each day? Did you have a poor relationship with your supervisor(s)? Did you get along with your coworkers? Was the work meaningful and enjoyable? You may have different answers for each of those questions, but if you take the time to reflect on the importance of each question, you will begin to see the value in organizational behavior. Personal experiences and relationships with coworkers are a hallmark of research within organizational behavior, and this is due to the importance of the topic regarding organizational effectiveness. While scholars of organizational behavior are concerned with organizational outcomes, they also seek to improve employees' work experiences. Given this concern, organizational behavior scholars have developed mechanisms to improve employees' experiences by enlisting concepts such as leadership, diversity, and interpersonal skills (all of which are covered in this textbook). This chapter begins with a brief introduction to organizational behavior in sport, followed by an overview of an exciting new concept that is beginning to gain popularity in sport management, positive organizational behavior. Then, sport managers and employees will be discussed, with the intention of providing a glimpse into what is required of various sport organization employees. This chapter concludes with a presentation on some of the external influences (and their impacts) on sport organizations.

1.1.1 History of Organizational Behavior in Sport

The field of sport management's initial focus was on the management of sport organizations, and organizational behavior was a primary topic. Early scholars such as Chelladurai, Slack, and Zeigler all brought forth critical discoveries that helped inform our understanding of how sport organizations are managed and how such organizations' management can be improved. Initial studies included topics such as leadership, work environment factors such as stress, burnout, and motivation.[1] Perhaps due to the heavy influence of coaching in sport, leadership has long been a popular topic within sport management. Forms of leadership, including transformational leadership and transactional leadership, often in the form of coaches and athletes, have seen a steady stream of scholarly attention. Chelladurai's[2] review of the Leadership Scale for Sport also included an argument to expand the scope of leadership within sport. Since then, theories involving leadership in sport have evolved and moved into exciting new areas, including leader-member exchange, servant leadership, authentic leadership, psychological contracts, and political skill. A recent review of leadership literature in sport by Welty Peachey, Zhou, Damon, and Burton[3] details the growth and expansion of leadership in sport. As leadership has been a core feature within sport organizational behavior, an entire chapter of this book is dedicated to the topic.

Leadership might be the most prominent area of research in sport organizational behavior but is not the only area with a long history of scholarship. Scholars have begun to explore other areas of organizational behavior in sport, including diversity, motivation, organizational structures, attitudes, and communication. All of these topics, plus many others, will be covered in this book.

Another exciting aspect of studying organizational behavior in sport is the diverse set of participants available to researchers. Previously, fitness and college recreation employees have been studied under the umbrella of sport organizational behavior. Recent trends in sport management have been concentrated on interviewing and surveying collegiate and professional sport employees. As sport organizations increase the value they place on their employees, and by extension, expand their scope and capabilities, there will likely be increased efforts to study the thoughts, feelings, and behaviors of sport employees.

The important thing to keep in mind as you read this book is that sport management has changed dramatically since its inception, and it is almost assuredly likely to continue to evolve as we gain a deeper understanding of sport organizations and their employees. Many new exciting horizons await scholars and practitioners for further study and application to the sport workplace. One of those areas is positive organizational behavior, of which we will turn to next.

1.1.2 Positive Organizational Behavior

An emerging paradigm in organizational behavior is known as positive organizational behavior (POB). This concept has been championed by scholars such as Fred Luthans, Bruce Avolio, and Carolyn Youssef-Morgan (although many other scholars have endorsed this approach to OB). One of POB's main functions is to create a growth approach for organizations but, more specifically, employees. Within POB, scholars seek to advance employees' functionality and thereby promote a competitive advantage for organizations.[4] As such, POB has been defined as[5] "the study and application of positively orientated human resource strengths and psychological capacities that can be measured, developed, and effectively managed for performance improvement in today's workplace" (p. 59). In short, POB focuses on positive personal capabilities in order to improve the experience of the employee and simultaneously supporting the organization. While POB scholarship is inclusive to any positively focused endeavor, specific theories have emerged from the paradigm.

▷ **Psychological Capital** An individual's positive psychological state of development is characterized by: (1) having confidence (self-efficacy) to take on and put in the necessary effort to succeed at challenging tasks; (2) making a positive attribution (optimism) about succeeding now and in the future; (3) persevering toward goals, and when necessary, redirecting paths to goals (hope) in order to succeed; and (4) when beset by problems and adversity, sustaining and bouncing back and even beyond (resilience) to attain success.

1.1.3 Psychological Capital and the HERO Model

Human capital[6] is a form of personal resources that are used to improve one's circumstances. There are numerous forms of human capital. For example, intellectual capital is known as "what you know" or social capital, known as "who you know." These forms of human capital are quite common. One of the more developed constructs to surface from POB is known as *psychological capital* which explores "what one can become." Psychological capital offers a new means to develop employees to meet their full potential.[7] Psychological capital is "an individual's positive psychological state of development characterized by: (1) having confidence (self-efficacy) to take on and put in the necessary effort to succeed at challenging tasks; (2) making a positive attribution (optimism) about succeeding now and in the future; (3) persevering toward goals, and when necessary, redirecting paths to goals (hope) in order to succeed; and (4) when beset by problems and adversity, sustaining and bouncing back and even beyond (resilience) to attain success[8]" (p. 2). As one can see, there are currently four components to psychological capital, which stand for the HERO within (i.e., Hope, Efficacy, Resilience, and Optimism). Although Luthans et al. have called for other constructs (e.g., courage, authenticity, and creativity) to be studied within psychological capital, little is known about how such constructs can serve employees and organizations, specifically in the sports industry.[9]

Yet, sport organizational scholars have begun to examine psychological capital within the sports industry. One of the leading scholars in this area of sport management is Dr. Minjung Kim, who has published several studies of conceptual and empirical nature. Dr. Kim's work includes the development of HEROES, which is similar to the HERO model previously described, but the HEROES model has been developed specifically for sport organization employees. Interestingly, concepts such as meaningful work and a supportive organizational climate have been found to improve the hope, efficiency, resilience, and optimism of sport organization employees. More so, having such capacities can improve sport employees' well-being and job satisfaction.[10] Psychological capital is also being expanded specifically in the sports industry by infusing the concept of authenticity to psychological capital.[11] In this work, the authors argued for creating A-HERO by stating that being true to oneself (i.e., authenticity) is a vital component of psychological capital. As such, employers and employees should begin to consider how they present themselves and behave at work. Being authentic to one's self could have positive influences on their well-being. As scholars begin to explore new concepts such as psychological capital and authenticity (of course, many other variables are being investigated), a unique opportunity is created for sport organizations to grow and prosper, not only financially, but culturally. Both scholars and practitioners need to find common ground and merge their interests, and POB represents one method to deliver positive influences on sport organizations and employees.

1.2   Managers and Employees

If you are reading this book, you have likely considered what life would be like as an employee of a sport organization. Employment opportunities in sport are numerous, yet they are still difficult to acquire. To better understand what is required of sport organization employees, this portion of the chapter is designed to provide you with a better understanding of sport organization employees' qualifications and job experiences. What follows is a brief description of who sport organization employees are and then an explanation of what their roles consist of by providing a detailed account of their various duties.

1.2.1   Who Are They?

Employees of sport organizations are generally thought of as anyone employed by an organization in the sport industry, but there are a few caveats to that statement. Most scholars in sport organizational behavior would not consider professional athletes to be "sport employees." Instead, an emphasis has been traditionally placed on the managerial and administrative employees. Generally, administrators are those in an organization who create and design policies, rules, campaigns, and so on. The managers are the employees who carry out the policies or campaigns and are in charge of implementing the administrators' directives. Hence, the popular term "middle-management" is often associated with those who carry out the boss's orders but have little if any authority to make large-scale decisions on their own. Many studies, particularly in the leadership context, examine the leadership style of an athletics director (i.e., administrative) and the influence of that leadership on the employees of the sport organization (i.e., managerial). It is important to note that other areas of sport organizations' personnel are also studied, including entry-level employees and interns.

From a more individual standpoint, scholars have begun to explore the psychological processes of sport employees. One such area that is receiving growing attention is the relationship between being a sport employee and being a fan of their organization's team(s). There is an old adage in the sports industry: sport organizations do not hire their fans. Many sport management students have been warned *not* to wear their favorite team's jersey to a job interview. The prevailing wisdom is that sport organizations seek to hire employees and *not* fans. They expect their employees to be working during games and not cheering on the team or being distraught after a close loss. This is generally excellent advice, but recent research has been conducted that might tell a slightly different story. Through multiple studies, scholars have begun to posit a new concept that suggests sport organization employees do not identify as traditional fans of the team, but instead, they feel a strong linkage with sport in general.[12] Put another way, many sport organization employees are drawn to sport and relish the opportunity to be involved in sport. This could explain why so many employees of sport organizations are willing to work evenings and weekends, in addition to working the traditional 40-hour workweek. They may enjoy being a part of a group that values sport and competition.

Another thought-provoking finding concerning sport organization employees is how they react during sporting events. In describing accepted and inappropriate sport employee behaviors during March Madness, participants in a recent study explained that they felt watching the games of March Madness was expected behavior, and focusing on work instead of watching the games would bring concerns about not being able to fit in at the workplace. The study participants explained that there is an appropriate level of decorum, such as getting your job done during games and not being a cheering fan or showing your emotions. Still, it was also crucial for other employees to be interested in sport and stay involved and knowledgeable about the sport organization's team or teams.[13] This dichotomy presents a unique work environment for sport employees. They are expected to follow along with the team or teams, watch major sporting events, but not be emotionally engaged when watching a game while they are "on the clock." The sports industry is undoubtedly unique, and these circumstances are one prominent example of how working in sport is strikingly different from working for a traditional business company.

1.2.2 What Do Sport Employees Do?

Sport employees hold a diverse set of jobs and responsibilities. First, it is worthwhile to re-examine the previous discussion on managers and administrators. Many readers of this book likely seek to, one day, be a leader of a sport organization (e.g., General Manager, Athletics Director, or Team President). These positions take years of experience to attain (along with a bit of luck and social connections!), which is for a good reason. The people in these positions are required to make difficult and often arduous choices, and having years of experience can go a long way to making the best possible decision for the organization. Individuals at this level of administration arc charged with designing the missions and plans of their organizations. This could be a wide-ranging operation to install a new organizational culture, a new marketing plan, or a specific fundraising campaign for a new arena. There are very few of these top-level leadership positions available, and worse yet, there is little job security meaning that if you earn such a position one day, you could lose that job very quickly! Professional sports are rife with examples of executives being removed from their positions after just a few, or even one, season!

The next level of sport employees includes the aforementioned "middle" managers—those employees who carry out the administrators' directives. These positions are often "lost in the shuffle" and not discussed by people outside of the sports industry. These circumstances are why many sport organization employees view their jobs as being "behind the scenes" and refer to their positions as "thankless jobs." This is a grim outlook on life as an employee, but the work environment of sport is not very different from other industries in that middle managers feel undervalued. However, some circumstances contribute to the distinction of the sports industry. One of the more prominent factors is the concept of time. Odio[14] explained how sport is subjected to cyclical and seasonal characteristics, which are due to the nature of sport, more so than other industries. That is, sport revolves around the various seasons for each sport. For example, in collegiate athletics departments, the months of August and September are notoriously busy as many sports (e.g., football, soccer, volleyball) are starting their seasons, and school is beginning as well. Conversely, the months of May and June are viewed as less hectic as many sports have finished or are winding down, and school is also ending for an extended time. The unique time sequences can add increased stress for employees and further separates sport organizations from those in other industries.[15]

Another layer of responsibility in sport organizations are those completed by entry-level employees and interns. Almost all aspiring sport employees begin their careers as interns, frequently serving as interns multiple times at multiple sport organizations. The sports industry is highly competitive, and it cannot be stressed enough that students who seek entry into the sport organizations should attempt to begin interning while they are an undergraduate student. Interns gain practical experience by performing duties such as selling tickets, assisting in marketing campaigns, helping with gameday presentations, and, in some cases, having duties similar to fulltime employees. While internships are often not a glamorous period in one's professional career, they are a needed step in the process. Beyond the practical experience, which helps students build their resumes, internships also expand students' social networks by introducing them to professionals in the field. Social networks are often the mechanism through which future job opportunities are accessed. While the hours are long and the pay is not great (many interns are unpaid), interning in sport organizations can help to provide a pathway to future employment in the sports industry.

1.3   External Influences of Organizational Behavior

Sport organizations are highly dependent on their environments in their quest for success on and off the field, and this dependence means that their internal management processes are impacted by their environments. The field of organizational behavior is predominantly focused on the micro- (i.e., individuals) and, to a lesser extent, meso-level (i.e., groups) groups. A related field of study is known as Organizational Theory, which is broader in scope and fixated on the macro-level

(i.e., industry). However, both organizational behavior and organizational theory are interrelated in different manners. In this section, we will focus on how organizational environments affect sport organizations' ability to achieve their goals and the method by which they can organize and perform.

▶ **Resource   Dependency** Organizational attempts to manage constraints and uncertainty that result from the need to acquire resources from the environment.

1.3.1   Resource Dependency

Many theories exist that attempt to explain external influences on organizations, the vast majority of which describe how the organization's environment impacts its capacities, profitability, and maneuverability. Two of the more prominent theories are resource dependency theory[16] and institutional theory.[17] Resource dependency theory is a reasonably straightforward concept in that the theory proposes that organizations depend on and are limited by the resources available to them within their environment to succeed and prosper. In other words, "resource dependence predicts that organizations will attempt to manage the constraints and uncertainty that result from the need to acquire resources from the environment" (p. xxiv).[18] As Pfeffer and Salancik[19] noted, organizational survival is based on the ability to be effective, namely acquiring resources from the organizational environment. The term "resources" is meant to convey anything that is of value to an organization. The phrase "organizational environment" generally reflects the geographic region and the industry of the organization and the practices thereof. Yet, the process of gathering resources is not simple, given that resources within an organizational environment are finite or limited. For example, there are only so many potential fans in a given city or state; therefore, it is unlikely that a professional sport organization will advertise in a neighboring (but separate) city or state to grow their fanbase (i.e., resources). Instead, that sport organization will need to compete with the other sport and entertainment organizations of the city for patrons' business. Another issue with acquiring resources from the organizational environment is that such environments (especially the sport environment!) will experience constant change and require adaptation. For example, a team could win a championship one year and lose many of their best players before the next season. While this might be understandable to most loyal fans, many possible sources of resource acquirement (i.e., other fans) could choose to spend their money (i.e., resources) with a different local team or venue. As you can see, there would be many unique challenges that would face this hypothetical sport organization as they began to prepare for the upcoming season and still acquire enough resources to survive.

1.3.2   Open Systems Theory

Another way to describe how resource development theory is believed to affect organizations is via open systems theory, which describes a process whereby resources are taken in (i.e., inputs), processed (i.e., throughputs), and put back into the environment (i.e., outputs) all within a bounded environment. Importantly, throughputs are what an organization does to manipulate, change, or enhance a given input before submitting it back into the environment, with the hope of the resource becoming an input yet again. Much like resource development theory's emphasis on exchange, open systems theory explains the interdependent activities (i.e., outputs to inputs) of organizations and their environments.[20] Here is an example of how the theory works: a professional basketball team that is preparing for an upcoming season will need to obtain enough resources to pay their coaches, players, and staff, maintain the facility, pay for travel expenses, and a host of other costs. To gather the necessary resources to pay for these expenses, the sport organization will need to go into the external environment and convince people to spend money on team merchandise or tickets to games beyond what they receive from media contracts. With an open systems perspective, fans decide to

go to a game, and purchase tickets would be considered inputs. Once they come to the arena and experience the game, they are considered throughputs. When the contest ends and the fans leave the arena, they are viewed as outputs.

For a sport organization to survive, they need to provide positive experiences during the game, the throughput stage, for those fans to desire to return to another contest on a later date. Therefore, the throughput stage is critical as it provides the link between input and output and allows for the intercedences of resources in a constrained environment. Without repeat customers, and those customers providing positive feedback to other potential customers, it is incredibly difficult for a sport organization to bring in enough resources to pay for their expenses. Consequently, there are several external influences on sport organizations from this perspective. One example is the influence on customer service and outreach as such many sport organizations have entire departments dedicated to community/public relations. Sport organizations also employ large-scale efforts in their marketing campaigns to garner attention and new consumers. These efforts can be seen at the collegiate level of sport as well as the professional level. More so, professional sport organizations have begun to attempt to grow their fanbases internationally.

The National Football League (NFL) plays games each year in the United Kingdom and Mexico. The National Basketball Association (NBA) has attempted to take advantage of its immense popularity in Asia, and Major League Baseball (MLB) has also played games in countries beyond North America. One professional league that has taken advantage of an environment full of untapped resources is the English Premier League (EPL). The various clubs play matches in the United States in the summer months, and they have made a television deal with NBC to grow the popularity of the EPL in the United States. This tendency has extended to collegiate football with the University of Notre Dame playing games in Ireland. Although it would not make much sense for the Denver Broncos to advertise their organization in Kansas City, reaching international markets is one example of sport organizations attempting to grow their popularity and reach new resources in the form of fans. The throughput stage is vital to bringing fans back as future inputs, and the throughput stage can be defined by how well a sport organization is run. This concept adds value to the study of organizational behavior. It can help a sport organization become more efficient and provide better services to their fans.

▶ **Legitimacy** A generalized perception or assumption that the actions of an entity are desirable, proper, or appropriate within some socially constructed system of norms, values, beliefs, and definitions.

1.3.3 Legitimacy and Institutional Theory

Institutional theory is the other common form of external control on sport organizations. The institutional theory perspective is concerned not with resource acquisition, but rather with the attainment and perpetuation of institutional legitimacy. Put another way, the institutional theory view is that the appearance as a legitimate entity is valued and drives the success of an organization. Several aspects of institutional theory have had considerable attention and have significant application to the sports industry. These forms include isomorphism and institutional work, both of which will be explained below. But first, the concept of legitimacy needs to be discussed. Suchman[21] defined legitimacy as a "generalized perception or assumption that the actions of an entity are desirable, proper, or appropriate within some socially constructed system of norms, values, beliefs, and definitions" (p. 574). As such, legitimacy is determined by society and can change depending on the beliefs of society. All institutions (including organizations) seek legitimacy, as it serves as a stamp of approval from relevant groups. Without legitimacy, organizations will predictably suffer. After all, people tend not to do business with organizations that they deem to be not legitimate. Therefore institutional theory posits that legitimacy is the goal of all institutions, and organizations will alter their practices to achieve and maintain legitimacy. We now turn to two popular theories that describe how organizations attempt to gain and preserve their legitimacy.

▶ **Isomorphism** Organizations tend to appear or behave similarly in order to achieve and preserve legitimacy.

1.3.3.1 Isomorphism

One area of institutional theory that has seen considerable scholarship in sport management is isomorphism, which describes how organizations tend to appear or behave similarly in order to achieve and preserve legitimacy. There are three forms of isomorphism: coercive, normative, and memetic.[22] Coercive isomorphism results from binding rules and regulations that force organizations to become or appear to be similar. An example of coercive isomorphism would be sports leagues with policies that govern uniforms and roster sizes. This presents to the public that all of the teams are part of a larger, equal group of organizations.

▶ **Coercive Isomorphism** Similarities between organizations resulting from compliance to rules and regulation.

▶ **Normative Isomorphism** Similarities between organizations that are the result of commonly accepted business practices, tradition, and industry culture.

▶ **Memetic Isomorphism** Similarities between organizations cause by imitation or replication of successful practices.

Another form of isomorphism is normative, which entails following specific resources such as professional certifications, qualifications, or licensure. An example of normative isomorphism in the sports industry can be seen in collegiate sport. Many athletic departments require a master's degree for head coaches. The last form of isomorphism is memetic, which is true to its name. Organizations will mimic successful organizations to gain legitimacy. There are numerous examples of memetic isomorphism in the sports industry, much of which is done unknowingly. The NFL is known as a "copycat league" where teams will use plays or design their rosters in an attempt to appear legitimate by following the lead of the most successful teams.

Another example is the explosion of multiple uniforms and helmets in college football made popular by the University of Oregon Ducks. Once the Ducks became known as a successful team and brand, the practice of using multiple helmets and uniforms was accepted as legitimate because of the positive impact it had on recruiting and on the field. Consequently, almost all college football teams now have multiple helmets and uniforms in an attempt to appear to be as similar as possible to a successful team.

1.3.3.2 Institutional Work and Disruption

The final form of institutional theory that will be discussed, although there are many more, is known as institutional work. This form of institutional theory has been described as the means by which institutions are created, maintained, or disrupted.[23] As such, institutional work explains what organizations actually do in their attempts to reach and keep a desired level of legitimacy. New organizations, or those that are reconfiguring, are often in the creation stage where they are likely to engage in memetic isomorphism by organizing their front office staff in a similar manner to already successful organizations by hiring employees with ties to successful individuals. In the maintenance stage, organizations seek to preserve or retain their legitimacy. This is an active process whereby organizations must remain aware of their institutional environment to appear to be legitimate. Also, institutions that have gained legitimacy will perform rituals that support the existing belief and rule systems.[24] Put another way, these organizations will reproduce the actions and customs deemed legitimate as long as the institutional environment believes such actions legitimate. A sport example of insti-

tutional maintenance would be the practice of tailgating before football games. Tailgating is a popular ritual for many football consumers; removing the opportunity to do so would harm the sport organization's legitimacy, and consequently, such practices are supported and encouraged by sport organizations.

Institutional disruption occurs when institutions or practices are deemphasized or removed altogether. This is done when a given institution or practice is no longer viewed as legitimate. An example of institutional disruption is the recent efforts that both professional and collegiate football have made to make the game safer by altering their tackling rules.

1.4 Summary

Sport organizations are inherently controlled by their environments. The two perspectives discussed provide different viewpoints, one where sport organizations are controlled by the amount or lack of resources and the other by whether or not a sport organization is viewed as legitimate based on the perceptions of those within the institutional environment. Moving forward, it is important to take into account the ability of the sport organization to support its employees is often dictated by the environment. There simply may not be enough resources available to support employees fully. Perhaps implementing programs that are not well known or unproven would be seen as weird and illegitimate by peer institutions or other employees, which would make the organization appear less attractive to some employees. Regardless, sport organizations need to be aware of how their environment impacts their capabilities and limitations.

Discussion Questions

1. How has the study of organizational behavior in the sports industry evolved?
2. What are the differences between the HERO, HEROES, and A-HERO models?
3. Why is legitimacy important to sport organizations?

4. Distinguish between coercive, normative, and memetic isomorphism. Provide examples of each.

Notes

1. Soucie, D., & Doherty, A. (1996). Past endeavors and future perspectives for sport management research. *Quest, 48*(4), 486–500.
2. Chelladurai, P. (1990). Leadership in sports: A review. *International Journal of Sport Psychology, 21*(4), 328–354.
3. Peachey, J. W., Zhou, Y., Damon, Z. J., & Burton, L. J. (2015). Forty years of leadership research in sport management: A review, synthesis, and conceptual framework. *Journal of Sport Management, 29*(5), 570–587.
4. Luthans, F., Youssef-Morgan, C. M., & Avolio, B. J. (2015). *Psychological capital and beyond.* Oxford University Press, USA.
5. Luthans, F. (2002). Positive organizational behavior: Developing and managing psychological strengths. *Academy of Management Executive, 16*, 57–72.
6. Becker, G. S. (1964). *Human capital: A theoretical and empirical analysis with special reference to education.* Columbia University Press.
7. Luthans, F., Youssef-Morgan, C. M., & Avolio, B. J. (2015). *Psychological capital and beyond.* Oxford University Press, USA.
8. Luthans, F., Youssef-Morgan, C. M., & Avolio, B. J. (2015). *Psychological capital and beyond.* Oxford University Press, USA.
9. Luthans, F., Youssef-Morgan, C. M., & Avolio, B. J. (2015). *Psychological capital and beyond.* Oxford University Press, USA.
10. Kim, M., Kim, A. C. H., Newman, J. I., Ferris, G. R., & Perrewé, P. L. (2019). The antecedents and consequences of positive organizational behavior: The role of psychological capital for promoting employee well-being in sport organizations. *Sport Management Review, 22*(1), 108–125.
11. Oja, B. D., Kim, M., Perrewé, P. L., & Anagnostopoulos, C. (2019). Conceptualizing A-HERO for sport employees' well-being. *Sport, Business and Management: An International Journal, 9*(4), 363–380. https://doi.org/10.1108/SBM-10-2018-0084.
12. Oja, B. D., Bass, J. R., & Gordon, B. S. (2015). Conceptualizing employee identification with sport organizations: Sport Employee Identification (SEI).
Sport Management Review, 18(4), 583–595; Oja, B. D., Bass, J. R., & Gordon, B. S. (2020). Identities in the sport workplace: Development of an instrument to measure sport employee identification. *Journal of Global Sport Management, 5*(3), 262–284.
13. Oja, B. D., Hazzaa, R. N., Wilkerson, Z., & Bass, J. R. (2018). March Madness in the Collegiate Sport Workplace. *Journal of Intercollegiate Sport, 11*(1), 82–105.
14. Odio, M. A. (2019). The Role of Time in Building Sport Management Theory. *Journal of Global Sport Management,* 1–17.
15. Kim, M., Perrewé, P. L., Kim, Y. K., & Kim, A. C. H. (2017). Psychological capital in sport organizations: Hope efficacy, resilience, and optimism among employees in sport (HEROES). *European Sport Management Quarterly, 17*(5); Odio, M. A. (2019). The Role of Time in Building Sport Management Theory. *Journal of Global Sport Management,* 1–17.
16. Pfeffer, J., & Salancik, G. R. (2003). *The external control of organizations: A resource dependence perspective.* Stanford University Press.
17. Meyer, J. W., & Rowan, B. (1977). Institutionalized organizations: Formal structure as myth and ceremony. *American journal of sociology, 83*(2), 340–363; Washington, M., & Patterson, K. D. (2011). Hostile takeover or joint venture: Connections between institutional theory and sport management research. *Sport Management Review, 14*(1), 1–12.
18. Pfeffer, J., & Salancik, G. R. (2003). *The external control of organizations: A resource dependence perspective.* Stanford University Press.
19. Pfeffer, J., & Salancik, G. R. (2003). *The external control of organizations: A resource dependence perspective.* Stanford University Press.
20. Scott, W. R. (2003). Organizations: Rational. *Natural, and Open Systems, 5.*
21. Suchman, M. C. (1995). Managing legitimacy: Strategic and institutional approaches. *Academy of Management Review, 20*(3), 571–610.
22. Washington, M., & Patterson, K. D. (2011). Hostile takeover or joint venture: Connections between institutional theory and sport management research. *Sport Management Review, 14*(1), 1–12.
23. Lawrence, T., Suddaby, R., & Leca, B. (2011). Institutional work: Refocusing institutional studies of organization. *Journal of Management Inquiry, 20*(1), 52–58.
24. Lawrence, T. B., & Suddaby, R. (2006). 1.6 institutions and institutional work. *The Sage Handbook of Organization Studies,* 215–254.

> **Learning Objectives** After reading this chapter, students should be able to:

- Identify components of organizations.
- Distinguish sport organizations from other types of organizations.
- Identify internal and external factors that influence behaviors of sport organizations.

2.1 Introduction

In Chap. 1, we defined organizational behavior and explored some of the internal and external factors that influence the behaviors of employees and managers. As you likely grasped, effective managers develop an understanding of how their actions, the organization's actions, and the organization's external environment influence the behaviors of employees. You may have also noticed that many of the theories discussed in this book are based on broader management and organizational theory. So, why the need for a book on organizational behavior in sport?

Sport management is a subdiscipline of management. It evolved from conversations that Brooklyn Dodgers owner, Walter O'Malley, had with university professors Clifford Brownell (Columbia University) and James Mason (University of Miami and Ohio University)

regarding the lack of adequately trained individuals to work in the sports industry. O'Malley recognized that business principles had to be adapted by sport managers to meet the unique needs of sport organizations.[1] This chapter explores the unique characteristics of sport organizations. Beginning with the definitions of organizations and sport organizations, this chapter will then discuss the impacts of organizational size, bureaucratic structures, and financial constraints on the behavior of sport organizations and their employees. The second half of this chapter will further explore the environments in which sport organizations function, including sociocultural impacts of sport organizations on their communities and influences of public scrutiny on organizational practices.

> **Organization** Organizations are groups of people, working interdependently, and providing specialized contributions toward a common end or purpose.

2.2 Defining Organizations

Organizations are groups of people, working interdependently, and providing specialized contributions toward a common end or purpose.[2] This broad definition allows for many different groups of people to meet the definition of an organization, including athletic teams, community sport organizations, governing agencies, and many other sport-based entities. However, not every group of people can be considered an organization. Chelladurai outlined several attributes that delineate organizations from other groups.[3]

2.2.1 Identity and Permanency

To be considered an organization, an entity must have a separate and distinct identity from those with which it is associated. Further, if a member leaves, the organization must continue to exist and function toward its goals. In other words, the organization is bigger than any of its members.

Jim Delany served as Commissioner of the Big Ten Conference from 1989 through 2020. During this period, Delany oversaw many changes to the Big Ten, including expansion to 14 member schools and the creation of the Big Ten Network. He also used traditional and new media effectively to advocate for the conference and was often seen as the public face of the Big Ten. However, when Delany decided to step down, the Big Ten Conference did not cease to exist. Instead, he was replaced by a new commissioner, Kevin Warren. Delany will long be associated with the Big Ten, but his identity and the identity of the Big Ten Conference are distinct.[4]

2.2.2 Instrumentality

Instrumentality refers to an organization's ability to achieve goals beyond the scope of what members can accomplish individually. Through effective use of processes and coordination/allocation of resources, organizations can take advantage of economies of scope and economies of scale.[5] This is particularly true of larger organizations.[6]

Girls on the Run uses sport to strengthen confidence in elementary and middle school-age girls.[7] It is quite possible for a coach to have an impact on children at his or her school

or even in the local community, but eventually, even the hardest working individual is limited in the resources they can access. As an organization, Girls on Run can use its size to access resources and organizational knowledge to replicate successful procedures across many communities. ◄

2.2.3 Membership

Organizations maintain controls on who can become a member. These controls include entry procedures, requirements to maintain membership, and systems to replace members that leave the organization. Suppose you browse job and internship postings on job boards such as Teamwork Online. In that case, you will notice that most include minimum and/or preferred qualifications such as education levels, experience levels, and skillsets desired. These requirements allow organizations to sort applicants and select interview candidates as part of their entry procedures. Sport organizations receive an abundance of applications for open jobs. In 2018, the Chick-fil-a Peach Bowl received over 700 applications from students interested in joining the organization as an intern. Thus, entry procedures are needed to make selection processes effective and efficient.

Once new employees are hired, organizations use appraisal methods such as performance appraisals to determine to evaluate the individual's position within the organization. Evaluations can be used by managers to shift members between roles or remove members from the organization. It is important to note that organizational members are often employees, but members can have many other affiliations with their organization. The previous chapter pointed out that unpaid interns are considered employees by many sport organizations. Sports councils and other community sport organizations rely heavily on volunteers.[8] It is not uncommon for experienced volunteers to be placed in positions of authority or assigned interdependent tasks to achieve the desired outcome. A youth hockey tournament, for example, may have volunteers in charge of finding teams to compete, scheduling games, arranging officials, running concessions, and accounting for finances. Although these members are volunteers, sport organizations still put processes to control who is occupying these positions.

2.2.4 Division of Labor

Organizations divide labor to create efficiencies in workflow. Labor division allows organizations to take advantage of members' specialized knowledge in a rational manner consistent with organizational goals. It is the division of labor that enables organizations to achieve instrumentality or possibly economies of scope.

Like many professional sport organizations, the National Women's Soccer League (NWSL) franchise, North Carolina Courage, divides its employees into the following functions: ticket sales, corporate partnerships, creative and marketing, operations, communications, broadcasting, merchandising, finance, and team operations.[9] Employees working in creative and marketing generate plans to develop community interest in the team, the ticket office staff makes sales and delivers tickets to customers, and the merchandise office sells team-branded apparel at the games. These departments work together to ensure they present a consistent brand to the public but undertake their primary functions independently to create efficiency. The organization utilizes economies of scope when using these same departments to serve their partner club's needs, North Carolina FC. ◄

2.2.5 Hierarchy of Authority

Synchronization of interdependent members and their responsibilities requires individuals to serve as administrators and managers whose task is to coordinate processes and employee functions. Individuals in management roles must have the necessary authority to make decisions that affect the tasks of others. Organizational charts indicate positions of authority, as well as which members and functions that position oversees. Some organizations include many layers of bureaucracy, while others are relatively flat. This concept will be discussed further later in this chapter as well as in Chap. 4.

2.2.6 Formal Policies and Procedures

Policies and procedures allow managers to control the behaviors of employees, protect organizational norms, and create consistency in processes throughout the organization. Most organizations utilize policy manuals and other formal documents designed to educate members on organizational rules. Organizations may also create policies that govern who is to complete tasks and how tasks are to be completed. Formal policies and procedures assist managers by outlining authority and providing provisions for fair and equal treatment.

2.3 Sport Organizations

The features outlined by Chelladurai are common to organizations in any industry. Sport organizations share similarities with non-sport organizations. Business functions such as marketing, sales, financial management, strategic management, and regulatory compliance are just as crucial for Manchester United as they are for Coca-Cola. Yet, Walter O'Malley and many other sports industry practitioners continue to argue that sport organizations are unique.

Chapter 1 emphasized some of the broader external and industry-related factors that contribute to this perspective. The remainder of this chapter will provide a more detailed examination of macro and micro industrial environmental factors that shape sport organizations' behaviors. We will also introduce sociocultural issues to the conversation. However, to understand what makes sports organizations unique, we must first define the concept of a sport organization. This is actually a difficult task.

2.3.1 Sport Defined

Sport can be defined as officially governed, competitive physical activity in which participants are motivated by internal and external rewards.[10] If we use this definition for sport organizations, that would mean sport organizations are organizations that govern competitive physical activities in which participants are motivated by internal and external rewards. By this definition, leagues, conferences, associations, and other bodies that govern professional and amateur competition would be considered sport organizations. Teams, clubs, and franchises would also likely meet the definition as they could be regarded as participants.

Unfortunately, this definition of sport organization is inadequate as it does not capture the full nature of sport. For example, esports is an emerging sector within the sports industry, although some argue that it lacks the physical component necessary to be defined as sport. Yet, many traditional sports franchises such as the Los Angeles Lakers and Manchester City FC have invested in esports teams. During the shutdowns caused by the spread of Covid-19, leagues such as NASCAR and the United Soccer League (USL) turned to esports as a way to provide content when traditional operations were not an option. In a similar vein, organizations that use sport and physical activity to affect their communities, such as Girls on the Run and Sport for Good, fall short of the proposed definition. Their activities are not competition-based. Equipment manufacturers, media, and other entities that aid in producing and promoting sport would also be excluded because they do not provide governance.

A broader definition of sport offered by the European Sports Charter[11] states, "Sport means all forms of physical activity which, through casual or organized participation, aim at expressing or improving physical fitness and mental well-being, forming social relationships or obtaining results in competition at all levels." This definition captures organizations, such as community agencies but still excludes organizations that support or facilitate sport participation such as manufacturers and regional sports com-

missions. In reality, what has been defined as or accepted as sport evolves with societal norms. Once accepted as a mainstream sport, events such as gladiator matches in ancient Rome are considered barbaric by modern standards. Esports, which are still seen by many as problematic because they do not promote physical activity, is increasingly accepted as a form of sport. Because societal perceptions of sport are fluid, including a strict description of sport in the definition of sport organizations is impractical. If we cannot rely on the academic definitions to set the book's scope, maybe economic categorizations will help.

2.3.2 Sport as an Industry

Estimates of the global sports industry size in terms of value-added to the economy range from $489 billion[12] to $1.5 trillion.[13] Economists struggle to generate an accurate estimate of the sports industry's size because the sports industry is not classified as a separate segment of the economy by the world's governments. The US Department of Commerce classifies sport under the broad segment of arts, entertainment, and recreation. Organizations such as for-profit recreation providers and professional spectator sports franchises are included within this segment. However, sport-related businesses can fall into numerous segments based on the Bureau of Economic Analysis (BEA) guidelines.[14] Major sporting equipment and apparel manufacturers such as Nike and Adidas are categorized into the retail trade segment of the US economy. Sports facilities could be classified as arts, entertainment, and recreation segment, but may also be classified as part of the government or real estate segments. Amateur sport organizations may be classified in the government, educational services, or non-profit segments of the economy. Therefore, if we use the BEA definitions of the sports industry, organizations such as the US Olympic Committee would be excluded. Economic classification is also of no help for identifying the scope of the sports industry. Luckily, organizational behavior theory provides an answer!

▷ **Organizational Identity** Organizational identity is the organizational members' perceptions of "who" the organization is, and "how" the organization is different from other organizations.

2.3.3 Organizational Identity

From an organizational behavior perspective, neither the academic and economic definitions are relevant in determining which organizations are sport organizations. Organizations seek to differentiate themselves from other organizations, both within and outside of their identified industries.[15] Organizations such as Soccer in the Streets, Reviving Baseball in the Inner Cities (RBI), and Sport for Good are non-profit organizations that work to provide opportunity to disadvantaged youth in inner-city Atlanta. However, each holds its own organizational identities. Soccer in the Streets is an independent, grassroots organization that builds soccer fields and classrooms for youth. RBI is a non-profit affiliated with Major League Baseball and the Atlanta Braves that build athletic fields and sponsors baseball and softball leagues for youth. Sport for Good Atlanta is affiliated with Laureus, an international non-profit sport development organization that uses sport to achieve numerous community initiatives.

Although the aforementioned organizations may not fit perfectly with the academic or economic definitions of sport organizations, employees at these organizations generally view themselves as sport employees (social identity theory) and their organizations as sport organizations (organizational identity). Organizational identity is the organizational members' perceptions of "who" the organization is and "how" the organization is different from other organizations.[16] In other words, if the employees of an organization feel like sport is a defining characteristic of the organization's culture, mission, brand, or identity, the organization is a sport organization. How outsiders perceive the organization as a sport organization is irrelevant.

Using organizational identity as the defining factor in determining which organizations qualify as sport organizations may seem daunting for studying organizational behavior. The sports industry becomes a huge tent. Large international corporations such as Nike and small organizations, such as community recreation departments, identify as sport organizations. However, because organizational identity is strongly tied to employees' in-role and extra-role behaviors (i.e., actions they take on behalf of the organization), attitudes toward their job (i.e., how they feel about working for an organization), and cognitions (i.e., how they interpret the organization's messages and actions), scholars argue it could be one of the most important factors in understanding organizations.[17] Additionally, as you understand how external factors related to resource limitations and sociocultural issues influence many sport organizations similarly, you will be able to apply organizational behavior theories to issues facing sport organizations across the sports industry's broad spectrum. At the same time, you will appreciate that organizations in any sector are actually quite unique regardless of how similar they appear to an outsider. In other words, the St. Louis Blues and Detroit Redwings are two distinct organizations despite both being members of the National Hockey League (NHL). Yet, perhaps shockingly, they also likely share some similarities with the Durham Bulls (MiLB) and Chunichi Dragons (Nippon Professional Baseball).

To be a successful sport manager, you will need to understand your organization's identity and will likely have a role in helping shape it. You will also need to adapt and apply your knowledge of organizational behavior to the circumstances your organization confronts, be they internal, uniquely based on your organization's identity, or external forces confronting all sport organizations. Throughout the remainder of this chapter, we'll explore some of the internal characteristics of sport organizations and factors in the organizational environment that influence sport organizations' behaviors.

2.4   Internal Organizational Factors

As mentioned in the previous section, every sport organization is unique. Organizational mission, culture, and structure, to name a few, are all unique to the organization but have significant influences on the behavior of administrators, managers, and other organizational members. This section will provide a brief overview of these factors. A more in-depth discussion is available in Chap. 6.

2.4.1   Mission, Vision, and Values

All organizations should have a reason for their existence (*mission*), ambitions for their future (*vision*), and ethical underpinnings for how they will achieve current and future goals (*values*). Often espoused in written documents shared with the public, mission, vision, and value statements can shape organizational identification, therefore influencing employees' attitudes and behaviors. They can also influence external perceptions of the organization, potentially influencing perceptions of potential employees before they enter the organization.

2.4.2   Organizational Culture

Organizational culture refers to the shared values and assumptions held by organizational members regarding how employees should act and how work should be conducted.[18] In other words, organizational culture is the shared beliefs or norms that influence the workplace atmosphere. Organizational culture often manifests in rituals and ceremonies such as "Casual Fridays" or "Ringing the Bell" following a sale.

2.4.3   Organizational Structure

All organizations have, to some degree, a formal hierarchy of oversight. Organizational structure refers to the division of labor within the organization, as well as the patterns of communication, coordination, workflow, and authority designations that direct organizational activities.[19] Organizational structure, often illustrated in the form of an organizational chart, creates the division of labor and supports specialization and departmentalization.

▶ **Specialization** Separation of labor based on job attributes and competencies.

An effective organizational structure can create a more efficient organization. Using a college athletics department as an example, compliance, facility management, ticket sales, marketing, and fundraising are critical functions of the organization. It would not make sense for one individual to do more than one of these jobs because there is little overlap in the competencies needed from one job to the next. Some people are better salespeople, while others are better at oversight. It makes more sense for the salesperson to sell tickets while the person who is better at oversight applies their competencies in the compliance office. This separation of labor based on job attributes and competencies is known as specialization.

▶ **Departmentalization** Grouping   similar specialized positions to take advantage of similar workflows.

Departmentalization occurs when similar specialized positions are grouped to take advantage of similar workflows. In the athletic department example, it may make sense to group people in ticket sales, marketing, fundraising into a department since all of the positions are unique but interrelated. Departmentalization can improve communication. Oversight of this department by an upper level manager (i.e., Associate Athletic Director for External Relations) creates a hierarchy within the organizational structure.

As you will learn in Chap. 4, there are many different organizational structures used by sport organizations. In general, organizational structures can be classified by organizational "height." Tall organizational structures have many different levels of management (*bureaucracy*). In sport, large organizations, including manufacturers and elite professional and amateur sport, generally have taller structures. Smaller organizations are usually flatter, meaning that they have less distance between upper management and lower level employees. The width of an organization's structure is dictated by the number of functional areas in which the organization is engaged.

Example

Atlanta United's organizational structure contains nine bureaucratic levels from the organization's owner: Owner → President → Vice President → Director → Assistant Director → Manager → Coordinator → Assistant → Associate. The organization is also reasonably broad, containing 14 different departments. Suppose we take a look at AMBSE, Atlanta United's parent firm. In that case, we find a complex organization that also includes the Atlanta Falcons (NFL), Mercedes Benz Stadium (Venue), PGA Superstores (Retail), Mountain Sky Ranch (Tourism), The Arthur M. Blank Family Foundation (Non-Profit), and AMB Group (Financial) creating a very complex organizational structure. ◄

Organizational structure, along with organizational culture, affects communication. In more formal organizations, communication only occurs top-down through channels that run from authority figure to next level subordinate. Cross-departmental communication occurs only at the executive level. Lower tier employees in formal organizations rarely, if ever, directly interact with executive-level employees. In less formal organizations, communication may flow more directly across departments, but formal communication channels remain important to information flow.

Smaller organizations have fewer levels of bureaucracy. Minor league/lower division professional clubs and lower tier competitive amateur sport organizations have flatter organizational structures. The Durham Bulls (MiLB) have only three to four levels of management between the team president and interns. National Pro Fastpitch's league office has three levels of management from commissioner to intern. Similarly, Oxford United of the English Football League, League One has a flat organizational structure with two to four levels of bureaucracy, but because the organization has numerous youth teams, a women's team, and a walking football team, the structure is wider than you would see in North American professional sports franchises. Community sport and many other smaller sport organizations may have a completely flat structure with only one level between management and employees. In flatter organizational structures, information is more likely to flow directly from executives to lower tier employees or vice versa, and organizations tend to be less formal due to frequent interaction between employees across management levels and departments.

2.4.4   Organizational Size and Resources

Large professional sport organizations tend to draw the most attention from industry outsiders. The New York Yankees, FC Barcelona, and Los Angeles Lakers are known by fans worldwide and often skew public perceptions of sport organizations. In fact, many sport management students have dreams of working for a handful of teams, but the industry is much more diverse than the EPL, NFL, and Nike. Barnhill and Smith[20] highlighted that a majority of sport organizations fit the definition of small business enterprises. That means they have less than 50 employees and operating with limited resources and limited profit margins.[21] This is particularly true if we remove sport operations personnel (coaches, athletes, trainers, scouts, etc.) from the equation and focus on business operations. Small organizations tend to be flat, informal organizations with frequent interactions between executives and other employees. Frequent interaction influences the psychological contract that employees form with the organization.[22] Limited resources can also create an atmosphere where creativity and other beneficial employee behaviors are valued. At the same time, employees are more likely to see their ideas rejected, not because they are viewed as bad ideas, but because the organization lacks resources (human, financial, time) to implement them. Research has indicated that some organizational behavior theories developed through studies at larger organizations become unreliable in smaller organizations. This creates a challenge in sport.

2.5 Sport and Culture

In Chap. 1, we noted that, like all organizations, sport organizations are controlled by their environment. This is particularly true in terms of resource acquisition, where sport organizations compete with other organizations for both employees and financial resources. However, unlike some other industries, sport organizations also make direct impacts on their external environments. In this section, we'll introduce some of the ways sport organizations are acted upon or act themselves act upon their external environments. We will also explore how organizational interactions with their environments can impact relationships with current and future employees.

2.5.1 Impact of Politics on Sport Organizations

Sport organizations rely on local, regional, or national governments for support. This support can take many forms. For community sport organizations, their entire budget may be a line-item in the city budget. These same organizations may also be affected by the availability of government grants or programs. For example, a sport organization may contribute to a community program with a broad initiative to improve local residents' health and welfare. Votes by the city council or community residents can dramatically alter access to funding depending on the political climate. During recessions, municipalities reduced funding for non-essential services, and community sport organizations can be targets for cuts.

Government support also comes in the form of legitimacy. Public support from community officials can legitimize a sport organization's efforts in the eyes of other community organizations. This can make it easier for that organization to seek support from sponsors, donors, and other community members who now view the organization's mission as having value. Correspondingly, outside support for the organization can affect how employees view their employer and career, influencing attitudes and behaviors.

More broadly, sport organizations may be used as symbols in broader political issues. Fights for racial and gender equality and LGBTQ rights have often seen sport organizations become symbols of progress or discrimination. Because of their influence, sport organizations can influence public opinion. Therefore actions such as the Brooklyn Dodgers signing Jackie Robinson become emblematic of larger movements happening in society. This can occur without intention or action of the organization. For some sport organizations, such as many women's teams, mere existence can be seen as political by some citizens.

Understanding emotional attachments the public can have with teams and athletes, sport organizations can find themselves co-opted by politicians and fans into larger political movements. Nelson Mandela used South Africa's National Rugby team's popularity to increase unity between Black and White South Africans during the 1995 Rugby World Cup.[23] US President, Donald Trump, has used sport organizations such as NASCAR and the NFL to signal his positions on various political issues, drawing distinction between he and his opponents.[24]

Fans also co-opt teams to signal political affiliation. The El Classico rivalry between FC Barcelona and Real Madrid can be traced to the Spanish Civil War. Catalonians sided with FC Barcelona to represent their region and culture while Real Madrid became the favorite of Spanish Nationalists. Today, Catalonia flags and chants are prevalent at FC Barcelona home matches.[25] The question is, how do these political fights affect organizations? Employees look for alignment between their values and the values of their employer. In many cases, professional and amateur sport organizations attempt to maintain neutrality. Political fights involving their organization can alter employees' work-based feelings.

2.5.2 Impact of Sport Organizations on Their Communities

Many organizations use community outreach initiatives or corporate wealth to influence their communities. Relative to the overall size of the industry, sport organizations have an outsized impact on culture. As such, sport organizations have a tremendous ability to influence their own communities, beyond the scope of their own outreach and financial investment. Sometimes, this can take the form of politics or community activism.

Sport for development organizations exist to influence their communities by using sport to create positive health, social, and economic outcomes in their communities. Similarly, sports commissions exist to bring events that have positive economic impacts and also market their communities to potential tourists. Governing bodies, amateur and professional teams, equipment and apparel manufacturers, and other sport-associated organizations are also increasing community outreach efforts and other forms of corporate social responsibility programs.

Increasingly, sport organizations are willing to use their standing to in support of political causes. Whether it is Nike's support of social justice organizations, the WNBA's Take A Seat, Take A Stand initiative, or local sports organizations supporting local ballot initiatives, sport organizations' political stances have the power to influence community members but also alienate fans and customers who disagree. These stances are indicators of an organization's values for current and potential employees, possibly influencing perceptions of organizational fit.

2.6 Summary

A sport organization is an organization where employees identify as sport organization employees. In many ways, sport organizations are similar to organizations in other industries. Sport organizations select employees, structure and divide labor to create efficiencies, and control processes. Sport organizations, like all organizations, must maintain cultures and develop organizational structures that attract talented employees and allow them to perform their roles productively. However, sport organizations are generally smaller than other organizations. They must contend with outsized cultural and sociopolitical influences while also dealing with limited access to resources. These factors together influence organizational behavior.

Discussion Questions

1. Why are academic and economic definitions of sport inadequate for determining which organizations qualify as sport organizations?
2. What attributes delineate organizations from other types of workgroups?
3. How could you determine if a community development non-profit qualified as a sport organization?
4. What is the difference between specialization and departmentalization?
5. How does society affect sport organizations? How do sport organizations affect society?

Notes

1. Mason, J. G., Higgins, C., & Owen, J. (1981). Sport administration education 15 years later. *Athletic Purchasing and Facilities*, 44–45; Ohio University (n.d.). *Walter O'Malley: History of the Founder*. Retrieved from http://https://business.ohio.edu/4812.aspx.
2. Chelladurai, P. (2014). *Managing Organizations for Sport and Physical Activity: A Systems Perspective* (4th ed.). Routledge; McShane, S., & Von Glinow, M. (2018). *Organizational Behavior* (8th ed.). McGraw Hill.
3. Chelladurai, P. (2014). *Managing Organizations for Sport and Physical Activity: A Systems Perspective* (4th ed.). Routledge.
4. Rosenthal, P. (2019, March 7). The Big Ten grew bigger and richer under Jim Delany—but that's not a full accounting of his legacy. *Chicago Tribune*.
5. Babiak, K., Heinze, K.L., & Thibault, L. Management concepts and practice in sport organizations. In Pedersen P.M. & Thibault, L. (Editors). *Contemporary Sport Management* (6th Edition), Human Kinetics, 2017; Miozzo, M., Lehrer, M., DeFillippi, R., Grimshaw, D., & Ordanini, A. (2012). Economies of Scope through Multi-unit Skill Systems: The Organization of Large Design Firms. *British Journal of Management, 23*(2), 145–164.

6. Wicker, P., Breuer, C., Lamprecht, M., & Fischer, A. (2014). Does club size matter: An examination of economies of scale, economies of scope, and organizational problems. *Journal of Sport Management, 28*(3), 266–280.
7. Girlsontherun.org.
8. Harman, A., & Barnhill, C. (2018, November). Psychological contract development in community sport organizations. Paper accepted for presentation at the biannual Psychological Contract Small Group Conference, Melbourne, Australia.
9. nccourage.com.
10. Coakley, J. (2021). *Sports in Society: Issues and Controversy* (13th ed.). McGraw Hill.
11. Council of Europe (2001). Recommendation No. R (92) 13 Rev of the Committee of Ministers to Member States on the Revised European Sports Charter.
12. Business Insider (2019, July 17). *Increasing Sports Sponsorships Will Drive the Global Sports Market to $614 Billion by 2022: The Business Research Company.* Retrieved from https://markets.businessinsider.com/news/stocks/increasing-sports-sponsorships-will-drive-the-global-sports-market-to-614-billion-by-2022-the-business-research-company-1028360019#.
13. Plunket Research, Ltd. (n.d.). *Sports & Recreation Business Statistics Analysis, Business and Industry Statistics.* Retrieved from https://www.plunkettresearch.com/statistics/sports-industry/.
14. Bureau of Economic Analysis (n.d.). *Industry List A.* Retrieved from https://apps.bea.gov/regional/rims/rimsii/download/372IndustryListA.pdf.
15. Gioia, D. A., Price, K. N., Hamilton, A. L., & Thomas, J. B. (2010). Forging an identity: An insider-outsider study of processes involved in the formation of organizational identity. *Administrative Science Quarterly, 55*(1), 1–46.
16. Gioia, D. A., Patvardhan, S. D., Hamilton, A. L., & Corley, K. G. (2013). Organizational identity formation and change. *Academy of Management Annals, 7*(1), 123–193. https://doi.org/10.1080/19416520.2013.762225.
17. Marique, G., Stinglhamber, F., Desmette, D., Caesens, G., & De Zanet, F. (2013). The relationship between perceived organizational support and affective commitment: A social identity perspective. *Group & Organization Management, 38*(1), 68–100.
18. Schein, E. H. (2010). *Organizational culture and leadership* (Vol. 2). John Wiley & Sons.
19. McShane, S., & Von Glinow, M. (2018). *Organizational Behavior* (8th ed.). McGraw Hill.
20. Barnhill, C. R., & Smith, N. L. (2019). Psychological contract fulfillment and innovative work behaviors in sport-based SBEs: The mediating role of organizational citizenship. *International Journal of Sport Management and Marketing, 19*(1/2), 106–128.
21. Small Business Council (2004) *Evaluation of Government Employment Regulations and Their Impact on Small Business*, Small Business Council, London.
22. Atkinson, C. (2008) 'An exploration of small firm psychological contracts', *Work, Employment and Society, 22*(3), 447–465 [online] https://doi.org/10.1177/0950017008093480.
23. Smith, D. (2012, December 8). Francois Pienaar: 'When the whistle blew, South Africa changed forever.' *The Guardian.* Retrieved from https://www.theguardian.com/world/2013/dec/08/nelson-mandela-francois-pienaar-rugby-world-cup.
24. Thrush, G., & Haberman, M. (2017, September 25). Trump's N.F.L. Critique a Calculated Attempt to Shore Up His Base. *New York Times.* Retrieved from https://www.nytimes.com/2017/09/25/us/politics/trump-nascar-nfl-protests.html.
25. Fitzpatrick, R. (2012). *El Clasico: Barcelona v Real Madrid: Football's Greatest Rivalry.* Bloomsbury Publishing.

3

Diversity in Sport Organizations

▶ **Learning Objectives** After reading this chapter, students should be able to:

- Define the terms diversity and inclusion in sport organizations.
- Identify sport-specific examples to each of the four major areas of diversity and inclusion.
- Analyze current issues and solutions to improving diversity and inclusion in the sports industry.

Calvin Claggett: Associate Director of External Operations, ETSU Athletics
To listen to the interview <click here>

Supplementary Information The online version of this chapter (https://doi.org/10.1007/978-3-030-67612-4_3) contains supplementary material, which is available to authorized users.

3.1 What Does It Mean to Be a Diverse Organization?

Diversity is brought up more than ever in organizations, including sport organizations. Partially these conversations are occurring because in many countries, such as the United States, census demographics indicate there is or soon will be no majority ethnic group,[1] but also due to cultural shift and the rise of social media. Those conversations have often stopped at asking how many people of different ethnicities or genders an organization has. Diversity is so much more than counting demographic numbers. There needs to be conversations around lived experiences and perceptions of inclusivity, and these experiences are impacted by multiple levels, such as at the individual level, the social level, structurally, and societally.[2] Therefore, for a sport organization to be truly diverse, it must not only include employees from different demographic groups; it should also strive to be representative of the community that it serves. This chapter explores diversity in sport organizations by examining essential aspects of diverse organizations, as well as systems and practices that facilitate the development of diversity within an organization. In the next section, we will be talking about these topics as they relate to sport organizations.

C. R. Barnhill et al., *Organizational Behavior in Sport Management*,
https://doi.org/10.1007/978-3-030-67612-4_3

3.1.1 Ethical Aspects

While the sports industry often focuses on the financial or legal aspects of diversity (covered later in this chapter), managers must also consider diversity as an ethical issue. What is the right thing to do according to your ethical principles? Ethics vary from one person to another. For managers, the bottom line (i.e., profit) can often influence their ethical decision-making process. However, other influences can include but are not limited to friendships, power dynamics, public pressure, and biases. The Rooney Rule in the NFL, for example, is the requirement that a Black candidate must be interviewed for a coaching vacancy. The rule continues to be stymied by a pervasive culture of "you end up calling your friends, and the typical coach has not been exposed to many black coaches," as legendary coach Bill Walsh highlighted.[3] If a GM chooses to only speak to their friends about hiring, it may violate an established rule, but it is also an ethical decision. Each coach has made an ethical decision when seeking out new candidates. Unfortunately, there is a long history of unethical treatment in sport management for people based on race, gender, or sexuality. For example, since the beginning of the NCAA, sexist and racists beliefs were a part of college athletics.[4] We will talk more in later chapters about ethical leadership and other ethical considerations.

3.1.2 Financial Aspects

Diversity is also impacted by and impacts the financial aspects of sport organizations. Researchers have found that diverse organizations are more successful financially and on the field.[5] For example, a more diverse organization with employees that are representative of all neighborhoods in the community may generate ideas to understand why ticket purchase patterns differ across the neighborhoods and generate different marketing plans based on employees' insights. As sport organizations deal with a more competitive landscape for sponsorship money, viewership, grants, or participants, coming up

with new, creative ideas are more important than ever. As was introduced in the previous chapter, employees align themselves with organizations that share similar values. One of the benefits for organizations that demonstrates their value of a diverse workforce is improved performance from employees who feel valued by their organization. Employees may also work harder for organizations that they think values them as individuals.[6] There could be some financial costs associated with having a diverse employee group, such as physical changes to the workplace to accommodate a physical disability or scheduling difficulties due to differing religious holiday schedules. However, these are usually outweighed by the benefits of decreased employee turnover, increased creativity, and better customer service.

▶ **Discrimination** Prejudiced treatment of and/or systematic exclusion of a particular group.

3.1.3 Legal Aspects

In a large portion of the world, there are legal requirements related to diversity. These federal, state, and local regulations usually focus on eliminating discrimination. Discrimination is the prejudiced treatment of and/or systematic exclusion of a particular group. For example, it is illegal in the United States to discriminate based on someone's age, sex, and physical ability. A key component of these laws is the willingness to enforce these rules. In the United States, filing complaints with the Equal Employment Opportunity Commission (EEOC) can be a helpful way for employees to signal that an organization is discriminating. Suing an organization can be a powerful way to enforce legislation. For example, in 2017, a former athletic administrator and former coach successfully sued the University of Iowa for sex discrimination, highlighting the continued work that needs to be done surrounding discrimination in college athletics. Title IX and the Americans with Disabilities Act are two examples of legislation that impact sport organizations in the United States.

3.1.3.1 Title IX of the Educational Amendments

Part of the Educational Amendments of 1972, Title IX is a federal law regarding equal access to educational opportunities for women and bars discrimination based on sex in any educational institution or program that receives federal support. Initially, this act was about giving women access to law and medical schools (until 1972, many of these schools had only a small number of slots for women to be admitted). However, it is now better known for its influential part in the growth of college sports in the United States. Despite being a federal statute for nearly 50 years, there are still examples of college athletic departments violating this law. Dozens of high schools and universities have been successfully sued for Title IX violations. In recent instances, San Diego State University settled with a former coach for $4 million, and St. Cloud State University in Minnesota was ordered to pay over $1 million in legal fees after six of their student-athletes were sued over Title IX violations. Title IX violations are often blamed on the financial costs associated with running women's sports. This is despite the fact that men's sports generally have more expenses than women's sports. Compliance with Title IX is nearly always more cost effective than paying out settlements once violations occur.

▶ **Reasonable Accommodation** Organizations must provide accommodations for disabilities of otherwise qualified individuals unless the accommodation would cause an undue hardship.

3.1.3.2 The Americans with Disabilities Act

The Americans with Disabilities Act of 1990 (ADA) is another example of federal legislation to eliminate discrimination against a specific demographic. There are many similar laws in countries like Canada, the UK, and others. Because this act was not passed until 1990, many facilities are still not ADA compliant. If an organization avoids major renovations on a facility, then it is not required to make buildings or facilities ADA compliant. Knowledge of the ADA is vital in facility planning, but the ADA also covers

reasonable accommodation in hiring, too. Reasonable accommodation is a legal term, which means organizations must accommodate an individual's needs within reason. For example, the volunteer manager of a running event company is focused on successfully managing the hundreds of volunteers it takes to put on a large 10 k race. Many would assume that person would need to be able to walk and lift a certain amount of weight, often seen in job descriptions for these operations roles. However, as management is the allocation and coordination of resources, why couldn't a person in a wheelchair accomplish this task. A reasonable accommodation would be for other volunteers to move items around the event. Beyond hiring, think about ways organizations can be more accommodating to their consumers or participants with disabilities. Simple things like subtitling social media videos can signal to potential participants, consumers, and employees that the organization cares about them.

3.1.4 Consumer/Participant Aspects

As sport continues to globalize and access to technology allows anyone to become fans of any sport, customer bases and participant pools are diversifying for most sports. The globalization of the game of golf provides an example. Increased interest in the Ladies Professional Golf Association (LPGA) in countries such as South Korea has permanently altered the fan base and participant pools in women's golf. The increased popularity of the LPGA in South Korea can be traced to the success of golfers such as Se Ri Pak in the 1990s and early 2000s. This leads to an influx of interest in the sport and more South Korean golfers qualifying for the tour. Today, South Korea hosts its own regional LPGA tour and a major tournament on the main LPGA tour.

Even within organizations that value diversity, implementing actions that demonstrate values and give voice to underrepresented populations can be challenging. Recruiting applicant pools that mirror communities is important as it allows organizations to hire qualified employees while maintaining diversity. By hiring people who reflect your fan base, your fan base may feel better represented and increase their loyalty to your brand.[7] Note of warning, though, hiring one person of a group will not provide access to the entire group. For example, if we want gender diversity in the boardroom, having only one woman-identified person will not influence outcomes, due to gender norms and the vast differences within the subscribed group. Yet, research indicates that having as few as two or more members from underrepresented groups provides a significant impact in terms of decision-making and productivity.[8]

▶ **Stereotype** Positive or negative attributes assigned to a particular group.

3.2   Types of Diversity

Diversity is often portrayed as having representatives from multiple races, genders, or sexual orientations on staff. While these are elements of diversity, this view is incomplete. As managers, it is essential to understand our employees and all the different ways we are categorized by others or ourselves. Stereotypes are attributes assigned to a particular group and can be negative or positive. Think about stereotypes surrounding extroverts, for example. Stereotypical behaviors for extroverts include having a loud, gregarious nature, thinking before they speak, and having the need to be around people all the time. This may be true for some extroverts but not all meet this description. People are not merely an extrovert or an introvert, it is a more complicated spectrum. If we make assumptions about an employee by their perceived extroversion, we could pigeonhole them into specific work tasks. This could be limiting an organization's success. While that example is a simple one, more harmful stereotypes hurt whole groups of people. It is important to be self-aware about any stereotyping you might be doing of your coworkers, participants, or consumers.

▶ **Intersectionality** People experience simultaneous identities, such as their race,

gender, social class, religion, and so on and those identities can interconnect to distinctly impact their lived experience.

Another aspect of diversity to understand is intersectionality. Intersectionality means people experience simultaneous identities, such as their race, gender, social class, religion, and so on. Those identities can interconnect to distinctly impact their lived experience.[9] Indeed research into the experience of Black, female athletic directors in American college athletics found that most experienced multiple challenges based on stereotypes that intersected their gender and race.[10] There are numerous ways to think about diversity, including demographic differences, psycho-social differences, and cultural differences. Some of these differences are more apparent as you meet someone, whereas others may need to be revealed by the individual.

3.2.1   Demographic Differences

Demographic differences are based on age, race, religion, socioeconomic class, gender, sex, physical ability, and sexual orientation. These are the categories that might be checked off on a census survey or an employment application. When thinking about demographic differences, there are often categories related to our cultural history. For example, race in the United States is often categorized by federal or state regulations (i.e., box-checking) grouped into these categories: American Indian or Alaska Native, Asian, Black or African American, Native Hawaiian or Pacific Islander, White, or more than one race, whereas, Hispanic or Latinx is an ethnic category. However, in other countries, they may have different categories related to race. For example, in New Zealand, individuals are grouped into ethnic groups of European, Asian, Maori, and other Pacific Islander. Over 16% of New Zealanders identify as Maori, the original people of the country. History, geography, and culture can influence how a country or industry categorizes people into demographic groups. These can also be contentious. For example, some individuals do not identify with being only male or only female, but some governments ask only for individuals to identify as such. This was the case in the 2016 Canadian Census; the Canadian government asked individuals for their "sex" and gave the option for male or female. However, reports indicate in 2021, the census will ask about sex at birth and current gender in separate questions.[11] The sex of an individual is referring to the biological attributes of an individual, whereas gender refers to the socially constructed roles, behaviors, and expressions that are prescribed to each sex. All of these demographic differences play a role in an employee's lived experiences within and beyond your organization.

▶ **Sex** The sex of an individual is referring to the biological attributes of an individual.

▶ **Gender** Gender refers to the socially constructed roles, behaviors, and expressions that are prescribed to each sex.

3.2.2 Psycho-Social Differences

When we think about psycho-social differences, there are several areas to consider. Usually, one cannot tell psycho-social differences without getting to know a person. Many organizations ask their employees to take different personality tests. These tests can help individuals become more aware of their tendencies and personality traits, as well as learn more about their coworkers. Rather than trying to have all the same personality types in the same workgroup or organization, consider how each personality brings something positive to the table. Understanding the psycho-social differences within an organization or workgroup can help prepare for how each person may react to change or uncertainty, or how communication styles may lead to expectation gaps.

There are a number of archetypes that people use to differentiate psycho-social differences. For example, the Enneagram Typology has recently emerged as a popular typology, and many organizations use the historically popular Myers-Briggs Test. Other ways to think about psycho-social differences include the extroversion-introversion spectrum, or big-thinkers versus detail-oriented, but there are many more tools to use. Like all aspects of diversity, balance the use of typologies to better understand employees with seeing each person as complex and ever-changing. While sometimes steady, personality traits can change depending on the context, environment, and time.[12] Do not use these differences to create in-group, out-group scenarios, but to increase your organization's diversity and inclusion.

▶ **Cultural Diversity** Cultural diversity relates to the norms, behaviors, and values that permeate a particular culture. These could include cultural elements from our national origin, region, hometown, language, family culture, religion, or social class.

3.2.3 Cultural Diversity

Another way to think about diversity is cultural diversity. We all have different cultural experiences. Cultural diversity relates to the norms, behaviors, and values that permeate a particular culture. These could include cultural elements from our national origin, region, hometown, language, family culture, religion, or social class. Different combinations of these elements can intersect to create unique cultures. Residents from across the state of Georgia share similar cultural norms due to shared geographic history. However, residents of Atlanta, Georgia, share many similar cultural norms with New Yorkers because both cities are very large metropolitan areas. Residents of rural Vidalia, Georgia, cannot relate to some of the norms shared between Atlanta and New York.

Cultural differences can also play a role in sport participation. For example, historically in the United Kingdom, soccer was considered a working-class sport played in urban areas like Liverpool and Manchester, whereas rugby was played more by upper-middle and upper-class men at private boarding schools. Beyond sport, class-related cultural norms can influence norms and behaviors around clothing or music choices. These are not always uniform within a specific social identity, but people often prescribe stereo-types to these differences.

▶ **Prejudice** Having negative attitudes toward someone based on their culture or other social identities.

Stereotypes about people can lead to negative feelings and behaviors. Having negative attitudes toward someone, based on their culture or other social identities, is called prejudice. Sometimes it isn't a negative feeling toward other groups, but instead is a positive bias toward those within your own group. That positive bias can still result in prejudice against other groups because you over-value those within your own group. Let's think about an example some of you might have expe-rienced: student-athletes as dumb jocks. If you are a college athlete or know a college athlete, you likely know they reflect the overall student population; some college athletes are great stu-dents, while others are not. However, hiring man-agers may believe the stereotype of dumb jocks and be prejudiced against every college athlete. This unfairly hurts former college athletes in their hiring prospects. In contrast, a hiring man-ager, who was a college athlete themselves, could have a positive bias for anyone who also played a college sport. This unfairly hurts non-athletes in the hiring pool. There is plenty of evidence that prejudice exists in sport organizations. Now let's think beyond merely how many different types of people we have in our organization, but also how they feel they fit within the company.

▶ **Diversity** Having an assortment of demographics, cultures, and psycho-social types present in the organization.

▶ **Inclusion** Inclusion refers to making everyone in the organization feel involved and valued.

3.3   Diversity Versus Inclusion

As mentioned, diversity means having an assort-ment of demographics, cultures, and psycho-social types present in the organization. On the other hand, inclusion refers to making everyone in the organization feel involved and valued. In other words, diversity means you get into the party. Inclusion means you are asked to dance. Several organizations study diversity in sport organizations. Annually, The Institute for Diversity and Ethics in Sport (TIDES) reports on diversity percentages within various sport organi-zations in college athletics and professional sports leagues, and the Tucker Center for Research on Girls & Women in Sport creates a similar report card on women in coaching. Both these centers provide relevant diversity demo-graphic data, where we can compare organiza-tions and observe changes over time, but these do not give a picture of how inclusive these organi-zations are. While diversity is important, inclu-sion supersedes it by effectively engaging all employees in the organization's vision, strate-gies, and day-to-day operations. Indeed, organi-zations are less effective if they engage in compliance diversity strategies rather than proac-tive, inclusive strategies.[13] Feelings of inclusion are not monolithic in an organization. Relationship building, providing employees a voice, and demonstrating a commitment to employees' growth are essential inclusion strategies.

3.4   Benefits of Diversity and Inclusion

Perhaps you already care about diversity and inclusion in your current and future organiza-tions. In some sport organizations, however, traditions and nostalgia reign supreme, so get-ting people to care about making organizations more diverse may be difficult. Offensive nick-names, traditions, or slogans historically asso-ciated with the team can discourage some people from applying, hindering diversity recruitment efforts and limiting pools of quali-fied applicants. Some managers may also believe that people from other cultures, races, or genders are not interested in their organiza-tion's sport. Hiring managers may face push-back from others within the organization who do not value or are threatened by a diverse workforce. These obstacles can be overcome through outreach and ethical persuasion, but managers may also have to convince their colleagues of the benefits of fostering a diverse, inclusive workforce.

3.4.1 Organizational Success

One of the most significant benefits of diversity is often better organizational performance and success toward achieving organizational goals. There are many ways to evaluate organizational success. One common way to evaluate organizational success is financially analyzing profit margins. Sport organizations may also measure success through increased participant numbers, shareholder value, on-field success, community or environmental impact, or various participant-based outcomes. Thus, organizations like a local YMCA or local recreation department could measure success in the number of members, revenue, or community partnerships. An NFL franchise could count successful performance based on profits, franchise values, or victories.

Regardless of which goals the organization uses to measure its success, diversity and inclusion help achieve that success. There are a few possible reasons for this success through diversity and inclusion.

First, by expanding their applicant pool, organizations increase their chances of finding the best-qualified candidate. In less diverse sports industry segments, accessing a larger applicant pool can provide an organization with a competitive advantage due to greater human capital access. Secondly, employees' diverse experiences can bring new ideas to organizations or new ways to consider a problem. Those new ideas could build a competitive advantage for the organization and help it grow its share of the marketplace. As has been mentioned several times throughout the book, employees want to work for organizations that share similar values. How does that benefit the organization? Engaged employees are more invested in their roles and the organization's

success. They have a greater sense of urgency, focus, and enthusiasm for their tasks than less engaged employees.

However, organizations must exhibit an actual commitment to diversity. Statements are not enough to generate engagement and may hurt the organization if not backed with action. Suppose an organization made claims to be diverse and inclusive, but didn't achieve that. How frustrating would that be to employees? As you will see in later chapters, not following through on organizational commitments can substantially damage employees' attitudes toward the organization and workplace behaviors. Frustration and a lack of feeling that everyone is in this together can spur employees to disengage, making them less productive or willing to go above and beyond for your organization.

Example

Women have historically been denied access to top-level leadership roles in sport organizations. Many still have senior staffs that are entirely male and mostly white. Imagine being a part of one of these organizations and being vocal about the need to have female representation in leadership. Your colleagues are also vocal and it appears the organization is listening when a highly qualified woman, Mary, is hired for a senior leadership position. Mary is excited and ready to join the leadership team with ideas to improve the company. You are excited to be a part of her department. However, at senior leadership meetings, Mary is consistently talked over. Her ideas are either ignored or repeated by a male colleague, who receives the credit for those ideas. ◄

After reading the example, how do you think Mary will begin to feel about her new organization? How will you and the rest of your departmental colleagues feel about their manager being discounted because of her sex? Maybe not right away, but eventually, Mary will move on. So might you and your colleagues. The organization has spent valuable time and money hiring and training someone new but didn't get to enjoy the benefits of those new ideas. As you can see, organizations that ignore diversity and inclusion are

not just falling short on ethical and legal obligations. They are missing out on opportunities to
improve the organization's overall success.

3.5   Organizational Aspects of Diversity and Inclusion

If an organization decides to become more
diverse, and more importantly, more inclusive,
there are several aspects to consider. First, it
should seek feedback from people within the
organization. Employees who identify as part of
an underrepresented or marginalized group often
have ideas on making their organizations more
diverse and inclusive.[14] In fact, they've likely
been trying to share them with the organization
for a while but have been ignored. Committees/
task forces, public statements, recruitment, hiring, programming, and structural/policy changes
are possible avenues for improving diversity and
inclusion. As you can see, all elements of an
organization should be touched by diversity and
inclusion efforts. Let's take a look at common
actions in the sports industry.

3.5.1   Committees on Diversity and Inclusion

As Cooper et al.[15] argued in their research about
college athletics that having committees dedicated to diversity and inclusion efforts are a
great beginning step within any sport organization. They also note that committees should
include internal and external stakeholders such
as athletes, employees, and partners. The key
aspect being that these committees or task
forces are "given organizational power to create
policies, practices and methods of evaluation to
reduce and eliminate systematic racism and
sexism and improve diversity and inclusion"
(p. 11). These committees, when given
resources, can help shape the organizational
statements, recruitment efforts, and hiring processes, as well as programming and structure of
sport organizations.

3.5.2   Diversity and Inclusion Statements

Increasingly, sport organizations are producing
diversity and inclusion statements. These
statements aim to demonstrate the organization's
dedication to diversity and/or inclusion to both
internal and external stakeholders. Diversity and
inclusion statements signal organizational values
to both employees (internal) and participants,
consumers, businesses, or community partners
(external). Such statements can be an effective
way to communicate organizational values to
prospective applicants. However, suppose the
actions of the organization are contrary to these
statements. In that case, it can be harmful to
employee morale or external partnerships and
hurt recruitment and hiring efforts.

3.5.3   Diversity and Inclusion Recruitment

The only way to increase diversity within an
organization is to hire a diverse workforce.
Organizations must be intentional in their recruiting practices. An oft-cited argument for lack of
diversity is the absence of interest by a particular
group; however, the issue is generally related to
inadequate efforts in the recruitment process.
One of the most common recruitment efforts is to
post a job announcement on a sport-related job
board (i.e., *Teamwork Online, Sports Job Finder,*
etc.). Research has found that men are likely to
apply for a posted position if they meet at least
60% of the listed qualifications whereas women
generally only apply to positions in which they
already meet 100% of qualifications. According
to the study, which included more than 1000 professionals, women don't apply because they follow the hiring post's written guidelines.[16] As a
result, applicant pools are overloaded with men,
partly because men are more willing to apply
when they are less than qualified, and also
because women already receive few opportunities to achieve qualifications jobs in the sports
industry. Organizations can remove this barrier

by focusing less on achieved qualifications and more on talent and potential. To seek out the best possible talent, organizations should expand their recruitment beyond posting the job online.

Sport organizations can learn more about applicants' potential through conversation and interaction. To gain access to more diverse talent pools, organizations can consider conferences, clubs, mentoring programs, and other physical locations where you are more likely to meet diverse groups of people. For example, in esports, 22% of African-Americans in the United States indicated fanship of esports, yet the professional teams and managers are primarily white and Asian.[17] If esports organizations want to seek out more African American representation, creating mentoring programs, hosting conferences, and recruiting at events will be more effective than posting on job boards. Increasingly, sport organizations are hosting hiring events where potential applicants must pay to attend. This strategy is a successful revenue-generating strategy but also prohibits applicants from lower socioeconomic classes from entering the applicant pool.

▷ **Explicit Bias** Biases that one is consciously aware of and willingly allows to influence decision-making.

▷ **Implicit   Bias** Predispositions   that unconsciously guide decision-making.

3.5.4   Hiring Process

How does an organization choose the right candidate from its applicant pool? One thing to consider is the implicit bias of hiring managers. We often think about explicit bias, which is the acting on a bias of which one is consciously aware. Explicit biases are very harmful because they result in blatant discrimination, but they are also more visible to all involved parties. Implicit biases are predispositions that unconsciously guide our decision-making. We often do not even realize we have them which is what makes implicit bias so damaging. Hiring managers act-

ing on implicit bias believe they are making the best and fairest decisions without any intention to do harm.

There are ways to either acknowledge our implicit biases or reduce its impact on the hiring process. One way is to simply acknowledge that decision-makers are biased and learn to recognize them. Organizations can have their hiring committees take implicit bias tests, which can reveal biases toward specific groups. This allows hiring managers to better recognize when their decisions are discriminatory. Another possible consideration would be to create a rating system based on each of the criteria of job announcement, or adopt some form of analytical or scientific assessment to evaluate candidates. This will reduce bias for an in-group member (maybe the son of a friend), who is clearly not as qualified as other candidates.

Organizations must also reexamine their interview processes to eliminate implicit bias. Search committees should be expanded to include broad representation. Having a diverse hiring committee allows for collaboration and discussion of candidates that include more viewpoints. In addition, interview questions should be standardized for all candidates. This ensures that all applicants are evaluated on the same criteria. Finally, organizations can ask candidates to complete a task so they can be assessed directly on job-related skills or potential.

Example

Men's sports leagues have a long-held bias against women's ability to coach male athletes. Acknowledging that bias, several teams in the NFL, NBA, and MLB have hired women for coaching positions in recent years. Katie Sowers became the first female to coach in a Super Bowl, when she coached as an offensive assistant for the San Francisco 49ers in Super Bowl LIV. ◄

3.5.5   Diversity and Inclusion Programming

Diversity trainings are becoming more common for both incoming and current employees. These are meant to help encourage inclusivity and help people understand their biases. However, sometimes they can be detrimental if not done productively. The classic American TV show *The Office* had an episode about a disastrous way to do diversity training. In the episode, managers drew attention to racial, gender, and LGBTQ stereotypes but did not discuss the dangers of holding such prejudices. In the end, everyone in the office felt more awkward around each other than they had before. It is satire, so an exaggeration, but there are stories of real diversity training going horribly wrong. This generally makes life worse for those within the organization, especially those from underrepresented groups.

Recognizing how training efforts may be implemented in a context-specific way, understanding the inter-personal dynamics of each workgroup is most effective. While not addressing the larger structural issues, the Six-stage framework (Fig. 3.1) can help design individualized education modules for employees. Various employees within your organization will be somewhere along this spectrum (and in different places depending on the type of diversity). Thus, knowing their stage has utility in building more effective and useful programming.

As Kim mentions[18] in the early stages of the framework, individuals seek psychological safety as their default placement. Although it is hard to imagine people being unaware of bias, most do not automatically explore prejudices in society unless they are affected. Once they become aware, the apathetic stage is one of acknowledgment but also downplaying the impact bias has on others. At this stage, you may hear an employee say, "Well, we all have problems," or "I just have too much going on to care right now." The third stage, curious, is when employees will begin to ask questions. Statements like "I want to learn more, but I am afraid of saying the wrong thing" is common.

In the later stages, employees begin choosing to address bias, even if it makes them uncomfortable. In the informed stage, employees develop an understanding of the issues surrounding their biases and start making efforts to make changes in their own attitudes. At the empowered stage, individuals now feel more comfortable acknowledging their biases publicly. They care less about their own reputation compared to making changes in the organization. In the final stage, employees join the fight for change within the organization.

To ensure programming is successful, organizations must keep in mind a few important lessons. First, the effort to mitigate bias should not fall on the shoulders of the marginalized group. This is unfair, and the extra work may hurt their careers. Second, training must be an ongoing process, championed by the organization. Once-a-month workshops are generally not useful. Most importantly, initiatives should garner a sense of belonging for everyone in the organization, focus on both a top-down and bottom-up approach, and involve small actions regularly to build real and lasting feelings of inclusiveness for all the employees.

3.5.6 Organizational Culture and Structure

In the previous chapter, you were introduced to the concepts of organizational culture and structure. Both can encourage or discourage diversity and inclusion. Building diversity and inclusion into the organizational culture and championing initiatives as essential organizational functions inform employees of their importance. Tangible programs, such as the Bill Walsh Diversity in Coaching Fellowships in the NFL[19] and NASCAR's Drive for Diversity, signal organiza-

Fig. 3.1 Six-stage framework (Kim, J. [November, 2017]. How to design original, impactful diversity and inclusion programming. Presented at the Lever Talent Innovation Summit. Retrieved from: https://www.jennifer.kim/inclusion)

tional commitments to inclusion that are evident to employees from underrepresented groups and employees from privileged populations. Structural changes like the ones referenced can be powerful mechanisms for change. But small changes to policy and norms to be more inclusive also make significant impacts.

Many organizations hold important meetings at 8:00 am. This seems rather benign. Holding meetings at 8:00 am allows people to complete the meeting and move into their day. However, for parents, especially single parents, or parents who are the primary caregiver, early meetings can be a considerable obstacle to their success and growth. It places parents in a position where they may be unable to get their children to school and make that early meeting. This seemingly innocent organizational tradition could signal that the organization does not value their family to working parents. Similarly, a tradition of socializing at a local pub after work can effectively build morale and improve team cohesion. However, employees who abstain from drinking for religious, health, or addiction issues may feel left out, especially if work-based discussions are conducted. Simply altering organizational policies or rotating team-building activities so that more can participate goes a long way toward making everyone feel included.

3.6 Conclusion

As you can see, diversity and inclusion are essential parts of today's sports industry. No matter what part of the industry you choose to work in, conversations are being had about this important topic. There are many opportunities and challenges when it comes to diversity and inclusion in the sports industry. There is now overwhelming evidence from both academic and industry-sponsored research indicating that diversity and inclusion are beneficial to both employee well-being and the bottom line (i.e., profit margins). Thus, you will see references to diversity and inclusion in nearly every chapter of this textbook.

Discussion Questions

1. Think about the different aspects and types of diversity written in this chapter. How do you identify in terms of race, gender, sexual orientation, or socioeconomic status? What other types of identity are important aspects to who you are as a person?
2. Recall a time when you did not feel included or noticed someone else was not being included in a team or work setting. How did it make you feel? What concrete, specific ways could you help someone feel more included in your sport organization?
3. Part of inclusion in an organization is getting to know your coworkers and building empathy for them and their lived experiences. List different ways you would get to know and build empathy for your coworkers.

Notes

1. Kotkin, J. (August, 2010). The Changing Demographics of America. *Smithsonian Magazine*. Retrieved from: https://www.smithsonianmag.com/travel/the-changing-demographics-of-america-538284/.
2. Olushola-Ogunrinde, J., & Carter-Francique, A. R. (2020). Beyond the Xs and Os. In (Eds. Bradbury, S., Lusted, J., & van Sterkenburg, J.) *'Race', Ethnicity and Racism in Sports Coaching*. London: Routledge.
3. Proxmire, D. (December, 2008). Coaching Diversity: The Rooney Rule, Its Application and Ideas for Expansion. *American Constitution Society for Law and Policy*. Retrieved from: https://www.acslaw.org/wp-content/uploads/old-uploads/originals/documents/Proxmire_Issue_Brief.pdf.
4. Cooper, J. N., Newton, A. C., Klein, M., & Jolly, S. (2020). A Call for Culturally Responsive Transformational Leadership in College Sport: An Anti-ism Approach for Achieving Equity and Inclusion. *Frontiers in Sociology, 5*, 65, 1–17.
5. Cunningham, G. B., & Melton, E. N. (2011). The benefits of sexual orientation diversity in sport organizations. *Journal of Homosexuality, 58*(5), 647–663.
6. Cooper, J. N., Newton, A. C., Klein, M., & Jolly, S. (2020). A Call for Culturally Responsive Transformational Leadership in College Sport: An Anti-ism Approach for Achieving Equity and Inclusion. *Frontiers in Sociology, 5*, 65, 1–17.
7. Cooper, J. N., Newton, A. C., Klein, M., & Jolly, S. (2020). A Call for Culturally Responsive

Transformational Leadership in College Sport: An Anti-ism Approach for Achieving Equity and Inclusion. *Frontiers in Sociology, 5,* 65, 1–17.

8. Loop, P. & DeNicola, P (Feb., 2019). You've Committed to Increasing Gender Diversity on Your Board. Here's How to Make it Happen. *Harvard Business Review.* Retrieved from https://hbr.org/2019/02/youve-committed-to-increasing-gender-diversity-on-your-board-heres-how-to-make-it-happen.

9. Walker, N. A., & Melton, E. N. (2015). The tipping point: The intersection of race, gender, and sexual orientation in intercollegiate sports. *Journal of Sport Management, 29*(3), 257–271.

10. McDowell, J., & Carter-Francique, A. (2017). An intersectional analysis of the workplace experiences of African American female athletic directors. *Sex Roles, 77*(5–6), 393–408.

11. Leblanc, D. (April, 2020) Ottawa adding new census questions on gender, Indigenous, linguistic, and ethnic minorities. *The Globe and Mail.* Retrieved from: https://www.theglobeandmail.com/politics/article-ottawa-adding-new-census-questions-on-gender-indigenous-canadians/.

12. Damian, R. I., Spengler, M., Sutu, A., & Roberts, B. W. (2019). Sixteen going on sixty-six: A longitudinal study of personality stability and change across 50 years. *Journal of Personality and Social Psychology, 117*(3), 674

13. Fink, J. S., Pastore, D. L., & Riemer, H. A. (2001). Do differences make a difference? Managing diversity in Division IA intercollegiate athletics. *Journal of Sport Management, 15*(1), 10–50.

14. Singer, J. N., & Cunningham, G. B. (2018). A collective case study of African American male athletic directors' leadership approaches to diversity in college sport. *Journal of Intercollegiate Sport, 11*(2), 269–297.

15. Cooper, J. N., Newton, A. C., Klein, M., & Jolly, S. (2020). A Call for Culturally Responsive Transformational Leadership in College Sport: An Anti-ism Approach for Achieving Equity and Inclusion. *Frontiers in Sociology,* 5, 65, 1–17.

16. Mohr, T. S. (August, 2014). Why women don't apply for jobs unless they're 100% qualified. *Harvard Business Review.* Retrieved from: https://hbr.org/2014/08/why-women-dont-apply-for-jobs-unless-theyre-100-qualified.

17. Peterson, L. (March, 2018). Why aren't more black kids going pro in esports? *The Undefeated.* Retrieved from: https://theundefeated.com/features/why-arent-more-black-kids-going-pro-in-esports/.

18. Kim, J. (November, 2017). How to Design Original, Impactful Diversity and Inclusion Programming. Presented at the Lever Talent Innovation Summit. Retrieved from: https://www.jennifer.kim/inclusion.

19. Agyemang, K., & DeLorme, J. (2010). Examining the Dearth of Black Head Coaches at the NCAA Football Bowl Subdivision Level: A Critical Race Theory and Social Dominance Theory Analysis. *Journal of Issues in Intercollegiate Athletics*, 3, 35–52.

Part II

Understanding the Organization

In their essence, organizations in sport are groups of people segmented and structured in a manner to accomplish tasks. The efficiency with which managers structure the employees can greatly influence the success of an organization. Therefore, understanding the organization is vital to organizational success. This unit will explore how organizations are structured and communication channels function in sport organizations. Next, we'll examine how organizational culture is created and experienced by organizational members. Finally, we'll discuss the key aspects of organizational change. Organizations are dynamic and complicated. In the sports industry, society provides them with great prominence. As such, their behaviors and changes are influenced by and are critiqued by their external environment.

Dr. Miriam Merrill: Director of Athletics, Pomona-Pitzer Colleges
  To listen to the interview <click here>

4.1 Concepts of Structure Within Organizations

Look at your favorite team's roster. In most sports, players are assigned a position that defines their role and dictates how they interact with other teammates. In sports with high degrees of specialization and complex playing structures, positions may also tell us which grouping the player belongs. In soccer, a player's position also lets us know if they are a defender, midfielder, or a forward player. In football, the position tells us if the player is on the offensive or defensive side of the ball. It also communicates how close to the line of scrimmage they position themselves. Much like teams, employees are placed in a specific role, and that role may be a part of a larger grouping of employees with similar functions. How people are placed within an organization influences communication patterns, culture, and execution of organizational goals.

As you begin reading this chapter, you may wonder, what is the best organizational structure. As you will see, there is no correct structure for sport organizations. The optimal organizational structure depends on an organization's vision and goals. Organizational structures are the patterns or grouping of tasks and individuals that determine reporting relationships. Imagine an organization with a strict hierarchical structure, where entry-level employees rarely interact with the president, CEO, or athletic director. That organizational structure means the power resides mainly

Supplementary Information The online version of this chapter (https://doi.org/10.1007/978-3-030-67612-4_4) contains supplementary material, which is available to authorized users.

with the middle managers, who relay information and directives between those entry-level workers and those in top leadership positions. Conversely, with a flatter organizational structure, meaning middle managers are not a part of the design, the communication patterns are quite different. New interns may find themselves in meetings with upper administration to discuss strategy. In determining which organizational structure is most important, firms should account for six building blocks to organizational structure: specialization, departmentalization, formalization, centralization, span of control, and chain of command. This chapter will begin by addressing each block. The later parts of the chapter will explore the influence of sport on these organizational structures and different structure options for a sport organization.

▶ **Organizational Structure** Organizational structures are the patterns or grouping of tasks and individuals that determine reporting relationships.

▶ **Specialization** Specialization refers to the degree to which the tasks of an organization are broken down into specific roles.

4.1.1 Specialization

In the front office of most Class A-level Minor League Baseball teams, one person is in charge of the team's ticket operations. Their duties would include selling tickets, processing ticket orders, and overseeing gameday operations of the box office. In a larger organization, such as an MLB franchise, ticket sales are a separate department from box office operations. Further, the ticket sales department likely has workers solely focused on selling single-game tickets, season tickets, group tickets, or premium tickets. This is an example of specialization. Specialization refers to the degree to which the tasks of an organization are broken down into specific roles. Specialization allows individuals to become highly knowledgeable in their particular roles.

This helps the employee become more efficient at executing those tasks and introduces creative ideas because of their focus on one particular topic.

Specialization is more common in larger sport organizations that have resources to hire people that serve only one role. In smaller sport organizations, specialization is difficult to achieve as resource limitations prohibit firms from hiring enough workers to complete all organizational functions. Thus, employees have to complete roles in multiple functional areas. More recently, smaller organizations have begun outsourcing functions that require specialization, such as ticket sales. However, larger organizations also outsource work when the required specialization is far outside of the organization's primary function. For example, Major League Baseball Advanced Media paid several NYU computer science professors to develop Statcast, an innovative visual analytics tool.[1] Although specialization is a critical component in organizational efficiency, it can have adverse outcomes. One issue with increasing specialization is a lack of flexibility in the organization. Individuals who only have expertise in one area cannot be easily assigned new tasks that don't fit within their knowledge area. In addition, if employees become bored in their role due to a lack of task variety, they can actually become less engaged and less productive.

4.1.2 Departmentalization

Departmentalization is defined as grouping roles and tasks within the organization's structure to accomplish specific elements of its operational needs. The idea is to group employees with similar functions or related processes to make workflow, decision-making, and communication more efficient. Deciding which roles to group into a department can vary based on the organization's size and focus, as well as the nature of the task. Suppose we look at the departmentalization of ticket operations across the industry. Ticket operations is generally tasked with seating allocation, ticketing software selection, printing and distribution of tickets, and gameday gate operations. If we were to survey organizational structures across the industry, we would see ticket operations personnel placed in sales offices, marketing offices, business operations, and facility operations. If ticket operations and facility operations were together, department meetings would include discussions of people flow and security, in business operations, discussions would be focused on accounting of revenues, whereas with sales or marketing, department meetings would include conversations around incoming groups and increase in suite sales. Each of those impacts the ticket operations staff, but in different ways. It is not to say ticket operations wouldn't learn about both of these task areas regardless of their department grouping, but departmental groups expedite this information sharing. While departmentalization can lead to several issues (see Chap. 14), effective use of the tactic does increase efficiency. Therefore, thinking about the most effective and efficient way to group an organization's tasks can improve organizational success.

▶ **Formalization** Formalization is the degree to which the organization relies on and documents operating procedures to maintain structure.

4.1.3 Formalization

Formalization is the degree to which the organization relies on and documents operating procedures to maintain structure.[2] Job duties, listed in both position announcements and human resource manuals, represent a level of formalization within the organization's structure, but formalization can take many other forms. Many factors influence the degree of formality within a sport organization. For many long-time, amateur-run community sport organizations, there is a struggle between complete flexibility and increasing formalization, due to pressure from funding resources.[3] But, access to resources is not the only driving in formalization. As discussed in Chap. 2, most sport organizations are relatively small. Smaller organizations have little need nor capacity to formalize.[4] On the other hand, organizations that experience a lot of employee turnover desire more formality. When an individual leaves the organization, it may be difficult for the organization to replace them, as their supervisors may not be aware of their whole task list. Employee turnover has long been an issue for sport organizations.[5] Depending on the formalization level required for a role, sport organizations often ask current employees to write out their duties, including those not previously formalized. This allows the organization to understand better what tasks will not be fulfilled should the person leave.

Beyond turnover, formalization can help employees and administrators manage expectations. When an employee is encouraged to do whatever is asked of them and more, it can create frustration, confusion, and burnout. Formalization of tasks allows employees to understand what is within their role and what is beyond. However, similar to many of these other elements of organizational structure, too much formalization can create extreme rigidity, making organizations inflexible to shifts in their environment. Organizations should seek a balance based on their needs and their operational environment.

▶ **Centralization** Centralization refers to the consolidation of decision-making in an organization.

4.1.4 Centralization

Centralization refers to the consolidation of decision-making in an organization. If the decision-making process requires consistent approval from a singular role, such as president or CEO, then the organization is highly centralized. Contrariwise, when decision-making responsibility lies with department heads and other middle managers, we can say that the organization is decentralized. Many non-profit and community sport organizations adopt decentralized structures where a significant amount of decision-making is done by a governing board of directors, who are democratically elected by the association members. These organizations seek to involve as many stakeholders as possible, and maintain a fair and inclusive environment. This relates back to their missions as a community-focused organization. An issue with decentralized decision-making is it can slow down decision-making and could create sub-unit competition.

Conversely, a highly centralized organization can be more agile in its decision-making processes. Many sport organizations leave decisions regarding player acquisition up to specific individuals. This allows them to beat out other teams when a coveted talent becomes available. Smaller organizations and those with more visionary leadership are also more likely to adopt a centralized structure. In a highly centralized organization, employees in those decision-making roles take on increased importance.

▶ **Span of Control** The number of employees who report to a manager.

4.1.5 Span of Control

In organizations with a hierarchical structure, one person may manage three to four people, but in flatter organizations, individuals may directly manage ten to fifteen people. The number of employees who report to an individual within an organization's structure is their span of control. When hiring individuals for a supervisory position, it is important to think about a potential applicant's span of control capabilities. After all, managing two to three direct reports is quite different than overseeing the 15 employees. Similarly, managing entry-level employees is quite different from overseeing highly experienced workers. Determining the appropriate span of control for managers depends on a number of elements, such as geographic distance, level of competency, and complexity of tasks. Span of control considerations are more important in hierarchical structures than in other typologies discussed later in this chapter. Unique to event-based organizations, such as many sport organizations, is how an employee's span of control shifts between game day and non-game day. In day-to-day operations, a game day manager may

have a coordinator and an intern under their span of control, but manage a significantly higher number of people on the day of an event. Determining each manager's capabilities to coordinate employees, along with organizational needs and directives, will allow sport organizations to develop proper spans of control and become more efficient in staffing.

4.1.6 Chain of Command

Chain of command refers to the line of authority that extends from upper-level management through middle management to lower tiered employees. Depending on the organization's structure and formality, the chain of command dictates who reports to whom. Often, the chain of command also dictates communication flow through the organizational structure. The chain of command is ever-present, giving managers oversight over daily decisions like approving advertising campaigns, employee travel, and other routine functions. But, the chain of command in sport organizations is also highly evident and relevant during time-sensitive situations and crises. When difficult decisions need to be made, it becomes clearer to most employees why it is relevant. For example, the Covid-19 pandemic forced sport organizations to make very tough choices about if, when, and how to play games. Decisions were made based on the chain of command for each organization, which looked very different in the German Bundesliga compared to NCAA athletic programs. Even within various athletic departments, there were differences based on structure. Coaches and operations staff reported to athletic directors, who, in turn, reported to university presidents. University presidents are usually governed by a board of trustees, and potentially the state government. Most college athletic programs also belong to a conference. The NCAA and most universities deferred to their conferences to make decisions regarding competition during the pandemic. Universities and their athletic departments then made decisions using their own chains of command to determine how to react to conference decisions.

Understanding who has decision-making power in organizations can help employees or potential employees better comprehend how decisions are made.

4.2 Type of Organizational Structures

After understanding the elements of organizations, let's discuss the different organizational structure types and how sport may influence these structures. Most organizations adopt one of the following organizational structures: simple, bureaucratic/hierarchical, matrix, and self-managed team structures. Sport's history and culture have influenced how many sport organizations are structured. As sport becomes more globalized, professionalized, and competitive, sport organizations have adapted their organizational structures to meet new goals.

4.2.1 Simple Structure

A simple organizational structure is often found in smaller sport organizations. For example, in a minor league hockey franchise, there may only be a general manager (GM) and an assistant general manager (AGM) as full-time employees. They may also have game day staff and interns, but the organization's front office structure would still be relatively simple, with everyone reporting to either the GM or AGM. As seen in Fig. 4.1, there are not multiple layers of communication. Everything generally flows through one or two people.

This structure makes the organization extraordinarily fluid and flexible. As everyone is in close proximity and communicate frequently, they are able to shift duties as the situation arises. An example of this, when MiLB canceled the 2020 season, most MiLB franchises shifted quickly to survive. If an organization grows larger, a simple structure can still be effective if it maintains a strong organizational culture and effective communication channels.

The Johnson City Cardinals, a rookie league affiliate of the St. Louis Cardinals, had their 2020

Fig. 4.1 Simple organizational structure

season canceled due to the Covid-19 pandemic. The front office quickly pivoted as an organization and used their stadium to host high school tournaments and other events. The quick pivot allowed the organization to earn revenue while being unable to perform its primary function. Having only two full-time employees, the organization was able to make decisions quickly and act decisively. ◄

4.2.2 Hierarchical or Bureaucratic Structure

In larger organizations, hierarchical structures often emerge. These structures rely on layers of reporting mechanisms (bureaucracies) to create a laddered pyramid within its chain of command. This structure usually is highly organized, which creates formality within reporting structures and communication channels. As seen in Fig. 4.2, a singular person or a small group of upper-level administrators possess final decision-making power. Authority and decision-making capabilities recede further down the structure.

Remembering the section on departmentalization, these organizations are generally segmented into departments. There are clear lines of work delineation and who is in command of what area. Departments are often clustered by a specialization. For example, in Fig. 4.2, there is a marketing department, a ticket sales department, a sponsorship or business development department, and an operations department. Depending on the organization's size, these

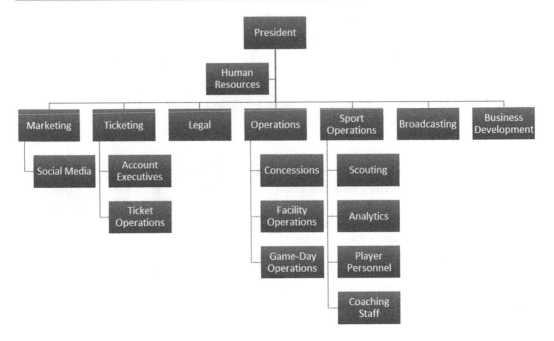

Fig. 4.2 Hierarchical organizational structure

department or work team groupings can be highly specialized. With their clear chain of command, hierarchical structures can reduce anxiety for individual roles, make individual employees more replaceable, and quickly execute directives from above.

Hierarchical structures are not right for every organization, and the structure's bureaucracy presents problems in some scenarios. The structure makes the organization less adaptable or quick to change, an issue in today's ever-changing society. Ideas from lower tiered employees are often drowned out in the numerous layers of the chain of command. Additionally, depending on its rigidity, the hierarchical structure makes it easier to cover up abuse by individuals. See sexual abuse scandals at Michigan State and USA Gymnastics. Organizational mechanisms for reporting abuse or addressing other serious issues are essential in hierarchical structures.

An important note regarding hierarchical structures, an organization can appear on paper and in written policy to be highly bureaucratic but function much differently. Informal communication channels allow for information to bypass the formal chain of command. This creates poten-

tially confusing expectations for employees housed within these structures as they no longer know whom to report to and who is making decisions. This informality has been accelerated by modern communication (see Chap. 5).

Analyzing an organizational structure on both paper, and in reality, provides utility for leaders. The hierarchical structure creates clarity for employees and organizes long lists of tasks. However, it also limits adaptability and could create problematic power dynamics.

4.2.3 Matrix Organizational Structure

As the name suggests, a matrix organizational structure consists of people and projects built into a matrix, where individuals will report to multiple stakeholders depending on the project or process. As seen in Table 4.1, the operations director answers to a different event director for each event. They may also manage a different team for each event, depending on what is needed.

This type of structure gives organizations flexibility in utilizing individual skills for mul-

Table 4.1 Matrix organizational structure

	Event A	Event B	Event C
	Event A director	Event B director	Event C director
Marketing director	Marketing team	Marketing team	Marketing team
Sponsorship director	Sponsorship team	Sponsorship team	Sponsorship team
Public relations director	PR team	PR team	PR team
Operations director	Operations team	Operations team	Operations team

tiple projects or teams. For organizations with multiple geographic locations, having someone leading in each geographic location can address location-specific issues. For an organization headquartered in Paris but hosting events in Toronto, London, and Melbourne, it makes sense to have project leaders headquartered at each site. At the same time, support staff in Paris may be working with each project leader as needed.

This structure also occurs frequently in the sports industry when there is a need for a highly specialized workgroup. For example, sport organizations that host multiple teams, such as FC Bayern Munich or The Ohio State University athletics, must support the needs of individual teams. Coaches and other specialized support staff serve in dedicated roles to their team. That is, the basketball coaches only coach basketball and soccer coaches only coach soccer. On the other hand, athletic trainers may serve multiple teams within the organization and report to different leaders for each team. Thus, the trainer for rowing reports to both the head of sports performance and the rowing team's head coach. Matrix structures can be a great use of resources, leveraging the time and expertise across multiple teams or workgroups. Communication is fundamental within these types of organizational structures. Destructive forms of conflict between managers of different projects or teams (see Chap. 16) can create difficult situations for those within the matrix structure.

command and span of control, a self-managed team structure provides a great deal of latitude for employees to organize themselves and tasks to achieve the goals set forth by the organization. In fact, some organizations allow the self-managed team to set its own goals. We see examples of this all throughout sports. For instance, head coaches often enable their players to have input on team goals. Similarly, ticket sales departments can have tremendous input regarding revenue goals. This strategy allows upper administration, be they a coach or director of ticket sales, to gauge what success looks like to the team. This approach enables top-level administrators to become facilitators rather than using the typical top-down approach.

Self-managed teams can increase employee engagement because the employees helped shape the roles and goals of the group. This is based on the assumption that humans enjoy autonomy in their work rather than only working for money. This makes self-managed teams an interesting option for sport organizations since many sport employees are highly identified with either the sport or team they work for.[7] However, self-managed teams can also be hard to execute, particularly if there is confusion or fear of change within the group. A great deal of autonomy can be difficult for employees who have never experienced such freedom, so clarity of expectation and consistency of action by the team leader is fundamental to team success.[8] These structures offer options but are only as effective as they are implemented and aligned with the organization's vision.

4.2.4 Self-Managed Teams

A somewhat-new structural option is the self-managed team, first popularized in the 1990s by Taco Bell.[6] Moving away from a focus on chain of

4.2.5 Fluid and Complex Structures

When observing sport organizations' structures, it becomes evident that many organizations use elements of more than one type. For example, in a college athletic department or a multi-sport club, there may be a matrix style for the sport performance staff, a bureaucratic structure for the coaching or operations departments, and a self-managed team structure for the sales department. It is about what will make the organization most effective in meeting its needs and goals.

More frequently, sport organizations are moving beyond separate structures for different departments toward blurred or hybrid configurations. Changes to the operating environment, in terms of business environment, organizational missions, and in employees' expectations, are forcing even the most traditional sport organizations to rethink their structures. For example, as sports fans have adopted more globalized consumption habits and access to financial capital has tightened, smaller sport organizations with local and regional followings have had to adapt. In recent years the Scottish soccer clubs in existence for over a hundred years have had to restructure in a variety of ways, such as becoming a social enterprise or owned by the club's foundation.[9] Other clubs have merged, blending cultures and structures.[10] The emergence of sport development and peace organizations has created structures that adopt from voluntary organizations, health organizations, or governmental organizations, and non-governmental organizations (NGOs).[11] Internal and external forces will continue to affect sport organizations' structures, as will the desire to spur innovation, creativity, and entrepreneurial outcomes.

4.3   Influences and Issues in Sport Organizations

In sport organizations, the organization's history, resources, and size can significantly affect the structure. Unique aspects within the structures of sport organizations, such as the creation of the Senior Woman Administrator role in intercollegiate athletics, were shaped by the history of codifying modern sport. As discussed throughout the text, the generally smaller size of sport organizations limits bureaucracy but also

forces employees to have multiple duties or place non-full-time employees in decision-making roles. There is also the concept of coopetition, that is, the unique element of the sports industry where organizations compete on the field but are also business partners. League structures and the simultaneous competition and cooperation create organizational structures where various interests from different organizations are represented.

4.3.1   Influence of Sport's Origin on Current Organizational Structures

Sport was originally formed through loosely organized clubs and associations. These associations had voting processes, thus major decisions were made through a democratic process. These origins still influence many sport organization's structures. Research regarding Swedish sport clubs found conflict between the professionalization of these and the historical precedent of democratic decision-making processes. The hierarchical structure made these clubs more efficient, but the association structure made the clubs more democratic.[12] As we mentioned before, understanding the goals and vision of a sport organization is crucial to determine what structures are most appropriate.

Another aspect of sport history that has fundamentally shaped sport organizations, especially in the Olympic movement and intercollegiate athletics, is the idea of amateurism. The founders of the Olympic movement built sport organizations around the concept of amateurs competing against each other. Sport organizations today are still influenced by that history. A whole department within almost every college athletics program addresses compliance with NCAA rules related to keeping college athletics an amateur endeavor. Whether or not that is successful is not the point of this example. Amateurism remains a powerful influence in the structure of college athletic programs. Likewise, as a part of Title IX-impacted higher education, college athletics has created a unique role, the Senior Woman Administrator (SWA). An SWA is a designation provided by the

NCAA to help provide women with more representation in leadership. The actual functioning of this role is disputed.[13] Regardless, college athletics provides a useful example of how sport's origins can influence organizational structure.

4.3.2   Small-Medium Enterprises in Sport

Despite being one of the largest and most powerful sport organizations globally, FIFA only reports having 947 employees in 2019.[14] Conversely, the cumulative number of grassroots sport employees is more extensive than FIFA, yet each one may consist of one to a dozen employees. Therefore, it has been argued that the vast majority of sport organizations are actually small-medium enterprises.[15] Why does this matter? For one, working in a smaller sport organization means the specialization, departmentalization, and centralization capabilities may be limited based on the number of employees versus the number of tasks required to achieve the organization's goals. A ticket manager may also be in charge of accounting and social media. The organization's size may require a flexible organizational structure, one for standard operating procedure and one for game-day events. Similarly, if a non-profit sport-for-development organization realizes the organization needs to increase its grants to maintain the level of programming to reach its goals, but it does not have a grant writer on staff, this may alter role descriptions as needed. The resource constraints associated with smaller organizational size provide both opportunity and challenge to building a useful structure for small-medium sport enterprises.

4.3.3   League and Coopetitive Influences

Many sport organizations are stand-alone enterprises, such as Nike, the multi-national sporting goods company, or a local afterschool youth sports program. Their organizational structure is entirely up to the leadership of that organization. However, for sport organizations that are affiliated with a league or conference, structure is highly influenced by their affiliation. For example, Major League Soccer (MLS) has a single-entity ownership structure. This makes it quite different from most other soccer leagues in the world, which are formed as associations of clubs. MLS clubs essentially operate as one organization.[16] English Premier League (EPL) clubs are highly independent, but their association in the EPL and the Football Association (FA) demand some behaviors that are in the interest of the collective. Coopetition is the idea used in management or economics, to refer to organizations that both compete and cooperate simultaneously. From the earliest studies of sport management and economics, this has been argued as one of the differentiation factors in sport.[17]

Example

The National Lacrosse League (NLL) is a new professional men's lacrosse league with 13 teams in the United States and Canada. Those teams compete against each other on the field, being an obvious and fundamental part of sport. However, consider that if they didn't cooperate as organizations. (1) Those on-field competitions would never exist. Teams have to cooperate on multiple levels, including an agreed-upon set of rules, time and location for the game, what are the punishments for breaking agreed upon rules, and who will be enforcing these rules. Without cooperation, ground rules for competition would not be set. (2) Without financial cooperation, some franchises would founder while others prosper. The NLL has teams in Rochester and Buffalo, New York. Those cities are only about an hour apart. They may be inadvertently, or purposely, compete for fans' attention and affiliation. If one team, say Rochester, had more on-field success, they are likely to become more popular. That would certainly benefit the owners and front office of the Rochester team. League-wide agreements mean Rochester's also benefits the Buffalo franchise through increased league awareness, league-wide sponsorship agreements, and better attendance when Rochester plays in Buffalo. Television rights and licensing agreements help both popular and less popular teams. ◄

Another way a sport organization may cooperate as it relates to organizational structure is through role designation. Teams may cooperate, or be forced to cooperate, as it relates to certain roles within each front office. Leagues often require organizations to place personnel in defined roles, thus defining elements of their structures. These positions are often related to competition-specific roles, but not always. When social media first rose in popularity for marketing purposes, some leagues eager to engage with their fans or increase their visibility required their teams to have someone running social media accounts.

In other incidences, league-wide trends can require changes to structure without a mandate. When analytics, such as sabermetrics in baseball, were first adopted by sport organizations, not every team jumped on board.[18] Over time, many organizations have created departments and handed substantial decision-making authority to analytics personnel.

4.4 Conclusion

As Dr. Merrill, the AD at Pomona-Pitzer Athletics, pointed out in her interview at the beginning of this chapter that while she plans to build a collaborative organizational structure, the key to her success is the engagement of her employees and a clear understanding of the organization's vision and goals. As we will discuss later in the unit (Chap. 8), being able to adapt an organization to the changing context or external environment, while simultaneously maintaining alignment with the organization's vision, is fundamental. When thinking about organizational structure, remember to consider the six elements outlined in the chapter, as well as compare and contrast the structure types mentioned above. Consider alternative structures not addressed in this chapter. Understand their strengths and weaknesses and how they might help a sport

organization achieve the vision and goals they set out. Organizational structure is only as effective as the people in it.

Discussion Questions

1. Which types of sport organizations might choose a simple organizational structure? What types of organizations might adopt a matrix structure?
2. Explain how historical factors have influenced the structures of sport organizations.
3. Explain the concept of coopetition. How does it influence sport organizations?

Notes

1. Boulton, C., & Hickins, M. (2014, March). Billy Beane Expects Big Things from MLB's Big Data Play. *The Wall Street Journal*. Retrieved from http://blogs.wsj.com/cio/2014/03/05/billy-beane-expects-big-things-from-mlbs-big-data-play/.
2. Hitt, M. A., Miller, C. C., Colella, A., Triana, M. (2017). *Organizational Behavior* (5th ed.). Wiley.
3. Nichols, G., Wicker, P., Cuskelly, G., & Breuer, C. (2015). Measuring the formalization of community sports clubs: Findings from the UK, Germany and Australia. *International Journal of Sport Policy and Politics, 7*(2), 283–300.
4. Nichols, G., & James, M. (2008). One size does not fit all: Implications of sports club diversity for their effectiveness as a policy tool and for government support. *Managing Leisure, 13*(2), 104–114.
5. Anderson, B. (2020, October). Why MLB has a brain drain problem in front offices; and how COVID-19 pandemic accelerated it. *CBS Sports*. Retrieved from https://www.cbssports.com/mlb/news/why-mlb-has-a-brain-drain-problem-in-front-offices-and-how-the-covid-19-pandemic-accelerated-it/.
6. Heskett, J. (2006, September). Are We Ready for Self-Management? *Harvard Business Review*. Retrieved from https://hbswk.hbs.edu/item/are-we-ready-for-self-management.
7. Oja, B. D., Bass, J. R., & Gordon, B. S. (2015). Conceptualizing employee identification with sport organizations: Sport Employee Identification (SEI). *Sport Management Review, 18*(4), 583–595.
8. Graham, J., & Trendafilova, S. (2016). Implementing Self-Managed Teams at Western Field University: A Human Resource and Leadership Case Study. *Case Studies in Sport Management, 5*(1), 64–72.
9. Adams, A., Morrow, S., & Thomson, I. (2017). Changing boundaries and evolving organizational forms in football: Novelty and variety among Scottish clubs. *Journal of Sport Management, 31*(2), 161–175.

10. Byun, J., Leopkey, B., & Ellis, D. (2020). Examining post-merger sociocultural integration in sport. *European Sport Management Quarterly*, 1–22.

11. Misener, K. E., & Misener, L. (2017). Grey is the new black: Advancing understanding of new organizational forms and blurring sector boundaries in sport management. *Journal of Sport Management, 31*(2), 125–132.

12. Fahlén, J., & Stenling, C. (2019). (Re) conceptualizing institutional change in sport management contexts: The unintended consequences of sport organizations' everyday organizational life. *European Sport Management Quarterly, 19*(2), 265–285.

13. Tiell, B., & Dixon, M. (2008). Roles and tasks of the senior woman administrator (SWA) in intercollegiate athletics: A role congruity perspective. *Journal for the Study of Sports and Athletes in Education, 2*(3), 339–361.

14. FIFA Annual Report (2019). FIFA. Retrieved from https://img.fifa.com/image/upload/ksndm8om-7duu5h8qxlpn.pdf.

15. Barnhill, C. R., & Smith, N. L. (2019). Psychological contract fulfilment and innovative work behaviours of employees in sport-based SBEs: The mediating role of organisational citizenship. *International Journal of Sport Management and Marketing, 19*(1–2), 106–128.

16. Coates, D., Frick, B., & Jewell, T. (2016). Superstar salaries and soccer success: The impact of designated players in Major League Soccer. *Journal of Sports Economics, 17*(7), 716–735.

17. Neale, W. C. (1964). The peculiar economics of professional sports. *The Quarterly Journal of Economics, 78*(1), 1–14.

18. Wolfe, R., Wright, P., & Smart, D. (2006). Radical HRM innovation and competitive advantage: The moneyball story. *Human Resource Management, 45*(1), 111–145.

▶ **Learning Objectives** After reading this chapter, students should be able to:

- Identify the elements of the communication process.
- Delineate between upward, downward, and horizontal communication.
- Identify and discuss various communication channels.

Gerald Jones: Founder and CEO, 5G Sports & Entertainment: Strategic Partnerships Consultant, NextUp Partners LLC

To listen to the interview <click here>

_____

Supplementary Information The online version of this chapter (https://doi.org/10.1007/978-3-030-67612-4_5) contains supplementary material, which is available to authorized users.

The Interns Have an Idea

When you're sitting in the pub after a match, everyone has a revolutionary idea. This time, it might be true. The interns for AFC Wimbledon meet at Murbury's Pub following each home match. The last few visits have been the setting for lively discussions regarding numerous topics, including how to solve the bottleneck at the stadium entrance. As part of their match day duties, the interns help check bags, hand out promotional items, and take tickets at the stadium entrance. At each match, they are met with complaints from angry fans who want to get in quicker.

The interns have an idea that they think can correct the issue, but getting their message up the chain of command is difficult. AFC Wimbledon has a very formal, very bureaucratic structure. Norms are for communication to be conducted with your immediate supervisor, who then relays ideas up the chain to management. Before the last match, several of the interns tried to share their ideas with the game operations director. That conversation is now the topic of discussion. "He just won't listen. He rolled his eyes and started to walk away before we finished speaking. How can we get our message to someone who will hear us?"

5.1 Importance of Communication

Did you ever play the game "telephone" as a child? In the game, one person whispers a message to another, who then repeats the message to another, who then does the same until the last person in the room hears the message. When the last receiver of the message compares what they heard to what the first person initially whispered, there is usually great laughter amongst the participants due to the discrepancies between the two. The longer the game's communication chain is, the more the message will change between the beginning and the end of the game.

Discovering how to communicate is one of the first things we learn as humans. There are likely people in your life with whom you can communicate seamlessly using only visual cues and gestures. Yet, you may struggle to find words with others to help them understand what you want them to know. In this chapter, we will discuss communication in sport organizations. We will begin by discussing the communication process before transitioning into examinations of different communication methods. But, before you read this chapter, take a minute and play a game of telephone as a class.

▶ **Communication** Communication is the sharing of information between parties to convey a message and achieve a common understanding.

5.1.1 Communication Defined

Communication is the sharing of information between parties to convey a message and achieve a common understanding.[1] Organizational behavior and communication scholar Joann Keyton argued that organizations could not exist without communication.[2] While that may sound extremist, which of the following could a sport organization achieve without communication?

- Planning of events?
- Creation of programs?

- Development of ticket and merchandise offerings?
- Implementation of successful marketing and promotional campaigns?
- Responding to the concerns of community members, customers, or stakeholders?
- Coordination of the actions of employees?
- Motivation of employees and volunteers?
- Expressing of concerns regarding social issues affecting their communities?

▶ **Formal Channels** Communication channels follow authority chains of organizational structures and are often outlined in organizational charts.

▶ **Informal Channels** Communication channels not explicitly designated by the organization.

As you can see, organizations really cannot conduct even their most basic functions without communicating. As discussed throughout this book (see Chap. 10), communication is often challenging, resulting in misunderstandings that can derail a project or even rupture relationships. On the other hand, effective communication enhances employees' identification with the organization.[3] In an effort to facilitate efficient communication, most organizations develop formal communication channels to facilitate information exchanges between members. Formal channels generally follow authority chains of organizational structures and are often outlined in organizational charts (See Chap. 4). However, since sports organizations are usually smaller and flatter organizations, formal channels can be less relevant. Informal channels, that is, those not explicitly designated by the organization, including social media networks and messaging applications, now play a significant role in communication for all organizations, especially sport organizations.

▶ **Sender** The person or entity that wants to communicate a message.

▶ **Encoding** Placing a message in text, images, symbols, emojis, gestures, or another form of communication so that it can be sent to the receiver.

5.2   The Communication Process

The communication process[4] (Fig. 5.1) begins with the sender of a message. The sender has information which they would like to convey to another party. It could be an idea for a new program offering at a community center, a promotional campaign for an NBA club, or details of a task to be completed before an event. The sender wishes to communicate their idea via a message. To convey the information, the sender must identify to whom they want to send the information, and how to send the information. Encoding involves creating a message to convey the information. During encoding, the sender chooses the best way to convey the information's meaning to their audience. Encoding most commonly involves placing the message into text, but messages can be encoded into images, emojis, symbols, and many other forms of communication. Next time you walk through a sports facility, take a moment to identify all of the ways organizations encode information. If you see a stick figure of a man or woman outside of a door, what does it mean? In addition to picking the visual or audio form of the message, encoding also involves picking the proper tone. Saying "you're great" can have different meanings depending on the tone used when saying the words. Communication competence, that is, the messenger's ability to convey a message clearly, is a major predictor of the interacting parties' satisfaction with one another. Managers' communication competency is significantly related to employees' job satisfaction.[5] Obviously, choosing the right message and encoding it correctly is essential.

▷ **Communication Competence** The messenger's ability to convey a message clearly.

▷ **Communication Channel** The medium used to send a message.

The channel is the medium used to send the message. A sender may ask themselves, if they should use a formal channel like a memo, company email, or meeting, or if they should use an informal channel like a text message. Choosing a channel is not that dissimilar to an advertiser trying to determine if their advertisement should be on television, radio, or Twitter. Just as with advertising, the chosen channel should be the one that is most likely to reach the target audience. However, the channel should also be the one that will allow the message to be perceived in the way it is intended.[6]

▷ **Receiver** The intended audience for the message.

▷ **Decoding** The process through which the receiver attempts to interpret the message's meaning.

The receiver is the intended audience for the message. Decoding occurs when the receiver attempts to interpret the message's meaning.[7] As Chap. 10 discusses, many different psychological, sociocultural, and structural factors influence how messages are interpreted. The factors are represented by noise in the model. For example, if the sender is excited about their idea, their encoding will be different from their encoding if they are frustrated. Similarly, the receiver's perception will be impacted by their emotions during decoding. Noise can be anything that affects message interpretation. Thus, contradictory mes-

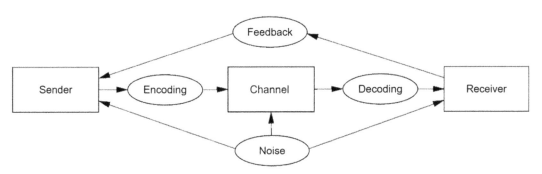

Fig. 5.1 The communication process

52   5 Communication in Organizations

sages from within the organization, others' opinions, or even distractions caused by personal matters can interfere with the process.

The final stage of the communication process is feedback, which allows for further discussion and message clarification. Feedback is actually a loop in which the communication process flips. The original receiver becomes the sender and vice versa. Thus, the parties go back and forth, relaying ideas and conveying their understandings, all while being acted on by the noise of their internal and external environments.

5.3   Direction of Communication

Encoding and decoding of messages, and the type of noise that influences the process often depend on the direction of communication. Communication can flow downward, upward, or horizontally through an organization.

5.3.1   Downward Communication

Downward communication flows from someone at a higher level in the organization's structure to someone at a lower level. Downward communication is used to provide instruction and evaluation, and informs employees of organizational goals and initiatives.[8] Downward communication is critical for the function of all types of organizations, but it is especially important for service organizations, the category to which most sport organizations belong.[9] Frontline workers, such as ticket sellers, event staff, volunteers, and many others in the sports industry that deal directly with customers, receive their training and instruction through downward communication.

5.3.2   Upward Communication

Communication that flows upward from subordinates to management is considered upward communication.[10] Upward communication is vital for an organization to function efficiently. First, it allows subordinates to provide feedback in the communication process, helping in the sensemaking process.[11] It also allows employees with problems or concerns to report those to the organization.[12] Additionally, upward communication allows subordinates to convey knowledge up the chain of command. Frontline workers, lower-level managers, volunteers, and others who contribute directly to the organization's operational functions develop knowledge regarding their roles that are often greater than those possessed by direct supervisors. For example, a Director of Facility Operations, who is concerned about the budget, may explore purchasing a different fertilizer brand for the stadium's grass playing surface. However, the Turf Manager has direct knowledge of how various products affect the facility's grass surfaces' quality. Suppose the Turf Manager cannot communicate their knowledge to the Director of Facility Operations. In that case, the playing surface could be damaged.

As important as upward communication is for an organization, many employees feel like they cannot communicate with those who are higher on the organizational chart.[13] These feelings may be based on actual experiences such as reprimands or instances where they were ignored by their bosses. However, many lower-level employees are either intimidated to communicate upward or do not know how to access the proper channels. In some collectivist cultures, upward communication may be looked down upon socially.[14] Managers can offset these feelings by demonstrating their concern for subordinates' ideas, including subordinates in decision-making processes, giving credit to subordinates for successful ideas, and creating an organizational atmosphere where artificial barriers between employees are removed. For upward communication that may be sensitive in nature (i.e., whistleblowing, reporting harassment, etc.), organizations can create anonymous channels for employees to access.

5.3.3   Horizontal Communication

Horizontal communication occurs between employees who are at similar levels within an organization's bureaucracy. This can include colleagues within the same work unit or with colleagues in other work units. Horizontal communication is absolutely vital within sport organizations. Imagine a marketing department trying to implement a game-day promotion without communicating with the event operations staff. The results would be a farce.

Horizontal communication allows basic organizational functions to occur efficiently as it leads to colleagues sharing ideas and resources. Horizontal communication can also lead to new idea generation. For example, an NBA team may see employees in its community outreach department communicate with colleagues in the public relations and ticketing departments to create an event that benefits underserved youth in the city while at the same time providing good publicity. Complex events and cross-organizational initiatives are only possible through horizontal communication. As crucial as horizontal communication can be, it isn't easy to achieve. Formality within organizational structures produces barriers that inhibit messaging between employees in different departments. Horizontal communication can be improved by exploring less formal structures or by grouping departments that interact frequently.

5.4 Communication Channels

The direction of communication has historically been determined by the formal communication channels offered by the organization as well as organizational norms. Relaxation of cultural norms toward formality and new technologies have altered how communication occurs in the workplace. As noted earlier in this chapter, choosing the proper communication channel to reach your intended audience is essential in the communication process. This section will explore oral, written, nonverbal, and electronic communication in both formal and informal forms.

5.4.1 Oral Communication

The most common form of communication, oral communication, includes all spoken forms of communication conducted in person or via telephonic delivery. Oral communication can be delivered more quickly than other forms of communication. It also provides the advantage of immediate feedback. The receiver can clarify any potential misinterpretations of the message by asking follow-up questions, and as long as the sender allows, free-flowing exchanges of ideas are possible.

Formal forms of oral communication include one-on-one communication, speeches, group discussions, and virtually any other oral communication format that is sanctioned by the organization. Informal oral communication occurs outside of channels formally recognized by the organization. This can include informal conversations within the work setting, such as discussions at the water cooler or in a break room. Informal oral communication can also occur outside the workplace—for example, conversations between colleagues at a restaurant after work.

Informal oral communication can be harmful to the organization. Rumor spreading and gossip can fuel dysfunctional conflict within the organization. Informal oral communication can also be exclusionary. Women, people of color, LGBTQ individuals, and other marginalized groups are often excluded from informal oral conversations. As a result, excluded employees are denied access to social and political capital within the organization.[15] The organization also loses out as it does not gain from the ideas, creativity, and knowledge of excluded individuals. On the other hand, if informal oral communication remains inclusive, water cooler conversations, weekend brainstorms via cell phone, and other idea exchanges generated via informal discussions can lead to enhanced organizational productivity.

5.4.2 Written Communication

Memos, letters, policy manuals, bulletins, faxes, ideas on a whiteboard, and other forms of tangible communication constitute written communication. Written communication offers the sender and receiver a verifiable copy of the communication. If a discrepancy arises, both parties can refer to the original communication for understanding.

Written communication holds several advantages over oral communication. First, it can contain more detailed information than oral communication. Because the receiver can continuously access written communication, initial retention is not a concern.[16] Thus, a sender might describe a new ticketing promotion orally, but they can detail the plan in a written document. Second, receivers spend longer analyzing written words than audio communication; thus, written communication is more likely to stir the receiver's critical thinking processes. Critical thought is an essential component of idea generation. Third, most forms of written communication are formal or considered formal by the receiver. Thus, receivers are more likely to interpret written communication as important and are more likely to trust it.

Written communication does have some disadvantages. First, it is slow. It takes time to craft a clear written document. Second, written communication does not create a mechanism for feedback. The sender generally has no foolproof way of knowing their message was received, and the receiver cannot quickly respond. Misunderstandings can take hours to resolve when oral communication takes minutes. To many, the time disadvantage of written communication has made them replaceable by electronic forms of communication, such as email. Thus, certain forms of written communication like faxes and memos have become obsolete.

5.4.3 Nonverbal Communication

Nonverbal communication includes facial gestures, hand gestures, body language, voice inflection, and physical distance between the sender and receiver. Nonverbal communication provides additional context for the receiver that helps with interpretation. For example, the statement, "We need to provide an event plan to the city commission," can be understood differently if it is said with a relaxed tone versus a more serious tone. A serious tone may lead the receiver to believe that the event plan is a top priority, but a more casual tone could be interpreted as an informative but not urgent piece of information. Similarly, a message can be interpreted differently if the speaker is smiling versus frowning, or making eye contact versus looking away.[17]

Nonverbal communication is not limited to the sender. The receiver's nonverbal cues also send a message back to the sender. Facial expressions and the receiver's body posture can provide the sender with feedback regarding comprehension, interest in the subject, and feelings toward the speaker's ideas. When a receiver makes eye contact and nods along with a speaker's key points, it indicates that the receiver is actively listening and digesting the message's content.[18] On the other hand, an eye-roll tells the speaker that the receiver doesn't agree with or doesn't care about the shared information.[19]

▶ **Emotional Contagion** Unconscious mimicry of another's body language, facial expressions, and other emotional behaviors.

Unlike oral and written communication forms, senders and receivers are less conscious of their nonverbal messaging. Written and oral communication requires individuals to think about what they want to say and how they want to say it. Yet, people rarely think about how their hand movements or body posture during conversations.[20] A form of noise that can influence nonverbal communication is emotional contagion—unconscious mimicry of another's body language, facial expressions, and other emotional behaviors.[21] For example, suppose a coworker is sharing about a stressful situation. In that case, we are likely to adopt a facial expression and voice inflection that demonstrates empathy. If a colleague is angry, the chances are that we will adopt a more serious posture and show anger with our expressions. Emotional contagion is an unconscious effort to make a connection with another. It demonstrates that we are listening and that we care about what the sender is saying. Emotional contagion has been shown to strengthen interoffice relationships as its presence reflects a bond between parties.[22]

5.4.4 Electronic Communication

Electronic communications are forms of oral and written communication that are enhanced by electronic means. Email, text messages, video conferencing, social media, and many other rapidly emerging forms of communication are frankly just evolutions of older communication forms. Email has taken the place of letters and office memos, video conferencing has taken the place of meetings and phone calls, text messages have taken the place of face-to-face conversations, and social media platforms such as LinkedIn and Twitter have become accepted forms of networking. Although each of these new forms of communication shares traits with its predecessors, electronic forms of communication are provided their own category because they also alter the communication process in some way. Let's take a look at some of the more common forms of electronic communication and how they impact the communication process.

5.4.4.1 Video Conferencing

Video conferencing was growing in acceptance as a communication tool over the last decade. However, the Covid-19 pandemic accelerated the adoption of platforms like Zoom, WebEx, and Google Meet, with each reporting record usage during the first nine months of 2020.[23] Zoom saw its usage increase 556% increase between January and September, 2020.[24] Video conferencing has opened up opportunities for remote work and virtual teams by allowing nearly any form of oral communication to take place in a virtual setting. They also offer opportunities to record meetings, which creates a record similar to a written communication form.

Video conferencing throws up some challenges compared to traditional oral communication forms. Nonverbal cues, which often help receivers decode messages, are difficult to decipher via video conferencing. Similarly, senders can have a difficult time deciphering nonverbal feedback from receivers. During a video conference, participants tend to look at their screen instead of their cameras; therefore, eye contact is not present. Other active listening cues are also challenging to detect. Participants can make their active listening cues more present by leaning slightly forward toward their camera and nodding along to the conversation. Accompanying chat features can also help with feedback.[25]

A second, more problematic issue with video conferencing is the feature that allows participants to turn off their cameras. Receivers generally have to turn off their microphones to avoid feedback or static. Once the audience turns off their videos, the speaker has no avenues left to receive feedback. Speakers often report feeling as if they're talking into the ether in this scenario. On the receiver's end, the ability to turn off microphones and video provides an opportunity to multitask undetected by others on the video call. Distractions from other work limit the receivers' abilities to listen and comprehend messages.

5.4.4.2 Messaging Applications

Messaging applications such as SMS, WhatsApp, and Remind allow colleagues to have conversations that would typically occur over the phone or in face-to-face environments. Messaging allows workers to share thoughts in real-time. This allows for colleagues to collaborate and share brainstorms as they happen. On the negative side, it is extremely difficult to convey emotions via messaging applications. Further, the medium's instant nature can create frustration for senders when receivers do not reply quickly. For messaging to be effective, senders should keep the following in mind:[26]

- Ask yourself, is texting the best medium for this conversation: Texting can be convenient, but it is not suitable for complex discussions.
- Keep texts short: If your text is long, a phone call or email is probably more appropriate.
- Be considerate: Texting after hours and on weekends puts pressure on the receiver to respond during personal time.
- Avoid emojis: Emojis are not effective conveyors of emotion. The receiver often misunderstands them.
- Use proper grammar: Texts are informal. This can make some feel more comfortable using colloquial or slang verbiage. This can create confusion if the receiver doesn't understand your terminology.

5.4.4.3 Email

Email has replaced letters, memos, and faxes within the workplace. Not only is it quicker than other forms of written communication, it also creates a natural archive that can be referenced as needed. Email is appropriate when:[27]

- It is difficult to reach the audience via other communication methods. Face-to-face and telephone conversations are more suitable when available.
- The information is not time-sensitive.
- To share a work file.
- To reach a large audience quickly.
- You need a record of the communication.

Do not use email when:[28]

- Your message is long or complicated. Receivers are less likely to dedicate time to long or complicated emails. Oral communication is best for complicated information.
- The message is confidential. Email leaves a record. It should never be considered a private medium.
- Your message contains an emotional message. Like other forms of written communication, emotion is not easily detectable in written form.

Emails are more effective when crafted appropriately. The subject line should be informative and attention-grabbing.[29] "Hello" does not tell the reader what the message is about. On the other hand, "Meeting Next Thursday?" conveys information to the receiver that you are asking to schedule a meeting. Next, work emails should contain appropriate greetings and signoffs. When communicating upward, use formal or professional titles unless the receiver has indicated to be less formal. It is not appropriate to email your boss with a greeting of "Hi, Judy" unless she has told you to use her first name. For men, Mr. is appropriate, and Ms. is an appropriate greeting for women. If the receiver is non-binary or you are unsure of the receiver's gender identification, you can use their first initial and last name (Dear P. Fisher). If the receiver has a professional title, you can use their title instead of a gendered salutation (Dear Coach Patterson). Commonly accepted signoffs in the English language are not gendered. Appropriate signoffs include sincerely, regards, cordially, and best wishes, to name a few.[30] Depending on your organizational culture, a team-related signoff such as "Go Giants!" could

be appropriate. Avoid religion-based signoffs as they may offend a receiver with beliefs that are different from your own.

When constructing your email, it is essential to keep your message clear and brief. Begin by stating the purpose of the email. This allows the reader to understand the context of the accompanying message. Next, separate thoughts by paragraph. If you need more than a few paragraphs, consider sending multiple messages instead of one long message. Wrap up your message by letting the receiver know what type of response you desire.[31] For example, "please email me the report by Tuesday," or "Let me know which meeting time best fits your schedule." Finally, before you send your email, proofread. If your email is a reply to another email, make sure only to use reply all if appropriate. It rarely is.

5.5 Communication and Cultural Norms

I'm sure that you know that the term "football" refers to entirely different sports in the United States and the United Kingdom. Did you know that the word "trainer," which refers to a medical position in the United States, refers to running shoes in the United Kingdom? Physiotherapists in the United Kingdom, they're trainers in the United States. These are just a few of the sports-related terms that could cause confusion between colleagues from the United States and the United Kingdom. There are many more terms and sayings that could be problematic. If you are visiting England from the United States and want to know where a Londoner purchased a pair of pants, you better ask about their trousers; otherwise, you will be asking where they purchased their underwear.

The sports industry is a global industry that reaches across national boundaries and cultures. Cultural norms not only affect how words and phrases are understood or translated, they also create numerous other communication barriers that can affect the availability of communication channels and perceptions of messages.[32] Organizational cultures in North America and

Western Europe are becoming less formal relative to Asia and Eastern Europe, where organizational cultures are more structured. Organizational cultures in South America tend to be more relaxed compared to cultures elsewhere in the world.[33] In more structured organizational cultures, communication occurs through formal channels. Informal communication is discouraged. Thus, an employee in Canada trying to communicate with a partner in Japan may find it more challenging to interact outside of recognized channels. Of course, this is a generalization, and organizations can develop unique cultures. Sport organizations that work with international partners or diversify their organization by adding employees from other cultures need to be aware of cultural norms that may affect communications before relationships are built.

In addition to the communication channel, the medium can also be influenced by culture. Some cultures value face-to-face interaction more than others. A text message will be well received in some cultures, whereas other cultures may expect a phone call or an email. More importantly, message content often needs adjusting to reach across cultural norms. As the first paragraph in this section illustrated, language barriers can exist between cultures that share a common language. When communication occurs across multiple languages, certain words and idioms may not translate to the same meaning. Even certain gestures and other nonverbal communications have different meanings in other cultures. It is essential to be sensitive to cultural differences when communicating.[34]

5.6 Summary

Communication is one of the most important functions that any organization undertakes. It seems simple, like riding a bike. But, just like riding a bike, it is easy to make a mistake that has serious consequences. Knowing how communication differs depending on the direction it flows through the organizational chart allows for a better understanding of the communication process. Picking the correct medium is vital for message comprehension, but so is cultural knowledge.

Discussion Questions

1. What are the critical elements of the communication process?
2. How does the direction of communication affect the communication process?
3. In what circumstances should the sender of a message opt for an oral communication channel? Written channel?
4. How do nonverbal cues influence message decoding?
5. What challenges do video conference, messaging applications, and email present?

Notes

1. Hitt, M. A., Miller, C., Colella, A., & Triana, M. (2017). *Organizational Behavior* (5th ed.). Wiley.
2. Keyton, J. (2011). *Communication and Organizational Culture: A Key to Understanding Work Experiences* (2nd ed.). Sage Publishing.
3. Neill, M. S., Men, L. R., & Yue, C. A. (2020). How communication climate and organizational identification impact change. *Corporate Communications: An International Journal, 25*(2), 281–298.
4. Berlo, D. K. (1960). *The Process of Communication*. Rinehart & Winston.
5. Steele, G. A., & Plenty, D. (2015). Supervisor–Subordinate Communication Competence and Job and Communication Satisfaction. *International Journal of Business Communication, 52*(3), 294. https://doi.org/10.1177/2329488414525450.
6. Chen, I.-S. (2011). Choosing the right channels of communication and moderating stress levels during organizational change. *International Journal of Management and Innovation, 3*(1), 43–44.
7. Berlo, D. K. (1960). *The Process of Communication*. Rinehart & Winston; Clevenger, T., & Matthews, J. (1971) *The Speech Communication Process*. Scott Foresman.
8. Anderson, J., & Level, D. A. (1980). The Impact of Certain Types of Downward Communication on Job Performance. *Journal of Business Communication, 17*(4), 51–59. https://doi.org/10.1177/002194368001700405.
9. Trent, S. B., Allen, J. A., & Prange, K. A. (2020). Communicating our way to engaged volunteers: A mediated process model of volunteer communication, engagement, and commitment. *Journal of Community Psychology, 48*, 2174–2190.
10. Simpson, R. L. (1959). Vertical and horizontal communication in formal organizations. *Administrative Science Quarterly*, 188–196.
11. Tourish, D., & Robson, P. (2006). Sensemaking and the distortion of critical upward communication in organizations. *Journal of Management Studies, 43*(4), 711–730.

12. Hitt, M. A., Miller, C., Colella, A., & Triana, M. (2017). *Organizational Behavior* (5th ed.). Wiley.
13. Hitt, M. A., Miller, C., Colella, A., & Triana, M. (2017). *Organizational Behavior* (5th ed.). Wiley.
14. Suh, J., Harrington, J., & Goodman, D. (2018). Understanding the link between organizational communication and innovation: An examination of public, nonprofit, and for-profit organizations in South Korea. *Public Personnel Management, 47*(2), 217–244.
15. McGuire, G. M. (2000). Gender, race, ethnicity, and networks: The factors affecting status of employees' network members. *Work and Occupations, 27*(4), 501–523.
16. Robbins, S. P., & Judge, T. A. (2019). *Organizational Behavior* (18th ed.). Pearson.
17. Gentry, W. A., & Kuhnert, K. W. (2007). Sending signals: Nonverbal communication can speak volumes. *Leadership in Action, 27*(5), 3–7. https://doi.org/10.1002/lia.1220; Lybarger, J. E., Rancer, A. S., & Lin, Y. (2017). Superior–Subordinate Communication in the Workplace: Verbal Aggression, Nonverbal Immediacy, and Their Joint Effects on Perceived Superior Credibility. *Communication Research Reports, 34*(2), 124–133.
18. Lipetz, L., Kluger, A. N., & Bodie, G. D. (2020). Listening is Listening is Listening: Employees' Perception of Listening as a Holistic Phenomenon. *International Journal of Listening, 34*(2), 71–96. https://doi.org/10.1080/10904018.2018.1497489.
19. Ganguly, S. (2017). Understanding Nonverbal Cues: A Key to Success in Interviews. *IUP Journal of Soft Skills, 11*(2), 62–72.
20. Gentry, W. A., & Kuhnert, K. W. (2007). Sending signals: Nonverbal communication can speak volumes. Leadership in Action, 27(5), 3–7. https://doi.org/10.1002/lia.1220.
21. Banerjee, P., & Srivastava, M. (2019). A Review of Emotional Contagion: Research Propositions. *Journal of Management Research, 19*(4), 250–266.
22. Kelly, J. R., & Barsade, S. G. (2001). Mood and emotions in small groups and work teams. *Organizational behavior and human decision processes, 86*(1), 99–130.
23. Barrett, B. (2020, August 11). How Google Meet weathered the work-from-home explosion. *Wired.* Retrieved from https://www.wired.com/story/how-google-meet-weathered-work-from-home-explosion/;Novet, J. (2020, March 17). Cisco says Webex video-calling service is seeing record usage too, even as competitor Zoom draws all the attention. *CNBC.* Retrieved from https://www.cnbc.com/2020/03/17/cisco-webex-sees-record-usage-during-coronavirus-expansion-like-zoom.html.
24. Liedtke, M. (2020, August 31). Zoom rides pandemic to another quarter of explosive growth. *ABC News.* Retrieved from https://abcnews.go.com/Technology/wireStory/zoom-rides-pandemic-quarter-explosive-growth-72734420.
25. Navarro, J. (2020, March 31). Tips for improving communication during video conferencing. *Psychology Today.* Retrieved from https://www.psychologytoday.com/us/blog/spycatcher/202003/tips-improving-communication-during-video-conferencing.
26. Live and Learn (2019, October 16). 7 tips for effective communication using chat and text. Retrieved from https://livelearn.ca/article/digital-citizenship/7-tips-for-effective-communication-and-etiquette-using-chat-and-text/.
27. The Writing Center, University of North Carolina at Chapel Hill (n.d.). *Effective email communication.* Retrieved from https://writingcenter.unc.edu/tips-and-tools/effective-e-mail-communication/.
28. The Writing Center, University of North Carolina at Chapel Hill (n.d.). *Effective email communication.* Retrieved from https://writingcenter.unc.edu/tips-and-tools/effective-e-mail-communication/.
29. Indeed (2020, May 21). How to write a professional email. Retrieved from https://www.indeed.com/career-advice/career-development/how-to-write-a-professional-email; The Writing Center, University of North Carolina at Chapel Hill (n.d.). Effective email communication. Retrieved from https://writingcenter.unc.edu/tips-and-tools/effective-e-mail-communication/.
30. Indeed (2020, May 21). How to write a professional email. Retrieved from https://www.indeed.com/career-advice/career-development/how-to-write-a-professional-email; The Writing Center, University of North Carolina at Chapel Hill (n.d.). Effective email communication. Retrieved from https://writingcenter.unc.edu/tips-and-tools/effective-e-mail-communication/.
31. Hitt, M. A., Miller, C., Colella, A., & Triana, M. (2017). Organizational Behavior (5th ed.). Wiley; Indeed (2020, May 21). How to write a professional email. Retrieved from https://www.indeed.com/career-advice/career-development/how-to-write-a-professional-email; The Writing Center, University of North Carolina at Chapel Hill (n.d.). Effective email communication. Retrieved from https://writingcenter.unc.edu/tips-and-tools/effective-e-mail-communication/.
32. Smallwood, M. G. (2020). The Need for Cross-Cultural Communication Instruction in U.S. Business Communication Courses. *Business & Professional Communication Quarterly, 83*(2), 133–152. https://doi.org/10.1177/2329490620903730.
33. Cheng, Y. J., & Groysberg (2020, January 8). How corporate cultures differ around the world. *Harvard Business Review.* Retrieved from https://hbr.org/2020/01/how-corporate-cultures-differ-around-the-world.
34. McShane, S., & Von Glinow, M. (2021). *Organizational Behavior: Emerging Knowledge. Global Reality.* McGraw Hill.

▶ **Learn Objectives** After reading this chapter, students should be able to:

- Differentiate between integrated, differentiated, and fragmented organizational culture.
- Identify the underlying values that shape sport organizational culture, including personal, societal, and sporting values.
- Detect symbols, stories, written cues, verbal cues, and rituals that encompass an organizational culture in sport.
- Review the success of an organizational change based on the clarity and consistency of action and communication.

Anthony Horton: Vice President of Ticketing & Strategy, Arizona Coyotes
To listen to the interview <click here>

Supplementary Information The online version of this chapter (https://doi.org/10.1007/978-3-030-67612-4_6) contains supplementary material, which is available to authorized users.

6.1 Understanding Organizational Culture

Imagine it is your first day on the job at a sport organization. Someone comments, while giving a tour of the office, "Yeah, we work hard around here, but we also play hard." That is an example of organizational culture. The organization may not have 'work hard, play hard' in its official handbook or as part of its mission statement. But based on what was communicated to a new employee, a culture of long hours in the office punctuated by socializing is part of the ethos at your new employer. This chapter will discuss what organizational culture is, how it is signaled and reinforced to individuals in the organization, how it relates to organizational climate, and what employees do to maintain or change it.

6.1.1 Organizational Culture Defined

Organizational culture is a complicated concept. Schein's[1] generally accepted definition states that organizational culture is "a pattern of shared basic assumptions that the group learned as it solves its problems of external adaption and internal integration, that has worked well enough to be considered valid, and therefore, to be taught to new members as the correct way to perceive, think, and feel in relation to those problems" (p. 12). Schein's definition emphasizes that employees create the social environment of an organization, not the organization itself. Although Schein's definition is widespread, the focus on a shared experience can overlook profound differences in how individuals experience their work. Instead, Martin[2] provides a broader perspective on the organizational culture concept. Martin describes organizational culture as a three-perspective construct.

1. Integration—The shared aspects of an organizational culture.
2. Differentiation—Cultural elements as interpreted differently by subgroups.
3. Fragmentation—There is both consistency and inconsistency in employees' experiences and interpretations of cultural elements.

By observing an organization's culture through these three lenses, we can better understand how an organization's culture is experienced by employees.

▶ **Organizational Culture** A multilevel concept describing the shared and conflicting experiences of employees working for an organization.

▶ **Integration** Elements of organizational culture that garner broad consensus amongst employees relating to their own experiences.

▶ **Differentiation** Aspects of subcultures or differential perspectives on various elements of organizational culture held by groups within the organization.

▶ **Fragmentation** Ambiguous elements of organizational culture based on inconsistencies, ironies, and paradoxes within employees' experiences.

▶ **Clan Culture** A family-like atmosphere, where leaders are considered mentors and the organization is held together by loyalty and commitment.

▶ **Hierarchy Culture** An organizational culture focused on rules, regulations, mechanisms that promote efficiency and uniformity.

▶ **Adhocracy Culture** An organizational culture that is focused on flexibility, entrepreneurship, and creativity.

▶ **Market Culture** A results-focused organizational culture emphasizing competition amongst employees.

Another perspective analyzes organizational culture through a competing values framework which outlines four organizational culture archetypes: clan, adhocracy, market, and hierarchy culture types.[3] Clan culture epitomizes a family-like atmosphere, where leaders are considered mentors, and the organization is held together by loyalty and commitment.[4] Hierarchy culture is all about the rules, regulations, mechanisms that promote efficiency and uniformity. A hierarchy culture also maintains an internal focus. On the other hand, adhocracy culture is focused on flexibility, entrepreneurship, with an emphasis on creativity. Market culture is all about the result. It's a culture focused on goals and achievement with an emphasis on competition and winning. Colyer[5] recommended an organization equally balanced between all four quadrants. However, this may not always be ideal, depending on the goals of an organization. The various frameworks regarding organizational culture or organizational climate can provide a structure for analyzing a sport organization's work environment. However, these are complicated concepts and unique to each context. Despite the complexity of organizational culture, there is a connection between managing organizational culture and improvements in organizational effectiveness. Organizational culture is essential, and perhaps even more important than other key organizational elements such as organizational structure.[6] Therefore, learning the different aspects of organizational culture in sport can be beneficial for any manager.

6.2 Organizational Culture: Strength of Influence

Organizational culture can be a mechanism for reinforcing how the firm desires to execute its vision and goals. Rather than constantly looking over employees' shoulders to make sure they are behaving according to the organization's values, organizational culture can signal to everyone what is expected of them. When employees understand and agree with the elements of an organization's culture, it can make communication smoother, actions more cohesive, and interactions with external stakeholders more consistent across the organization. Imagine a well-coordinated sports team, passing the ball or puck in a way that seems to anticipate the moves of every person on the field/court/ice/pitch. A strong organizational culture provides an avenue for better understanding across the organization of what that organization represents. Researchers found sport organizations with stronger cultures performed better on the field and experienced higher attendance levels than their peers.[7]

However, a strong organizational culture can also be problematic if it reinforces negative behaviors. Consider the experiences of women with the NFL's Washington franchise[8] and with the Dallas Mavericks of the NBA.[9] Both organizations had cultures that reinforced notions that women were second-class citizens that led to hostile work environments. Sexist and bigoted attitudes can be found in organizations of every industry. However, there seems to be an overwhelming culture of sexism and acceptability of harassment in many professional sport organizations.[10] Therefore, managers need to learn how all employees experience the organization's culture throughout the firm. Doing so allows managers to understand potential harmful cultural elements better.

6.3 Organizational Culture and Values

Organizational culture relies on underlying values and assumptions from those within the organization. These values and assumptions are influenced by external forces, sport-specific values, and the organization's values.

6.3.1 Societal Values

Sport organizations are not immune to what's happening around them. Societal expectations or sport industry shifts can end up shaping organizational culture. For example, the sports industry was always viewed as recession-proof. This means that sports leagues would be relatively sustainable even in a recession because highly identified fans will sacrifice other goods before they stop purchasing sport products or participating in their chosen sports. This meant that even in times of great societal change, major sports such as men's soccer, men's basketball, or American football would remain relatively the same. Historically, this was never true. Sports leagues and organizations have always felt the impact of economic downturns and other societal events.[11] A fresh reminder that sports are not recession-proof impacted the industry in 2020. The Covid-19 pandemic forced sports to essentially shut down, with billions of dollars lost in revenue. At the same time, worldwide social unrest forced sport organizations to stake a position in ongoing fights for racial justice. These major external forces pushed sport organizations to adjust how things are done internally. Even the most traditional organizational cultures found being adaptable to change was the only mechanism for survival. In addition to pandemics, recessions, and social unrest, sport organization's values can be influenced by national identity, geographic location, technology, and religion.

6.3.2 Sporting Values

More specifically, for sport organizations, sport itself engenders certain values that can shape organizational culture. The emphasis on winning is not surprising in sport. The structure of most sports involves competition between two or more parties until a winner is decided. While winning and losing is a feature in many sports, it is not always the case. Initially, Tough Mudder challenge course events had no winners in their races. It was about all the participants completing rather than competing. This encouraged participants to help each other overcome obstacles. A similar culture can be found in many community sport organizations and in organizations like the Special Olympics. However, for many organizations, winning is the ultimate goal. In addition to competing and winning as underlying sport values, the value of being a team player also persists in many sporting cultures. This subservience to the team's good, while also competing against outside groups, can shape a sport organization's working culture. The emphasis on team identification through colors, mascots, and other symbols appears to be a unique and pervasive sporting culture element that reinforces the notion of team and unity.[12]

▶ **Individual Values** Beliefs a person might have about how they should act or behave.

6.3.3 Personal Values

The personal values of individuals can shape an organization's culture. For example, the International Olympic Committee's organizational culture is still shaped by the personal values of its founder, Pierre du Coubertin. His initial values of amateurism, moderate competition, and sport as a mechanism for peace between nations are still present in the Olympics and sport organizations in general today. This is why news of bribes related to hosting the Olympic Games and evidence of doping create such an uproar. They feel antithesis to the initial values of the founder of the modern Olympics. Learning about the values espoused by the founders of any organization can provide powerful insight into what were the foundations of the organizational culture.

Individual values are beliefs a person might have about how they should act or behave. Schwartz[13] espoused six main features of values:

1. Values are beliefs linked inextricably to affect.
2. Values refer to desirable goals that motivation to act.
3. Values transcend specific actions and situations.

4. Values serve as standards or criteria to follow.
5. Values are ordered by importance.
6. The relative importance of multiple values guides actions.

Schwartz[14] also identified 10 universal values, including self-direction, stimulation, hedonism, achievement, power, conformity, tradition, benevolence, security, and universalism See Table 6.1.

Schwartz's[15] theory has been a popular individual values framework due to its international universality, including in sport management.[16] Sometimes values can be contradictory between individuals and the organizations in which they work. For example, the value of being a team player (i.e. loyal) can come into conflict with the value of being kind to others, if the team president or the head coach is asking an employee to do something that the employee knows will hurt others. There are many examples of this conflict

Table 6.1 Universal values

1.	Self-Direction	Independence of thought and action deriving from the need for control or mastery.
2.	Stimulation	The desire for excitement, freshness, challenges in life.
3.	Hedonism	The desire to seek pleasure and gratification.
4.	Achievement	A drive to obtain personal success, demonstrate competence, and to excel, relative to social standards.
5.	Power	The desires to control resources and achieve social status over others.
6.	Conformity	Restraint over impulses that can harm others or be viewed negatively in society.
7.	Tradition	Respect for, and acceptance of customs.
8.	Benevolence	A desire to enhance the welfare of others.
9.	Security	The desire to live in a safe, stable society, and maintain social relationships.
10.	Universalism	An appreciation, tolerance, and acceptance of others with a desire to protect their welfare.

when looking at the recent scandals in sport (see Baylor football[17] or USA Gymnastics[18]). How organizations signal their culture can help employees or stakeholders identify these underlying organizational values.

6.4 Maintaining Organizational Culture

There are many avenues to learn about or reinforce an organization's culture, including verbal cues, nonverbal cues, as well as actions such as rituals. Sometimes knowing what is important in the culture of an organization is obvious from words, actions, and symbolism around organization facilities. Perhaps it is a phrase written on a wall that can be seen by many employees. An example of this is the large TNT painted at the Miami Dolphins (NFL) practice facility, which means Takes No Talent. The head coach reported it was meant to remind players that they aren't lacking in talent, but what it takes to succeed is effort and hard work.[19] This is an easy to spot cultural symbol; however, there are also many less obvious aspects of efforts throughout every organization—each designed to maintain organizational culture.

6.4.1 Verbal & Written Cues

One element of organizational culture is the verbal and written cues. In both verbal and written words, word choices can convey cultural norms and values. Here is one example to consider. How often is the word 'family' used in written cues, such as marketing materials or company value statements, or verbal cues such as during leadership speeches at an organization? The use of the term family can convey a sense of community and a place friendly to families. What can be confusing to employees is when they hear this word spoken about frequently, but the organization does not demonstrate actions in support of the espoused values. For example, an organization continuously uses the term family, but employees are refused time off to address family concerns or

are treated poorly by their superiors. Beyond word choice, the complexity of words used, or what words are considered professional, such as swear words, can all signal or encourage desired behaviors in employees. Also, the tone of voice is often used to reinforce norms. An acceptance of shouting in the office, use of sarcasm in meetings, even the pauses in between phrases, can all communicate to employees the organization's culture, as you learned in Chap. 5.

Word choice and consistent phrases can be both written and spoken. Reading through the written documents of an organization can shed light on the organizational culture. Training manuals for onboarding new employees help new employees quickly understand the organization's culture, but for current employees, there are also annual statements, dress codes, policies on sick leave or promotion, and other company documents. For example, written policies regarding hairstyles can convey a hostile work environment if those policies do not include cultural differences related to hair texture. Alternatively, by avoiding any policy, some workgroups can verbally encourage or discourage hairstyles, which may end up in opposition to the perspective of the organization's leadership. Another example common in sport organizations is wearing sporting clothes to work. In particular, what is the appropriateness of wearing the jersey or logo of an opposing team? For many regional college athletic programs, this is a common occurrence where a flagship school may dominate the fan identity of that state. Each leader in the organization, or the organization as a whole, needs to decide what actions, if any, to take. An organization encourages and reinforces values and organizational culture through its written and verbal cues, and thus should be taken seriously.

6.4.2 Symbols & Actions

As Chap. 5 noted, much of communication is nonverbal. Body language or symbols can carry incredible weight in an organization. They signal a multitude of attitudes or overarching values of the organization. Symbols are objects that stand in for words or an idea. In soccer, the star over the federation or team crest represents a championship. Every Brazilian national soccer team jersey has five stars on it, symbolizing their men's team's five World Cup wins. This conveys a culture of soccer excellence in Brazil to anyone who sees the national team crest. Interestingly, the women's national team also wears that symbol, although they have never won a tournament. To many, this nonverbal cue represents the cultural disvalue of women's soccer within the Brazilian federation. Symbols can play as influential a role as logos or mascots. These visual cues provide brand recognition and nostalgia related to the sport organization. For smaller sport organizations, changing away from a logo or mascot perceived to have locally specific connotations can have financial consequences.[20] For those within the organization, symbols provide a touchpoint reminder of the large organizational culture.

Beyond symbols, other nonverbal cues can communicate the values of an organization. For example, answering emails at all hours of the night or on weekends communicates that working long hours is an expected part of that organization's culture. Even if the team leader verbally espouses work-life balance, by working themselves at all hours, they are setting an example that employees feel pressured to follow. Inviting only white men to a meeting signals to people of color and women that they are not included or valued by the organization. While these are seemingly small actions, they all add up to creating an organizational culture over time and thus are powerful.

6.4.3 Stories

For thousands of years, stories have communicated societal values and culture to the members of a community. Whether they are fictional stories, or rooted in actual events, stories are told over and over again to convey what is expected of those who live within a society. This is also the case in sport organizations. In the summer of 2020, it was announced a National Women' Soccer League (NWSL) franchise was coming to Los Angeles. This new organization's first action was to tell their origin story and thus communicate their values and vision. The story was about a unique collaboration between actresses such as Natalie Portman and Eva Longoria, entrepreneurs Kara Nortmann and Alexis Ohanian, and some of the best retired women's soccer players, such as Mia Hamm and Abby Wambach.[21]

This storytelling communicates to any future employees what they should expect when hired by Angel City. Whether on purpose or otherwise, the storyteller is communicating organizational culture elements to the listener. Is it a story about scrappiness, resiliency, innovation, triumph, or hardship? Pay attention to the themes and messages being communicated because it is part of the organization's culture.

6.4.4 Artifacts

Artifacts in the sports industry are not referring to old clay pots in a museum, the common image conjured up by the word, but they play a similar role. Artifacts are physical objects used to convey cultural values to an organization's stakeholders. Sport organizations have used artifacts to convey norms and values to its employees, participants, consumers, and fans. Think about the statues at every stadium. They are used to communicate the organization's history, and thus values, to those who pass by. For example, The University of Tennessee–Martin erected one of the first statues of a female sports figure, that of former women's basketball head coach Pat Summitt, along with two other influential women in basketball, Nadine Gearin and Bettye Giles. She played at the university before becoming the winningest coach in basketball and winning 8 National Championships with the University of Tennessee-Knoxville. The statues positioned outside their arena remind fans, players, coaches, and staff of Summitt's legacy in women's basketball. It also communicates the importance of women's sports to the athletic program.

Statues are obvious and large symbols of an organization's culture, but there are smaller examples as well. Displaying trophies that the team has won, or photos of past successful players attempts to convey a winning culture. However, some research indicates this can be interpreted in a variety of ways by participants.[22] Individual employees may display autographed memorabilia to convey a sense of importance due to their proximity to a sporting celebrity. Looking around the offices in a sport organization, one can observe types of physical objects that may convey both organizational culture as well as individual values.

6.4.5 Rituals

Whether it is ringing a bell when someone closes a ticket sale or lunch break group workouts, ritual activities can reinforce organizational culture. Rituals can be seemingly mundane activities, but they communicate values, create feelings of an in-group and identity, and build emotional ties between employees. Varying in formality, rituals provide opportunities for explicit communication of values but also a celebration of the organizational culture. In e-sports, a simple ritual has become part of the whole culture of e-sports, not just one organization. Before each match, players or fans often say or type out GLHF. Which means 'Good Luck, Have Fun.' This small ritual can signal to those who love e-sports that they are a part of something larger than themselves.[23] In another example, sport organization employees talked about how the organization's gifts when an employee had a baby signaled the organization cared about them as people.[24] These can vary in terms of the level of publicness as well. While those gifts may have been sent individually, another organization may use a year-end meeting to hand out logoed gear to top performers in front of the whole organization. Unchecked, rituals can be damaging if they reinforce abuse or are counter to the desired culture. Rituals such as hazing tell newcomers that they are unwelcome or that the organization has an abusive culture. A key element, as well, is the level of authenticity in a ritual. As they are meant to symbolize the organizational culture and connect employees emotionally to their organization, one must remember rituals need to be true to the organization's ethos.

6.4.6 Organizational Systems

Organizations can reinforce their cultural values and norms through policies and systems. For example, disciplinary policies like the NFL's suspension rules related to domestic violence and their suspensions related to marijuana use are attempts to enforce the desired culture. By creating policies and doling out suspensions for each of these actions, the NFL is communicating to players and the public what they stand for and what they are less concerned about. The NFL wants to be seen as an organization that opposes both domestic violence and marijuana use. The interesting part of how systems can play a part in communicating values is when these policies are compared. Players have seen larger game suspensions for marijuana use than for domestic violence. Individuals in the organization could infer stopping marijuana use is more important than stopping violence against women. Even if that value assessment was not their intention in creating the policies, systems in organizations could communicate values and culture to both internal and external stakeholders.

Organizations can also build out reward systems that reinforce organizational culture. It doesn't need to be only monetary either. The criteria for an employee award can provide an opportunity to communicate elements of an organization's culture. Let's say the leader of a sport organization seeks to increase collaboration within the organization. Providing incentives for collaboration can help build that. A typical example of this as a mechanism is in ticket sales. Individual incentives encourage a competitive spirit between colleagues, whereas team-level sales goals encourage helping each other out to close sales. Both have their benefits and downsides, but it is key for a manager to consider how these systems reinforce organizational culture.

6.4.7 New Employees

New employees can maintain culture through a few avenues. First, hiring managers can try to attract individuals who would maintain the current culture of an organization. Now, as mentioned previously, creating an incredibly strong (i.e., integrated) organizational culture has fallbacks. Suppose an organization only recruits people who fit into the organizational culture. they might miss out on interesting, divergent ideas if the organization values a hierarchical, tradition-focused culture. However, if the organizational culture reinforces inclusion and divergent thinking values, then hiring individuals who espouse those ideas would still bring innovation to the organization. Beyond hiring, new employee programming provides a key touchpoint for organizations.

Training of new employees occurs in almost every organization, some more formally than others. However, consider other programming or actions those within an organization do related to new employees. This can include how a new employee is introduced to their co-workers, after-work social activities, or organization-level programming versus team-based programming. A powerful way to communicate organizational culture is in that first week of employment, or even beforehand. Imagine an employee starts at an organization in a month, and they are in town looking at places to live when their supervisor texts and invites the new hire out to trivia with some of their future colleagues. That simple gesture can communicate a culture of fun, caring about employees as humans, and community. Also, while orientations help new employees understand the organizational culture, the training manuals can be a helpful written reminder. It is often overwhelming to learn and experience everything in the first week of employment somewhere new; so written communication that employees can refer back to, helps reinforce organizational culture.

6.5 Altering Organizational Culture

Now that we spent all this time talking about maintaining a culture, it is imperative we also discuss how to alter an organizational culture. Changing an organizational culture requires effort and consistency. In some industries, researchers found 80% of reorganizations failed to achieve their intended goals.[25] Don't despair too much when thinking about your future leadership roles. There are examples of leaders turning their organizations around and building effective, positive organizational cultures. Organizational change will be discussed in more depth in another chapter, but specific to organizational culture, using the same elements to reinforced culture as outlined above can also help change a culture.

Not all organizational cultures are altered based on the desires and motivation of its leadership. External forces can play a powerful in changing organizational culture. Societal shifts on cultural issues place pressure on an organization through its stakeholders, be they fans or sponsors, which can be mechanisms to force or inspire change. When problems related to organizational culture for the Dallas Mavericks was reported on in February of 2018, employees talked about issues related to acceptance of harassment and domestic violence within the organizational culture. While this culture had been in place for years, public outrage surrounding the news led to substantial changes within the organizational culture of the team's front office.[26]

As mentioned previously, organizational culture is a complex concept, involving multiple stakeholders, complicated interpretations and shifting levels of buy-in, and layers of meaning. Utilizing the elements outlined above, employees can alter organizational culture. Building new rituals collaboratively with employees can increase feelings of autonomy and identification with the organization. One recent experiment found that a democratically designed ritual could be an effective way to build the desired organizational culture.[27] New policies, artifacts, and symbols can also signal a change of culture.

Another important element in altering organizational culture is clarity of communication and action. For example, if a manager wants the workplace to be more fun, it would help to give some examples or provide activities that define what fun means. While the manager might have imagined playful jokes and lunch break nerf basketball competitions, another employee might have imagined beer pong and complex pranks played on interns. Obviously, these different versions of fun would lead to different perceptions of culture. Words can have multiple meanings, so providing explicit examples can help everyone be on the same page. Paying attention to the communication process (Chap. 5) can help ensure that your message is received as intended.

Finally, consistency in behavior and word is incredibly useful for employees to understand how the organization's culture will change. It is the classic phrase, talk the talk and walk the walk. Suppose an organization has a history of discussing change, only to return to the status quo, it will be harder to get employees to buy into new efforts. For example, if your organization desires to build a more anti-racist organizational culture, following through on diversity statements with systematic and consistent action would be a powerful change mechanism.

6.6 Organizational Culture vs. Organizational Climate

A concept similar to organizational culture is organizational climate. The climate in an organization "represents signals individuals receive concerning organizational expectations for behavior and potential outcomes of behavior."[28] In other words, the organizational climate represents how employees feel about the work environment whereas culture is a broader representation of what the organization actually represents. Both constructs are measurable, but organizational culture is broader, more abstract, and is generally explored from a qualitative perspective. Organizational climate, which is based on psychological underpinnings, can be measured using quantifiable measures.[29] This perspective assumes someone can objectively measure organizational climate without bias from their values. This perspective also assumes that organizational climate can be manipulated more easily by the organization.

A more simplistic explanation of culture versus climate would be that culture is the way things are, and climate is the way we feel about it. Organizations can use both concepts to determine an organization's culture and its impact (climate) on employees. Work environment is often studied through the lens of organizational culture in sport management. Maitland, Hills, and Rhind[30] conducted a systematic review of organizational culture in sport management literature, finding that questionnaires and other forms of quantitative insight allow organizations to determine how employees feel about various culture and climate elements. Thus, the research could make it easier for managers to manipulate how the organization operates.

The purpose of highlighting differences between culture and climate perspectives is not to persuade but to help anyone thinking about their work environment consider the purpose of their observations or programming. By understanding if the perception of organizational culture is one of prediction and control, getting to a mutual understanding, or exposing and removing cultural domination, managers can better understand the purpose of any programming or analysis conducted.

Consider any team or group you've been a part of. Think about what was perceived to help or hurt the success of that group. Consider whether what was said by the leader of the group aligned with everyone's experience in the group. Viewing organizational culture more as a climate that can be manipulated or reinforced and is experienced by everyone uniformly is easier for managers. There is less complexity in that viewpoint. However, there is also utility in understanding organizational culture as everyone experiences it. Valuing everyone in the organization as an individual can uncover biases, discrimination, and other detrimental actions or feelings that harm individuals in the group.

6.7   Conclusion

Whether considering joining an organization or you are currently part of an organization, take a critical eye to these elements discussed. Organizational culture and climate are complex aspects of an organization. It is an intangible concept experienced through tangible elements. Analyzing the integrative, differentiated, and fragmented aspects of an organization's culture through the elements of verbal and written cues, symbols, rituals, stories, and systems can give insight into how the organization can improve. This could be through reinforcing or altering cultural elements. Anyone who claims to build or change organizational culture easily misses out on fundamental aspects of the concept.

Discussion Questions

1. What do you value in a team? How do you convey that value? Write down your thoughts and list out words, artifacts, symbols, and stories that you use to communicate what you value in a team.
2. Imagine you desired to have employees who feel a sense of fulfillment as part of your organizational culture. How would you go about helping achieve that desire? What symbols would you use to convey that? What rituals would you consider creating to help facilitate this feeling?
3. Pick a sport organization that you care about or work for currently. What feelings or words come to mind when you think of them? Then take each word and pick out specific examples of why you wrote down those feelings or words.

Notes

1. Schein, E.H. (1992). *Organizational Culture and Leadership: A Dynamic View* (2nd ed.). Jossey-Bass.
2. Martin, J. (2002). *Organizational culture: Mapping the terrain.* Sage.
3. Cameron, K. S., & Quinn, R. E. (2005). *Diagnosing and changing organizational culture.* Jossey-Bass.
4. Eckenhofer, E. M., & Ershova, M. (2011). Organizational culture as the driver of dense intra-organizational networks. *Journal of Competitiveness, 3*(2), 28–42.
5. Colyer, S. (2000). Organizational culture in selected Western Australian sport organizations. *Journal of Sport Management, 14*(4), 321–341.
6. Zheng, W., Yang, B., & McLean, G. N. (2010). Linking organizational culture, structure, strategy, and organizational effectiveness: Mediating role of knowledge management. *Journal of Business Research, 63*(7), 763–771.
7. Choi, Y. S., & Scott, D. K. (2008). Assessing organisational culture using the competing values framework within American Triple-A baseball. *International Journal of Sport Management and Marketing, 4*(1), 33–48.
8. Kaufman, E., Muntean, P., & Robinson, L. (2020, July 18). At least 15 women are accusing Washington Redskins staffers of sexual harassment, report says. *CNN.* Retrieved from https://www.cnn.com/2020/07/16/us/washington-redskins-sexual-harassment-allegations/index.html
9. Evans, M. (2018, September 19). Investigation into Dallas Mavericks reveals sexual misconduct over 20 years. *NPR.* Retrieved from https://www.npr.org/2018/09/19/649615551/investigation-into-dallas-mavericks-reveals-sexual-misconduct-over-20-years
10. Hindman, L. C., & Walker, N. A. (2020). Sexism in professional sports: How women managers experience and survive sport organizational culture. *Journal of Sport Management, 34*(1), 64–76.
11. Surdham, D.G. (2011) *Wins, Losses, and Empty Seats: How Baseball Outlasted the Great Depression.* University of Nebraska Press.
12. Smith, A. C., & Shilbury, D. (2004). Mapping cultural dimensions in Australian sporting organisations. *Sport Management Review, 7*(2), 133–165.
13. Schwartz, S. H. (2012). An overview of the Schwartz theory of basic values. *Online Readings in Psychology and Culture, 2*(1), 2307–0919.
14. Schwartz, S. H. (2012). An overview of the Schwartz theory of basic values. *Online Readings in Psychology and Culture, 2*(1), 2307–0919.
15. Schwartz, S. H. (2012). An overview of the Schwartz theory of basic values. *Online Readings in Psychology and Culture, 2*(1), 2307–0919.
16. Trail, G., & Chelladurai, P. (2002). Perceptions of intercollegiate athletic goals and processes: The influence of personal values. *Journal of Sport Management, 16*(4), 289–310.; Peachey, J. W., & Bruening, J. (2012). Are your values mine? Exploring the influence of value congruence on responses to organizational change in a Division I intercollegiate athletics department. *Journal of Intercollegiate Sport, 5*(2), 127–152.
17. Brown, S. (2018, October 2). It's Been 2 Years Since Scandal Erupted at Baylor. Yet the Allegations Continue. *The Chronicle of Higher Education.* Retrieved from https://www.chronicle.com/article/its-been-2-years-since-scandal-erupted-at-baylor-yet-the-allegations-continue/

18. Stiernberg, B. (2020, July 20). USA Gymnastics' Culture of Abuse Runs Far Deeper Than Larry Nassar. *Inside Hook*. Retrieved from https://www.insidehook.com/article/sports/usa-gymnasticss-history-of-abuse

19. Wolfe (June 2019). Brian Flores experience: T.N.T. wall, one-line mantras and more in Miami. *ESPN*. Retrieved from https://www.espn.com/blog/miami-dolphins/post/_/id/29333/brian-flores-experience-t-n-t-wall-one-line-mantras-and-more-in-miami

20. Agha, N., Goldman, M., & Dixon, J. C. (2016). Rebranding: The effect of team name changes on club revenue, *European Sport Management Quarterly*, *16*(5), 673–693.

21. Sigal, J. (2020, July 21). Los Angeles awarded NWSL expansion with star-studded ownership group, eyes 2022 start. *MLS*. Retrieved from https://www.mlssoccer.com/post/2020/07/21/los-angeles-awarded-nwsl-expansion-star-studded-ownership-group-eyes-2022-start

22. Mills, C., & Hoeber, L. (2013). Exploring organizational culture through artifacts in a community figure skating club. *Journal of Sport Management*, *27*(6), 482–496.

23. Li, R. (2016). *Good Luck Have Fun: The Rise of Esports*. Skyhorse Publishing.

24. Smith, A. C., & Shilbury, D. (2004). Mapping cultural dimensions in Australian sporting organisations. *Sport Management Review*, *7*(2), 133–165.

25. Heidari-Robinson, S., & Heywood, S. (2016). Getting reorgs right. *Harvard Business Review*, *94*(11), 84–89.

26. Towsend, B. (Sept 2018). One year later: How the Mavs' culture transformed from 'corrosive' to inclusive. The *Dallas Morning News*. Retrieved from: https://www.dallasnews.com/sports/mavericks/2019/09/18/one-year-later-how-the-mavs-culture-transformed-from-corrosive-to-inclusive/

27. Ozenc, F. K., & Hagan, M. (2018). Ritual design: Crafting team rituals for meaningful organizational change. *Advances in Intelligent Systems and Computing*, *585*, 1–12.

28. Scott, S. G., & Bruce, R. A. (1994). Determinants of innovative behavior: A path model of individual innovation in the workplace. *Academy of Management Journal*, *37*(3), 580–607.

29. Denzin, N. K., Lincoln, Y. S., & Guba, E. G. (2005). Paradigmatic controversies, contradictions, and emerging confluences. *The Sage handbook of qualitative research*. Sage Publications, 163–188.; Ehrhart, M., & Schneider, B. (2016, December 22). Organizational Climate and Culture. *Oxford Research Encyclopedia of Psychology*. Retrieved 20 Oct. 2020, from https://oxfordre.com/psychology/view/10.1093/acrefore/9780190236557.001.0001/acrefore-9780190236557-e-3.

30. Maitland, A., Hills, L. A., & Rhind, D. J. (2015). Organisational culture in sport–A systematic review. *Sport Management Review*, *18*(4), 501–516.

▶ **Learning Objectives** After reading this chapter, students will be able:

- Comprehend the history of labor and its influence on the sport workplace.
- Examine how the law has shaped labor in the United States.
- Discuss the pros and cons of viewing collegiate student-athletes as employees.
- Explain how not all labor is physical.

Lauren Aldridge: Compliance Coordinator, University of Mississippi Athletics

To listen to the interview <click here>

_____

Supplementary Information The online version of this chapter (https://doi.org/10.1007/978-3-030-67612-4_7) contains supplementary material, which is available to authorized users.

Lessons from the Pandemic

Sitting on her back porch, Alaina felt a sense of calm. What a strange feeling to have in 2020! It had been a long six-months. Alaina and her colleagues in the Charlotte Checkers marketing and promotions department were preparing for the AHL playoffs when the pandemic hit. Fourteen-hour days were the norm, and then, everything stopped. Alaina and her team were told to stay away from the office. The season was canceled. The team's offices were shut down and have yet to fully reopen. In the months that followed, Alaina and the other department heads were given limited access to their offices, but her team has worked from home since April.

Why did Alaina feel so calm this morning? Working from home was far from ideal. Meetings are harder. Zoom fatigue is real. Those impromptu brainstorming sessions in the break room don't happen when you eat lunch on your own. But, there were some elements that were unexpected when the pandemic started. Her team was rested, which is something that they now talk about often. They never realized how tired they were. They were able to carry out most elements of their jobs without being in the office. Perhaps because of the rest, or the ability to work in comfortable places, the team had thought of some innovative promotions to try once fans return. Everyone wants normal to return. The long hours will come back, but perhaps some lessons will be learned from the pandemic.

7.1 The Concept of Labor

This chapter is dedicated to a very important and yet commonly overlooked concept in sport management: labor. The concept of labor affects all of us, as we all need to work in order to earn wealth, which in turn allows us to purchase the goods and services necessary to live the lives we want. We will discuss a common idea during this chapter: does one work to live, or do we live to work? What this concept asks is, have we as a society properly balanced our priorities, so employees can work a reasonable number of hours as well as be paid an amount of money that enables them to enjoy meaningful time with their families or participate in leisure activities? Or, have society and its economic systems created an environment whereby some individuals are paid so little that they have to take multiple jobs or work so many hours that they are unable to enjoy leisure time or activities? Of note are the two components to this perspective: time and wages. Both are needed for employees to enjoy a healthy work-life balance.

This chapter is organized into several sections. First, we will discuss perceptions of labor both inside and outside of sport. Although this book is centered on the sport industry, it is valuable to have an in-depth understanding of how labor is interpreted and managed by organizations. We will explore a brief history of labor in the United States because of the prominence of the sport industry in the U.S. Other topics include legal issues and the unique challenges that sport organizations and their employees face from a labor perspective. Not all labor is physical, and so we will also review how emotional labor impacts sport employees. Overall, this chapter is meant to convey the importance of labor to sport organizations and its employees, but also to help you understand how the concept of labor impacts your professional and personal lives.

7.2 Perceptions of Labor

Hard work is a virtue that is held throughout nations and cultures. We all value those who work hard. Although working hard is something that we can all agree is a "good" thing, when does it become "too much of a good thing"? In discussing the finances and commercialization of American higher education and the role that athletics departments play within such intuitions, an interesting perspective of exploitation has been raised.[1] Bass and colleagues make a persuasive argument that labor, and more so, who does the actual physical labor, are socially constructed norms. From this perspective is the dichotomy of those in the leisure class who are also known as "the capitalists" and the actual workers (i.e., laborers). The capitalists (keep in mind that capitalist in this sense is not a reflection of an economic system but rather used to depict a certain class of individuals) have the power to force the laborers to make things for them, which can then be sold for greater profits than what was paid to acquire the raw materials and labor. It is also important to keep in mind that this viewpoint includes labors producing physical goods (i.e., products) but also contributing to services, which is more pertinent to the sports industry. Regardless of a product or service perspective, the end result is a form of exploitation.

Imagine a scenario where a capitalist contacts homeowners in a neighborhood and agrees to have their lawns mowed twice a month at $50 a month each. The capitalist recognizes that there is a college in town that has many undergrads who are eager to make an extra few dollars to participate in their favorite social activities. The capitalist contacts several college students and offers to pay them $30 for each lawn that they mow twice a month. For the college students, they now have an additional avenue to finance their social lives, but for the capitalist, they have just made $20 per lawn each month for minimal (in this case almost no) labor. This is a form of (legal) exploitation, and it is not the point to have a legal discussion (yet). Instead, this example demonstrates how a capitalist can accumulate wealth without any (or at least comparable) labor and the increasing gaps between financial classes.

More so, when capitalists are able to accumulate wealth with limited physical labor, this allows more time to set up similar mechanisms to acquire even more wealth. In turn, with more wealth comes more influence. Later in this chapter, we will discuss an increasingly popular and divisive topic that pertains to labor and potential exploitation in the sports industry: college student-athletes as employees. For now, we will turn our attention to the expectations of labor for sport employees.

It is no secret that sport employees (and even more so interns) are required to work long and arduous hours. More so, these hours commonly occur at odd times as sporting events are in and of themselves leisure activities or events, at least for spectators and consumers. Because sport events are leisure activities for many, they usually take place during evenings or on weekends. While this may be convenient for sport fans and spectators, it also means that sport organization employees are forced to spend their evenings and weekends at work. This creates a difficult proposition for sport employees when the sports they work in are in full swing. They often have to work during the "traditional" workday to prepare for that evening or the coming weekend sport events. These circumstances result in the reality that sport employees consistently work 80 or more hours in a week, and the traditional 40-hour workweek is a luxury reserved for the off-season. On that note, let's take a look back at the history of labor and its relationship with the law.

7.2.1 History of Labor

The concept of labor has a long and complicated history which includes some truly awful displays of treatment of people and a disregard for humanity. Our focus in this section will be on the modern applications of labor, but this does not diminish the struggle or importance of those who battled through cruel and unjust conditions as this chapter is also meant to describe how labor impacts all individuals. However, it is essential for a history of labor to acknowledge the influence of slavery. From the plantations in the United States to the pyramids in Egypt (many more examples exist), slavery was used to advance the will and the wealth of many in power. Slavery and indentured servitude are both reprehensible social systems, and because of their sinister natures, the institutions that supported them were eventually removed or weakened (there have been allegations of modern-day slave labor in constructing the facilities for the World Cup in Qatar).[2] Another example of a social arrangement designed to manage labor is the concept of serfdom in the feudal system, which has been used in a variety of time periods and geographic locations but perhaps the most well-known is medieval Europe. This system broadly involved surfs (i.e., peasants) harvesting grains and other agricultural goods for those who held land and maintained castles or other forms of shelter. In feudalism, the surf would provide their agricultural goods in exchange for protection from knights if bandits or vandals came into the area. Although an improvement, this was still not a great system for the laborers.

Another significant advancement occurred during the Industrial Revolution, which saw a transition from labor occurring in the fields and farms that produced the food for society to labor in the factories that enabled significant technical advancements for individuals, including cars and home appliances, which made our lives much easier and convenient. The technological advances of the Industrial Revolution also saw harsh working conditions for employees, which included long hours and unsafe working conditions. Moreover, employees had little to no bargaining power for wages, hours, or working conditions. Instead, those who owned businesses had so much power that they were able to set wages and hours. These circumstances would eventually change globally as workers gained more power and influence.

In the United States, the labor movement has had stops and starts. Before exploring the various legal issues of labor in the United States, it is important to first understand the recent historical developments. Steven Greenhouse[3] has chronicled the labor movement in the United States. One of the signature moments in the American labor movement was the conclusion of World War II and the Great Depression. Greenhouse[4] explained how the might of American labor, particularly in the car manufacturing industry, was a product of the American consumer's desire to purchase items like cars and a lack of European competition as the region had been decimated by war and would take decades to return to prominence. As a result of the lack of competition and a strong desire for their products, car factories' employees had unprecedented power that allowed them, through the use of labor unions, to negotiate favorable agreements for wages and hours with their employers. Because of these favorable agreements, America had a robust middle class that enjoyed leisure activities because of their strong wages and amble time away from work.

Today's work environment has seen a drop in labor power, unionization, wages, and an increase in productivity. In other words, American employees' productivity has grown over the past few decades, and yet their wages have actually gotten smaller.[5] The reason for this is complicated and ranges from circumstances such as increased foreign competition, changes to employment law, and corporate greed.[6] Despite these changes to labor in the United States that have harmed the laborer's interest, American workers enjoy improved working conditions and higher wages than employees in other countries. Interestingly, there are several parallels to working conditions and the American sports industry. For example, Nike continues to come under fire for paying low wages to workers and even forced labor in China.[7] As noted above, the World Cup organizers for Qatar have been scrutinized for their use of labor where there have been accusations of slave labor.[8] In an effort to protect workers, governments have enacted laws that regulate businesses to provide meaningful wages and working conditions.

7.3   Legal Issues and Labor

Although this book is dedicated to the management of sport organizations, it is valuable to examine various facets that are technically outside of the realm of management. This is because management interacts with almost every aspect of an organization. To highlight the importance of management, we would point out that all areas of organizations, including marketing, finance, ticketing, and legal (just to name a few), all require some degree of management and coordination to be fully functional. The reverse is true for legal issues as the law dictates how organizations can be managed. Thus, we will now turn our attention to how the law impacts sport organizations' management and specifically how the law influences employment in sport organizations.

One of the landmark moments in the history of labor was the passing of the Fair Labor Standards Act (FLSA). You may have never heard of this law but rest assured that this law has and will continue to impact you as you move forward in your career. As we learned in the history of labor section, workers have not always enjoyed weekends or a standardized work week in terms of hours, and yet when the FLSA was enacted, workers in the United States were able to enjoy newfound advancements in their labor rights. As we will review, there are exceptions to the rules that are put forth in the FLSA, but we will start with a look at a few of the highlights of the FLSA and how they will influence your career in sport. The FLSA established the standard of a 40-hour workweek for employees. Interestingly, 40 hours per week is the maximum number of hours that are supposed to be completed in a given week. The law does not regulate when these hours occur, but employees are not supposed to work more than 40 hours in a given seven-day period. Of course, this is not always practical and rarely is in the sports industry. The law does take this into account with a term that you have surely heard of: overtime. According to the FLSA, when an employee works more than 40 hours in a given seven-day period, they are entitled to overtime pay for time over the 40-hour threshold. Overtime is stipulated as at least one's normal pay × 1.5. So, if your base pay is $10 an hour, and you work 41 hours during the workweek, you have to be paid $400 for the 40 standard hours, as well as $15 for the one extra hour (base pay $10 × 1.5 = $15 per hour of overtime). If you worked 42 hours that week, your employer would owe you $30 of overtime pay. In this scenario, you are owed $15 per hour for every hour you work over 40 hours in a seven-day period.

Not surprisingly, businesses are not fond of paying overtime and will sometimes do all they can to avoid paying overtime. Greenhouse[9] provides some pretty disappointing examples, including how some companies would change their employees' timecards! There are very important lessons for sport employees and managers concerning this overtime rule. One of the most prominent lessons is that all employees are entitled to overtime pay when they work over 40 hours in a week (unless they are salaried, which requires an exemption). This means that if you are an employee and are paid an hourly wage (and you are NOT salaried and NOT an intern), your organization is (very likely) to owe you overtime if you work over 40 hours. Conversely, if you are a sport manager and you have your employees work more than 40 hours in a week you will have to pay them overtime for time worked beyond 40 hours. More so, employees cannot agree to not be paid overtime for hours worked over the 40-hour limit. To be completely clear, employees who are paid a wage must be paid overtime for any amount of time worked beyond the 40-hour threshold. However, as has been alluded to, there are several exemptions to this rule. We will save a more in-depth look into this exemption for your class on sport law, but for now, we will examine the Executive/Administrative exemption.

One way to think of this exemption is that it applies to white-collar workers or those at the very top of an organization. At least, that is how it is supposed to work. Sport organizations heavily rely on this exemption to avoid paying their employees overtime. This exemption has three qualifying tests, but we will focus on one that stipulates that the minimum salary an employee can receive and still be considered exempt (from the FLSA standards) is $23,660. Depending on where you are in your career, you might think that such a salary could go a long way to satisfy your everyday needs, but it is not nearly enough for most. A few important considerations: (a) $23,660 is the minimum, and many sport employ-ees are salaried at a higher amount, (b) if an employee is exempt and salaried, they are not eligible for overtime pay, and (c) the 40-hour workweek no longer applies to the salaried employee. As we have previously discussed, most sport employees are required to work evenings and weekends on top of working during the traditional 8 to 5 time period. As a result, many sport employees work more than 40 hours in a week. Prominent sport employees like coaches at the professional levels or the higher levels of American collegiate sport are salaried, but their salaries are at very high levels. Yet, for sport employees who are middle managers or entry-level employees, their salaries are much lower than coaches. This is a widespread misunderstanding of the sports industry. Yes, some jobs pay incredibly well, even exuberantly well, but a vast majority of jobs in the sports industry are not well compensated. This is particularly problematic when coupled with a lower salary as well as many hours worked. When we take into account the number of hours someone works, the "value" of their salary further diminishes as more hours are worked. As such, being able to set a sport employee's salary at a specific amount, requiring many hours over 40 in a week, and being shielded from paying overtime is a huge benefit for sport organizations.

Although sport economists disagree about how many college athletic departments are profitable (i.e., college athletic departments have little incentive to report a profit and not spend their revenues), the ability to equitably pay sport employees is becoming a popular topic. Interestingly, the $23,660 figure for salaried employees was almost moved to $47,476 in the spring of 2016,[10] but due to a lawsuit and a change in the executive branch of the United States' government, this was never fully implemented. For much of 2016, many American sport organizations were very concerned about this change. This was because it would have required significant pay increases for their employees that they had not budgeted for, or they would have had to start paying overtime for hours worked over 40 in a week. This is a telling circumstance for how sport organizations pay their employees and the amount of labor they need from them in order to function at a high level. It also tells us that many jobs pay less than $48,000 a year in sport and that you should not expect overtime for extra labor while working in the sports industry.

7.3.1 Interns and Volunteers

Two areas of the FLSA that are critical to the sports industry are interns and volunteers. The FLSA does not require interns to be paid, but they can be paid if the business decides to do so. Sport organizations rely heavily on interns, and most sport management programs require or suggest an internship near the end of their academic programs. This is done because it is believed that internships are an excellent mechanism to enter the sports industry, as they allow students to gain experience and expand their social and professional networks. There is a critical consideration that all students and sport organizations should be aware of, which is that in order to be considered an "intern" there needs to be an educational component to the internship. In other words, internships must consist of actual work that will allow interns to gain meaningful experience. Additionally, internships are not meant to be designed for interns to run the copy machine or make coffee runs as their primary duties. To be clear, an organization can ask or require a traditional full-time or part-time employee to handle copy or coffee duties as they see fit, but for unpaid (or lower than minimum wage) interns, there needs to an educational element that allows them to gain the necessary skills to obtain a full-time position in the future. This is the government's way of allowing organizations to have interns and their cheap labor, but also making sure the intern is able to receive a meaningful experience if not paid for their labor.

Another area that the FLSA covers is volunteers. What is significant about the FLSA and volunteering is that organizations cannot force their employees to volunteer for work and not be paid for those hours. The FLSA does allow for volunteering, but volunteering for a for-profit organization to which one is employed requires careful consideration to ensure that the employee is willingly volunteering to help the organization. One last word on the FLSA and its importance: violating the FLSA can result in severe fines and back wages (e.g., if it is found that a company should have paid an employee overtime, they will have to provide them with those lost wages). As such, understanding and following the FLSA is of critical importance for sport organizations. Of course, it is also important to treat employees fairly and equitably!

7.3.2 Unions

Another area of the law that directly impacts labor in sport organizations are labor unions. We will only offer a brief review of labor unions and focus on the impact unions have on the sports industry. To be sure, unions in sport are mostly known because of their prominence with players at the professional sport level. There are few instances of unionized sport employees, and student-athletes are beginning to explore the possibility of unionization. Thus, it is important to have a deeper understanding of how labor unions impact employees' lives and organizations. Broadly, for-profit organizations bemoan labor unions, and will make every attempt to squash the initial organizing required to begin a union (whether doing so is legal or not).[11] Yet, sport organizations welcome unions in order to form a collective bargaining agreement, in which owners and players agree to restrictive practices. Because both groups agree to these practices (e.g., a salary cap), owners are able to avoid antitrust litigation. However, labor unions will cause certain "headaches" for sport industries as various lockouts (i.e., owners' actions) or strikes (i.e., players actions) have caused entire seasons of professional sport to not be played or having a season interrupted and not completed. The history of labor in the United States as well as sport has not been an easy or straightforward journey.

The National Labor Relations Act (NLRA) became law in 1935 and had the effect of enabling employees to form unions (and protections for doing so) even in private companies. Essentially, the NLRA gave employees the right to collectively (i.e., as a group) negotiate for wages and other working conditions. This process is called "collective bargaining," and it was what professional sport players' associations negotiate with their leagues' owners. The NLRA also established the National Labor Relations Board (NLRB), when is meant to facilitate the certification (and decertification) of labor unions, as well as regulate unfair practices by owners or management. The NLRB was at the center of a recent attempt by the Northwestern University football team to unionize. In this case, the regional board stated that Northwestern's football players did have the right to unionize. At this point, the team voted on whether or not they wanted to form a union. However, the national board essentially stopped the process by refusing to recognize the student-athletes' ability to unionize, and the ballots were not counted.[12] Had a majority of the student-athlete football players voted to not form a union, the point would have been moot, and no labor union would have been produced, but if a majority had voted in favor of forming a union, then a union would have been established. Unfortunately, we will never know how the votes were cast and the intentions of the Northwestern University football players.

The case of the Northwestern football players is germane to our discussion of labor and sport management. While this event was unfolding, many inaccurate statements were put forth about how unions function. For example, head coach Pat Fitzgerald stated that he did not want a third party coming between the student-athletes and the coaches, claiming that a union would be such a party.[13] Labor unions are made up of the organization members, and forming a union does not involve hiring outside groups to serve as the union; the members are the union. Labor unions will indeed hire lawyers or negotiators to help them (and the Northwestern players were receiving support and guidance from other union officials), but it is the members of the union (in this case, it would have been the football players) that have to vote to ratify any collective bargaining agreement. The reason why Northwestern football player Kain Colter began the process of starting a union was not to so much as to bargain over wages (although this would have opened this door), but instead to "have a seat at the table" when it comes to issues such as medical and mental health issues.[14] Student-athletes are in a unique position whereby they need to attend practices, follow team rules, participate in games, as well as perform well in the classroom to keep their scholarships. Yet, some student-athletes cannot pursue their preferred major of study at their university because some of their mandatory classes take place during practice times. As a result, many student-athletes do not have the opportunity to realize their career dreams.

7.4 Student-Athletes as Employees

A topic that might well be on its way to being resolved is the employment status of student-athletes. The NCAA has maintained that college students who play on their university's varsity teams are "student-athletes" and the student aspect comes first (see what they did there?). This perspective is grounded in the concept of "amateurism," which Branch[15] points out, is a made-up term that is not well defined. Still, the NCAA has avoided having to pay student-athletes compensation beyond their tuition and, until recently, their cost of living by using terms such as "student-athlete" and "amateurism." Essentially, the NCAA's argument is that if you are paid for your labor, you are a professional, which goes against everything the NCAA stands for: "amateur" athletics are students who go to school and just happen to play a sport of their choosing.[16]

When making this argument, NCAA representatives conveniently avoid discussing what their perspective would mean if all students were held to the same standard. Students who work at a university bookstore would be considered a "professional." From a practical (and ethical) perspective, the NCAA and its member schools have to rely on slogans that they created to avoid having to pay student-athletes, but their strongest shield is likely the fact that many who enjoy college sport are attracted to the notion of "amateur" athletics and that if student-athletes were paid, most of the enjoyment would cease to exist (this premise has not been tested).

Interestingly, one of the main reasons college sport organizations may not want their student-athletes classified as employees is because doing so would mean the responsibility of paying workers' compensation (i.e., when employers have to pay for their employees' injuries that occur while performing work duties). It is a misnomer that college sport organizations pay for surgeries for their student-athletes. Many indeed provide excellent care with athletic trainers and rehabilitation facilities, but when a student-athlete is injured, they must use their own private insurance to pay for the surgery (there are exceptions to this, and some universities do sell student-athletes affordable health insurance). In a recent twist, several states have begun to implement state laws that require student-athletes to be paid. The NCAA would have a difficult time claiming that everyone plays on an even playing field in college sports if some schools can offer pay to student-athletes and others unable to provide the same. In response, the NCAA is might explore asking congress for antitrust exemption.

7.5   Emotional Labor

Labor and the influence of the law are critical components of the sports industry. The happiness and enthusiasm of sport employees, coaches, and players can significantly influence a sport organization's ability to function and perform at a high level. All managers need to be mindful that employees have lives outside of work, and although they may love working in the sports industry, they still need to pay bills and support their family financially and socially. One unique aspect of working in sport is the prestige of some organizations, and it is relatively well known that some sport organizations pay their employees less because it is viewed as prestigious to work at that organization. Low pay and long hours might seem great from an organizational perspective. Still, the reality is that these circumstances cause many to leave sport organizations (or the industry

in general). Turnover is no friend of any organization due to its effect on performance and the cost of training new employees. People will leave organizations because they are burnt-out or have lost the will to continue working in their current working conditions. As such, sport managers must understand the importance of taking care of their employees financially and providing appropriate time away from the office.

▶ **Emotional Labor** The management of feeling to create a publicly observable facial and bodily display.

As we have alluded to, working in sport organizations is difficult due to long hours and low pay (for most employees). While physical labor is certainly one of the main causes of these difficulties and eventually turnover, the concept of emotional labor is attuned to the emotional efforts employees have to invest in their jobs. Emotional labor has been defined as "the management of feeling to create a publicly observable facial and bodily display" (p. 7)[17] In the first chapter of this book, we briefly discussed how organizations desire legitimacy and put in place rules to help them maintain or obtain legitimacy. Within emotional labor theory, organizations provide norms of emotions within the workplace, and if such norms are in conflict with how an individual actually feels, they will have to act or "labor" to provide the standardized, expected, or required response.[18] There are three primary forms of emotional labor: surface acting, deep acting, and genuine expression.[19] Surface acting is when one changes how they present themselves in order to "fit in" to a given social setting within the organization. Another way to look at surface acting is being "fake" by showing positive emotions when actually in a poor state of mind or not displaying an adverse effect. Deep acting involves individuals altering their perceptions in order to try and experience the appropriate or desired emotions, which then allows for a more natural expression. Deep acting is usually viewed more favorably than surface acting because in deep acting, individuals are at least attempting to experience the emotions that the situation calls for, whereas those who are surface acting are merely trying to get through the experience without trying to realize a more profound meaning.[20] Genuine expression extends the spectrum of emotional labor as it refers to displaying the situation-specific appropriate emotions with little to no effort.[21] In other words, one's natural reaction to an event in an organization is also the appropriate emotional response. This form of emotional labor does not require such labor.

▷ **Surface Acting** When one changes how they present themselves in order to "fit in" to a given social setting within the organization.

▷ **Deep Acting** When individuals alter their perceptions in order to try and experience the appropriate or desired emotions, which then allows for a more natural expression.

▷ **Genuine Expression** Displaying the situation-specific appropriate emotions with little to no effort.

Think back to various experiences in your past or current workplaces and imagine the times where you were "fake" to get through a situation, or tried to "fit in" with your displays of emotions. Compare that to a time when your natural reactions seemed to be appropriate; when you could just be your natural self. Which situation was more taxing? Can you see how taxing emotional labor can be? If you had to continually act like someone you are not or had to put in great effort to experience certain emotions or perspectives, there could significant impacts on your mental health and well-being. Deep acting and genuine expression are generally viewed as a positive feature of emotional labor, but surface acting can be harmful. Recent studies have begun to show such effects in the sport workplace. For example, surface acting was found to increase coaches' burnout and harm their satisfaction, while the opposite was true for deep acting and genuine expression.[22] As such, it is important to consider both physical and emotional forms of labor when exploring how sport organizations support their workforce.

7.6 Summary

Labor is an important consideration for all employees, but it is especially so for sport employees who are tasked with working nights and weekends in addition to standard working hours. Labor is further complicated with laws and regulations that seemingly work against employees and allow organizations to limit pay and require many hours of labor. Not all labor is physical, and this chapter provided a review of some of the basic emotional labor concepts. Labor has yet to receive much attention in the sport management discipline, but as you can see, consideration of sport employee labor is critical for all who work in the sports industry.

Discussion Questions

1. How has the status of labor changed in the United States over the past several decades?
2. How does the law influence labor?
3. What is the case for viewing collegiate student-athletes as employees?
4. What are the components of emotional labor, and how do they impact employees?

Notes

1. Bass, J.R., Schaeperkoetter, C. C., & Bunds, K.S. (2015). *The "Front Porch": Examining the increasing interconnection of university and athletic department funding*. Hoboken, NJ: Wiley.
2. Ganji, S. K. (2016). Leveraging the World Cup: Mega sporting events, human rights risk, and worker welfare reform in Qatar. *Journal on Migration and Human Security, 4*(4), 221–259.
3. Greenhouse, S. (2009). *The big squeeze: Tough times for the American worker.* Anchor Books; Greenhouse, S. (2020). *Beaten down, worked up: The past, present and future of American labor*. Anchor Books.
4. Greenhouse, S. (2009). *The big squeeze: Tough times for the American worker.* Anchor Books.
5. Greenhouse, S. (2009). *The big squeeze: Tough times for the American worker.* Anchor Books.
6. Greenhouse, S. (2009). *The big squeeze: Tough times for the American worker.* Anchor Books; Greenhouse, S. (2020). *Beaten down, worked up: The past, present and future of American labor*. Anchor Books.
7. Fifiled, A. (2020, February). China compels Uighurs to work in shoe factory that supplies Nike. *Washington*

Post. Retrieved from: https://www.washingtonpost.com/world/asia_pacific/china-compels-uighurs-to-work-in-shoe-factory-that-supplies-nike/2020/02/28/ebddf5f4-57b2-11ea-8efd-0f904bdd8057_story.html.

8. Ganji, S. K. (2016). Leveraging the World Cup: Mega sporting events, human rights risk, and worker welfare reform in Qatar. *Journal on Migration and Human Security, 4*(4), 221–259.

9. Greenhouse, S. (2009). *The big squeeze: Tough times for the American worker*. Anchor Books.

10. Pokorny, B., & Rotman, S. K. (2016, May). New rules announced: $47,476 minimum salary, effective 12/1/2016. *Wagehourinsights.com*. Retrieved from: https://www.wagehourinsights.com/2016/05/new-rules-announced-47476-minimum-salary-effective-1212016/.

11. Greenhouse, S. (2009). *The big squeeze: Tough times for the American worker*. Anchor Books.

12. Nocera, J., & Strauss, B. (2016, February). Fate of the union: How Northwestern football union nearly came to be. *Sports Illustrated*. Retrieved from: https://www.si.com/college/2016/02/24/northwestern-union-case-book-indentured.

13. Nocera, J., & Strauss, B. (2016, February). Fate of the union: How Northwestern football union nearly came to be. *Sports Illustrated*. Retrieved from: https://www.si.com/college/2016/02/24/northwestern-union-case-book-indentured.

14. Nocera, J., & Strauss, B. (2016, February). Fate of the union: How Northwestern football union nearly came to be. *Sports Illustrated*. Retrieved from: https://www.si.com/college/2016/02/24/northwestern-union-case-book-indentured.

15. Branch, T. (2011, October). The shame of college sports. *The Atlantic*. Retrieved from: https://www.the-atlantic.com/magazine/archive/2011/10/the-shame-of-college-sports/308643/.

16. Branch, T. (2011, October). The shame of college sports. *The Atlantic*. Retrieved from: https://www.the-atlantic.com/magazine/archive/2011/10/the-shame-of-college-sports/308643/.

17. Hochschild, A. R. (1983/2003). *The managed heart: Commercialization of human feeling*. Berkeley: University of California Press.

18. Diefendorff, J., Croyle, M., & Gosserand, R. (2005). The dimensionality and antecedents of emotional labor strategies. *Journal of Vocational Behavior, 66*, 339–357.

19. Diefendorff, J., Croyle, M., & Gosserand, R. (2005). The dimensionality and antecedents of emotional labor strategies. *Journal of Vocational Behavior, 66*, 339–357.

20. Diefendorff, J., Croyle, M., & Gosserand, R. (2005). The dimensionality and antecedents of emotional labor strategies. *Journal of Vocational Behavior, 66*, 339–357; Grandey, A. (2000). Emotional regulation in the workplace: A new way to conceptualize emotional labor. *Journal of Occupational Health Psychology, 5*, 95–110.

21. Diefendorff, J., Croyle, M., & Gosserand, R. (2005). The dimensionality and antecedents of emotional labor strategies. *Journal of Vocational Behavior, 66*, 339–357.

22. Lee, Y. H., & Chelladurai, P. (2018). Emotional intelligence, emotional labor, coach burnout, job satisfaction, and turnover intention in sport leadership. *European Sport Management Quarterly, 18*(4), 393–412.

Minji Ro: Chief Operating Officer and Co-Founder of Elites Optimization Services

To listen to the interview <click here>

Supplementary Information The online version of this chapter (https://doi.org/10.1007/978-3-030-67612-4_8) contains supplementary material, which is available to authorized users.

▷ **Change** A reweaving of actors' webs of beliefs and habits of action to accommodate new experiences obtained through interactions.

▷ **Organizational Change** Organizational change occurs when an organization alters its function, resource allocation, the form an organization takes, or even employees or stakeholders.

8.1 Organizational Change

Time has proven that change is inevitable. Change can be defined as the "reweaving of actors' webs of beliefs and habits of action to accommodate new experiences obtained through interactions."[1] Organizational change occurs when an organization alters its function, resource allocation, the form an organization takes, or even employees or stakeholders.[2] The cause of that change can vary between organizations. In some instances, change might be expected. Alterations to league rules or structures are voted on in advance, giving organizations time to prepare for changes. For example, the NWSL announced in July of 2020 that a new Los Angeles franchise, Angel City FC, will join the league in 2022. Other NWSL franchises now have two years to prepare for an expansion draft and scheduling changes.

Of course, not all changes are agreed to well in advance. Forced change, such as the Covid-19 pandemic, often requires organizations to adjust quickly. There weren't many in the world who imagined a delayed Olympic Games, yet the 2020 Tokyo Summer Olympic Games were not played in 2020. Not all forced change is rapid. Many teams with indigenous group-based mascots have been forced to change due to public outcry. Pressure has been growing on the NFL's Washington franchise and the Canadian Football League's (CFL) Edmonton franchise for many years. These will be discussed later in the chapter. For whatever reason, change is ever-present in the sports industry. It is going to happen. How organizations respond can have a lasting effect going forward. Let's take a look at expected change and forced change in greater detail.

▶ **Expected Change** Organizational change that is inevitable or predictable.

8.1.1 Expected Change

Change is often necessary for organizational growth. Change can be as small as one person leaving or a new hire moving in. A change could be something as substantial as an overhaul of the organization's culture. Expected organizational change is defined as a change that is inevitable or predictable. MLB's transition to using instant replay could be considered an example of this. It took three home runs in four days being disputed to instigate implementation of replay in MLB games.[3] While the technology existed to ensure accuracy on some major calls, there was resistance from many stakeholders. MLB took this change very slowly. At first, only homeruns and some other "easy" calls, like fan interference, were reviewable. Although these were incredibly small changes compared to replay technology readiness, it was revolutionary for an organization that is generally resistant to change. There are many instances of expected change in sport. The draft process, a change of athlete personnel, is a predictable yearly event in all North American sports leagues. Similarly,

the transfer window is a set time period when European soccer clubs can obtain new players. Clubs build their plans around that window. Expected change is usually easier for sport professionals, as they can address questions of uncertainty and prepare for unintended consequences. It is generally forced change that is more difficult to manage.

▶ **Expected Change** Organizational change that occurs due to pressures from the operating environment.

8.1.2 Forced Change

Forced change occurs because of pressures from the environment that the organization is operating in, whether socially, financially, or culturally motivated. Shipping giant FedEx pressured the NFL's Washington franchise to change its name due to the racist implications of the team's nickname. FedEx holds the naming rights to the team's home venue. The owner of the team, Dan Snyder, had been on record for years saying that he would never change the organization's name, regardless of how people felt about it.[4] However, due to the pressure from the public and substantial sponsors like FedEx, Mr. Snyder changed his stance, and soon after, the derogatory nickname was officially retired.[5] This was a forced but not a sudden change.

Although the example of the now Washington Football Team retiring the nickname due to push back from the sponsors and fans can be an example of forced change, it could also be an example of expected change as it relates to larger societal changes. With the hundreds of other high schools, colleges, and other professional franchises retiring their Native American nicknames over the years, it seemed eventual for Washington to do so as well. Interestingly, Washington's name change appears to have been a catalyst for another football team, the CFL's Edmonton franchise, who announced three weeks after Washington that they would no longer maintain their indigenous group-based nickname.[6]

It may have taken new ownership in the company or policy by the NFL banning these kinds of nicknames for teams, but the change would have eventually taken place. The Washington Football Team is an excellent example of organizational change, as well as resistance to change. In 1949, the NFL began allowing African Americans into the league. Washington refused until the franchise was forced to integrate in 1962. That change was spurred by the United States government who threatened to bar the franchise from using its venue.[7]

The Washington example illustrates forced change that is slow. Often, forced change happens much quicker than expected change. This is because forced change depends on the demands of the surrounding environment. However, the speed and intensity of a forced change depend entirely on context. A series of bad results can put a coach's job in jeopardy. However, a scandal may lead to an immediate firing.

The outsized role/influence of sport in society increases pressures on sport organizations. Social media and other modern technologies provide more access for outsiders who desire to pressure an organization. It's important to remember that an organization is not a singular unit but a combination of workgroups, departments, subsidiaries, or individual employees.[8] So, when considering expected or forced change, keep in mind the application of a change can vary wildly within an organization as well. One example could be the application of a new intra-office communication system such as Slack. For some employees or workgroups, this would seem like an expected change, as they came from organizations that already utilized these systems or followed business trends. However, others in the organization may feel this is an unexpected change being forced upon them. These employees are either not as technologically adept or may not understand why this change is happening. We'll talk more about this issue later in this chapter.

▶ **Incremental Change** Organizational change that happens slowly, often in the form of numerous small actions that alter the organization.

▶ **Radical Change** Organizational major change that often occurs rapidly and can fundamentally alter the organization.

▶ **Revolutionary   Change** Organizational change that is sudden and brief in implementation.

▶ **Evolutionary Change** Organizational change that is slow and continuous.

8.1.3 Incremental versus Radical and Revolutionary versus Evolutionary Change

While a change may be expected or forced on an organization, organizational change can be differentiated within an organization based on intensity of scale and intensity of time.[9] When thinking about intensity of scale, researchers have distinguished between incremental changes versus those that are radical. Organizational change is quite different if the change is radical, such as a football team worth well over a billion US dollars changing its identity. Whereas small, incremental changes may happen every day in a sport organization without much notice, such as fine-tuning marketing documents or rewriting a policy to improve clarity. The radical change process can be jarring. Communicating with both internal and external stakeholders has been shown to help garner support for such radical change.[10]

While a change may land somewhere along the spectrum of incremental to radical change, the pace at which the change occurs is also important. Evolutionary change refers to the slow, continuous change within an organization, whereas revolutionary change is sudden and brief. Considering the intensity and speed at which a change occurs can help employees manage the transition more successfully.

▶ **Structural Change** Change that alters the structure of the organization.

▶ **Cultural Change** Change that alters an organization's culture.

▶ **Personnel Change** Change that adds or removes organizational members.

8.1.4   Structural, Cultural, and Personnel Organizational Change

Organizational changes can leave their mark on an organization in multiple ways. As discussed in the chapter on organizational structure (Chap. 4), each organization is organized differently, be it reporting relationships or communication channels. Sometimes these organizational structures are very hierarchical, and sometimes they have a flatter structure. While it's common to see personnel changes due to structural change, losing or gaining an individual does not constitute structural change (see Chap. 2). The focus remains on how responsibilities are distributed across the organization or how work teams are organized. For example, the US Olympic Committee restructured its entire organization, consolidating locations, creating new departments, and adding new employees with particular expertise. This was done to address the serious concerns stemming from the Nassar abuse scandal.[11] Structural changes in an organization can sometimes be as complicated as this one, or they could be as simple as transferring duties from one person in the organization to another.

Beyond structure, another avenue for change is through organizational culture (see Chap. 6). Structural changes can solve organizational issues by removing employees or regrouping individuals for better fits. Sometimes, this is a sufficient change in solving a cultural problem. However, when problems are embedded in the organizational culture, structural shifts are not adequate, and broad organizational culture change is needed. Due to sport's societal importance, calls for culture change can often come from whistleblowers or outside sources. Multiple instances in sport provide illuminating examples, such as the 2015 corruption case against FIFA by United States federal prosecutors. While the scandals surrounding FIFA were not just organizational culture issues, it was evidence of the

influence of FIFA's organizational culture in the illegal actions of various stakeholders.[12] Changing organizational culture is difficult and requires consistent, comprehensive efforts.

Finally, personnel changes within an organization offer up even more signs of change. Some personnel changes can involve shifting employees to provide additional resources for an overstretched workgroup or to a new role that better fits their skills. Employees who are actively acting in opposition to the organization's vision, goals, and culture may need to be removed entirely from the organization. Leadership personnel changes are often the most prominent in these instances. For example, at Texas Tech, women's basketball coach Marlene Stollings was fired because of the culture she created in the women's basketball program. She created a hostile environment for players that resulted in 12 of the 21 players leaving the program after her first season.[13] This is one of many examples where athletic programs chose to make a leadership personnel change to improve the environment and improve the image of the university to the public. Personnel changes are a very common type of change in an organization and offer a short-term solution to fixing an organization's negative culture. Personnel changes can be an effective way of addressing organizational change if that person is hindering or opposing organizational goals or change. However, if the issues are more systemic in an organization, personnel changes will not be an effective solution.

8.2   Key Aspects of Organizational Change

Several factors influence organizational change and its success within a sport organization. Considering organizational change holistically, remember that an organization is a collection of individuals, potentially workgroup departments, and even multiple subsidiaries acting as individual organizations while being under one umbrella. No organization runs entirely independently of its environment, especially sport organizations.

Many sport organizations run within or are ancillary to a governing body. Change can happen organically over time as new people are hired, or people within the organization make small changes impacting the organization as a whole. However, change can also happen quickly and on a large scale. A great example to think about is the adoption of social media by professional sport organizations. Social media adoption by sport organizations only occurred at a full-scale in the last decade, yet it is now fundamental to organizational success. Change can happen from the top-down, directives from the CEO or President, or bottom-up, such as with employee strikes.

There are several key aspects to change: (1) resistance to change, (2) stress and change, and (3) learning organizations. An interesting new development in organizational change is the concept of learning organizations, and how these sport organizations are influenced by or are influencers in the broader society. Change may be resisted or encouraged by both internal and external stakeholders, such as the 2009 rule increasing the pitchering circles's distance in interscholastic softball.[14] Some fans and players were opposed to the change due to resource constraints and field usage. However, it was adopted by most high school programs within the following years. External and internal stakeholder resistance does not always stop change, but it can succeed at delaying change or adapting change to fit the needs of an area. Conversely, outside factors or internal champions can be a push or a voice for change.

8.2.1 Resistance to Change

Resistance to change is almost as certain as change itself. As the saying goes, "if it ain't broke, don't fix it." While some level of change may not be required to execute organizational goals, it could improve the process. Imagine if we had never incorporated the airplane into our global transportation infrastructure. We could still travel but it would be less efficient. United States' Olympic teams would still be braving the Atlantic Ocean by boat to participate in an Olympics, as they did for the 1924 Paris Summer Olympic Games. Although an exaggerated example, there was a time people thought that flying was something only to be done by birds. Without accepting change and the push for innovation by the Wright brothers, people would not have access to the rest of the world as we do now.

Resistance to change occurs for many reasons. Change involves going from the known to the unknown and therefore engenders feelings of anxiety and discomfort. Change often involves additional work for the individuals involved. Change can have unintended consequences not apparent to management at the time of implementation. Sometimes change can even involve job loss for various employees. Depending on the circumstance, resistance can even seem like a logical response to change.[15] Resistance to change can also be linked to bias of thought. For example, incorrect theories about the female body influenced the sports in which women were allowed to compete. It was once believed that women's bodies would give out under the stress of sport competition, and so women were banned by the IOC from running longer than 200 meters from 1928 to 1960. Not until 1984 did women participate in the marathon at the Olympics.[16] Since then, this has been proven utterly false by the increasing popularity of long-distance running for women. Sport is tradition-laden, thus resistance to change permeates on-field and office aspects of sport organizations.

Resistance to change by employees is linked to a large percentage of organizational change failures.[17] While managers may be inclined to focus on the technical aspects of organizational changes, they must consider the implications for employees as well. For example, adopting a new Customer Relations Management (CRM) system involves many technical issues, such as software integration, hardware updates, and budgetary matters. Employees being asked to adopt a new system may also have serious objections or confusion surrounding this new system. Understanding employees' reasons for their

Table 8.1 Employee defense mechanisms

Humor	Dealing with stress by emphasizing amusing and/or ironic aspects of the situation.
Denial	Refusal to acknowledge particularly distressing elements of a situation that are readily apparent to others.
Dissociation	Dealing with stress through a breakdown in integrated functions of consciousness, memory, perception of self, and the environment.
Isolation of affect	Separating stressful ideas from the feelings associated initially with them.
Projection	Falsely attributing stressors and their outcomes to another.
Acting out	Reacting to stressors through inappropriate actions.

resistance can help an organization address those concerns. Employees may use six different defense mechanisms when dealing with organizational change: humor, anticipation, denial, dissociation, isolation of affect, projection, and acting out[18] (see Table 8.1). While humor was found to be a useful mechanism for adapting to change, the projection mechanism was the most maladaptive to change. This mechanism tends to blame others, and the individual lacks self-reflection on their own resistance impulses.

8.2.2 Stress and Change

Change can be challenging, but stress can be managed by both the individual and the organization through preparation and consistent responsiveness. As we discussed above, some individuals will be more resistant to change, but change can be stressful even for those who embrace it. Depending on the type of change, there could be financial consequences, upending of schedules, a more immense workload, or even layoffs. Another concern is unintended consequences which may occur when the change is complex or disruptive. For example, in research conducted with Swedish Regional Sport Federations, Stenling and Sam[19] found that professionalization in sport governance undermined the democracy found in these sport organizations' elected boards. The push for efficiency essentially undid the operating processes of these

organizations. Unlike some organizational change ideas, such as a move toward anti-racism, there is often no clear-cut answer as to which perspective is better or more effective in driving efficiency until after the change has occurred. Therefore, many throughout the organization may carry stress until outcomes are known.

Some of this stress comes from an individual's previous experiences with organizational change. Perhaps they have experienced negative results of earlier changes or heard about it in other organizations. Even if those seeking change have a strong belief in this change, listening to those resistant concerns and fears will substantially help the process. Communication or lack thereof can also be stressful throughout organizations.

Employees and stakeholders may have stress with how change will affect them personally, but also with the on-field product. Many employees and fans revere the traditions of their favorite sport.[20] When billionaire Stan Kroenke bought Arsenal soccer club, a top club in both the men's and women's game, there was some consternation regarding the American ownership of Arsenal, by both players and fans. They were concerned his American business perspective of profit maximization would overshadow the storied club. This came to a head with the global pandemic as players were asked to take a pay cut, and a few players resisted due to concerns about club finances.[21] This has caused a great deal of stress for many stakeholders of the organization. While there is likely going to be stress-related to any organizational change, understanding the process of change within an organization can equip managers in better handling the emotions that will come.

8.2.3 Learning Organizations

Sport organizations, like all organizations, utilize the collective memory of the organization to interpret and learn from incoming information.[22] It takes a learning organization to understand what is going on in the world, the country, and the community and integrate any new knowledge or insights into their organization. First-order organizational learning focuses on achieving organizational goals through existing learning patterns. Second-order organizational learning provides radical change opportunities.[23] Second-order learning involves seeking out new routines and ways of thinking. Removing learned behaviors can be incredibly hard, but if the current organizational routines are ineffective in achieving the organization's goals, this unlearning and new learning are necessary.

The NBA and the WNBA are current examples of learning organizations, as the push for corporate social responsibility in sport has increased dramatically in recent years.[24] During the second half of their respective 2020 seasons, the WNBA and NBA provided both players and teams opportunities to voice their concerns regarding racial justice. In March 1996, Denver Nugget's guard Mahmoud Abdul-Rauf refused to stand for the national anthem, citing it against his Islamic faith. He was fined $31,707 for every game that he kneeled.[25] The WNBA and NBA have allowed their players to wear social justice messages on their jerseys, along with the phrase "Black Lives Matter" painted on courts. This example highlights the NBA and WNBA's learning perspective and addressing both player and societal concerns. As preliminary evidence suggests, athletes can play an influential role in society. Thus, learning organizations are essential in helping reshape cultures and communities.[26]

8.3   The Change Process

Organizational change usually does not happen instantaneously. Even in the most urgent situations, a process occurs through which change happens. Frameworks can be useful to guide an organization through change. Research encourages analyzing and preparing for change through multiple theoretical frameworks and perspectives.[27]

8.3.1   Lewin's Three-Step Model

Lewin's three-step model of change provides a linear and straightforward perspective to organi-

zational change. The first step involves unfreezing the organization. During this stage, the need for change is discussed throughout the organization to gather support and address concerns from employees. The second stage, known as the change stage, is when the transition begins. Management should encourage participation from employees but be quick to dismiss false information that can spread among the ranks. Engagement with employees is critical during the change stage. The final stage is the freeze stage, during which change is embedded and sustained throughout the organization, success is celebrated, and employees are supported as they adapt to a new organization.[28]

To further expand on the model, let's analyze a sport-specific context with that framework in mind. The United States Women's National Soccer Team (USWNT) has had tremendous success on the field, winning four World Cups and two Olympic Gold Medals. Following their World Cup win in 2015, the players filed a wage discrimination complaint against their employer, US Soccer Federation (USSF), citing unequal pay with their male counterparts. This is despite their overwhelming success in comparison to the men's national team. In Lewin's Three-Step-Model, by instigating a lawsuit, the players have unfrozen the current level. The change stage will occur when they renegotiate a new collective bargaining agreement. If they are successful, the freezing stage will occur once the agreements are in place and the USWNT and USSF reform their partnership. Lewin's model, often criticized for being too simple, still provided utility for understanding organizational change even in its straightforwardness.

8.3.2   Kotter's Eight-Step Plan

In Kotter's eight-step plan, managers are able to visualize a potential path for their intended change. The eight steps are as follows:

1. Establishing a sense of urgency
2. Creating the guiding coalition
3. Develop a vision and strategy

4. Communicating the change vision
5. Empowering broad-based change
6. Generating short-term wins
7. Consolidating gains and producing more change
8. Anchoring new approaches in the culture

There are many similarities between Kotter's eight-step plan and Lewin's model. In essence, Kotter breaks the processes within each of the three steps of Lewin's model into a more detailed procedure. This makes Kotter's eight-step plan a helpful, understandable, how-to in implementing organizational change. It focuses on a top-led management perspective. Therefore, managers need to be mindful to engage with all the stakeholders affected by the change. Additionally, while the plan is presented linearly, most literature has found that a more iterative process actually occurs.[29]

A distressing mechanism for creating urgency is for an individual employee to release information regarding your organization's issues publicly. Some recent examples include scandals at Baylor Athletics, Michigan State, Rutgers Athletics, Dallas Mavericks, Utah Royals, among many others. This can be an effective way to create a sense of urgency regarding a needed change because the public may build an outcry over your organization's issue. While a potentially effective way to instigate change, it is essential to refer back to the ethical decision-making process in choosing an avenue for jumpstarting desired change. In the cases above, employees made information public after internal change mechanisms failed or were ignored.

8.3.3 Integrative Model of Organizational Change

Specific to sport, Cunningham[30] developed the Integrative Model of Organizational Change. The model, which integrates elements of human ecology, institutional theory, strategic choice, and resource dependence, was designed to understand how sport organizations institute radical change, where those involved in change may have competing interests. For example, many athletic departments outsource their ticket sales to various agencies (IMG Learfield, Taymar, etc.). A Director of Ticket Sales employed by the athletic department will be faced with conflicting motives if their employer decides to outsource sales. Their loyalty to the athletic department and knowledge of sales may help the employee see the advantage an agency provides. On the other hand, outsourcing to an agency may fundamentally alter their role or eliminate it altogether. Colleagues who are friends with the Director of Ticket sales will be torn between their loyalties to their friend and their employer.

In this case, management can adopt a holistic approach addressing the various aspects of the institution, including political pressures, operational pressures, and social pressures this change will place on employees. Sport-specific research based on the integrative model found misunderstandings and lack of communication and collaboration all hinder change processes in sport organizations.[31]

8.3.4 Other Models

There are at least ten different organizational change models in the research. Many come from business and management more generally, such as the McKinsey 7-S framework, which indicates employees should focus on Strategy, Structure, Systems, Shared Values, Style, Staff, and Skills, or the ADKAR model: Awareness, Desire, Knowledge, Ability, and Reinforcement. An interesting new development regarding institutional change is the understanding of "muddling through" as a reality of organizational change. Somewhat of a counter-point to institutional change theory as a clear, guiding framework, this perspective recognizes the reality of sport organizations that are changing without a guiding framework. In other words, while these frameworks are interesting and have utility for radical change, in reality, trying to find solutions to problems may result in larger organizational change through small, incremental "muddling through" actions.[32]

8.4 Summary

Change is constant and comes in many different forms. There are changes at the individual, group, or organizational levels, and they all vary in intensity of scope and speed of implementation. Without change, we would still be seeing basketball with peach baskets; women would not be able to participate in sport, and stadiums would be without videoboards. Change is essential for a sport organization to keep up with changing demands and expectations of our society. How successful a change becomes depends on how well it is managed.

Discussion Questions

1. Self-reflect on a time you've dealt with change. How did you feel about the change? How did you react? What about those around you? What would you do differently next time?
2. Discuss one change currently happening in the sports industry. Why do you think the organization chose to implement that change? How do you think it's going?
3. Write down ten changes you've seen in the sports industry in the last five years. Create a graph with incremental on the left side, radical on the right side, evolutionary on the top side, and revolutionary on the bottom side. Plot each change on those spectrums based on how you perceive them. Find a partner and compare how you differ in your perceptions of changes in the sports industry?

Notes

1. Tsoukas, H., & Chia, R. (2002). On Organizational Becoming: Rethinking Organizational Change. *Organization Science, 13*(5), 567–582. https://doi.org/10.1287/orsc.13.5.567.7810.
2. Huber, G. P., Sutcliffe, K. M., Miller, C. C., & Glick, W. H. (1993). Understanding and predicting organizational change. In Huber, G. P. & Glick, W. H. (Eds.), *Organizational Change and Redesign* (pp. 215–65). New York: Oxford Univ. Press.
3. Deveney, S. (2008). MLB is overreacting on instant replay. *Sporting News*, 232(25), 38.
4. Goldberg, R. (May, 2013). Dan Snyder Says He Will Never Change Washington Redskins' Controversial Name. *The Bleacher Report*. Retrieved from: https://bleacherreport.com/articles/1634935-dan-snyder-says-he-will-never-change-washington-redskins-controversial-name.
5. Keim, J. (2020, July 2). Stadium sponsor FedEx asks Redskins to change nickname. *ESPN.com*. Retrieved from: https://www.espn.com/nfl/story/_/id/29401445/stadium-sponsor-fedex-asks-redskins-change-nickname.
6. McCarriston, S., & Fernandez, G. (2020, July 21). Edmonton CFL team confirms they will change name from 'Eskimos' after sponsors threatened to bow out. *CBS Sports*. Retrieved from: https://www.cbssports.com/general/news/edmonton-cfl-team-confirms-they-will-change-name-from-eskimos-after-sponsors-threatened-to-bow-out/.
7. Banks, P. (2014). Who you calling a Redskin? (Washington Redskins). *USA Today* (Magazine), 142(2824), 24–28.
8. Bovey, W. H., & Hede, A. (2001). Resistance to organisational change: The role of defence mechanisms. *Journal of Managerial Psychology, 16*(7/8), 534.
9. Greenwood, R., & Hinings, C. R. (1996). Understanding radical organizational change: Bringing together the old and the new institutionalism. *Academy of management review, 21*(4), 1022–1054.
10. Thompson, A., & Parent, M. M. (2020). Understanding the impact of radical change on the effectiveness of national-level sport organizations: A multi-stakeholder perspective. *Sport Management Review*.
11. Etchells, D. (Feb. 2019). United States Olympic Committee Chief Executive Outlines Restructuring of Organization. *The Sport Digest*. Retrieved from: http://thesportdigest.com/2019/02/united-states-olympic-committee-chief-executive-outlines-restructuring-of-organization/.
12. BBC News (May 2015). Fifa corruption inquires: Officials arrested in Zurich. *BBC News*. Retrieved from: https://www.bbc.com/news/world-europe-32895048.
13. Associated Press (2020, August 7). Texas Tech women's coach fired one day after report of abuse. Retrieved from: https://apnews.com/article/sports-womens-basketball-womens-college-basketball-basketball-tx-state-wire-ab0b4e84eaa024b490e51995ce99e085.
14. MHSAA (2009, December 8). Softball Pitching Rule—Part 2. Michigan High School Athletic Association. Retrieved from: https://www.mhsaa.com/News/Blog-From-the-director/articleType/ArticleView/articleId/78/Softball-Pitching-Rule-Part-2.
15. Bovey, W. H., & Hede, A. (2001). Resistance to organisational change: The role of defence mechanisms. *Journal of Managerial Psychology, 16*(7/8), 534.
16. Carroll, J. (2019, July 3). A history of women's running. *Runner's World*. Retrieved from: https://www.runnersworld.com/uk/training/motivation/a26748147/a-history-of-womens-running/.
17. Waldersee, R., & Griffiths, A. (2004). Implementing change: Matching implementation methods and

change type. *Leadership & Organization Development Journal, 25*(5), 424–434.

18. American Psychiatric Association. (1994). *Diagnostic and Statistical Manual of Mental Disorders* (4th ed.). American Psychiatric Association; Bovey, W. H., & Hede, A. (2001). Resistance to organisational change: The role of defence mechanisms. *Journal of Managerial Psychology, 16*(7/8), 534.

19. Stenling, C., & Sam, M. (2019). Professionalization and its consequences: How active advocacy may undermine democracy. *European Sport Management Quarterly*, 1–21.

20. O'Brien, D., & Slack, T. (2004). The emergence of a professional logic in English rugby union: The role of isomorphic and diffusion processes. *Journal of Sport Management, 18*(1), 13–39.

21. Rathborn, J. (Aug. 2020). Mezil Ozil defends decision to reject Arsenal pay cut. *The Independent*. Retrieved from: https://www.independent.co.uk/sport/football/premier-league/mesut-ozil-arsenal-contract-pay-cut-transfer-news-2020-arteta-a9668161.html.

22. Newman, K. L. (2000). Organizational transformation during institutional upheaval. *Academy of Management Review, 25*(3), 602–619.

23. Cunningham, P. M. (2001). *Making space: Merging theory and practice in adult education*. Greenwood Publishing Group.

24. Zeimers, G., Anagnostopoulos, C., Zintz, T., & Willem, A. (2019). Organisational learning for corporate social responsibility in sport organisations. *European Sport Management Quarterly, 19*(1), 80–101. https://doi.org/10.1080/16184742.2018.1546752.

25. Schoenfeld, B. (Sept. 2017). The Justice League: A growing number of NBA stars and coaches are raising their voices about the most pressing social issues of the day. *Esquire*, 168(4), 90.

26. Willis, L. (Aug. 2020). WFU professor study whether pro athletes political statements and race are influencers. *Wake Forest University News*. Retrieved from: https://news.wfu.edu/2020/08/31/wfu-professors-study-whether-pro-athletes-political-statements-and-race-are-influencers/.

27. Slack, T., & Hinings, B. (1992). Understanding change in national sport organizations: An integration of theoretical perspectives. *Journal of Sport Management, 6*(2), 114–132.

28. Burnes, B. (2019). The Origins of Lewin's Three-Step Model of Change. *The Journal of Applied Behavioral Science, 56*(1), 32–59. https://doi.org/10.1177/0021886319892685.

29. Pollack, J., & Pollack, R. (2014). Using Kotter's Eight Stage Process to Manage an Organisational Change Program: Presentation and Practice. *Systemic Practice and Action Research, 28*(1), 51–66. https://doi.org/10.1007/s11213-014-9317-0.

30. Cunningham, G. B. (2002). Removing the Blinders: Toward an Integrative Model of Organizational change in Sport and Physical Activity. *Quest*, 54(4), 276–291.

31. Legg, J., Snelgrove, R., & Wood, L. (2016). Modifying tradition: Examining organizational change in youth sport. *Journal of Sport Management, 30*(4), 369–381.

32. Fahlén, J., & Stenling, C. (2019). (Re)conceptualizing institutional change in sport management contexts: the unintended consequences of sport organizations' everyday organizational life. *European Sport Management Quarterly, 19*(2), 265–285.

Part III

Getting to Know Employees and Volunteers of Sport Organizations

The people who constitute sport organizations are essential. More so, they represent more than the tasks they perform or the positions they hold. Without employees and volunteers, sport organizations would simply cease to exist. This chapter takes a deep look into who sport employees and volunteers are and how the sports industry's unique aspects require special talents and perspectives. In this unit, we will review how various personalities and values interact in the sport workplace. From there, we will discuss different socialization tactics and perceptions within sport organizations. We will also explore how emotions are a mainstay in sports but have unique properties for those working in sport. Sport employees and volunteers also need to be motivated, and so this unit also covers the various motivational factors in sport workplaces. Lastly, the unit includes a critical discussion pertaining to the creative behaviors of sport employees and volunteers and such behaviors wherewithal in the sports industry.

- Distinguish between the different personality frameworks.
- Explain the importance of personality within the sport workplace.
- Specify personal beliefs and values.
- Explain the various subcomponents of the person-environment fit paradigm.

Layne Doctson: Assistant Annual Fund Coordinator, Colorado State University Athletics
To listen to the interview <click here>

9.1 Introduction

As we begin our section on getting to know the employees and volunteers of sport organizations—something you may aspire to be one day—it is essential to look at concepts such as the personalities of individuals as well as a brief look into the personalities within sport organizations. This chapter focuses on the various personality frameworks that describe the mindset of people. From there, we can better understand how individuals, specifically sport employees, function and how their personalities help dictate their behaviors. We will also discuss belief systems and values, as these determine how individuals frame their perceptions of others and of organizations. This area will include a deeper exploration of how psychological capital (i.e., beliefs of oneself) can be a powerful asset to any person who is willing to adventure for their highest potential. The chapter will also explore the concept of Person–Environment Fit, which will help us further understand why some individuals are drawn to and remain members of certain organizations.

9.2 Personality Frameworks

When searching the Internet for content to help you write a paper for class, you have likely come across a link to take a "personality test." While

Supplementary Information The online version of this chapter (https://doi.org/10.1007/978-3-030-67612-4_9) contains supplementary material, which is available to authorized users.

not elaborating on the validity of such tests, they are fascinating opportunities. We all seek to understand ourselves better, and personality is one way to increase our awareness of ourselves. There are quite a few typologies of personality, and we will focus on a few of the more popular versions.

▶ **Type A Personality** Personality type characterized by individuals who are independent, confident, and even callous.

▶ **Type B Personality** Personality type characterized by individuals who are more concerned with getting along well with others and are generally laid-back and considered good listeners.

9.2.1 Type A versus Type B

One description of personalities is broken down into Type A and Type B groups.[1] The "Type A" personality is characterized by independent, confident, and even callous individuals. Type As desire achievement, and visible achievement at that due to their drive for accomplishment and the resulting control that comes from being viewed as a high achiever. Because of the drive that comes from the desire for achievement, power, and control, Type As are not as concerned with others' thoughts or positions. One word that sums up Type As would be "aggressive." Conversely, Type Bs are more concerned with getting along well with others and are generally laid-back and considered good listeners. A word to describe Type Bs is "follower." It is not difficult to recognize how these two types could work in harmony but also be detrimental to relationships in the sport workplace. For example, suppose a boss is a Type A personality type and their subordinates are Type Bs. In that case, there could be a strong possibility that the individuals could work well together if the leader (i.e., Type A) provides direction and guidance to the employees (i.e., the Type Bs) for organizational goal achievement. However, if the boss is too overbearing or forceful, there is a chance that the Type Bs could strug-

gle to perform. Additionally, if a supervisor is more of a Type B and some of their subordinates are Type As, there is a high potential for conflict.

▶ **Dominance Behaviors** Self-confidence, directness, lacking patience.

▶ **Inspiration Behaviors** Attention seeking, social, creative, problem-solving.

▶ **Submission Behaviors** Calm, thoughtfulness, averse to change.

▶ **Compliance Behaviors** Inquisitive, intellectual, socially withdrawn, task-focused.

9.2.2 The DISC Profile

Building off the cornerstone of Type A and B personalities, we will review Thomas Erikson's[2] four types of human behavior. Erikson's book is centered on understanding the behavior of individuals, but the four types of behaviors that are described can be positioned as types of personalities. Erikson utilizes a color scheme to differentiate the four personality types, but the core of his book is based on the DISC profile. D stands for "dominance" (Red, according to Erikson), which is exemplified by individuals who are very self-confident, have little patience, and are very direct. I represents "inspiration" (Yellow for Erikson) and consists of people who thoroughly love to be the center of attention and always seem to be the one who is talking. Another aspect of this personality type is the willingness to be creative and think of solutions to complex problems, but when it comes to doing the actual work required to implement these plans, there is often a bit of a struggle for such individuals to follow through. The S signifies "submission" (Green, according to Erikson); those within this framework are calm, thoughtful, and are generally averse to change. Lastly, C stands for "compliance" (Erikson uses the term analytical and is represented by Blue), and are exemplified by those who value having a clear understanding of the problem, willingness to research an issue to gather a complete understanding, and a focus on work activities rather than developing friendships at work. It is very common for people to have a combination of two or three types of colors.[3] Although this is a very brief overview of the DISC profile, we encourage you to take some time and consider which color or combination of colors you might be.

9.2.3 "Big Five" Model of Personality

One of the benefits of examining personalities is categorizing groups of people. Doing so helps us understand others and ourselves. It is much easier to understand 2, 4, or 5 categories than, say 20 or 30 categories. The "Big Five" personality types have received a great deal of attention from scholars and practitioners.[4] The Big Five consists of neuroticism, extraversion, openness to experience, agreeableness, and conscientiousness. *Neuroticism* consists of contending with forms of anxiety and detractors of well-being from insecurities and is thus a reflection of the lack of emotional stability.[5] For example, neuroticism has elements such as hostility, anxiety, vulnerability, impulsiveness, self-consciousness, and depression.[6] *Extraversion* is typified by individuals who are "social butterflies" and those who are generally outgoing and enjoy being in crowds. Such individuals also tend to reflect positive qualities such as being ambitious, assertive, and adventurous.[7] *Conscientiousness* is a form of responsibility and the desire for accomplishment through rigorous planning. There are three components of conscientiousness: achievement, organization, and dependability.[8] *Openness to experience* reflects one's willingness to engage their imagination and generally be unconventional.[9] The last personality type in the Big Five typology is *Agreeableness*, which is the willingness to work with and help others. Others broadly like those who fit within this personality type. Some common qualities of those who are considered agreeable are trusting, caring, and cheerful.[10]

It is important to note the degree to which each of the Big Five types has positive and nega-

tive qualities. Neuroticism is undoubtedly a quality that many of us would not want to be associated with, but it is still important to comprehend neuroticism to avoid the pitfalls associated with this personality type. Judge et al.[11] warned of potential negative consequences of neuroticism, such as increased fear, anxiety, and irritability. We can all likely think of friends, family members, or coworkers who always seem to be in a bad mood or struggle to find happiness. The Big Five perspective informs that this can be a function of personality and that it can harm one's work (and personal) life. The other Big Five personality types are generally positive in nature as they can support human growth and development. The other four types have different impacts on growth and development, with extraversion and conscientiousness being viewed as the most impactful on career success.[12] As a part of human growth and development, it is also important to note that people change. If you feel that you might align with neuroticism upon self-reflection, that does not mean you are confined to such a distinction. As we live and learn about ourselves, we can adjust our perceptions (and consequently behaviors) to help us reach improved interactions with others. Lastly, although the Big Five typology is quite persuasive and has generally been accepted and supported by academics, these types are not hard and fast rules for personality among humans.

9.2.4 Myers–Briggs

We will conclude our discussion about personality types with another popular personality categorization perspective: The Myers–Briggs Type Indicator. There are four groupings in the Myers–Briggs view of human personality: extroversion-introversion, sensing-intuiting, thinking-feeling, and judgment-perception. According to this typology, there are two options per category, resulting in four letters that each represent the option selected. For example, this could be INFJ or ESTP. The first category is a measure of one's willingness to engage with others (i.e., extroverts seek interactions with others, while introverts tend to keep to themselves). The second category represents a distinction between those who need to "see it to believe it" as opposed to "trusting my gut" (i.e., sensing individuals focus on tangible facts and data and intuiting people trust their subconscious). The third category is focused on the differences between seeing the world from a black and white perspective and seeing the world with shades of gray (i.e., thinking people rely on clear rules, guidelines, and order while feeling individuals attempt to look at all angles of an issue). The last category defines how people receive new information (i.e., judgment-based individuals are generally closed to new information and perceptive people are willing to listen to new information). Have you taken this test? Do you remember your categories? Have they stayed consistent throughout time?

In finishing up our conversation about personality types, we must emphasize that there are many forms of personality forms and tests, some of which are more valid than others. However, we must also emphasize not to let any personality test be self-defining. You are your own person, and your strengths and weaknesses should be regularly self-evaluated as well as celebrated and improved upon. Finally, our personalities are thought to be relatively stable, but that does not mean that your "category" will not change. What is most important is that you are aware of your own personality and are comfortable with it.

▶ **Self-Concept** How we view ourselves.

▶ **Values** What we hold dear in life.

9.3 Belief Systems and Values

Before engrossing ourselves in the concepts of belief systems and values, we need to start with the idea of self-concept, which is simply how we view ourselves. Self-concept refers to many aspects of ourselves including thoughts on our strengths and weaknesses, in addition to belief systems and values. Our values are what we hold dear. One way to understand values consists of equating a semblance of money to a given idea or

object. Let's use a fictitious example of a company that is realizing record profits; what will they do with it as a response? Suppose they provide an increased salary for their well-paid administrators and decide against providing higher wages to middle-managers or other staff members. In that case, we have a pretty good idea of what that company values. The same is true for individuals. People will support, proliferate, and protect that which they value.

▶ **Belief System** One's thoughts on how the world works.

Belief Systems are broader than values, as they represent one's thoughts on how the world works. In some respects, one's belief systems could be viewed as morals, a broad outlook on how people should behave, or their general outlook on life. When individuals have conflicting belief systems, there is potential for conflict. This is why many workplaces attempt to keep their internal and external operations as neutral as possible. Organizations have their own belief systems (see Chap. 6), but having a clear understanding of the differences between individual values and belief systems will help enhance your understanding of the organizational forms of these constructs in future chapters.

Another way to view your self-concept is from the lens of identity theory. In a sense, your self-concept is your identity. One area of identity theory that is used to understand individuals better is role theory, where people define themselves based on their roles in life, or more pertinent to our discussion, their work roles. Burke and Stets[13] explained a prominent view of identity theory and its relation to one's roles, "Identities are a person's internalized role expectations in the sense that individuals take these expectations to be their own, as part of who they are. For each role a person plays out in a social network, there is a corresponding identity attached to it" (pp. 45–46). In our case, a "social network" can be viewed as a sport workplace or department, and the internalization aspect of the quote means that individuals take on meanings of their roles that they self-assign. In this way, we create our own meanings for our work and our roles at work. Social identity theory, which is discussed in multiple chapters, posits that individuals first need to understand who they are, as this helps them find groups which they desire to join. However, recognizing that people create their own realities and meanings for the roles which they engage in work is important to understand. As such, you are the one who determines if your work role is essential (or valued) and can then frame or reframe your perspective of your work roles. Interestingly, sport organizations might offer a unique opportunity to enhance the role identity of sport employees. This could be a function of sport holding distinct properties of athletic competition as well as the pride and prestige of working for visible sport organizations.[14]

Another important aspect of identity theory is identity salience, which determines when individuals make concerted efforts to evoke their identity or "act out" in certain situations. As such, we can recognize others' personal identities and role identities by observing their behaviors. Burke and Stets[15] presented a model of individual identification that holds four components and describes how individuals adjust their personal identities. The first stage is referred to as one's "identity standard." This is a baseline understanding for individuals of a held identity. The next stage involves an environmental conflict whereby individuals find themselves in a situation that is at odds or is a threat to their held identity. Once an individual recognizes this conflict, they will modify their behavior to either improve their fit or congruence with the environment, or the more likely reaction is to assert or evoke their held identity to emphasize the differences between themselves and others within the context of the environment. The demonstration of an emphasized identity leads to the fourth stage, a strengthened identity, because the behavior modification becomes normalized. That is, enacting a held identity helps to reinforce the identity. Interestingly, the strengthened identity is then thought to eventually become the new identity standard. As a result, we can take away that the environments that we interact in significantly influence our personal identities.

Burke and Stets[16] used the dichotomy of masculinity/femininity in their example where an individual who identifies as masculine (note: masculinity or femininity is not determined by one's gender) could enter into an environment that they interpret as feminine. To make others aware of their held identity and reinforce the identity for themselves, the individual is likely to act in an overtly masculine manner, which could then lead to a strengthened masculine identity and eventually a new masculine identity standard. While this example is informative, let's consider a more sport-centric example. If you have ever attended a sporting event involving one of your favorite teams, but at an opponent's area or stadium, this example might resonate with you. Imagine being at the game, wearing your favorite team's colors, and being surrounded by rival fans. You certainly would not want any confusion as to which team you are cheering for, and so you will loudly and overtly cheer and demonstrate for your team at every chance you get (of course, you would not be rude or demonstrative). After the enjoyment of cheering for your team, you may walk out of the stadium with a stronger identity of being a fan of your favorite team. If this were to occur, you would have gone through the adjustment cycle of identity. You went to the game with a held identity. After finding yourself in a "hostile" environment, there was an urge to make everyone around you aware that you were separate from them and that you were not a fan of your rivals. In turn, this modification to your behavior could have caused a more profound and stronger sense of individual fandom. Identity theory is a fascinating concept, and we will expand our knowledge concerning the topic with a discussion about social identity in later chapters. We will now turn our attention to how one's self-concept or, more specifically, one's belief in oneself can lead to positive experiences for sport employees.

▶ **Hope** A positive motivational state that is based on an interactively derived sense of successful (1) agency and (2) pathways.

In the opening chapter of this book, we briefly reviewed the concept of psychological capital.[17]

As a quick reminder, psychological capital is described as "who you are" and "who you are capable of becoming."[18] In the traditional view of psychological capital, the construct comprises the elements: hope, efficacy, resilience, and optimism. These elements combine to form the psychological capital construct known as the "HERO within," with each element being represented by one letter. Within the realm of psychological capital, hope is not simply the belief that good things will happen. In fact, the theoretical view of hope is much deeper, as demonstrated by its definition: hope is "a positive motivational state that is based on an interactively derived sense of successful (1) agency (goal-directed energy) and (2) pathways (planning to meet goals)."[19] Then, hope requires both the ability and drive to meet goals as well as a route to goal achievement, which also reinforces one another. Suppose one has the requisite drive and determination for their goals. In that case, they are more likely to seek alternative pathways for goal achievement and creating new pathways through such developments as innovation can strengthen one's desire for goal achievement.[20] An interesting byproduct of a lack of hope, specifically the perception of a dearth of pathways to goal achievement, is the conduction of learned helplessness[21] and can result in inactivity and self-victimization.[22] For a sport employee to avoid a fate of learned helplessness, they would need to be empowered not only by themselves but also by their sport organizations in order to realize the required drive and belief that pathways exist for them to achieve their goals.

▶ **Efficacy** An individual's conviction (or confidence) about his or her abilities to mobilize the motivation, cognitive resources, and courses of action necessary to successfully execute a specific task within a given context.

The next aspect of the HERO model is efficacy, which is the belief in one's abilities. Stajkovic and Luthans[23] defined efficacy as "an individual's conviction (or confidence) about his or her abilities to mobilize the motivation, cognitive resources, and courses of action necessary to successfully execute a specific task within a given

context" (p. 66). Within this view of efficacy, challenges are welcomed as those who possess efficacy believe they will master challenges, which will then result in personal growth and development.[24] Another aspect of efficacy is the need for practice. Practice helps one improve and grow their efficacy, which indicates that efficacious individuals actually seek out opportunities for practice in order to hone their crafts. One last note on efficacy is that it is not synonymous with success, and Luthans et al.[25] explained that "success does not just equal efficacy, in that we must also include how success is interpreted" (p. 53), which suggests that success and efficacy are often interpreted at the individual level. A sport employee who has efficacy will take on challenges presented at work; they believe that by doing so, they will be able to improve their skillset and have the confidence that their current skillset will allow them to grow professionally by accepting the challenge.

▶ **Resilience** The positive psychological capacity to rebound, to 'bounce back' from adversity, conflict, failure, or even positive events, progress, and increased responsibility.

The third aspect of the HERO model is resilience, which is a fairly straightforward concept as it relates to perseverance. The definition of resilience within the psychological capital paradigm is "the positive psychological capacity to rebound, to 'bounce back' from adversity, conflict, failure, or even positive events, progress, and increased responsibility."[26] Based on the definition, it is important to keep in mind that continuing to progress because of (or despite) success is also essential. The world of sport is filled with stories of athletes experiencing a "sophomore slump" after a superb season. It is then vital to keep in mind that we ought to aim for continual growth and avoid complacency when we achieve our goals. Another critical facet of reliance is the existence of adversity. Within the psychological capital perspective, adversity is not considered to be inherently negative; instead, adversity is an opportunity for growth. In other words, one who has a positive outlook on life is able to view a setback or adversity as a chance to improve themselves. This is done through adapting to the adversity at hand, and through this adaptation, personal development is realized (Luthans et al. 2015).[27]

▷ **Optimism** Optimism is comprised of both positive beliefs and one's ability to compartmentalize their successes and failures in terms of internal or external forces.

The final component of the traditional form of psychological capital is optimism. Much like the HERO model's other components, optimism is a more profound construct than what many view as merely having a positive outlook. Within psychological capital, optimism comprises both positive beliefs[28] and one's ability to compartmentalize their successes and failures in terms of internal or external forces.[29] In terms of positive beliefs, those with optimism will be able to put a positive light on difficult circumstances that are believed to be within their control.[30] The other aspect of optimism is the assigning of causality for positive or negative outcomes. Specifically, optimistic individuals can recognize their accomplishments as a result of their hard work and dedication to expanding their skillsets. Yet, when a failure occurs, optimistic individuals acknowledge that forces are out of their control and avoid blaming themselves (at least entirely) for failing.[31] It is relevant to note that this perspective should not be viewed as avoiding responsibility; rather, the understanding that our failures are not always strictly because of our shortcomings. In the sports industry, optimistic sport employees are valuable because of their ability to maintain a positive outlook and continue to believe in their ability to perform at a high level. For example, if an optimistic sport employee plans an outdoor fundraising event, resulting in a successful fundraising drive that will help build new facilities, they would find satisfaction from a job well done. However, if a storm causes the event to be canceled, that optimistic sport employee would understand that a storm coming through is not their fault, and some things are out of their control. In turn, they will continue and plan ways to have the event take place indoors or on a different

date. All of these components are powerful tools that anyone can develop, and we encourage you to consider how you can improve yourself by better understanding your own self-concept.

9.4 Person-Environment Fit

Now that we have a deeper understanding of the personalities, identities, self-concepts, and personal resources of individuals, we will now focus on how such concepts influence their ability to fit in at work. As we have seen, people have different personalities and perceptions. This means that people will have different experiences at work based on the environment within that organization. In this way, it is important to appreciate the congruence between employees and their workplace, because such an understanding opens the door to a better work experience for employees and the potential for improved organizational performance because of the benefits of a fit between employee and organization.

▷ **Person-Environment Fit** A concept that explains the compatibility between employee and their work environment.

The comprehensive concept that described the congruence between employee and organization is person-environment fit, which broadly explains the compatibility between employee and their work environment.[32] Within person-environment fit, there are several specific elements used to depict certain areas of fit within the organizational setting, which are used to determine the overall fit between an employee and their organization. One specific area of fit is known as person-vocation fit, which describes the similarity between a person and their occupation (i.e., vocation). As Kristof[33] explained, one's personality plays a critical role in the degree of fit between a person and their vocation as some occupations facilitate the strengths of certain individuals, which causes the perception of fit. Conversely, an occupation that limits one's strengths or reinforces areas for improvements would prohibit a perception of fit. Importantly, one's person-vocation fit is not specific to an organization but rather their career choice. In other words, a sport employee who feels like working in sport fits well with their personality is likely to recognize a sense of fit working in sport, but this would not preclude them from working for a different sport organization in a similar capacity. In this way, sport represents an occupation that would fit well for some but cause burnout and turnover for others due to a lack of fit.

▶ **Person-Group Fit** A concept that describes the congruence between an employee and their colleagues.

Another area of fit is known as person-group fit, which describes the congruence between employees and their coworkers.[34] There is a wide range of potential for coworkers as its distinction can range from those in a specific workgroup to any other member in the organization.[35] This area of person-environment fit is seemingly a critical aspect of work experiences. In many circumstances, the degree to which you enjoy coming to work every day will likely be impacted by how well you get along with your coworkers. If you genuinely enjoy your coworkers and their company, then it is quite likely that going to work might even be an enjoyable experience. But working with coworkers you despise is not likely to have you jumping out of bed in the morning to rush into work. As we have alluded to, emotions run high in sport organizations because of fandom and the public display of organizational performance. As such, person-group fit appears to be an essential concept when evaluating your current and future career paths.

▶ **Person-Job Fit** The similarity between the strengths and aptitudes of an employee and the duties required by their specific job.

A more specific form of person-environment fit is person-job fit, which is the similarity between an employee's strengths and aptitudes and the duties required by their specific job.[36] This form of fit is distinct from person-vocation fit as person-job fit is explicit in its relationship

with the demands of a job, while person-vocation fit is focused on one's career and the industry they work in. In the sports industry, an equipment manager's role will be wildly different depending on what level of sport they work in. Sport organizations that play at higher levels of sport tend to provide their athletes with as many resources as possible (e.g., equipment managers packing bags for players) as opposed to those at lower levels of sport where sport organizations do not have as many resources to provide their athletes (e.g., equipment managers having other duties and players having to pack their own bags). In short, although the profession might be the same, different jobs will have unique responsibilities, thus the degree of fit will be dissimilar for some individuals.

▶ **Person-Organization Fit** The compatibility between people and organizations.

The last form of fit that we will discuss is person-organization fit, which is "the compatibility between people and organizations that occurs when: (a) at least one entity provides what the other needs, or (b) they share similar fundamental characteristics, or (c) both" (p. 6).[37] There are two facets of person-organization fit (although it can be used with other forms of fit) which are objective and subjective or perceived fit. The objective fit distinction refers to collecting information about a given organization and then weighing how well one fits with an organization, and the perceived fit is more of a personal decision by employees as to whether or not they believe they fit well with their organization.[38] This area of fit is dedicated to how well an employee fits with the overall organization and, therefore, represents another level of fit within the person-environment fit spectrum (i.e., vocation, organization, group, and job). This level of fit has recently received attention of sport management scholars as they have attempted to find ways for sport organizations to retain their coaches[39] and its impact on recreational sport employees' motivations and work engagement.[40] Then, person-organization fit in sport organizations measures how sport employees sense an alignment with the values of the organization, such as a dedication to excellence and competition or supporting participants. Fit is an important and emerging concept in sport management, and we would encourage you to evaluate how well you feel you would fit in at an organization when interviewing (or at your current sport organization).

9.5   Summary

This chapter broadly covered the personalities of individuals and how personalities impact the lives of sport employees in and outside of the sport workplace. It is critical to keep in mind that one's personality is malleable (or flexible) as it can be shaped or formed over time. In other words, you are not "stuck" with a personality type that you do not feel represents whom you want to be. To this point, the chapter included content on psychological capital, which is viewed as "who you can become," to provide an understanding of the ways by which individuals can improve their emotional and mental perspectives. The chapter concluded with a discussion concerning fit between employees and their workplaces and the importance of finding an organization that fits your personality to have an enhanced work-life.

Discussion Questions

1. What is the DISC profile and which do you feel most aligns with your personality?
2. Which of the Big 5 personalities fits you best?
3. What are some of the belief and value systems that you have encountered?
4. What are the subcomponents of the "person-environment fit" perspective?

Notes

1. Bowditch, J. L., Buono, A. F., & Stewart, M. M. (2008). *A primer on organizational behavior.* Hoboken, NJ: John Wiley & Sons, Inc.
2. Erikson, T. (2019). *Surrounded by idiots: The four types of human behaviour.* Vermilion: London, UK.
3. Erikson, T. (2019). *Surrounded by idiots: The four types of human behaviour.* Vermilion: London, UK.
4. Goldberg, L. R. (1990). An alternative "description of personality": The Big Five factor structure. *Journal of Personality and Social Psychology, 59,* 1216–1229.; Judge, T. A., Higgins, C. A., Thoresen, C. J., & Barrick, M. R. (1999). The Big Five personality traits, general mental ability, and career success across the life span. *Personnel Psychology, 52,* 621–652.
5. Judge, T. A., Higgins, C. A., Thoresen, C. J., & Barrick, M. R. (1999). The Big Five personality traits, general mental ability, and career success across the life span. *Personnel Psychology, 52,* 621–652.
6. Costa, P. T., & McCrae, R. R. (1992). Four ways five factors are basic. *Personality and Individual Differences, 13,* 653–665.
7. Judge, T. A., Higgins, C. A., Thoresen, C. J., & Barrick, M. R. (1999). The Big Five personality traits, general mental ability, and career success across the life span. *Personnel Psychology, 52,* 621–652.
8. Judge, T. A., Higgins, C. A., Thoresen, C. J., & Barrick, M. R. (1999). The Big Five personality traits, general mental ability, and career success across the life span. *Personnel Psychology, 52,* 621–652.
9. Judge, T. A., Higgins, C. A., Thoresen, C. J., & Barrick, M. R. (1999). The Big Five personality traits, general mental ability, and career success across the life span. *Personnel Psychology, 52,* 621–652.
10. Judge, T. A., Higgins, C. A., Thoresen, C. J., & Barrick, M. R. (1999). The Big Five personality traits, general mental ability, and career success across the life span. *Personnel Psychology, 52,* 621–652.
11. Judge, T. A., Higgins, C. A., Thoresen, C. J., & Barrick, M. R. (1999). The Big Five personality traits, general mental ability, and career success across the life span. *Personnel Psychology, 52,* 621–652.
12. Judge, T. A., Higgins, C. A., Thoresen, C. J., & Barrick, M. R. (1999). The Big Five personality traits, general mental ability, and career success across the life span. *Personnel Psychology, 52,* 621–652.
13. Burke, P. J., & Stets, J. E. (2009). *Identity theory.* New York, NY: Oxford University Press.
14. Todd, S., & Kent, A. (2009). A social identity perspective on the job attitudes of employees in sport. *Management Decision, 47,* 147–190.
15. Burke, P. J., & Stets, J. E. (2009). *Identity theory.* New York, NY: Oxford University Press.
16. Burke, P. J., & Stets, J. E. (2009). *Identity theory.* New York, NY: Oxford University Press.
17. Luthans, F., Youssef, C. M., & Avolio, B. J. (2015). *Psychological capital and beyond.* New York, NY: Oxford University Press.
18. Luthans, F., Youssef, C. M., & Avolio, B. J. (2015). *Psychological capital and beyond.* New York, NY: Oxford University Press.
19. Snyder, C. R., Irving, L. M., & Anderson, J. R. (1991). Hope and optimism, in Ramachandren, V. S. (Ed.), *Encyclopedia of Human Behavior,* Academic Press, San Diego, CA, pp. 535–542.
20. Snyder, C. R. (2002). Hope theory: Rainbows in the mind. *Psychological Inquiry, 13,* 249–275.

21. Seligman, M. E. P. (1972). Learned helplessness. *Annual Review of Medicine, 23*, 407–412.
22. Luthans, F., Youssef, C. M., & Avolio, B. J. (2015). *Psychological capital and beyond.* New York, NY: Oxford University Press.
23. Stajkovic, A. D., & Luthans, F. (1998). Social cognitive theory and self-efficacy: Going beyond traditional motivational and behavioral approaches *Organizational Dynamics, 26*, 62–74.
24. Luthans, F., Youssef, C. M., & Avolio, B. J. (2015). Psychological capital and beyond. New York, NY: Oxford University Press.
25. Luthans, F., Youssef, C. M., & Avolio, B. J. (2015). *Psychological capital and beyond.* New York, NY: Oxford University Press.
26. Luthans, F. (2002). Positive organizational behavior: Developing and managing psychological strengths. *The Academy of Management Executive, 16*(1), 57–72.
27. Luthans, F., Youssef, C. M., & Avolio, B. J. (2015). *Psychological capital and beyond.* New York, NY: Oxford University Press.
28. Carver, C., Scheier, M., Miller, C., & Fulford, D. (2009). Optimism, in S. Lopez, & C. R. Snyder, (Eds.), *Oxford Handbook of Positive Psychology* (2nd ed.), Oxford University Press, New York, NY, pp. 303–312.
29. Seligman, M. E. P. (1998). *Learned Optimism.* Pocket Books: New York, NY.
30. Luthans, F., Youssef, C. M., & Avolio, B. J. (2015). *Psychological capital and beyond.* New York, NY: Oxford University Press.
31. Seligman, M. E. P. (2011). *Learned Optimism: How to Change Your Mind and Your Life.* Random House LLC: New York, NY.
32. Kristof-Brown, A., & Guay, R. P. (2011). Person-environment fit. In S. Zedeck (Ed.), *American psychological association handbook of industrial and organizational psychology* (pp. 1–50). Washington, DC: American Psychological Association.
33. Kristof, A. L. (1996). Person-organization fit: An integrative review of its conceptualizations, measurement, and implications. *Personnel Psychology, 49*, 1–49.
34. Kristof, A. L. (1996). Person-organization fit: An integrative review of its conceptualizations, measurement, and implications. *Personnel Psychology, 49*, 1–49.
35. Kristof, A. L. (1996). Person-organization fit: An integrative review of its conceptualizations, measurement, and implications. *Personnel Psychology, 49*, 1–49.; Seong, J. Y., Kristof-Brown, A. L., Park, W. W., Hong, D. S., & Shin, Y. (2015). Person-group fit; Diversity antecedents, proximal outcomes, and performance at the group level. *Journal of Management, 41*(4), 1184–1213.
36. Kristof, A. L. (1996). Person-organization fit: An integrative review of its conceptualizations, measurement, and implications. *Personnel Psychology, 49*, 1–49.
37. Kristof, A. L. (1996). Person-organization fit: An integrative review of its conceptualizations, measurement, and implications. *Personnel Psychology, 49*, 1–49.
38. Kristof, A. L. (1996). Person-organization fit: An integrative review of its conceptualizations, measurement, and implications. *Personnel Psychology, 49*, 1–49.
39. Oja, B. D., Schaeperkoetter, C. C., & Clopton, A. W. (2015). Slowing the coaching carousel: The benefits of person-organization fit. *Journal of Issues in Intercollegiate Athletics, 8*, 162–182.
40. Hazzaa, R. N., Oja, B. D., & Jung, H. (In Press). The importance of value congruence: An analysis of college recreation employees and organizations. *Managing Sport and Leisure*, DOI: https://doi.org/10.1080/23750472.2020.1728703

> **Learning Objectives** After reading this chapter, students should be able to:

- Identify socialization methods utilized by sport organizations.
- Understand how information is perceived.
- Explain how schemas and bias affect perception.

Jared Orton: President, Savannah Bananas
To listen to the interview <click here>

Abby's First Day at Talon Sports Promotions Abby's first morning with Talon Sports Promotions was a whirlwind. She had sat through training all morning with other new employees. To be honest, the company was sharing so much information. It was all a blur. One thing that stood out to her as she looked around the room was the number of women in the room. There must have been 30 employees at the training, and about

ten were women. Abby had worked in the sports industry for eight years, and she was used to being the only woman in the room. The itinerary said that there would be a lunch served and then a speech from the company president in the afternoon. Abby decided lunch would be an excellent chance to meet some of her new colleagues.

Abby approached a young woman who was sitting by herself. "Hello, my name is Abby. Can I join you for lunch?" "Sure, my name is Stephanie. Please sit down." The two chatted throughout the lunch session. Stephanie had just graduated and was very excited to work with Talon. One of her friends landed an entry-level position with Talon out of college and had advanced to a middle management position in just two years.

The ending speech from Talon's president struck an inspirational tone. He spoke about how the organization was different from other sports marketing firms, how the workplace valued all of its employees, valued creativity, and that anyone could advance to management. After the speech, Abby and Stephanie met each other in the parking lot. Stephanie could hardly contain her excitement. "Wasn't his speech great? I think we have a real future with Talon." Abby nodded along but did not share Stephanie's enthusiasm. She had heard

Supplementary Information The online version of this chapter (https://doi.org/10.1007/978-3-030-67612-4_10) contains supplementary material, which is available to authorized users.

similar pep talks from managers before, but she had been passed over for promotions repeatedly by less qualified colleagues.

10.1 Introduction

Have you ever read a situation differently as compared to your friends? Maybe you understood an email from a manager or professor to mean one thing when others took it another way? Perhaps your feelings toward a political discussion are different from those of your roommate? As we move through our day, we receive thousands of messages from managers, co-workers, friends, family, community members, and marketers. Many of these messages are intentional in that they are explicitly trying to convey information to us. However, in Chap. 5, we learned that interpretation of all information, both intentional and unintentional, is in the receiver's mind. In other words, you can tell your employees that financial resources are going to be tight this season, but you cannot control how they interpret your words.

Sport organizations use many different methods to convey messages about their culture to current and potential employees. Social media posts, websites, job announcements, and emails from supervisors carry information meant to influence perceptions about the organization. This chapter will explore how organizations use various communication channels to influence current and future employees' perceptions of organizational culture and person-organization fit. We will also explore how individuals interpret information and develop implicit agreements with their organizations that actually govern the formal relationship.

10.2 Socialization

If you were to begin working for the St. Louis Cardinals organization upon graduation, you would quickly be educated in the "Cardinal Way." Throughout much of the organization's history, the Cardinal Way has been a philosophy for developing and integrating players into a specific style of play.[1] But, it also serves as a philosophy for how front office employees conduct themselves, operate, and interact with the public.[2] The organization has passed down knowledge of the Cardinal Way to new employees via conversation and storytelling from longtime organizational members. However, at some point in the last 15 years, the Cardinal Way was published in an internal document that is passed around the organization. Considered part of the organization's competitive advantage, the document is not to be shared with outsiders.[3] As a new employee, you would likely feel the need to learn the Cardinal Way, not just to ensure you were doing your job correctly, but also to fit in with your colleagues.

Every organization has its version of the Cardinal Way, that is, its way of doing things. We call these customs, traditions, languages, and philosophies of organizational culture (see Chap. 6). Out of organizational culture, organizational norms develop. Organizational norms influence how people within the organization act, communicate, dress, and interact with others within and outside the organization. It is possible for organizational newcomers to pick up on elements of the broader organizational culture through observation; however, norms are much more challenging to decipher. For example, suppose you are interested in a job at your local sports commission. In that case, you may have seen employees out in the city talking about their casual workplace. The job posting may have mentioned a laid-back workplace leading you to believe something about the organization's culture. During your interview, you see employees dressed casually and having informal conversations throughout the building, and you conclude that the sports commission has a very relaxed organizational culture. You are likely correct in that assumption, given the evidence from your observations. At the same time, you still have a lot to learn about the organization. Who do you contact when you have an idea? How should you dress when you meet a client? How does the organization mentor and promote employees? Of course, there are likely organizational norms related to each of these questions, but for an organizational newcomer, you'll need more information to understand how the organization functions.

▷ **Socialization** The process through which new employees acquire attitudes, behaviors, and knowledge necessary to function as part of the organization.

Socialization is the process through which new employees acquire attitudes, behaviors, and knowledge necessary to function as part of the organization.[4] Many organizations refer to their socialization efforts as onboarding. These efforts can take many forms, including large-scale orientations, meetings with human resources and managers, mentoring, new employee guides, and handbooks, to name a few. The Cardinal Way document is an example of a socialization effort used by a sport organization. Fang, Duffy, and Shaw[5] examined research on socialization and found that most organization-led efforts, what they referred to as institutional socialization, and what organizations frequently refer to as onboarding, use one or more of six tactics (Table 10.1).

Many common institutional socialization activities meet definitions of multiple categories.

Table 10.1 Onboarding tactics

Category	Description
Formal activities	Officially recognized activities designed to welcome and provide uniform education to all organizational newcomers.
Collective experiences	Group gatherings and activities involving large numbers of newcomers.
Sequential experiences	Activities and experiences that are scaffolded to build on prior socialization experiences.
Fixed experiences	Socialization efforts scheduled at prescribed intervals in the organizational calendar designed to enhance newcomers' acclimation to the organization.
Serial tactics	Socialization activities designed to pair organizational newcomers with experienced employees.
Investiture efforts	Trainings designed to provide newcomers with positive feedback from experienced employees.

Fang, R., Duffy, M. K., & Shaw, J. D. (2011). The organizational socialization process: Review and development of a social capital model. *Journal of Management, 37*(1), 127–152

For example, large orientations or welcome week programs could be considered both formal activities and collective experiences. Similarly, monthly trainings designed to help newcomers understand organizational policies on sexual harassment, diversity, cyber safety, and other organizational issues would be considered formal activities and fixed experiences. If those trainings were conducted in a group setting, they would also be regarded as collective experiences. Mentoring falls under the category of serial tactics. However, a sales training class that allows newcomers to participate on calls and receive feedback could be considered a sequential experience, a collective experience, a serial tactic, and an investiture effort.

It would be difficult in this book to state that one socialization activity is more effective than another. Organizations have different structures and relationships with new employees, meaning what works for one organization may not be effective at another organization. The welcome week activities used by the Savannah Bananas to socialize new interns would not work to socialize the new Assistant General Manager for the Charlotte Hornets. Overall, new employees generally report that group orientations, meetings with human resource managers, manuals, and training are more helpful in understanding their new employer's policies and general processes. However, socialization efforts that emphasize the interaction between newcomers and experienced employees, such as mentoring programs, are more effective in conveying organizational norms and culture, while also helping new employees build social capital.[6]

Regardless of which socialization methods an organization employs, we need to be aware of several factors. First and foremost, organizations must be consistent in their messaging. If a new employee receives conflicting messages, it will lead to confusion and damage trust. It is also essential to use accessible communication channels with simple, understandable language. As you will see later in the chapter, communication clarity is vitally important. Next, organizations must be aware that socialization efforts will be occurring outside of their control. Employees who are both happy and unhappy with their role in the organization are often eager to help new employees adapt to the organization. At the same time, newcomers will seek out information about their new employer to help them understand their new workplace. Finally, the newcomer's perceptions will influence how they receive and interpret messages delivered during institutional socialization and other less formal socialization efforts. Throughout the remainder of the chapter, we will explore perception and how it influences socialization and the broader relationship between individuals and organizations.

▶ **Perception** The process of receiving and interpreting information to make sense of our environment.

10.3 Perception

Perception can be defined as the process of receiving and interpreting information to make sense of our environment.[7] Individuals are inundated with information throughout their day. From the moment you wake up until the moment you fall asleep, you are exposed to advertisements, news, emails, phone calls, text messages, conversations, websites, and many other information sources. Even nonverbal communication, such as another person's facial expressions or willingness to extend a handshake, can convey useful information in a given circumstance (see Chap. 5). Once a message is sent, verbally, textually, or visually, how it is perceived or whether it is even noticed is out of the sender's control. Employees, in particular newcomers, receive so many messages during the course of a day that it is impossible to process them all. Not all messages make enough impact to enter the perception process. Our brains filter stimuli that are deemed too insignificant to warrant further consideration. Other stimuli are retained and interpreted for meaning. This is known as selective attention.[8] For information that is retained, three sets of factors influence how it will be perceived (see Fig. 10.1).[9]

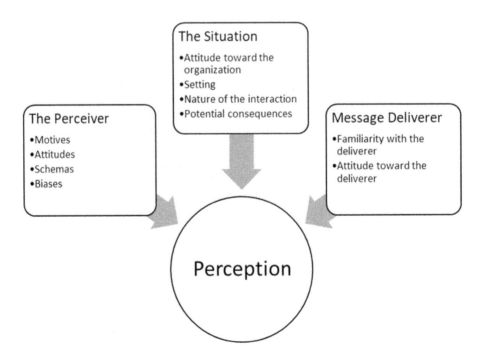

Fig. 10.1 Factors influencing perception

10.4   The Perceiver

If we think back to the case study at the beginning of the chapter, two new employees sat
through the same orientation, but they had very
different impressions regarding the message
being delivered. There were several differences
between the two newcomers, including their
career motives, attitudes, and past experiences. In
reality, every employee is unique. Everyone in
the organization has different career motives,
attitudes, schemas, experiences, and biases that
affect how they interpret messages.

10.4.1 Motives

People are influenced by many different intrinsic
and extrinsic outcomes. Some employees may be
driven by a desire to earn more pay. Others may
crave recognition or responsibility. Common
employee motivators include compensation, job
security, accomplishment, skill acquisition, promotion, and recognition, but there are many others.[10] For sample, a social media coordinator may
be motivated to seek opportunities to be creative,
while their colleague may appreciate opportunities to work independently.

Of course, people are often influenced by several motivators at once, and motivations may
change over time. As an intern, you may be seeking opportunities for skill acquisition and recognition, but later in your career, you may be driven
by opportunities for promotion and responsibility. Coming out of a recession, an employee may
be seeking job security, but pay motivations
could be more influential if that employee wants
to buy a house.

These various motivators primarily influence
perception because of selective attention.
Employees are both more attuned to, as well as
more likely to seek out information as it relates to
their self-interests.[11] Therefore, a new employee
who is motivated by career advancement is more
likely to notice messages pertaining to training,
mentorship, and promotion opportunities.[12] At
the same time, this employee may miss information related to pay structures. Further, confirma-

tion bias (discussed later in this section) makes it
more likely that we will perceive information as
favorable to motive related desires.

10.4.2 Attitudes

Workplace attitudes (discussed in Chap. 11) are
critical to how employees and prospective
employees interpret information. Employees
who exhibit higher levels of workplace/occupa-
tional satisfaction and organizational/occupa-
tional commitment are more likely to perceive
information in a manner that enhances their view
of the organization.[13] For example, an employee
who is highly committed to the organization may
interpret a memo discussing restructuring of the
ticket sales office as an opportunity for the club
to focus on new business opportunities. An
employee in the same department who is less satisfied and less committed may read that memo as
the club is looking for an opportunity to lay off
workers.

▶ **Schema** Mental models that allow individuals
to compartmentalize past experiences and make
generalizations of new information.

10.4.3 Schema

Schemas are mental models that allow individuals
to compartmentalize past experiences and make
generalizations of new information.[14] In essence,
schemas are our brain's organization of perceptions of past experiences—your brain's C-Drive.
When confronted with a unique experience, such
as understanding the norms of a new organization,
schemas provide a frame of reference against
which to evaluate further information.[15]

Past experiences are the primary drivers of
schema formation. Suppose an employee was the
victim of discrimination at a previous employer.
In that case, they might look at a new organization's anti-discrimination policies with more
skepticism than other newcomers, especially if
the new organization's anti-discrimination policy
is similar to that of their previous employer. The

new organization will need to overcome the sins of the last employer through actions that prove to the new employee that its values are different.[16]

The internationalization of the sports industry can also impact schemas. An individual moving from a club in the Japanese Professional Football League (J League) to a club in the Bundesliga will have different work and cultural experiences than an employee that was educated in Germany and has only worked for German clubs. Therefore, the two will have different schemas through which they understand organizational communication. It will be up to the employee to gain an understanding of cultural norms in their new club and country, but the organization also must figure out how to communicate so that messages are received as intended.

▶ **Heuristics** Mental models that allow people to make decisions without comprehensive information.

Further complicating the role schemas play in perception is the concept of heuristics. Heuristics are mental models that allow people to make decisions without comprehensive information. In essence, heuristics are shortcuts that the human brain uses to understand complex situations.[17] When confronted with a new experience, such as a new position in the company or a change in management, our minds want to quickly make sense of it with readily available information. Although related to past experiences, influenced by bias, and lacking in knowledge about the current situation, schemas provide the foundation for our brains to take the heuristic shortcut and make a generalization about a complicated situation.

10.4.4 Bias

Bias occurs when individuals allowed erroneous predispositions to interfere with rational judgments. Like heuristics, biases are methods to shortcut the perception process. The following are some of the most common biases that affect perception and decision-making.

▶ **Self-Evaluation Bias** Self-evaluation bias occurs when a person misunderstands their own abilities relative to their position or situation.

▶ **Overestimation** False belief in one's ability, knowledge, performance, or control over success.

10.4.4.1 Self-Evaluation Bias

Self-evaluation bias occurs when a person misunderstands their own abilities relative to their position or situation.[18] Self-evaluation bias is often exhibited in the overestimation of one's ability, knowledge, performance, or level of control over their success. Many sports fans display overestimation of their abilities to run a team. See any message board or Twitter after a team loses. Employees also exhibit overestimation, which is often in the form of beliefs that they should be in a more prominent role, have more responsibility, or receive more credit from the organization. Overestimation clouds both perception and decision-making. Individuals are more receptive to information that confirms, or that they perceive to confirm their overestimated beliefs, but less responsive or even offended by contradictory information.[19]

▶ **Overplacement** Occurs when a person overestimates their abilities relative to the average person.

The second element of self-evaluation bias is overplacement, which occurs when a person overestimates their abilities relative to the average person. In other words, it is the belief that they are better than average.[20] Evidence of overplacement bias can be seen in studies where more than half the respondents indicated they were better than average producers,[21] managers,[22] drivers,[23] and problem solvers.[24] Barnhill, Czekanski, and Pfleegor[25] surveyed students about their abilities to work in the sports industry before taking their first sport management course. They found that a considerable majority of students believed they had above-average capabilities to work in the sports industry. The people you manage will overplace their abilities. Thus, any information that an employee may be average or below average is likely to be rejected by the individual. However, it should be noted that some employees will be prone to underconfidence where they will underestimate and underplace themselves relative to others.[26]

▶ **Confirmation Bias** Seeking or interpreting of evidence in ways that are partial to existing beliefs or expectations.

10.4.4.2   Confirmation Bias

Confirmation bias is defined as "the seeking or interpreting of evidence in ways that are partial to existing beliefs or expectations" (p. 175).[27] If you've spent any time on social media during an election year, you've likely seen confirmation bias as well as fallen prey to it. People generally search for information that confirms their political beliefs while ignoring contradictory information. The same can be seen in the workplace. If a person sought employment with an organization because of its commitment to social responsibility, they will look for examples that cement their view but ignore incidents or information that contradicts their beliefs. In other words, this employee would be excited to see their organization have a booth at an event raising funds for underserved communities but ignore its efforts to gentrify the area around its stadium.

10.4.4.3   Anchoring Bias

You've likely heard first impressions are important. This is due to the anchoring bias. The initial information we receive on a topic has the most significant influence on our perceptions, whereas information or experiences that occur after perceptions are formed are less impactful.[28]

10.4.4.4   Availability Bias

While some individuals are very active in their information seeking, others rely on readily available information. This is known as availability bias.[29] Availability bias is especially prevalent when the accessible information is intense or evokes emotions.[30] As sport naturally provokes emotion in both fans and employees, availability bias can be incredibly widespread. However, issues pertaining to workers' personal lives can also be emotional, evoking availability bias. For example, a parent who receives a memo regarding limitations for leave to care for sick children may perceive that the organization is not family-friendly. These perceptions can persist even if later policies are more family-friendly.

10.5   The Situation

The situation in which the information was received will also influence how an individual perceives its meaning. Would your perceptions of information regarding potential layoffs be different if you heard about it from a friend in the parking lot versus in a board room from your boss? Are you more likely to believe a speaker who exudes confidence or a speaker who appears nervous? Which is more believable, a story from an anonymous source in the paper, or your organization's Twitter account? There are many elements related to the situation that can influence perception. In this section, we'll discuss four elements that can be particularly influential.

10.5.1   Attitudes Toward the Organization

In a verbal exchange, there are one or more information deliverers along with an information receiver. How the information receiver feels about the organization will influence their interpretation of the interaction. But, the receiver's perceptions of how the others in the exchange view the organization will also affect how the receiver interprets the conversation. If the information receiver believes the others in the organization are biased in favor of the organization, it will influence how the information is received.[31] In other words, positive news will be viewed with skepticism, but negative information will be magnified. "How could this person who loves the organization say something negative? The situation must be bad." On the other hand, if the information deliverers are thought to be biased against the organization, negative information would carry less weight, but positive information would be powerful. "Bill hates working here, and even he thinks the new Director of Marketing will make a positive impact."

10.5.2 Setting

The setting in which the information is delivered can have a tremendous impact on how it is perceived. How would you feel if you heard you would be put in charge of the team's community outreach initiative? Would your perceptions of this information be different if you heard it from your boss in the hallway, in an email, or a staff meeting? What about if you heard this at a company picnic versus at a pub with colleagues after work? More official settings, such as at the office or an official document, lead employees to put more trust in the message's content. Information received in a less formal setting, such as at a bar after work, may be dismissed or need confirmation before the employee believes the message.

10.5.3 Nature of the Interaction

During conversations, humans attempt to read the body language and voice inflection of the speaker. Words can be interpreted to have different meanings based on the speaker's mannerisms, posture, and voice tone.[32] Let's use the words, "This club is committed to diversity and inclusion." Spoken with confidence, these words may lead employees to trust the organization's commitment. Spoken with empathy, and employees may feel a sense of caring and safety from their employer. However, suppose the speaker appeared nervous or unsure. In that case, employees may question whether the speaker believed the message, leading to feelings of doubt. If the same words were delivered in a flippant manner or with a sarcastic tone, employees might feel the speaker was joking and be offended by the organization's position on the topic.

Modern communication methods have made it more challenging for people to read body language and tone. Video conferencing allows listeners to hear a speaker's words, but facial expressions are more difficult to pick up. Usually, the speaker's body is not visible, so visual cues available in face-to-face conversations are lost. Further, speakers often adjust their tone so that they are not too loud, too soft, or inaudible via their microphone. These adjustments mask verbal cues that listeners use to judge intention.[33] Text messaging and other text-based channels also hide tone. See Chap. 5 for a more detailed discussion on communication in organizations.

10.5.4 Potential Consequences

The potential consequences of the interaction can also influence how it is perceived. If just meeting with an individual is seen as a positive for an employee, then the interaction itself is likely to be perceived positively. For example, suppose an intern is told the president has seen your work and would like to meet you. In that case, it is expected that the intern will be excited about the meeting. Being invited indicates a positive in the intern's career, and even criticisms will be seen as beneficial. On the other hand, if an employee breaks the chain of command in a manner outside organizational norms, the employee is likely to be nervous about the conversation. Any criticisms that arise could be viewed as detrimental to the employee's career ambitions.

10.6 The Message Deliverer

In addition to judging the situation in which the information is delivered, employees' perceptions will also be influenced by who is providing the information.[34] One factor that can affect how the message deliverer influences perception is familiarity. Employees are more likely to trust message deliverers with whom they have a relationship or know to be trustworthy. This is, of course, if the messenger is believed to be credible. Familiarity can lead to multiple reputations that could influence how an employee comprehends information.[35]

Along those lines, the employee's attitude toward the message deliverer influences perception. Employees and newcomers form attitudes toward colleagues and others at the organization that can influence judgment. As we have noted throughout this chapter, it is impossible to take in all information received. That includes information about others. People unconsciously choose which information about a person affects their beliefs about another. This is called selective perception. Selective perception leads to several flaws in the judgment of others.

▶ **Halo Effect** Seeking or interpreting of evidence in ways that are partial to existing beliefs or expectations.

▶ **Projection** A belief that others share your own opinions or views.

▶ **Stereotyping** When an individual judges another based on false pretenses toward a group.

One such flaw is the halo effect in which the message receiver judges the deliverer entirely based on a single characteristic such as intelligence or appearance.[36] Projection is a judgment flaw in which we assume others are similar to us. Projection can lead employees to believe others share their values, views on politics, or experiences. A potentially harmful side effect of projection is the unwarranted discounting of others' attributes and experiences.[37] Another very dangerous flaw is stereotyping, which occurs when an individual judges another based on false pretenses toward a group.[38] In sport, racial minorities, women, and LGBTQ employees are often victims of stereotyping.[39] Further, stereotypes can lead employees to falsely interpret information because of an unrelated judgment error regarding the message deliverer.

▶ **Attribution** Attribution is the judgment of the locus of control of the individuals involved in the exchange.

Outside of judgments about the individual, employees may judge why the information is being shared. Attribution is the judgment of the locus of control of the individuals involved in the exchange.[40] When judging another's intentions, an employee may try to determine if the message deliverer is acting under their own intentions or being controlled by the organization. Messages may seem more official if the employee believes the deliverer is acting on the organization's will. On the other hand, messages deemed to have been shared at the deliverer's will could need additional confirmation.

10.7 Psychological Contracts

As individuals, be they newcomers, experienced employees, or even prospective applicants, gather information about an organization and develop perspective, they also begin to make assumptions about their relationship with the organization.[41] Think about your own experiences. You see a job announcement or learn of an opening from a friend. You begin seeking information to determine if you would like to work at the organization. Does the job pay well? What are the other people like? What are the organization's values? What would be expected of me? If the answers to your questions are satisfactory, you apply. Throughout the hiring process of questionnaires, phone interviews, and face-to-face interviews, you are asked many questions, but you also ask many questions. Some of the information you found earlier is confirmed, but some is discredited. At the end of the interview process, the organization makes a decision on whether you are a good fit for the organization, but you also decide on whether the organization is a good fit for you. These decisions are based on the perception of information exchanged. Once you are hired, you sign a contract that the legal relationship you will maintain with the organization and begin the socialization process prescribed by your new employer. You also continue seeking information and socializing yourself to understand the norms of where you are working. Perceptions are built, altered, or changed throughout the process. The cycle will repeat throughout your time with the organization.[42]

Psychological contracts are "individual's beliefs, shaped by the organization, regarding the terms of an exchange agreement between individuals and organizations" (p. 9).[43] Unlike legal contracts that are explicitly agreed upon transactional obligations between employees and employers, psychological contracts are the employee's perception of implied relational commitments between the parties. Whereas a legal contract may outline workers' obligations as the number of hours worked and the amount of revenue generated, in psychological contract, employees' obligations may include answering emails on weekends, following certain norms during sales calls, and acting a certain way in the office. For the organization, the legal contract outlines obligations to pay salaries and bonuses, but the psychological contract may include obligations to be flexible with working hours, opportunities for career advancement, and a pleasant office environment.[44]

Research has consistently shown that psychological contracts are the foundation of the employee-employer relationship, despite the fact that they are based on employee perceptions and may never be the subject of discussion between the parties. However, when employees believe their organization is fulfilling the psychological contract, numerous studies find that employees' attitudes such as commitment and satisfaction improved, as are measures of in-role and extra-role performance.[45] On the other hand, when the employee feels that the organization has failed to meet its obligations, the opposite effects are found.[46] Organizational behaviorists call this psychological contract breach. Following a psychological contract breach, employees will reevaluate their perceptions and adjust the psychological contract accordingly. Although, in cases where the breach is deemed to be overly egregious or causes emotional harm to the employee, the individual may consider leaving the organization.

Research on psychological contracts in sport has indicated several elements that are unique to the sports industry. First, because many sport organizations are small in terms of employees, there is more interaction between lower-level employees and upper management. Because of these interactions, it is more likely that terms of the psychological contract are explicitly discussed.[47] For example, a single parent working for a United Soccer League club may discuss their need to pick up their child from daycare each afternoon with the organization's president, allowing them to figure out a working plan. In a larger organization, it is less likely that such a conversation takes place. Psychological contract breaches are less likely when terms of the psychological contract are discussed openly.[48]

A second psychological contract feature unique to sports is perceived obligations toward the treatment of third parties. Research has indicated that sport organization employees believe their organizations have duties related to their treatment of athletes and are related to their responsibilities in the community.[49] These obligations are likely due to the nature of sport. Athletes are unique employees that are responsible for organizational success but may have less voice in decisions. At the same time, many team sport organizations represent their communities and are sometimes financially subsidized by their communities. Failures of the organization to meet these perceived obligations has a lower impact than other perceived breaches but can still damage attitudes and behaviors.

10.8 Summary

From the moment a person begins thinking about working for an organization, they start forming a psychological contract. At first, information seeking is imperfect. People seek information from any source that they trust, but much of the information lacks full context. Once the person becomes an employee, the organization begins socializing them into its organizational culture. This is a beneficial process that allows the employee to find their fit, and understand processes. However, socialization is only as adequate as the employee's perceptions of information. Numerous factors, including bias and credibility of information deliverers, influence how an employee perceives new information.

Discussion Questions

1. Think about an organization that you joined. What onboarding tactics did the organization use to educate you about its culture? Provide examples.

2. Is there a time when you overestimated your abilities? When did you realize that your abilities were not to the level you believed?

3. Think about an instance where you received good news but just couldn't believe it. Why were you skeptical? What did it take to believe the news finally?

4. We form psychological contracts with all of the organizations to which we belong. Think about your relationship with your university. What do they owe you? What do you owe the university (non-financial)?

Notes

1. Megdal, H. (2016). *The Cardinals Way.* Thomas Dunne Books.

2. Calandro, T. (2013, October 25). The Cardinal Way: Built to Last. *Huffington Post.* Retrieved from: https://www.huffpost.com/entry/the-cardinal-way-built-to_b_4164652?guccounter=1&guce_referrer=aHR0cHM6Ly9vbGluYYmxvZy53dXN0bC5lZHUv&guce_referrer_sig=AQAAAELzQv6bhNXjsLMfT-tsQxlyysDA9NQIcRCOYBOTYA99hAy3Y-WHqhuqfwQFINSU3eNgkgdFky_VbuByxS-76khluI1ELJyKkQPhDmugWrdnSyt7bEZNLr90JyUKykWULEGEAyEaWvZKZ3exYTZ6gk2dpVjqVSemuFPxEHwZjPf7z.

3. Goold, D. (2012, May 18). Now in book form: The Cardinal Way. *St. Louis Post-Dispatch.* Retrieved from: https://www.stltoday.com/sports/baseball/professional/now-in-book-form-the-cardinal-way/article_1c76331b-077e-57aa-9333-86a85b1f5ac2.html.

4. Van Maanen, J., & Schein, E. H. (1979). Toward a theory of organizational socialization. In B. M. Staw (Ed.), *Research in Organizational Behavior* (pp. 209–264). Greenwich, CT: JAI.

5. Fang, R., Duffy, M. K., & Shaw, J. D. (2011). The organizational socialization process: Review and development of a social capital model. *Journal of Management, 37*(1), 127–152.

6. Fang, R., Duffy, M. K., & Shaw, J. D. (2011). The organizational socialization process: Review and development of a social capital model. *Journal of Management, 37*(1), 127–152. https://doi.org/10.1177/0149206310384630; Hart, Z. P. (2012). Message content and sources during organizational socialization. *Journal of Business Communication, 49*(3), 191–209. https://doi.org/10.1177/00219436 12446731; Klein, H. J., Polin, B., & Leigh Sutton, K. (2015). Specific onboarding practices for the socialization of new employees. *International Journal of Selection and Assessment, 23*(3), 263–283. https://doi.org/10.1111/ijsa.12113.

7. McShane, S., & Von Glinow, M. (2021). *Organizational Behavior: Emerging Knowledge. Global Reality* (9th ed.). McGraw Hill.

8. Eagly, A. H., & Chaiken, S. (1984). Cognitive theories of persuasion. In L. Berkowitz (Ed.), *Advances in experimental social psychology* (Vol. 17, pp. 267–359). Orlando, FL: Academic Press.

9. Robbins, S.P., & Judge, T.A. (2019). *Organizational Behavior* (18th ed.). Pearson.

10. Morandin, G., & Bergami, M. (2014). Schema-based sensemaking of the decision to participate and its effects on job performance. *European Management Review, 11*(1), 5–20. https://doi.org/10.1111/emre.12019.

11. De Vos, A., Buyens, D., & Schalk, R. (2005). Making sense of a new employment relationship: psychological contract-related information seeking and the role of work values and locus of control. *International Journal of Selection and Assessment, 13*(1), 41–52.

12. Morandin, G., & Bergami, M. (2014). Schema-based sensemaking of the decision to participate and its effects on job performance. *European Management Review, 11*(1), 5–20. https://doi.org/10.1111/emre.12019.

13. Erwin, D. G., & Garman, A. N. (2010). Resistance to organizational change: linking research and practice. *Leadership & Organization Development Journal, 31*(1), 39–56.

14. Harris, S. G. (1994). Organizational culture and individual sensemaking: A schema-based perspective. *Organization Science, 5*(3), 309–321; Stein, D. J. (1992). Schemas in the cognitive and clinical sciences: An integrative construct. *Journal of Psychotherapy Integration, 2*(1), 45–63. https://doi.org/10.1037/h0101236.

15. Harris, S. G. (1994). Organizational culture and individual sensemaking: A schema-based perspective. *Organization Science, 5*(3), 309–321.

16. Sherman, U. P., & Morley, M. J. (2015). On the formation of the psychological contract: A schema theory perspective. *Group & Organization Management, 40*(2), 160–192. https://doi.org/10.1177/1059601115574944.

17. Wilkinson, N., & Klaes, M. (2012). *An Introduction to Behavioral Economics.* Palgrave Macmillan.

18. Wilkinson, N., & Klaes, M. (2012). *An Introduction to Behavioral Economics.* Palgrave Macmillan.

19. Moore, D.A., & Healy, P.J. (2008). The trouble with overconfidence. *Psychological Review, 115*(2), 502–517.

20. Wilkinson, N., & Klaes, M. (2012). *An Introduction to Behavioral Economics.* Palgrave Macmillan.

21. Cross, P.K. (1997). Not can, but will college teaching be improved? *New Directions for Higher Education, 17*, 1–15.

22. Larwood, L., & Whittaker, W. (1977). Managerial myopia: Self-serving biases in organizational planning. *Journal of Applied Psychology, 62,* 194–198.
23. Svenson, O. (1981). Are we all less risky and more skillful than our fellow drivers? *Acta Psychologica, 9,* 143–148.
24. Camerer, C.F., & Lovallo, D. (1999). Overconfidence and excess entry: An experimental approach, *American Economic Review, 89,* 306–318.
25. Barnhill, C. R., Czekanski, W. A., & Pfleegor, A. G. (2018). Getting to know our students: A snapshot of sport management students' demographics and career expectations in the United States. *Sport Management Education Journal, 12*(1), 1–14. https://doi.org/10.1123/smej.2015-0030.
26. Hallin, C. A., Øgaard, T., & Marnburg, E. (2009). Exploring qualitative differences in knowledge sources: A study of hierarchical effects of judgmental confidence and accuracy performance. *International Journal of Knowledge Management, 5*(4), 1–25.
27. Nickerson, R. S. (1998). Confirmation bias: A ubiquitous phenomenon in many guises. *Review of general psychology, 2*(2), 175–220.
28. Tversky, A., & Kahneman, D. (1974). Judgment under uncertainty: Heuristics and biases. *Science, 185*(4157), 1124–1131.
29. Dube-Rioux, L., & Russo, J. E. (1988). An availability bias in professional judgment. *Journal of Behavioral Decision Making, 1*(4), 223–237.
30. Robbins, S.P., & Judge, T.A. (2019). *Organizational Behavior* (18th ed.). Pearson.
31. Hitt, M.A., Miller, C.C., Colella, A., Triana, M. (2017). *Organizational Behavior* (5th ed.). Wiley.
32. Gentry, W. A., & Kuhnert, K. W. (2007). Sending signals: Nonverbal communication can speak volumes. *Leadership in Action, 27*(5), 3–7. https://doi.org/10.1002/lia.1220; Lybarger, J. E., Rancer, A. S., & Lin, Y. (2017). Superior–Subordinate Communication in the Workplace: Verbal Aggression, Nonverbal Immediacy, and Their Joint Effects on Perceived Superior Credibility. *Communication Research Reports, 34*(2), 124–133.
33. Navarro, J. (2020, March 31). Tips for improving communication during video conferencing. *Psychology Today.* Retrieved from: https://www.psychologytoday.com/us/blog/spycatcher/202003/tips-improving-communication-during-video-conferencing.
34. Hitt, M.A., Miller, C.C., Colella, A., Triana, M. (2017). *Organizational Behavior* (5th ed.). Wiley.
35. Luhmann, N. (2000). Familiarity, confidence, trust: Problems and alternatives. *Trust: Making and breaking cooperative relations, 6*(1), 94–107.
36. Hitt, M.A., Miller, C.C., Colella, A., Triana, M. (2017). *Organizational Behavior* (5th ed.). Wiley.; Nisbett, R. E., & Wilson, T. D. (1977). The halo effect: evidence for unconscious alteration of judgments. *Journal of personality and social psychology, 35*(4), 250.
37. Hitt, M.A., Miller, C.C., Colella, A., Triana, M. (2017). *Organizational Behavior* (5th ed.). Wiley.
38. Hitt, M.A., Miller, C.C., Colella, A., Triana, M. (2017). *Organizational Behavior* (5th ed.). Wiley; Sayce, S., Berry, D., & Bell, M. P. (2012). Inequality in organizations: stereotyping, discrimination, and labor law exclusions. *Equality, Diversity and Inclusion: An International Journal.*
39. Burton, L. J. (2015). Underrepresentation of women in sport leadership: A review of research. *Sport management review, 18*(2), 155–165.; Carton, A. M., & Rosette, A. S. (2011). Explaining bias against black leaders: Integrating theory on information processing and goal-based stereotyping. *Academy of Management Journal, 54*(6), 1141–1158.; Sartore, M. L., & Cunningham, G. B. (2007). Explaining the underrepresentation of women in leadership positions of sport organizations: A symbolic interactionist perspective. *Quest, 59*(2), 244–265.
40. Feldman, J. M. (1981). Beyond attribution theory: Cognitive processes in performance appraisal. *Journal of Applied psychology, 66*(2), 127.
41. Scholarios, D., Lockyer, C., & Johnson, H. (2003). Anticipatory socialisation: The effect of recruitment and selection experiences on career expectations. *Career Development International, 8*(4), 182–197.
42. Rousseau, D. M. (2004). Psychological contracts in the workplace: Understanding the ties that motivate. *Academy of Management Executive, 18*(1), 120–127.
43. Rousseau, D. M. (1995). *Psychological contracts in organizations: Understanding written and unwritten agreements.* Thousand Oaks, CA: Sage Publications.
44. Lee, C., Liu, J., Rousseau, D. M., Hui, C., & Chen, Z. X. (2011). Inducements, contributions, and fulfillment in new employee psychological contracts. *Human Resource Management, 50*(2), 201–226. https://doi.org/10.1002/hrm.20415.
45. Conway, N., & Coyle-Shapiro, J. A.-M. (2006). Reciprocity and psychological contracts: Employee performance and contract fulfillment. Paper Presented at the Academy of Management Annual Meeting. Atlanta, GA.
46. Zhao, H., Wayne, S. J., Glibkowski, B. C., & Bravo, J. (2007). The impact of psychological contract breach on work related outcomes: A meta-analysis. *Personnel Psychology, 60,* 647–680.
47. Barnhill, C. R., & Smith, N. L. (2019). Psychological contract fulfilment and innovative work behaviours of employees in sport-based SBEs: the mediating role of organisational citizenship. *International Journal of Sport Management and Marketing, 19*(1/2), 106–128.
48. Atkinson, C. (2008). An exploration of small firm psychological contracts. *Work, Employment and Society, 22*(3), 447–465. https://doi.org/10.1177/0950017008093480.
49. Barnhill, C. R., & Brown, L. E. (2017). Employee expectations of CSR: A psychological contracts perspective. *International Journal of Sport Management, 18*(2), 165–182.

▶ **Learning Objectives** After reading this chapter, students will be able to:

- Explain the traditional view of emotions.
- Comprehend Barrett's view on the construction of emotions.
- Discuss the differences and utilization of pride, passion, and well-being in the sport workplace.
- Understand the importance of emotions in the sport workplace.

Tanner Truelson: Ticket Operations Manager, Kroenke Sports and Entertainment
To listen to the interview <click here>

11.1 Introduction

Sport and emotions … they can go together incredibly well. Some might say they are made for each other. After all, what would sports be if not for the pure and even primal emotions that we experience when we watch our favorite team win an important game? Perhaps even more noticeable are the emotions we display after our favorite team breaks our hearts and loses a big game. In this way, emotions are a foundational element of the sport experience. In fact, the emotional spectrum that people display while participating or watching sport has an extensive range in that people can experience intense emotions while watching their favorite team, but they can also experience emotions that are maybe not as noticeable but are still equally relevant when they play a game or sport that they thoroughly enjoy. Not all sport is based on a profit-based format (the American college sport apparatus might be "technically non-profit," but a closer look at the amount of money made by coaches diminishes this stance); in fact, the vast majority of people who participate in sport do so in a non-profit system. Yet, emotions pervade throughout sport no matter if teams are popular and recognized throughout the world, or the teams are local or community-based. This makes understanding emotions an essential part of being a sport employee … no matter what level of sport you work in, emotions will be front and center to some degree.

In this chapter, we will review emotions first from a psychological perspective where we examine how emotions are constructed and compare this perspective to the classical view of emotions, which is starting to fade with more emphasis being paid to the former.[1] After we have

Supplementary Information The online version of this chapter (https://doi.org/10.1007/978-3-030-67612-4_11) contains supplementary material, which is available to authorized users.

a good handle on what emotions are, we will cover the importance of emotions and more so, controlling emotions by reviewing emotional intelligence. Afterward, we will review popular elements of emotions that are particularly relevant to the sports industry (i.e., pride and passion). We will then transition to a discussion about well-being and conclude by examining how emotions influence our behaviors.

11.2 Classical View of Emotions

Barrett[2] provided an overview of the classical view of emotions before describing her groundbreaking research on how individuals construct their emotions. Barrett explained that the classical view of emotions relies on the idea that we as humans have a natural predisposition to emotions, and we naturally understand when people are feeling, for example, angry or happy. This is done through the idea of "fingerprints" (this is a term Barrett uses to note how this perspective of emotions states that we have a natural knowledge of emotions, not actual fingerprints) that we supposedly have stored in our brains. In this perspective of emotions, our emotional reactions result from us witnessing an event. Then, our brain recognizes the event and utilizes the fingerprints that inform how we react. Once our brain recognizes the emotion that is at play (e.g., anger or happiness), we then provide our reaction that corresponds with the emotion that our brain has recognized. This theory of emotions was popularized with studies that involved participants viewing photos of people's facial expressions and then having a list of options to choose from. Barrett noted how participants responded with remarkable accuracy. These studies were replicated in many places throughout the world and even in areas with little to no exposure to the modern world. The success of these studies offered strong support and popularization for this theory. We will discuss some of the fallacies that Barrett noted in the next section but for now, let's look at a hypothetical situation to clarify this view of emotions. Suppose a sport employee encounters a coach who has just lost an important game. In that case, they may see a furrowed brow

(i.e., a typical representation of anger in the classical view) along with the coach yelling and storming down the hallway. The sport employee would recognize the facial expression, which would cause their brain to identify the emotion of anger. This will also cause a reaction for the employee, whereby they will experience emotions based on recognizing the coach's anger. This could mean the employee will feel anxious or nervous and then try and create as much distance from themselves and the coach as possible. In a more general example within the classical view of emotions, if we see a close friend who is upset and crying, we will recognize these emotions. Then a feeling of sadness will be activated or take over our own emotions. We will begin to feel sad and concerned.

The field of psychology is filled with experts who have varying views and perspectives concerning emotions, and while this is not a psychology textbook, it is important for you to have at least a basic understanding of how our brains work concerning emotions. So, before transitioning to Barrett's view of emotions as self-constructed, it is necessary to acknowledge that the debate between the classical view and Barrett's theory rages on, and we do not pretend to offer a precise answer for you. Instead, we hope to present to you both a widely used and understood theory of emotions and a cutting-edge theory that offers a nuanced perspective of how human beings create their own realities—emotions included.

11.3 Emotions as Self-Constructions

Before explaining Barrett's theory, it is essential to explain some of Barrett's critiques of the classical view of emotions. One of the central tenants of the classical view is that emotions are universal and that humans have an innate knowledge of emotions, which allows us to see pictures of people and then pick the correct emotion from a list of choices. However, Barrett demonstrated the importance of context when interpreting emotions by providing a short story along with a picture. When paired with a story, participant's accuracy plummeted, and so did the support for the idea that emotions are universal. Instead, Barrett argued that emotions are constructed or made by ourselves in response to our environment and the information that we take in.

In describing her theory, Barrett explained how our brains absorb information from our environment (Barrett is very thorough in her descriptions of the brain, our senses, and how our minds utilize the information we gather. Please note what follows is a very broad and simplified overview of Barrett's theory and rationale), which includes our senses, such as sight, smell, and hearing. In fact, our visual perceptions are strongly augmented by our other senses. We use this information to predict what occurs next, even visually. Yes, you read that correctly…what you are reading now is predicted by your brain (using the context surrounding you), and there is a subsequent series of predictions and corrections. Have you ever been at home and insist that you saw your pet walk by but look over and they are sleeping next to you? This would be an example of your brain making an incorrect prediction. Essentially, our brains are always taking in information, learning, guessing, and correcting. This also starts at a very young age when we start recognizing faces and words and begin to associate words with our own actions. In a fascinating description that connects the predictions of your brain to emotions, Barrett[3] explains this phenomenon as "your experience right now was predicted by your brain a moment ago" (p. 59). The emotions you feel are a prediction of what your brain is guessing will be the appropriate response based on the information it has received from the environment. In other words, your brain constructs your emotions to help you respond to a given situation.

Let's revisit our example from earlier with the upset coach storming down the hallway. In the classical view, the sport employee would recognize the coach's facial expressions, which would then inform their reactions and emotions. In Barrett's theory of constructed emotions, the employee's brain will make a prediction of the coach's behavior based on the sights and sounds of the moment, which will inform the emotions of the employee based on the learned experiences of past interactions with the coach. If the sport employee has had many interactions with this coach before in a similar situation, the brain will have data pertaining to past similar interactions and have a better chance to have their predictions be true or accurate. It could be that the sport employee has learned that when the coach appears to be in such a mood, they want someone to talk to and would welcome personal interaction. In Barrett's view, the brain is continually taking in information and using the information to guide its predictions, allowing the brain to create an emotional response, thereby constructing the emotion instead of having an emotion being activated from outside the brain.

Barrett's last critical point is that the emotional spectrum is incredibly broad and full of an array of emotions. The classical view is that there are clear boundaries between emotions and that being angry is, well, being angry. But as Barrett explained, a short reflection of our own emotional history would make it obvious that there are degrees of emotions or various levels of anger or happiness. A win over an archrival would surely bring a sense of happiness or even jubilance, but what about a win over an opponent that is not a rival. There would still likely be happiness in a victory over a non-rival opponent and potentially jubilance, but probably not as much as there would be over a rival, and yet the same name for the emotion would be used. This is a simple point that describes the complexity of emotions. While winning likely brings a feeling of "happiness," there are probably going to be different degrees of that happiness depending on the context of the victory. This again brings us back to Barrett's view on emotions and the importance of context or the environment. The circumstances that we find ourselves in provide unique information to our brains, which is then used to inform our emotions. For this reason, according to Barrett's theory, we feel a stronger sensation of happiness when your favorite team defeats their archrival as opposed to when they eke out a victory over a team that they have traditionally defeated. Now we will turn to emotional intelligence and the power that emotions can hold as well as the importance of managing our emotions.

11.4   Emotional Intelligence

The concept of emotional intelligence has been popularized by Daniel Goleman, who has been influential in developing the meaning and utilization of the construct. Interestingly, Barrett,[4] whom we just relied upon to help us understand what emotions are, specifically criticized Goleman's[5] view of the brain and how it works. In short, their differences are grounded in how the different parts of the brain work, with Goleman suggesting the brain's various compartments or sections are more separate than connected. Barrett, on the other hand, argues the entire brain is connected. Regardless, emotions play a powerful role in our daily lives. We experience a wide range of emotions every day. The manner by which we manage those emotions can have highly important influences on our health and career prospects.

Emotional intelligence is often referred to as "EQ," which draws comparisons to "IQ." One's IQ or intelligence quotient is meant to convey a degree of intellect. Someone who has a high degree of IQ is likely to be considered "book smart" or one who easily earns good grades. On the other hand, EQ is a measure of emotional understanding. While you might think that having a high IQ is more valuable than having a high EQ, you also might be mistaken. Goleman provides numerous benefits to having a high level of EQ, including improved career advancements and more fulfilling relationships. A high IQ is certainly a positive quality, but you will see there are many benefits to having a strong EQ. First, let's discuss the various definitions and components of emotional intelligence.

▶ **Emotional Intelligence** The ability to perceive accurately, appraise, and express emotion; the ability to access and/or generate feelings when they facilitate thought; the ability to understand emotion and emotional knowledge; and the ability to regulate emotions to promote emotional and intellectual growth.

There are a few different definitions of emotional intelligence, one being "a set of interrelated abilities at the interface of emotion and cognition, including perceiving, understanding, using, and managing emotions" (p. 316).[6] A different definition of emotional intelligence describes the construct as "The ability to perceive accurately, appraise, and express emotion; the ability to access and/or generate feelings when they facilitate thought; the ability to understand emotion and emotional knowledge; and the ability to regulate emotions to promote emotional and intellectual growth" (p. 10).[7] One common theme from these definitions is controlling one's emotions. There are four components of emotional intelligence, all of which help explain the various facets of emotional control. Wong and Law,[8] as well as Mayer and Salovey,[9] defined these four areas as self-emotional appraisal, regulation of emotion, others' emotional appraisal, and use of emotion. Goleman used a similar four-component approach (i.e., self-awareness, self-management, social awareness, and relationship management).

▶ **Self-Emotional Appraisal** Cognitive awareness of one's current emotional state.

11.4.1 Self-Emotional Appraisal

The first component, self-emotional appraisal (or self-awareness), is all about understanding your emotions at the moment. This is an essential aspect of emotional intelligence as without being able to understand our own emotions, we are likely to be "stuck" and unable to advance to the other areas or components of emotional intelligence. In a simple example, if we can recognize that we are feeling angry, we are more likely to change our reactions. Have you ever felt bad about how you acted when you were very emotional (usually being angry or upset)? First of all, do not be too hard on yourself … this happens to everyone. Goleman[10] alluded to emotions being addictive and almost like a drug whereby when we start to feel angry and nothing is done to bring us back to some equilibrium, we are likely to "overact" and behave in a manner that is not socially acceptable. These actions are taken because our brains have become "hijacked" by our emotions and we do not take the time to think about the meaning of our actions. These are natural human reactions, and there is nothing inherently wrong with being angry, but this comes with a caveat. Think about your personal and family relationships … is there someone that is continually in a poor or foul mood? If so, when around this person, do you seek them out, or do you avoid them? As Goleman explained, humans usually avoid being around people who have a bad attitude and instead would rather be around people who are happy and joyful. This is not exactly groundbreaking science, but it does underscore the importance of emotions and the ability to recognize them. If you find yourself as the person who is usually in a bad mood, your social circle, and potentially, your professional opportunities could shrink. The reverse is also true. If you can recognize when you are in a good mood and generally happy, you can then understand what environments help maintain a good attitude. This could lead to you learning how to keep yourself in a positive mood, which could then expand your circle and career opportunities.

▷ **Self-Management** One's ability to manage or control their emotions.

11.4.2 Self-Management

Although understanding our emotions is important, we also need to regulate our emotions as we will not prevent negative effects such as sadness or anger. In this component of EQ, those with higher levels of emotional intelligence are able to manage or control their emotions.[11] Going back to the example of feeling angry … recognizing being angry is important, as it allows us to start the process of "cooling down" and relaxing, but being able to control anger requires both the recognition of the emotion and the ability to continue to recede from an emotional overdrive. This allows individuals to keep their emotions "in check," which prevents embarrassing behaviors or actions. Please take a moment to think about the last time you were really angry … whether you are conscious of it or not, what helped you

calm down may have been when you realized you were angry and then you put yourself into a new state of mind or environment that allowed you to calm down. Interestingly, when someone who is very angry or even raging, and they are asked, "why are you so angry?" they might shout back, "I'M NOT ANGRY," and yet this could be the moment where they recognize they are acting inappropriately and begin to calm down. Mayer and Salovey[12] and Wong and Law's[13] use of the emotion component of emotional intelligence is relevant here. When individuals are able to master their emotions, they are able to improve their performance (potentially at work) and other productive activities, which represent the potential for personal growth. In all, these components are about the individual and reflect how people can manage their own emotions to prevent or limit negative emotional outbursts, as well as prolong or amplify positive emotions.

▷ **Social Awareness** One's ability to recognize the emotions of others.

11.4.3 Social Awareness

The other components are related to how a person with higher levels of emotional intelligence can recognize others' emotions and provide the right response to those emotions. The third component, others' emotional appraisal, describes how one can recognize others' emotions.[14] If you see your best friend celebrating her favorite team winning a big game, is your response "they'll just lose the next game anyway"? Let's hope not, as doing so would be a poor "read of the room" or recognizing your friends' emotions.

▷ **Relationship Management** One's ability to act appropriately to the emotions of others.

11.4.4 Relationship Management

Identifying the state of emotions others are experiencing is a very powerful ability, and Goleman[15] explained that doing so can help us manage our relationships by knowing how to appropriately interact with our friends or strangers depending on the emotions they are experiencing. For example, do you have a friend who always seems to know the right thing to say no matter what the moment is … maybe they make you laugh when you are upset? These friends likely have a high level of emotional intelligence. They are so in tune with their emotions that they are able to recognize emotions in others, and because of that, they know the appropriate response. One could also view such individuals as empathetic. Regardless, those individuals who know the right thing to say or do are generally well-liked and often have a multitude of opportunities in terms of social circles and professional advancement. As such, the value of emotional intelligence should be obvious. Much like IQ, emotional intelligence comes naturally to some but can also be learned.[16] Based on the potential of emotional intelligence, we strongly encourage you to think about how well you recognize your emotions both in terms of yourself and with others. (We will revisit this aspect of emotional intelligence in Chap. 18 when we discuss leadership).

We have discussed emotional intelligence in depth, but how is it applied in sport? As we have noted, sport and emotions are interrelated. One does not need to watch nightly sports highlights for a long time before seeing a coach or player verbally (hopefully not physically!) berating an official. Sport management scholars have begun to investigate the impact of coaches and athletics directors' emotional intelligence on constructs such as emotional labor, job satisfaction, turnover intentions, and goal orientation.[17] In another example, sports have also begun to explore how sport employees' emotional intelligence influences their job engagement and creative behaviors.[18] The authors found that sport employees with a higher level of emotional intelligence are likely to have greater job engagement and creative behaviors. Another interesting aspect of this study was that emotional intelligence was a stronger predictor of creative behaviors than

authentic leadership (this form of leadership actually hurts creative behaviors), which positions emotional intelligence as a potentially valuable construct in the contemporary sport workplace and one that sport organizations and leaders might consider offering training programs for. In continuing the progression of showing how emotions are important in the sport workplace, we will now focus our discussion on specific constructs relevant to the sports industry.

11.5   Emotions in the Sport Workplace

In this section, we will review pride, passion, and well-being. The former can be viewed as an organizational-level construct (i.e., pride in an organization), and the latter two are usually studied at the individual level. These constructs were selected due to their relevance to the sport workplace, but there are a plethora of specific variables that could have been chosen. Instead, we will focus on these three and encourage you to research and review the references we have provided to discover other important variables in the sport workplace.

▶ **Pride** Feelings of importance, value, and admiration based on status evaluations of one's current job.

11.5.1   Pride

As noted above, pride can be viewed as an organizational-level variable in that pride felt by an individual, or in this case, employee, is reflective of the organization. Pride is an emotion that is "generated by appraisals that one is responsible for a socially valued outcome or for being a socially valued person" (p. 66).[19] In this way, when an individual determines that the organization they belong to behaves in an appropriate or legitimate (i.e., socially valued) manner, the result will be a feeling of pride in the organization, which then trickles down to the self. In regard to pride in the sports industry, the construct has been described as "feelings of importance, value, and admiration based on status evaluations of one's current job" (p. 355).[20] Having pride in oneself or an organization translates to improved self-efficacy, self-worth, and dignity because of an enhanced sense of achievement.[21] Additionally, there are two forms of pride: authentic and hubristic.[22]

The authentic version of pride results from accomplishments that provoke natural emotions related to self-esteem, support goal achievement, self-worth, and prosocial actions.[23] Those with authentic pride are motivated to accomplish their goals by taking on tasks with full effort.[24] Conversely, hubristic pride reflects a drive for accomplishment that comes from a selfish or conceited viewpoint.[25] Those who have hubristic pride are mostly concerned with their own desire to achieve their goals to propel themselves as compared to helping others. Essentially, this form of pride is egotistical and is strictly focused on individual desires and accomplishments, which results in poor or toxic relationships with others.[26] As you can see, pride can be a positive or a negative emotion; it all depends on how we use our emotions, and pride is no different.

Pride has begun to be studied by sport management scholars as they have examined the construct among sport employees. Scholars have argued that pride is likely to be an influential variable to help sport employees build their psychological capital and other variables.[27] In an empirical study, Swanson and Kent[28] were able to show a relationship between pride and employee satisfaction and organizational citizenship behaviors (i.e., extra efforts). Considering how pride in sport teams or organizations is likely to be a hallmark for many practitioners and participants, understanding how having pride in a sport organization would likely generate positive outcomes.

▶ **Passion** An individual's emotional and persistent state of desire and based on cognitive and affective work appraisals, which results in consistent work intentions and behaviors.

11.5.2 Passion

Much like pride, passion is a seemingly relevant construct to understand in the sports industry. To this point, passion among sport employees is beginning to see increased attention.[29] Also, similar to pride, passion has two dimensions, but we will first focus on a general definition for the construct. Passion, within a work perspective, is defined as an "individual's emotional and persistent state of desire and on the basis of cognitive and affective work appraisals, which results in consistent work intentions and behaviors" (p. 146).[30] This definition describes how those who are passionate about their work have a continuous desire to engage in work activities because they view their work as a means to experience self-efficacy.[31] Passion is further described with two dimensions: harmonious and obsessive. Harmonious passion is considered to be "a strong desire to freely engage" (p. 797)[32] and is generally thought of as a natural or internal appeal for work activities.[33] This form of passion is the positive aspect and is associated with a balance between work and the desires of the self. Erstwhile, the obsessive variety of passion occurs when individuals become so engrossed in their activities that they become fully consumed and minimize other duties or roles in their life. Obsessive passion has been defined as a "strong and uncontrollable urge to partake in the activity" (p. 128).[34] A transition from harmonious to obsessive passion is not a difficult trail, and as explained by Perrewé et al.[35] "Passion is often directed towards activities that employees find particularly meaningful and that they are generally skilled at performing, thus manifesting in conduct that is intentional, determined, and stable … as these behaviors become embedded, it may become more difficult to turn passion 'off'" (p. 147). As we have discussed, the sports industry requires many and demanding hours, and so passion is seemingly a critical construct to understand as having a passion for working in sport would seemingly support sport employees as they work through many evenings and weekends in the office or on the field. However, sport organizations and employees should be wary of having a harmonious passion for working in sport turn into an obsessive desire to be at work. Balance is essential for all things in life, and working in the sports industry is no different. Passion for work is a good thing, just do not allow it to become too much of a good thing!

11.5.3 Well-Being

The term "well-being" is one that you have likely heard before as it is a commonly used word to describe a sense of welfare or happiness. However, the construct of well-being is much deeper than just happiness. Well-being has been pervasive throughout Western philosophy, with some of the earliest conceptualizations of well-being coming from famous philosophers, and is generally viewed from two different perspectives: hedonic and eudemonic. The first form, hedonic, comes from the concept of hedonism and describes the desire for and attainment of pleasure and avoiding pain.[36] Hedonic well-being occurs when you are able to procure a box of your favorite cookies and are gleefully munching on them. Undoubtedly you would be experiencing some level of happiness as you taste the sweetness of the sugar in the cookies—this is the attainment of pleasure. This form of well-being is grounded in what scholars refer to as subjective well-being.[37]

The other form of well-being, eudemonic, is a deeper portrayal of happiness, as it represents the power of being true to oneself.[38] We will soon discuss authenticity and how it supports human functioning in Chap. 12, but eudemonic well-being represents this process. Within eudemonic well-being is the concept of psychological well-being. The psychological well-being paradigm has several components, including self-acceptance, positive relations with others, autonomy, environmental mastery, purpose in life, and personal growth.[39] The emphasis on human development, purpose, and growth differentiates subjective and psychological well-being, with the former centered on simple attainment of whatever feels "good" in the moment and the latter being concerned with improvements to one's psychological functioning.[40] Put another way, understanding one's subjective well-being is essential as it helps comprehend desires and motivations, but psychological well-being offers a more in-depth look into who we are and what we can potentially grow to be when we fully develop our psychological resources.

Unsurprisingly, psychological well-being (and to a smaller degree subjective well-being) has been viewed as an aspirational concept for sport organizations and employees to strive toward. Scholars have utilized psychological capital to better understand how sport employees can develop psychological well-being.[41] A similar research model has also been applied to understanding how to improve the well-being of collegiate student-athletes.[42] Emotions are diverse and powerful entities that are sometimes used to build on each other for desired emotional states such as psychological well-being. Pride and passion have also been viewed as concepts that can help support psychological well-being in sport employees.[43] As such, emotions can be considered a preferred outcome, but they are often used to induce certain behaviors. Essentially, when we are in a certain mood or are experiencing a given emotion, we are more likely to engage in certain activities than others. When we are in a positive affect state (e.g., happy), we are more likely to be friendlier with coworkers or willingly engage in our work tasks, but when our affect is negative, we are likely to avoid work or be rude with our coworkers. This positions emotions as a critical feature of human psychology as our emotions dictate our behaviors, and the importance of emotions also translates to the sport workplace. If happy sport employees tend to be more productive or help produce better work atmospheres, then it would stand to reason that sport organizations would prefer their employees to be in a good mood. What is unique about the sports industry is the game or competition element and the debate on whether sport employees are fans and if the performance of the organization's teams or other sporting events impacts sport employees' work productivity. Scholars have begun to look at this issue,[44] but this area of inquiry remains in its initial stages.

11.6   Summary

In this chapter, we reviewed both traditional and cutting-edge theories of human emotions and discussed the importance of emotions in sport. Emotions are an impactful concept that can influence certain behaviors, and as a result, the concepts of emotional intelligence, pride, passion, and well-being, were all discussed. Although psychologists are still learning about how emotions work and how humans are impacted by their emotions, it is clear that the sports industry is a particularly relevant arena for emotions to be considered. In sum, sport employees should pay special attention to their emotions and how they utilize them as they continue to progress through their careers.

Discussion Questions

1. What is Barrett's view of constructed emotions?
2. What is the traditional view of emotions, and how does it contract with Barrett's view?
3. What are the elements of emotional intelligence?
4. What are the different forms of well-being?

Notes

1. Barrett, L. F. (2017). *How emotions are made: The secret life of the brain.* Houghton Mifflin Harcourt Publishing Company: New York, NY.
2. Barrett, L. F. (2017). *How emotions are made: The secret life of the brain.* Houghton Mifflin Harcourt Publishing Company: New York, NY.
3. Barrett, L. F. (2017). *How emotions are made: The secret life of the brain.* Houghton Mifflin Harcourt Publishing Company: New York, NY.
4. Barrett, L. F. (2017). *How emotions are made: The secret life of the brain.* Houghton Mifflin Harcourt Publishing Company: New York, NY.
5. Goleman, D. (2005). *Emotional intelligence: Why it can matter more than IQ.* New York, NY: Bantam Dell.
6. Lopes, P. (2016). Emotional intelligence in organizations: Bridging research and practice. *Emotion Review, 8,* 316–321.
7. Mayer, J. D., & Salovey, P. (1997). What is emotional intelligence? In P. Salovey & D. Sluyter (Eds.), *Emotional development and emotional intelligence: Implications for educators* (pp. 3–31). New York, NY: Basic Books.
8. Wong, C. S., & Law, K. S. (2002). The effects of leader and follower emotional intelligence on performance and attitude: An exploratory study. *The Leadership Quarterly, 13*(3), 243–274.
9. Mayer, J. D., & Salovey, P. (1997). What is emotional intelligence? In P. Salovey & D. Sluyter (Eds.), *Emotional development and emotional intelligence: Implications for educators* (pp. 3–31). New York, NY: Basic Books.
10. Goleman, D. (2005). Emotional intelligence: Why it can matter more than IQ. New York, NY: Bantam Dell.
11. Wong, C. S., & Law, K. S. (2002). The effects of leader and follower emotional intelligence on performance and attitude: An exploratory study. Leadership Quarterly, 13(3), 243–274.
12. Mayer, J. D., & Salovey, P. (1997). What is emotional intelligence? In P. Salovey & D. Sluyter (Eds.), *Emotional development and emotional intelligence: Implications for educators* (pp. 3–31). New York, NY: Basic Books.
13. Wong, C. S., & Law, K. S. (2002). The effects of leader and follower emotional intelligence on performance and attitude: An exploratory study. The Leadership Quarterly, 13(3), 243–274.
14. Wong, C. S., & Law, K. S. (2002). The effects of leader and follower emotional intelligence on performance and attitude: An exploratory study. The Leadership Quarterly, 13(3), 243–274.
15. Goleman, D. (2005). Emotional intelligence: Why it can matter more than IQ. New York, NY: Bantam Dell.
16. Goleman, D. (2005). Emotional intelligence: Why it can matter more than IQ. New York, NY: Bantam Dell. Wong, C. S., & Law, K. S. (2002). The effects of leader and follower emotional intelligence on performance and attitude: An exploratory study. The Leadership Quarterly, 13(3), 243–274.
17. Lee, Y. H. (2019). Emotional intelligence, servant leadership, and development goal orientation in athletic directors, *Sport Management Review, 22*(3), 395–406; Lee, Y. H., & Chelladurai, P. (2016). Affectivity, emotional labor, emotional exhaustion, and emotional intelligence in coaching. *Journal of Applied Sport Psychology, 28*(2), 170–184; Lee, Y. H., & Chelladurai, P. (2018). Emotional intelligence, emotional labor, coach burnout, job satisfaction, and turnover intention in sport leadership. *European Sport Management Quarterly, 18*(4), 393–412.
18. Paek, B., Martyn, J., Oja, B. D., Kim, M., & Larkins, R. J. (in press). Searching for sport employee creativity: A mixed-methods exploration. *European Sport Management Quarterly*, https://doi.org/10.1080/1618 4742.2020.1804429.
19. Mascolo, M. F., & Fischer, K. W. (1995). Developmental transformations in appraisals for pride, shame and guilt. In Tangney, J. P. & Fischer,

K. W. (Eds.), *Self-conscious emotions: The psychology of shame, guilt, embarrassment and pride*, Guilford Press, New York, NY, pp. 64–113.

20. Swanson, S., & Kent, A. (2017). Passion and pride in professional sports: Investigating the role of workplace emotion. *Sport Management Review, 20*(4), 352–364.

21. Wärnå, C., Lindholm, L., & Eriksson, K. (2007). Virtue and health–finding meaning and joy in working life. *Scandinavian Journal of Caring Sciences, 21*(2), 191–198; Williams, L. A., & DeSteno, D. (2008). Pride and perseverance: The motivational role of pride. *Journal of Personality and Social Psychology, 94*(6), 1007–1017.

22. Tracy, J. L. & Robins, R. W. (2004). Putting the self into self-conscious emotions: A theoretical model. *Psychological Inquiry, 15*(2), 103–125; Tracy, J. L. & Robins, R. W. (2007). Emerging insights into the nature and function of pride. *Current Directions in Psychological Science, 16*(3), 147–150.

23. Carver, C. S., Sinclair, S., & Johnson, S. L. (2010). Authentic and hubristic pride: Differential relations to aspects of goal regulation, affect, and self-control. *Journal of Research in Personality, 44*(6), 698–703; Tracy, J. L. & Robins, R. W. (2007). Emerging insights into the nature and function of pride. *Current Directions in Psychological Science, 16*(3), 147–150.

24. Tracy, J. L. & Robins, R. W. (2004). Putting the self into self-conscious emotions: A theoretical model. *Psychological Inquiry, 15*(2), 103–125; Tracy, J. L. & Robins, R. W. (2007). Emerging insights into the nature and function of pride. *Current Directions in Psychological Science, 16*(3), 147–150.

25. Tracy, J. L. & Robins, R. W. (2007). Emerging insights into the nature and function of pride. *Current Directions in Psychological Science, 16*(3), 147–150.

26. Tracy, J. L. & Robins, R. W. (2007). Emerging insights into the nature and function of pride. *Current Directions in Psychological Science, 16*(3), 147–150.

27. Kim, M., Perrewé, P. L., Kim, Y. K., & Kim, A. C. H. (2017). Psychological capital in sport organizations: Hope, Efficacy, Resilience, and Optimism among Employees in Sport (HEROES). *European Sport Management Quarterly, 17*(5), 659–680; Oja, B., Kim, M., Perrewé, P., & Anagnostopoulos, C. (2019). Conceptualizing A-HERO for sport employees' well-being. *Sport, Business and Management: An International Journal, 9*(4), 363–380; Swanson, S., & Kent, A. (2017). Passion and pride in professional sports: Investigating the role of workplace emotion. *Sport Management Review, 20*(4), 352–364.

28. Swanson, S., & Kent. A. (2017). Sport identification and employee pride: Key factors in sport employee psychology. *International Journal of Sport Management and Marketing, 17* (1/2), 32–51.

29. Anagnostopoulos, C, Winand, M., & Papdimitriou, D. (2016). Passion in the workplace: Empirical insights from team sport organisations. *European Sport Management Quarterly, 16*(4), 385–412; Swanson, S., & Kent, A. (2017). Passion and pride in professional sports: Investigating the role of workplace emotion. *Sport Management Review, 20*(4), 352–364.

30. Perrewé, P. L., Hochwarter, W. A., Ferris, G. R., McAllister, C. P., & Harris, J. N. (2014). Developing a passion for work passion: Future directions on an emerging construct. *Journal of Organizational Behavior, 35,* 145–150.

31. Maslach, C. & Leiter, M. (2008). Early predictors of job burnout and engagement. *Journal of Applied Psychology, 93,* 498–512.

32. Marsh, H. W., Vallerand, R. J., Lafreniére, M. K., Parker, P., Morin, A. J., Carbonneau, N., … Paquet, Y. (2013). Passion: Does one scale fit all? Construct validity of two-factor passion scale and psychometric invariance over different activities and languages. *Psychological Assessment, 25*(3), 796–809.

33. Vallerand, R. J., Blanchard, C. M., Mageau, G. A., Koestner, R., Ratelle, C., Léonard, M., & Gagné, M. (2003). Les passions de l'ame: On obsessive and harmonious passion. *Journal of Personality and Social Psychology, 85*(4), 756–767.

34. Bélanger, J. J., Lafreniére, M. K., Vallerand, R. J., & Kruglanski, A. W. (2013). When passion makes the heart grow colder: The role of passion in alternative goal suppression. *Journal of Personality and Social Psychology, 104*(1), 126–147.

35. Perrewé, P. L., Hochwarter, W. A., Ferris, G. R., McAllister, C. P., & Harris, J. N. (2014). Developing a passion for work passion: Future directions on an emerging construct. *Journal of Organizational Behavior, 35,* 145–150.

36. Ryan, R. M., & Deci, E. L. (2001). On happiness and human potentials: A review of research on hedonic and eudemonic well-being. *Annual Review of Psychology, 52,* 141–166.

37. Ryan, R. M., & Deci, E. L. (2001). On happiness and human potentials: A review of research on hedonic and eudemonic well-being. *Annual Review of Psychology, 52,* 141–166.

38. Waterman, A. S. (1993). Two conceptions of happiness: Contrasts of personal expressiveness (eudaimonia) and hedonic enjoyment. *Journal of Personal Social Psychology, 64,* 678–691.

39. Ryff, C. D., & Keyes, C. L. M. (1995). The structure of psychological well-being revisited. *Journal of Personality and Social Psychology, 69*(4), 719–727.

40. Ryan, R. M., & Deci, E. L. (2001). On happiness and human potentials: A review of research on hedonic and eudaimonic well-being. *Annual Review of Psychology, 52,* 141–166; Ryff, C. D., & Keyes, C. L. M. (1995). The structure of psychological well-being revisited. *Journal of Personality and Social Psychology, 69*(4), 719–727.

41. Kim, M., Perrewé, P. L., Kim, Y. K., & Kim, A. C. H. (2017). Psychological capital in sport organizations: Hope, Efficacy, Resilience, and Optimism among Employees in Sport (HEROES). *European Sport Management Quarterly, 17*(5), 659–680; Kim, M., Kim, A. C. H., Newman, J. I., Ferris, G. R., & Perrewé, P. L. (2019). The antecedents and conse-

quences of positive organizational behavior: The role of psychological capital for promoting employee well-being in sport organizations. *Sport Management Review, 22*(1), 108–125; Oja, B., Kim, M., Perrewé, P., & Anagnostopoulos, C. (2019). Conceptualizing A-HERO for sport employees' well-being. *Sport, Business and Management: An International Journal, 9*(4), 363–380.

42. Kim, M., Oja, B. D., Chin, J., & Kim, H. (2020). Developing student-athlete school satisfaction and psychological well-being: The effects of academic psychological capital and engagement. *Journal of Sport Management, 34*(4), 378–390.

43. Kim, M., Perrewé, P. L., Kim, Y. K., & Kim, A. C. H. (2017). Psychological capital in sport organizations: Hope, Efficacy, Resilience, and Optimism among Employees in Sport (HEROES). *European Sport Management Quarterly, 17*(5), 659–680; Oja, B., Kim, M., Perrewé, P., & Anagnostopoulos, C. (2019).

Conceptualizing A-HERO for sport employees' well-being. *Sport, Business and Management: An International Journal, 9*(4), 363–380.

44. Oja, B. D., Bass, J. R., & Gordon, B. S. (2015). Conceptualizing employee identification with sport organizations: Sport Employee Identification (SEI). *Sport Management Review, 18*(4), 583–595; Oja, B. D., Bass, J. R., & Gordon, B. S. (2020). Identities in the sport workplace: Development of an instrument to measure sport employee identification. *Journal of Global Sport Management, 5*(3), 262–284. https://doi.org/10.1080/24704067.2018.1477521; Oja, B. D., Hazzaa, R. N., Wilkerson, Z., & Bass, J. R. (2018). March Madness in the sport workplace: Cultural implications for sport employees. *Journal of Intercollegiate Sport, 11*(1), 82–105; Swanson, S., & Kent, A. (2015). Fandom in the workplace: Multi-target identification in professional team sports. *Journal of Sport Management, 29*(4), 461–477.

▶ **Learning Objectives** After reading this chapter, students should be able to:

- Understand how motivation theories have evolved over time.
- Explain the different levels of Maslow's hierarchy of needs.
- Apply self-determination theory to the sport workplace.
- Comprehend the importance of authenticity and grit in the sport workplace.

Jay Larson: Senior Associate Athletic Director for Administration, University of California-Berkeley Athletics
To listen to the interview <click here>

"Why Am I So Tired?" "Why am I so tired?" Kim asked herself. Every day was a struggle. It was now hard to get out of bed.

It was hard to get to work on time. It was hard to stay focused during work. This wasn't always the case for Kim. She used to be so full of energy. Her lethargy now worried her so much that Kim visited her doctor last week for tests. When the results came back, Kim was relieved to find out that she had no health issues, but the results also confused her. She was hung up on a question that her doctor asked, "Has anything changed in your life?"

Six months ago, Kim left her position with her role as Community Relations Director for the Lotte Giants for a similar position with Busan IPark. Her new job paid more, and she worked less, but it was also more office work. With the Giants, Kim was out in the community. Her job was more hands-on. It required a lot of hours, but they seemed to fly by. Kim also had more freedom to take initiative than she has with Busan IPark. Could it be true? Was her new, more comfortable, better paying job causing her fatigue?

12.1 Motivation

The motivations of individuals are a critical feature of any workplace, but the sports industry is particularly dependent on a motivated workforce

Supplementary Information The online version of this chapter (https://doi.org/10.1007/978-3-030-67612-4_12) contains supplementary material, which is available to authorized users.

(as well as athletes and coaches). One of the main reasons that motivation and the study of motivation have become increasingly important in the sport workplace is the sheer number of hours and responsibilities that sport employees are required to provide. It is not uncommon to work 60, 70, or even 80 hours a week regularly as a sport employee. Beyond coaches, where it is not uncommon to hear such stories, some sport employees will sleep overnight in their office. Part of what makes the sports industry unique is the dedication of its employees. This is due to a plethora of reasons, such as the impact of fandom among sport employees and the ability to be a part of something bigger than themselves. Regardless, sport organizations have a considerable reliance on their employees, and as a result, we can better understand why having a motivated workforce is so important.

▶ **Motivation** Why an individual engages in a specific behavior.

In a very broad sense, one's motivation is a depiction of why a given action is taken. Much like the previous chapter, which informed our understanding of emotions and their roles in eventual behavior, studying individuals' motivation allows us to have a more comprehensive understanding of why individuals behave the way they do. For example, why are many sport employees willing to work 80-hour weeks while not being paid overly well? Why are they willing to miss family gatherings such as religious holidays or weddings in the name of work? Why are sport employees willing to endure very limited opportunities for recognition and reward? The answer likely lies in their motivations and the forces that drive their motivation for action. In this chapter, we will first review some basic forms of motivation from a theoretical lens before transitioning our focus to Self-Determination Theory, which is a popular theory in sport management literature that is used to explain why athletes, coaches, and employees engage in various activities. Lastly, we will review some exciting new concepts that will further expand your understanding of how motivation impacts the sport workplace.

12.2 Theoretical Concepts

In this section, we will review several pertinent theories of motivation. However, it is important to note that this is far from a robust list of motivation theories as scholars have continuously studied, reformed, and conceptualized various patterns of motivations among individuals. Instead, we have selected the theories that are best suited to improve your understanding of motivations and how they impact the sport workplace.

12.2.1 Expectancy Theory

Our first concept is expectancy theory, which has three aspects: (a) expectancy (i.e., increased effort will lead to improved functioning), (b) instrumentality (i.e., the belief that improved functioning will be rewarded), and (c) valence (i.e., the reward is valued by the person who is increasing their effort to attain the reward).[1] In a sense, this theory posits that people are motivated not only by the potential of a reward, but also by the belief that a given award is attainable with their increased efforts. Let's consider how this theory could be applied to the sports industry. Take, for example, an internal sales contest where the ticket sales representative who sells the most tickets in a month will be able to travel with the team to a road contest (chosen by the winner). For a sport employee to be motivated to put in the increased effort they will need to win the reward, they must view traveling with the team as valuable; otherwise, there will be no incentive to pursue the prize. Traveling with a team to a new city might seem like a great reward to some, but for others, they might value more time with their family instead (for these employees, a better reward might be an extra day off). Also, the employee will need to believe that any additional effort on their part will actually result in improved performance. So, suppose many of the ticket representative's contacts have no interest in purchasing more tickets. In that case, there likely will be little motivation to put in extra effort. Further, any improved performance will need to be perceived as likely to result in obtaining the reward. If the sport employee believes that no matter how much their performance improves, there is no feasible way for them to be the top seller (possibly due to long-time employees having the upper hand with a larger database), the motivation for action will be nullified. Yet, if the reward is valuable, and there is a belief that improved effort will lead to better performance, which is likely to result in obtaining the reward, there is now a good chance the employee will be motivated to work extra hard during that month.

12.2.2 Goal-Setting Theory

In the same vein as expectancy theory, Goal-Setting Theory describes the process of setting goals in order to achieve objectives. Goals are powerful tools that can be employed to achieve improved performance, and Goal-Setting Theory explains how goals lead to achievement. Broadly, goals provide us with purpose and direction. They allow us to focus our energy on specific tasks and provide a sense of accomplishment when recognizable goals are achieved. More succinctly, our goals motivate us. For many individuals, goals exist on a spectrum whereby there are lower- and higher-order goals. Lower-order goals reflect mini or everyday goals that we set for ourselves. For example, a sport employee might decide that they need to start getting into the office earlier than they have been, so they set a goal pertaining to their updated desired arrival time. Conversely, higher-order goals, or an individual's purpose, represent the long-term desires of an individual. Another way to look at goal hierarchies is that higher-order goals, which are long-term in nature, are why people behave the way they do[2] and lower-order goals, which are short-term goals, exemplify how one strategizes to achieve those higher-order goals.[3] Simply put, higher-order goals are one's life philosophy[4] and represent the purpose in one's actions.[5] Lower-order goals serve as the strategic plans that are crafted to reach one's life philosophies and purpose.[6]

Let's return to the example of the sport employee who wanted to start arriving at the office sooner…why would they want to do this? Surely no one would willingly want to wake up earlier unless there was a reward, or perhaps it was part of a plan. Within one's hierarchy of goals, the higher-order goals dictate the organization and content of the lower-order goals. In our example, it could be that the sport employee recognizes the potential for advancement within the sport organization, and by coming into work sooner, they might be able to demonstrate to their supervisors that they are serious about the job, thus improving the chances of a promotion. The reason for arriving at work sooner could result from a higher-order goal pertaining to the desire to one day become the General Manager or Athletics Director of the organization. Another function of one's goal hierarchy is specificity. The lower a goal is on the hierarchy, the more specific (and adjustable) the goal is likely to be. In the example, becoming a General Manager is likely to be a higher-order goal, but that does not mean there are no other higher goals on the spectrum. Just as goals become more specific the lower on the hierarchy they are, they also get more abstract and broader the higher they are. While being a General Manager could be a higher-order goal, being a kind and giving person would be an even higher-order goal. As you can see, setting goals is a pathway to motivation, as the desire to achieve our goals motivates us for action. If you have not already done so, we strongly encourage you to reflect on your goals (lower and higher order) and determine the best path for your achievement.

12.2.3 Equity Theory

Another important aspect of motivation is Equity Theory, which takes into account sociological influences on motivation. It is likely not surprising to read that humans often compare themselves with others in their proximity. Many of us simply cannot help ourselves and compare ourselves to others as soon as we walk into a room. Comparisons can also play a role in our motivations to act in the workplace. According to Equity Theory, individuals take note of their outputs (i.e., production) and their inputs (i.e., rewards or salary) and then compare them to that of a coworker. Any incongruency where an individual perceives they are receiving fewer inputs for comparable or superior outputs will likely result in a loss of motivation. As an example of how this could occur in a sport organization, let's consider a sport employee who has worked for the same sport organization for the last ten years, has never missed a day of work, has always received sterling performance reviews, and is up for a promotion. However, the promotion is given to an employee who has worked at the sport organization for three years and has had mixed performance reviews but happens to be a relative of the General Manager. It would not be difficult to see why the sport employee who lost out on the promotion would put in less effort moving forward, but Equity Theory is what explains why there is likely to be a decreased level of motivation.

12.2.4 Operant Conditioning and Reinforcement Theory

A theory that is very popular and one that you likely remember reading about is Skinner's theory of operant conditioning.[7] This theory suggests that an individual's motivations are determined by their surroundings and the resulting interactions with their surroundings. Put another way, behaviors are reinforced by the environment. According to Skinner's theory, as individuals engage with their environment, they experience positive and negative feedback. The behaviors that receive positive feedback are reinforced and are likely to be repeated. Conversely, the behaviors that are met with negative feedback are avoided. This results in a range of motivation for behavior, in that anticipated positive feedback will motivate certain behavior and anticipated negative feedback will motivate an individual to take a different course of action. While this may seem fairly obvious, Skinner's work significantly advanced our understanding of human motivations. In a simplistic example, a sport employee

who is thanked by athletes for providing them with quality attention and support is likely to continue to do so, while a sport employee who is screamed at "LEAVE ME ALONE!" by an athlete is unlikely to speak with that athlete in the near future.

12.2.5 Maslow's Hierarchy of Needs

We will now turn to the "needs" perspective of motivation. Any conversation about need-based motivation should include a discussion concerning Abraham Maslow's Hierarchy of Needs.[8] Many depictions of Maslow's Hierarchy of Needs are presented as a triangle. This is because the theory puts forth that the base of the triangle is required before moving to the next level and so on. That is, the Hierarchy of Needs theory requires fulfillment in the first stage before moving to the second, and fulfillment with the second stage before attaining the third level, and so on. The first stage consists of physiological needs, including air, water, and food. These are very basic but essential needs to sustain life. The next stage is security needs, which are typified by shelter and protection, such as living and resting comfortably. The third stage is social needs, or the need for relationships, friendships, and support. The fourth stage is self-esteem needs and the desire for recognition and feelings of expertise. The final stage, which, according to Maslow, requires the fulfillment of the other four stages, is self-actualization needs. This level represents the ultimate form of fulfillment in that all needs of the self are met, and the individuals' motivations then turn to behaviors that are meant to help and support others. This stage is difficult to attain, and many are not able to achieve this level of fulfillment. This popular theory has been revisited, adjusted, and amended several times, but the theory's foundation is still instrumental in our understanding of individuals' motivations.

The sport workplace is a seemingly ideal environment for a sport employee to achieve self-actualization. Of course, the first two stages would be indirectly related as the wages from employment with the sport organization would help employees purchase basic necessities. For social needs, the sport workplace would likely offer sport employees an opportunity to socialize and work closely with their colleagues. This is due to the need for sport organizations to coordinate their efforts when planning sport events. Self-esteem could potentially be problematic, given the aforementioned lack of recognition opportunities. However, sport employees are likely to take pride in watching a sport organization's highly visible and popular sporting events and knowing they played a critical role in the production of the event. Provided other needs are fulfilled, the sport workplace is uniquely positioned to support the self-actualization of sport employees, as there are plentiful occasions to help others.

12.2.6   Herzberg's Motivation-Hygiene Theory

The next theory that we will discuss focused explicitly on motivation in the workplace. Herzberg's Motivation-Hygiene Theory[9] was contrived to help develop employees in order to produce improved performance for an organization. This theory was in response to management styles that, at the time, were predominantly strict and cumbersome, which resulted in simple job tasks for employees. Resultantly, Herzberg suggested enriching employees' jobs, and to do so, jobs should be made to motivate employees by improving their sense of achievement, responsibility, growth, advancement, and recognition.[10] This represents the motivation aspect of the theory. The hygiene aspect is not focused on employee growth, but rather on preventing negative feelings or perceptions. In subsequent studies that built upon the Motivation-Hygiene Theory, scholars were able to better determine the relationship between tasks and motivation by examining concepts such as task variety, autonomy, knowledge, and responsibility.[11] Motivation-Hygiene Theory represents a significant advancement in our understanding of what motivates employees to work harder or "get ahead" in their careers. According to the Motivation-

Hygiene Theory, a sport employee would likely have an increased motivation to expand their job performance as well as initiative to put forth greater efforts to complete their work tasks when provided with more autonomy and opportunities to grow and develop. For example, a sport manager could allow their subordinates flexibility to determine the structure of a fundraising campaign with minimal oversight and direction. Doing so would likely invigorate the sport employees to craft a powerful campaign as it would represent an opening to grow professionally.

12.2.7   Self-Determination Theory

Self-Determination Theory (SDT), advanced by Richard Ryan and Edward Deci, describes the fulfillment of an individual's internal psychological need. An essential feature of SDT is the assumption that these psychological needs are a gateway to well-being and social functioning.[12] Another key facet of SDT is found in its name in that it is each individual who decides what level of importance is given to a specific action.[13] That is, an individual self-determines the need for certain behaviors or actions. SDT is further broken down into three components: competence, relatedness, and autonomy.[14] *Competence* is the recognition of proficiency in one's abilities. This often leads to a craving for greater challenges. *Relatedness* is similar to Maslow's social needs feature as individuals desire meaningful relationships with others. Ryan and Deci[15] elaborated, "Relatedness reflects the homonomous aspect of the integrative tendency of life, the tendency to connect with others and be integral to and accepted by others" (p. 7). *Autonomy* represents individuality, freedom of behavior, and independence. Ryan and Deci[16] added, "When autonomous, individuals experience their behavior as an expression of the self, such that, even when actions are influenced by outside sources, the actors concur with those influences, feeling both initiative and value with regard to them" (p. 8). These three components help to better understand individuals' motivation for behavior. In

other words, competence, relatedness, and autonomy are the needs that all individuals desire, and
their actions and behaviors are attempts to fulfill
these needs. Now, let's turn to SDT's three forms
of motivations that individuals utilize to gain fulfillment of their competency, relatedness, and
autonomy needs.

According to SDT, an individual's motivation
for behavior is found on a continuum. On one end
are self-determined behaviors, meaning that the
individual's reasons for behavior are strictly due
to their desires and wants. On the other end are
non-self-determined behaviors or, in some cases,
a lack of behavior or action, which is a result of
an individual having little or no desire to conduct
a specific behavior. In reality, most behaviors are
somewhere in the middle of this continuum, and
there are many specific names and terms for different landmarks on the continuum. We will
focus on three popular forms of motivation:
intrinsic, extrinsic, and amotivation (often known
as burnout).

▶ **Intrinsic Motivation** Desire to participate in
an activity because you genuinely enjoy the
activity.

12.2.7.1 Intrinsic Motivation
Intrinsic motivation is the "ideal" form of motivation in that it represents a "pure" desire of participants to engage in a given activity. The
intrinsic aspect of motivation is described as "the
inherent satisfactions of the behaviors per se,
rather than in contingencies or reinforcements
that are operationally separable form [sic] those
activities" (p. 10).[17] This means that those who
are intrinsically motivated perform a given action
because they genuinely enjoy that activity. In the
sports industry, an employee who is intrinsically
motivated to perform a specific task at work
would do so freely and would not require their
supervisor to ask them more than once to tend to
the task. For example, a sport employee who
enjoys supporting and working with collegiate
student-athletes and their studies would be intrinsically motivated to put in hard work to help
student-athletes improve their academics. Those
who are intrinsically motivated to complete their

work tasks would tell you that their work "does
not feel like work." That is, intrinsically motivated people naturally enjoy completing a given
task. As you can see, intrinsic motivation is a
powerful factor for sport and non-sport employees. While truly intrinsic motivation is difficult to
realize, it is likely to lead to beneficial personal
and organizational outcomes such as happiness,
well-being, and improved performance.

Extrinsic Motivation
A form of motivation where external rewards
drive behavior.

12.2.7.2 Extrinsic Motivation
Extrinsic motivation is a common form of motivation as it represents one's desire to engage in a
behavior because they believe there will be a
reward as a result of the action. Ryan and Deci[18]
described extrinsic motivation as "focused toward
and dependent on contingent outcomes that are
separable from the action per se" (p. 10). This
version of motivation requires a distal or an external reward, and it is the reward that spurs action.
A sport employee who is extrinsically motivated
to complete their job tasks would do so because
they view their work as a way to get paid and
allow them to live their desired lifestyle. One way
to compare intrinsic and extrinsic motivation is
by considering a hypothetical example of two
sport employees. Employee A loves working in
sport because they enjoy being in a competitive
environment and get excited for every game in
which their organization participates. Employee
B works in sport because they see an opportunity
to move up in the organizational hierarchy and
gain increased pay and power. Clearly, employee
A would be intrinsically motivated and employee
B would be extrinsically motivated. It is important to note that extrinsic motivation should not
be considered "bad" or in a negative light. In fact,
extrinsic motivation is quite common and does
influence many individuals. The key difference is
that work task completion will have a more substantial influence on personal well-being and
happiness when intrinsically motivated instead of
extrinsically. Lastly, intrinsic and extrinsic motivations are not universal for individuals as some

activities will be viewed as intrinsic while others are extrinsic depending on how a person views the task, and how the task is thought to enhance their competency, relatedness, and autonomy.

▷ **Amotivation**   A lack of desire to complete a task or engage in a behavior.

12.2.7.3   Amotivation

The last form of motivation that we will discuss is called amotivation, or as it is more commonly known, burnout. Importantly, this view of motivation does not indicate a lack of action but is more reflective of passive participation.[19] In this way, amotivation represents a lack of a desire or forced action and is the least self-determined form of motivation on the SDT continuum. Simply, amotivation occurs when one loses the desire to complete a task or only does so because they are forced to engage. In the sports industry, this is a common occurrence in youth sport when children become burnt out from competing in a highly competitive setting, the detriments of sport specialization, or abuse from coaches or parents. However, burnout and amotivation also occur in the sport workplace. The high turnover rate is one indication, but contributing factors are the lower pay rates and the excessive hours required in the sports industry. When a sport employee experiences burnout, they are likely to do shoddy work or avoid work, which is undoubtedly a situation that sport organizations would like to avoid. However, this means that sport organizations and managers need to take the time and provide the necessary effort to understand their employees. By having an improved understanding of their employees, sport organizations and managers will be able to design jobs in a matter that can avoid employee burnout and perhaps increase intrinsic motivation for task completion.

12.3   Motivation for One's Potential

A different view of one's motivation is based on the concept of "well-being." Although we learned about well-being in the previous chapter, its relationship to motivation runs deep. Specifically, Rogers' organismic valuing theory plays a key role in determining the motivations one has for improved life experiences.[20] The theory describes how people are motivated to participate in behaviors that will help them realize their true selves or, be authentic. Much like Maslow's work, Rogers suggested that individuals who are considered to be fully functioning, and thus realizing self-actualization, desire to participate in activities that allow them to be true to themselves, connect with the emotions, remain in harmony with others, and gravitate to meaningful goals.[21] Those who have achieved self-actualization, or are striving toward it, will seek to participate in activities that fulfill their sense of self. In other words, people are motivated to achieve a sense of self and are drawn to activities that reinforce our perceptions of who we think we are or what we represent. When individuals are on the pathway to self-actualization, they will construct goals and passions that will help them emphasize meaningful perspectives. For example, a sport employee who understands their emotional wants and needs, will craft or volunteer for activities that they believe reflect their own values.

Suppose you happen to believe that you are a creative and insightful person. In that case, you might feel drawn toward a career in sport marketing, as working on various marketing campaigns or coming up with new ideas would reinforce the perception of yourself that you are creative. Likewise, during your studies, you will likely set goals along the way that will help you work your way into the sport marking field. In other words, your motivations for goals and behaviors are an attempt to fulfill your perceptions of yourself. We would encourage you to reflect on how you view yourself, what skills you feel you excel at, and if those skills serve to reinforce perceptions of yourself that you consider to be valuable. Whether or not this is a consistent pattern for you is not immediately necessary, but it is important to begin the journey of understanding yourself to help you achieve self-actualization.

▶ **Grit** One's ability to set and pursue purpose-driven long-term goals and to effectively readjust short-term goals and goal-attainment strategies in the face of perceived or anticipated adversity or negative feedback.

12.4   New Concept: Grit

When watching a sporting contest, it is common to hear the phrase "She has SO much grit!" when describing an athlete, but have you thought about what grit really means? Phrases like toughness and determination are likely to come to mind. These would be accurate representations of the term, but there is a growing volume of literature that pertains to the theoretical development of grit as a psychological construct that can be applied in workplaces. This conceptualization of grit, popularized by Angela Duckworth and extended by authors such as Samantha Jordan, is grounded within motivation principles. This version of grit allows us to circle back to what we previously spoke about in terms of goal setting. Grit is a constant effort to take on challenges to help reach one's goals and the continuous determination to reach one's goals despite setbacks and failures.[22] Within grit theory literature, there are three traditional components: (a) perseverance, (b) passion, and (c) goals.[23] *Perseverance* describes the willingness to continue on in the face of difficulties. *Passion* is an emotional feeling where one feels engaged and even exhilaration. *Goals*, as we have noted before, are steeped within a hierarchy with lower- and higher-order goals. Recent adaptations of grit have described it as "a skill that influences purpose-driven goal setting and adjustment" (p. 322).[24] This updated version of grit emphasizes individuals' passion for their goals by focusing on their purpose or calling (i.e., motivation) for goal achievement. Also, the depiction of grit as a skill is noteworthy, as this indicates that grit can be developed, taught, and strengthened. Resultantly, the updated definition of grit is "one's ability (a) to set and pursue purpose-driven long-term (higher-order) goals and (b) to effectively readjust short-term (lower-order) goals and goal-attainment strategies in the face of perceived or

anticipated adversity or negative feedback" (p. 325).[25] As such, grit can be thought of as one's motivation to continue toward their purpose in life by forming and readjusting goals that have been developed to help facilitate the achievement of their higher-order goals.

More interestingly, Jordan and her colleagues' work[26] has been explicitly undertaken to contextualize grit to the workplace, specifically for employees. Utilizing the Jordan et al.'s perspective of work grit theory, there are two central features of the construct: goal hierarchies and work passion. Those who have grit are so motivated to accomplish their goals, they do not allow setbacks to get in their way. As a result, gritty individuals can alter their plans or create new action plans when faced with disruptions to their path to goal achievement.[27] More so, gritty people will request feedback, which will allow them to further specify their strategies to achieve their goals.[28] While many of us shy away from performance evaluations, gritty individuals (specifically employees) seek feedback and evaluation. For instance, a gritty sport employee would be motivated to ask their boss how their performance was in reorganizing the equipment room's layout, or they would ask for a one-on-one meeting with their supervisor to discuss ways where they can improve their performance. You might be thinking, "WHO does that?". The answer is gritty people as they have a motivation level that is so strong they welcome negative feedback as it is viewed as an opportunity for improvement.

The other work grit element is the passion one holds for their work and the tasks associated with their positions. When a person has found their purpose for work, they are likely to become almost wholly encompassed in their work with greater potential for achievement.[29] It is also important to note the definition of work passion, which is described as "an individual's emotional and persistent state of desire based on cognitive and affective work appraisals" (p. 146).[30] In other words, employees are motivated to engage in work activities because of the feelings and recognition that the activities engender. When one enjoys what they do, they are likely to have a passion for work, meaning there will be stronger motivations to complete work tasks. Moreover, passion connects to one's purpose, as recognizing that a given activity allows one to pursue, come closer, or achieve their purpose creates a passion for the activity. This is a similar concept to intrinsic motivation, and it should be recognized that the meaning of both is the same. When there are genuine, internal desires to engage in activities (in this case, work tasks), there is likely to be a stronger likelihood of the task being worked on and thoroughly completed. As a final example, consider a sport employee who has a strong emotional resonance with their job of working in ticket sales. They greatly enjoy seeing the joy and excitement when fans are entering the stadium on gameday. Because the sport employee recognizes the enjoyment they receive from witnessing positive emotions, they are likely to be motivated to continue working with great effort and see the purpose in their position. When combined with goals, one's purpose through their passions is an incredibly powerful tool that employees can rely upon for sufficient motivation to reach their higher-order goals.

12.5 Summary

In this chapter, we covered a wide range of motivation theories. We started with some of the more basic or fundamental theories that have provided a core foundation for scholars to continue to evolve our understanding of human desires and needs. Human beings are motivated by physical needs and emotional desires and will engage in behaviors that fulfill said desires and needs. From this chapter, we now know that sport employees are driven by an intrinsic connection to sport and their desire to remain a part of sport in some capacity. More so, new concepts such as grit offer exciting opportunities to expand the motivations and by extension the capabilities of sport employees.

Discussion Questions

1. Of the many motivation theories discussed, which is the most relevant to you?
2. What is self-actualization?
3. What are the components of self-determination theory?
4. What is authenticity, and why is it important in the sport workplace?
5. What is grit, and how can it be used in the sport workplace?

Notes

1. Vroom, V. H. (1964). *Work and motivation*. Wiley: New York, NY.
2. Bateman, T. S., & Barry, B. (2012). Masters of the long haul: Pursuing long-term work goals. *Journal of Organizational Behavior, 33*(7), 984–1006.
3. Jordan, S. L., Ferris, G. R., Hochwarter, W. A., & Wright, T. A. (2019). Toward a work motivation conceptualization of grit in organizations. *Group & Organization Management, 44*(2), 320–360.
4. Duckworth, A. L. (2016). *Grit: The power of passion and perseverance*. New York, NY: Simon and Schuster.
5. Kanfer, R., Frese, M., & Johnson, R. E. (2017). Motivation related to work: A century of progress. *Journal of Applied Psychology, 102*(3), 338–355.
6. Jordan, S. L., Ferris, G. R., Hochwarter, W. A., & Wright, T. A. (2019). Toward a work motivation conceptualization of grit in organizations. *Group & Organization Management, 44*(2), 320–360.
7. Staddon, J. E. R., & Cerutti, D. T. (2003). Operant conditioning. *Annual Review of Psychology, 54*, 115–144.
8. Maslow, A. H. (1943). A theory of human motivation. *Psychological Review, 50*, 370–396; Maslow, A. H. (1954). *Motivation and Personality*. Harper & Row: New York, NY.
9. Herzberg, F. (1966). *Work and the nature of man*. Cleveland: World.
10. Oldham, G. R., & Fried, Y. (2016). Job design research and theory: Past, present, and future. *Organizational Behavior and Human Decision Processes, 136*, 20–35.
11. Oldham, G. R., & Fried, Y. (2016). Job design research and theory: Past, present, and future. *Organizational Behavior and Human Decision Processes, 136*, 20–35.
12. Deci, E. L., & Ryan, R. M. (1985). *Intrinsic motivation and self-determination in human behavior*. New York, NY: Plenum; Ryan, R. M., & Deci, E. L. (2002). An overview of self-determination theory: An organismic-dialectical perspective. In E. L. Deci & R. M. Ryan (Eds.), *Handbook of self-determination research* (pp. 3–33). Rochester, NY: The University of Rochester Press.
13. Deci, E. L., & Ryan, R. M. (1985). *Intrinsic motivation and self-determination in human behavior*. New York, NY: Plenum.
14. Ryan, R. M., & Deci, E. L. (2002). An overview of self-determination theory: An organismic-dialectical

perspective. In E. L. Deci & R. M. Ryan (Eds.), *Handbook of self-determination research* (pp. 3–33). Rochester, NY: The University of Rochester Press.

15. Ryan, R. M., & Deci, E. L. (2002). An overview of self-determination theory: An organismic-dialectical perspective. In E. L. Deci & R. M. Ryan (Eds.), *Handbook of self-determination research* (pp. 3–33). Rochester, NY: The University of Rochester Press.

16. Ryan, R. M., & Deci, E. L. (2002). An overview of self-determination theory: An organismic-dialectical perspective. In E. L. Deci & R. M. Ryan (Eds.), *Handbook of self-determination research* (pp. 3–33). Rochester, NY: The University of Rochester Press.

17. Ryan, R. M., & Deci, E. L. (2002). An overview of self-determination theory: An organismic-dialectical perspective. In E. L. Deci & R. M. Ryan (Eds.), *Handbook of self-determination research* (pp. 3–33). Rochester, NY: The University of Rochester Press.

18. Ryan, R. M., & Deci, E. L. (2002). An overview of self-determination theory: An organismic-dialectical perspective. In E. L. Deci & R. M. Ryan (Eds.), *Handbook of self-determination research* (pp. 3–33). Rochester, NY: The University of Rochester Press.

19. Ryan, R. M., & Deci, E. L. (2002). An overview of self-determination theory: An organismic-dialectical perspective. In E. L. Deci & R. M. Ryan (Eds.), Handbook of self-determination research (pp. 3–33). Rochester, NY: The University of Rochester Press.

20. Rogers, C. R. (1961). *On becoming a person: A therapist's view of psychotherapy*. London: Constable.; Rogers, C. R. (1964). Toward a modern approach to values: the valuing process in the mature person. *Journal of Abnormal and Social Psychology, 68*(2), 160–167.

21. Vainio, M. M., & Daukantaitė, D. (2016). Grit and different aspects of well-being: Direct and indirect relationships via sense of coherence and authenticity. *Journal of Happiness Studies, 17*(5), 2119–2147.

22. Duckworth, A. L. (2016). *Grit: The power of passion and perseverance*. New York, NY: Simon and Schuster.; Duckworth, A., Peterson, C., Matthews, M. D., & Kelly, D. R. (2007). Grit: Perseverance and passion for long-term goals. *Journal of Personality and Social Psychology, 92*(6), 1087–1101.

23. Credé, M. (2018). What shall we do about grit? A critical review of what we know and what we don't know. *Educational Researcher, 47,* 606–611; Jordan, S. L., Ferris, G. R., Hochwarter, W. A., & Wright, T. A. (2019). Toward a work motivation conceptualization of grit in organizations. *Group & Organization Management, 44*(2), 320–360.

24. Jordan, S. L., Ferris, G. R., Hochwarter, W. A., & Wright, T. A. (2019). Toward a work motivation conceptualization of grit in organizations. Group & Organization Management, 44(2), 320–360.

25. Jordan, S. L., Ferris, G. R., Hochwarter, W. A., & Wright, T. A. (2019). Toward a work motivation conceptualization of grit in organizations. Group & Organization Management, 44(2), 320–360.

26. Jordan, S. L., Ferris, G. R., Hochwarter, W. A., & Wright, T. A. (2019). Toward a work motivation conceptualization of grit in organizations. Group & Organization Management, 44(2), 320–360.

27. Jin, B., & Kim, J. (2017). Grit, basic needs satisfaction, and subjective well-being. *Journal of Individual Differences, 38*(1), 29–35.

28. Jordan, S. L., Ferris, G. R., Hochwarter, W. A., & Wright, T. A. (2019). Toward a work motivation conceptualization of grit in organizations. Group & Organization Management, 44(2), 320–360.

29. Bureau, J. S., Vallerand, R. J., Ntoumanis, N., & Lafreniére, M. A. K. (2013). On passion and moral behavior in achievement settings: The mediating role of pride. *Motivation and Emotion, 37*(1), 121–133.

30. Perrewé, P. L., Hochwarter, W. A., Ferris, G. R., McAllister, C. P., & Harris, J. N. (2014). Developing a passion for work passion: Future directions on an emerging construct. *Journal of Organizational Behavior, 35*(1), 145–150.

> **Learning Outcomes** After reading this chapter, students should be able to:

- Differentiate between in-role and extra-role behaviors in the sport industry.
- Define organizational citizenship behaviors in the sport context.
- Articulate the key factors in increasing creative ideas in individual employees.
- Develop creative ideas in a sport-specific context.

Mayi Blanco Cruz: Global Head of Athlete Programmes at The Adecco Group
To listen to the interview <click here>

The Morning the Business Changed

"Okay, things are going to be very different now," Quentin Washington said to himself as he put on his tie. He awoke to the news that the US Supreme Court had ruled against the National Collegiate

Supplementary Information The online version of this chapter (https://doi.org/10.1007/978-3-030-67612-4_13) contains supplementary material, which is available to authorized users.

Athletic Association (NCAA). Student-athletes were now employees. He turned to ESPN and listened as studio hosts debated the ruling, and athletic directors from the Big Ten, SEC, and other major institutions cried that this was the end of college athletics. Washington calmly emailed his senior staff. "Meeting at 9 a.m. in the conference room."

Washington is the Director of Athletics at Greensboro State University (GSU). GSU is a Historically Black College and University (HBCU) located in North Carolina. The school competes in the Division I FCS Mideastern Athletic Conference. Under Washington's guidance, the school has been one of the more successful programs at their level of NCAA competition. The board room was humming with exasperated conversation when Washington walked in. Suddenly, the room went silent, and all eyes were on him. After a moment of silence, Zeta Jones, Director of Development, spoke, "Quentin, it's mass panic around college athletics. What are we going to do? Can we survive if the big schools are saying that they can't afford to pay their athletes?" Washington calmly looked at his senior staff, smiled, and said, "Let everyone else panic. That's their problem. I'm not sure what it is yet, but there is an opportunity in this ruling. The industry changed this morning, and the schools that adapt will thrive. Let the others panic. While they are, we'll plan for the new business model and become leaders. Let's get to work."

13.1 In-Role and Extra-Role Behaviors

In any organization, there are beliefs, values, verbal expressions, and behaviors. An individual may have beliefs or values they associate with their role, which shapes their behavior at work, but the prescribed or necessary actions of their job are what constitute in-role behaviors.[1] In-role behaviors could be reflected in their job descriptions, supervisor directives, or salary designations. Whereas extra-role behaviors are any behaviors employees engage in that are not assigned to them by their organization. These extra-role behaviors are not influenced by formal reward systems nor subject to punishment should they not be performed.[2] Think about often-used phrases: "going the extra mile," "going above and beyond the call of duty," or "giving 110%." Seeking out extra information or double-checking work, smiling at a customer when they are being mean, even if it is not expected of an employee, are all examples of extra-role behaviors. When a sport organization is tradition-focused, averse to risk, and top-down focused or micromanaged, engaging in creativity might also be an extra-role behavior.

▶ **In-Role Behaviors** Actions that are prescribed by the organization or necessary to one's position within the organization.

▶ **Extra-Role Behaviors** Actions that are beneficial to the organization but are not influenced by formal reward systems nor subject to punishment should they not be performed.

▶ **Organizational Citizenship Behaviors** Behaviors that employees engage in that improve the social and psychological environment of an organization, improving the organization through productivity or perceived service quality.

13.1.1 Organizational Citizenship Behaviors

Organizational citizenship behaviors (OCB) are behaviors employees engage in that improve the organization, whether through productivity or perceived service quality.[3] In differentiating organizational citizenship behaviors from other types of extra-role behaviors, OCB focus on behaviors that will enhance the social and psychological environment. Organizational citizenship behaviors have been differentiated into two types; OCB-O behaviors are those that are directly related to the organization, whereas OCB-I behaviors are those directed toward an employee's colleagues. Coming into work on a Saturday, under one's own volition, to finish a big project would be an example of OCB-O. An example of OCB-I would be staying late to assist a coworker who had to leave work early. These behaviors have been shown to have positive impacts on organizations.[4] Leaders should be careful not to be too encouraging of these behaviors because there are negative elements. If extra-role behaviors are overtly encouraged, they can be perceived as in-role by employees, losing the desired benefit and possibly leading to burnout.[5] OCB can also be negative if it interferes with in-role tasks. In an analysis of minor league baseball organizations, researchers found no relationship between increased OCB and organizational performance.[6] They supposed this is because of limited staff so that any OCB behaviors may have taken away from in-role behaviors necessary for the organization's basic functions. Additionally, there appears to be evidence of a "gray area" for athletes as it relates to what is extra-role and what is expected.[7] This role confusion could increase the likelihood of burnout. As with many aspects of organizational behavior management, a mindful balance should be considered with the encouragement of organizational citizenship behaviors to a healthy degree.

13.1.2 Creative Work Behaviors

Creativity is the buzzword in sports these days. National Basketball Association (NBA) teams and some college athletic programs have hired "Directors of Innovation" or "Chief Innovation Officers," all in an effort to become more creative. This wasn't always the way. Sports have historically been an incredibly tradition-focused industry. There is a tendency to not think for oneself, but copy and paste what others are doing in the industry. For example, even though baseball analytics was created long before the Oakland A's adopted it, Major League Baseball (MLB) franchises waited until they saw one team's success to slowly adopt the innovation.[8] In a few short decades, the sports industry went from being hesitant or even hostile to innovation to hiring employees specifically to encourage creativity. Increased competition for resources and consumers and changing perspectives within the sports industry to engage with external stakeholders have increased this desire for creative behaviors.[9] For some employees, though, these behaviors may still be considered extra-role behaviors.

While sport organizations may be moving toward more innovative and creative approaches due to external forces, there are many internal benefits to creativity. For the organization, creativity and innovation have been shown to increase the organization's value, increase the market share, and improve its competitive advantage in the market.[10] Some recent research in sport specifically has been mixed on its usefulness.[11] In Chap. 15, we'll discuss why that's the case. Despite the mixed results, there is enough evidence that pursuing creativity and innovation seems worth it. Beyond organizational improvements, innovation and creativity have shown to benefit employees as well. Encouraging innovation and creativity can increase employees' belief in themselves (self-efficacy), decrease turnover rates, and improve job satisfaction. Creativity involves independent thinking and playing around with ideas, which can be fun for employees. Also, if one of their new ideas works, employees tend to feel better about themselves and more engaged at work. While magically improving employee creativity by merely saying "be more creative" would be easier, that is not how creativity and innovation work. Therefore, we'll discuss how to increase creativity levels for sport employees.

▶ **Creativity** The production of new and useful ideas for the unit of measure.

13.2 Definition of Creativity in Management

Before discussing what aspects improve individual creativity in sport management, having a common definition of creativity is helpful. Creativity conjures up images of an artist painting on a canvas, a computer programmer developing the next big mobile app, or a trick shot going viral on social media. When talking about creativity in sport management, the definition refers to creativity in the management and business side of the sports industry. So in this context, creativity is the production of new and useful ideas for the unit of measure.[12] The unit of measure could be individual creativity and creativity within a workgroup or within an organization. For example, suppose a marketing manager has issues with productivity in their workgroup due to excessive chit-chat hurting task execution; they could decide to implement a flexible work schedule, where employees may work from home one day a week. For this specific context, the action works, and employees end up more productive while still remaining social with their colleagues. Since it is new and useful to the unit of measure (i.e., the workgroup), that change was a creative idea. Although the sports industry tends to focus on new products or services, such as luxury suites and analytics,[13] creativity is not merely a new output but could also be related to processes and structures. While the sports industry itself has historically been hesitant to be innovative, sport entrepreneurs have been known to promote change, look to future trends, be proactive, take risks, be receptive to opportunities, have optimism, and identify currently nonexistent products and ideas.[14]

13.2.1 Elements of Creativity in the Sports Industry

According to researchers, there are three key elements to being individually creative at work. These are domain-relevant skills, intrinsic task motivation, and engagement in creativity-related processes.

▶ **Domain-Relevant Skills** Any particular knowledge set or skills needed to come up with creative ideas for the unit of measure.

13.2.2 Domain-Relevant Skills

Knowing a significant amount about a particular topic or context gives employees the information they need to develop creative ideas. Domain-relevant skills include any particular knowledge set or skills needed to come up with creative ideas for the unit of measure.[15] These skills can include the ability to find information about a topic, such as through reading or listening to experts (like with this textbook!). It could also include building skills such as website design or how to stream online. Learning for a specific context or topic goes beyond what is learned in the classroom. There are many ways to learn about a domain and build the skills necessary to be creative in a sport organization.

Reading is the most obvious way to gain domain-relevant skills. This textbook is an example. Trade journals or blogs can also provide additional insight, especially for the most current information. Beyond reading, listening to podcasts or audiobooks, watching webinars, or attending conferences can also increase domain-relevant skills. Additionally, informational interviews with sports industry professionals provides unique insights into their context and experience. Informational interviews are when an individual asks questions of a professional in the field with the only purpose of learning information. This can be achieved in many different ways: reaching out to them over the phone, asking questions over social media, or going to conferences. Many sport professionals have expressed the desire to interact with students and young professionals, so taking advantage as a student can grow domain-relevant skills beyond what is learned in the classroom. These interactions will increase creativity through the knowledge gained in their specific context.[16] While an individual can be personally motivated to increase their domain-relevant skills, research has found HR programming can also improve these skills.[17]

13.2.3 Intrinsic Task Motivation

Any extra-role behavior requires employee motivation since they are behaviors not rewarded or punished by the organization. For creative behavior, specifically, researchers argue that intrinsic task motivation is a key factor in being creative at work.

As you'll remember from Chap. 12, when people are intrinsically motivated, they engage in behaviors because they genuinely enjoy an activity.[18] External motivation is not always negative. Bonuses, promotions, and public praise are still effective mechanisms at work. However, the research indicates that intrinsic task motivation may be more useful in increasing creativity.

This is a difficult situation for sport organizations because it is hard to inspire intrinsic motivation. Think about student motivations in class. These may include earning a good grade or remaining eligible for a scholarship, or to be able to play a sport. Those are external motivations and are useful in achieving exactly what is expected. Intrinsic motivation to find problems in an organization or find unique solutions requires extra effort, often effort that isn't rewarded if the organization is hierarchical or tradition-minded.[19] For example, engagement in online communities required extra effort for resource-constrained marketing managers in women's professional soccer, while it is now clear that early engagement in social media platforms such as Twitter laid a foundation for what is now considered an integral and successful part of the US women's professional soccer landscape. Initial efforts resulted from marketing managers just trying to find ways to break through barriers to coverage.[20]

Intrinsic task motivation increases creativity because the motivation to continue with a task, even when things get hard, can result in individuals taking the time to engage in the creative process. It can lead employees to spend more time on each aspect of the creative process and convince others in their organization to adopt their idea. What's interesting is that once an employee engages in a task and finds some success, or feels supported by the organization in that effort, it can have a snowball effect increasing the likelihood they will engage with even more effort. For organizations, building support for a sense of competency, alongside giving autonomy, has been shown to improve creativity in employees.[21]

13.2.4 Engagement in Creativity-Related Processes

Creativity does not appear out of thin air. For example, electronic video boards, a standard practice now in stadiums around the world, did not suddenly arrive at stadiums one day. People identified problems, found information, and came up with ideas on how to solve that problem. They probably did this many times before electronic video boards came to life. The creativity-related process includes these three stages: (1) Problem Identification; (2) Information Searching and Encoding, and (3) Idea Generation. Problem identification involves analyzing the unit of measure and highlighting any issues, both simple and complex. There are large problems and small problems in every organization. The sports industry faces many large and complex issues like systematic racism in college athletics and burnout in youth sports. Creativity is needed to tackle these complex issues that continue to plague sport organizations. However, even smaller problems like stadium toilets that continuously clog can require creative solutions. Of course, larger problems require much more effort.

Problem identification seems easy at first. Who can't find problems in sports? However, an essential part of problem identification is choosing problems and identifying underlying or sub-problems. As much as we would like to solve all the world's problems, we all have constraints, whether it be time, money, or another resource. Deciding which issues to pursue must be informed by the organization or workgroup's vision and goals. That will help any idea be both new and useful. For example, an employee at a non-profit youth swimming organization has identified pricing efficiency as an issue for the program. That's certainly a problem that needs to be addressed. However, the organization also lacks participants from a low-income neighborhood nearby. Referring to the organization's vision and goals helps determine which problem should be tackled first. For a non-profit organization with a strong mission of helping the local community, the second problem is probably more important to pursue first. Once a problem has been identified to pursue, an examination of any sub-problems needs to occur. Breaking down that problem and understanding the sub-problems gives a better understanding of potential areas for creative ideas.

Which brings us to the next step in the process: Information searching and encoding. This is where domain-relevant skills can come into play. Engaging in information searching and encoding is the act of using those domain-relevant skills. Seeking out a wide variety of information related to the problem is fundamental to this process engagement.[22] Sport is not the only industry dealing with safety in public spaces or increased use of mobile devices. Therefore, consider sources beyond the sports industry as well. Indeed, sport's interaction with a diverse set of stakeholders can allow for greater idea generation. It's also important to consistently engage in this stage, as information or situations can change rapidly in the sports industry. The information gathered provides utility for the next stage of the creative process.[23]

▶ **Idea Generation** The act of coming up with potentially new and useful ideas related to the specific unit of measure.

The final stage of creativity-related processes is idea generation. Idea generation is the act of coming up with potentially new and useful ideas related to the specific unit of measure. While idea generation is the stage of the creativity process where the new idea comes to light, it is really the culmination of the first two stages that leads to stage three. As research in professional sport indicated, these three stages are distinct actions.[24] While interaction improves creative idea generation, autonomy also plays a role. Imagine the loudest person in a workgroup; they often offer up their ideas before anyone else can participate.

That first response can shape the rest of the discussion. Simple idea generation activities can avoid this problem. Engaging in these three stages consistently and iteratively has been shown to produce more creative ideas.[25]

We'll discuss workgroups in greater detail in the next two chapters.

▶ **Divergent Thinking** The ability to be imaginative, flexible, or expand on the initial thought.

Beyond the creative process, factors such as personality and thinking style also affect creativity. Scholars found that those who had a positive perception of newness had more innovation in their organization in sport research.[26] For those who can think divergently, creativity comes easier. Divergent thinking means the ability to be imaginative, flexible, or expand on the initial thought. That makes sense. Coming up with new ideas requires some imagination. Another thinking style that helps is critical thinking. When employees use critical thinking, they analyze a situation, dig into the underlying sub-issues, and connect outside ideas to a specific industry. Finally, personality traits such as being independent, open to experience, and self-confident increase creative idea generation.[27] As we learned in Chap. 9, these traits can be found in multiple personality types. While these are harder to shift in employees for managers, engaging in the creative process or increasing domain-relevant skills can improve thinking styles.

13.3 Being Innovative as a Sport Manager

Creativity is the beginning step to innovation. So, while having creative ideas is great, it is only the starting point. After coming up with a creative idea, the next steps are to decide to adopt the innovation and implement it.[28] Implementing innovative ideas on a personal level for employees can benefit both the individual and the organization. Interestingly, innovation in sport organizations is different within the industry as

well, depending on the type of organization. Research has found declining sectors such as yachting and skiing focus more on process innovations, whereas newer sports, such as mountain biking and snowboarding, focused on product innovations.[29] Innovations are more common within organizations focused on emerging sports.[30] That makes sense because newer sports don't have as much tradition to leverage when it comes to luring in fans or participants. Newer sports don't have parents introducing their children to the sport. A common aspect of success in innovation implementation is the innovation champion. An innovation champion takes on the idea and preservers to get it implemented in their organization.[31]

Unless an employee is encouraged to be innovative at work, doing these types of actions would be considered extra-role behaviors. Research indicates that employees in sport organizations often view innovative work behaviors as something beyond what is expected of them at work, so they have to want to engage in these behaviors.[32] However, as mentioned previously, research also indicates that being innovative has benefits to the employee, including better job performance and higher job satisfaction.

13.3.1 Sport Entrepreneurs

One aspect of being innovative includes entrepreneurship in sport. Entrepreneurs in the sports industry are free to be open to new ideas and always looking for future trends and opportunities because they work for themselves. They are usually individuals who are proactive in taking risks so that they can develop a viable business within the sports industry.[33] Think about entrepreneurs who first developed professional sports teams and leagues. Something we take for granted now. There was a lot of failure in the early days of developing any professional sport. Some entrepreneurs failed multiple times but eventually developed franchises that endure today.[34]

Most sport entrepreneurs are focused on making their sport-related product or service into a profitable business; however, entrepreneurs can engage with any segment of the sports industry, including non-profits and sport for development.[35] These people are often optimists and able to handle risk. They also can see opportunities where others may not. A great example of this is the adventure racing sector of the sports industry. In a relatively recent phenomenon, these sport entrepreneurs were able to see a need in consumers to challenge themselves in difficult sport experiences, such as running through electrified wire or rope swing over muddy, icy water. This sector is now profitable, and those who invested early in companies such as Tough Mudder or Spartan Races have seen their bet pay off.

13.4   How Can You Be More Creative at Work?

As mentioned above, engaging in the creative process increases the likelihood of producing creative ideas, which can then generate innovation. There are a number of factors and actions managers can take to improve that likelihood as well. This includes providing resources, increasing autonomy, allowing for rest, and conducting effective idea generation exercises.

13.4.1   Resource Allocation

Obvious resources in an organization include money, facilities, or equipment. These are tangible resources that are often itemized and counted in an organization. However, a fundamental resource when discussing increasing creativity is time. Research in Minor League Baseball recently argued that time constraints might be an issue in connecting innovative work behaviors and organizational success.[36] Having time to engage in creative processes or build domain-relevant skills can pay dividends for an organization.[37] This may mean providing time away from the office. The sports industry is often a place where it is celebrated to work extreme hours, coming into the office at 9 a.m. despite the game going until midnight the night before. However, it is unlikely all those hours are spent produc-

tively, and they are likely contributing to burnout. This is where the sports industry could borrow ideas from tech. For example, Google built-in time for employees to work on passion projects. Think strategically about the hours you require your employees to be in the office or the task load you give them. Another resource to consider is space. The physical work environment affects an individual's ability to engage in creative thought. While an organization's realities limit changes to the physical environment and building or renovating spaces can be expensive, giving employees flexibility in their work environment can allow them to find or create spaces that inspire creativity.

13.4.2   Autonomy

Similar to Google's idea of providing time for employees to engage in passion projects, giving autonomy to individual employees can increase the production of creative ideas. While sport often encourages everyone to be a team player, that also means those individuals will not engage in creative or innovative behaviors unless explicitly encouraged to do so.[38] Giving autonomy doesn't mean letting employees do whatever they want whenever they want, but micromanaging how individuals work toward organizational goals will stifle innovative and creative ideas. A highly rigid work environment can stifle creativity because it doesn't allow individual employees to engage in extra-role behaviors, such as the creative process. Additionally, increased autonomy at work gives employees more opportunity to activate their intrinsic motivation.

13.4.3   Rest

There is a lot of evidence that seemingly silly things like going for a walk, gardening, or taking a shower can spark ideas. This is because these activities provide people with something for the body to do while leaving the mind open to process information. That gives the brain a rest to subconsciously connect previous information collected during the information searching and encoding stage. Detaching physically and emotionally, but not cognitively from work, allows for improved health while still grappling with challenging problems.[39] Likewise, research found dreaming specifically helps develop creative ideas.[40] So, when feeling stuck about an issue, taking a walk in the woods or getting some sleep can help. The neuroscience still isn't clear, but the specific act of looking at trees while walking can help spark those creative ideas.[41]

13.4.4 Engaging in the Creative Process

As mentioned above, idea generation is the last step in a three-stage creative process. Idea generation itself can involve a variety of activities. By practicing these exercises, individuals can help improve the likelihood that a creative idea will come about. Some simple exercises can help. While not an exhaustive list, here are a few of them:

1. *Idea Lists.* One way to inspire new connections in the brain is a time-constrained listing exercise. Focused on one particular problem, list as many ideas as possible in two minutes. The key here is not to think about each idea but to write them down. Handwrite them. It will be hard at first not to immediately evaluate each idea as they come up, but trying to focus on writing down as many ideas as possible can bring up unusual or unexpected possibilities. The point of this exercise is to pull out ideas that may not be on the surface. Usually, first-time attempts generate three to four ideas. This is because people get stuck and start overthinking each idea. Therefore, practicing this exercise more than once is a great way to push past those inclinations. With some practice, listing 15 to 20 ideas will come more naturally. The idea generation phase is not the place to decide if the idea is feasible or useful, but to develop possibilities.

2. *Juxtaposition Two Objects or Ideas.* Juxtapositioning is taking two things or ideas

and trying to see how they relate to each other. This can be practiced with random objects such as a flower and a ticket machine. By breaking down each one's elements and thinking about how they could be related, new synapses in the brain are formed. As a result, a new product or process could be discovered. In juxtaposing two seemingly unrelated items, interesting opportunities could arise. Take a moment to practice juxtaposition. Here are your two things—the internet of things and sport venues. Go! Juxtaposition should be a consistent practice. It is more about training the brain to think differently than producing immediate results.

3. *Worst Idea Ever.* This simple exercise provides an opportunity to reframe a problem. Reframing problems can inspire new ideas by analyzing the problem from another angle. Take one minute and come up with the worst idea ever related to a specific issue. Try to come up with a truly, completely, awful idea. Celebrate whatever idea emerges for its level of failure to be useful. Perhaps the idea is too expensive, or requires too much risk, or seems silly and childish, or takes up too much time. However, many ideas now useful in sport at one point may have been considered terrible. For example, virtual reality has taken years for technology to make it viable, but it has been part of the sport management discussion since the 1990s. Virtual reality is now being implemented in stadiums across the world. Thinking outside the box is much easier said than done. A great idea, but starting from a point of impossible and moving toward possible is much easier than starting from within the box and attempting to think outwardly. The purpose of this exercise is not to come up with a feasible idea but to reframe the problem through a unique lens. In turn, you may come closer to a creative idea than starting with what has already been done.

4. *Yes And.* The activities mentioned above are meant to be individual activities. As mentioned earlier, group dynamics can sometimes suppress creative expression. It is better to start with individual activities before moving

to group sharing or activities. The Yes And activity is a group activity inspired by improvised comedy. Take one possible solution to a problem and build on it from person to person. No one is allowed to eye-roll or reject the previous suggestion, but they must build on it. It promotes acceptance of unusual ideas in the group and seeing elements of possibility in even the craziest of ideas.

13.5 Summary

Understanding what employees in an organization consider in-role versus extra-role behaviors provides clarity for both employee and supervisor. Encouraging extra-role behaviors without impeding in-role behaviors toward core tasks is a balance managers must strive for. While personality traits and thinking perspectives are helpful in creativity in sport, sport employees' regular behaviors are what produce long-term creativity and innovation in the sports industry. Whether those are considered in-role or extra-role behaviors, building domain-relevant skills and intrinsic task motivation, as well as regularly engaging in creative processes, will help improve the creativity of sport employees.

Discussion Questions

1. What is the most interesting new idea or product you've seen in sports recently? How do you think that idea came about? Why do you think it has been successful?
2. What ways have you found helps you become more creative when you think about your future or current career in sports?
3. Do a few of the exercises in the chapter above. How did you feel doing those exercises? What did you notice about the ideas you came up with?

Notes

1. Katz, D. (1964). The motivational basis of organizational behavior. *Behavioral science, 9*(2), 131–146.
2. Van Dyne, L., & LePine, J. A. (1998). Helping and voice extra-role behaviors: Evidence of construct and predictive validity. *Academy of Management Journal, 41*(1), 108–119.
3. Husin, S., Chelladurai, P., & Musa, G. (2012). HRM practices, organizational citizenship behaviors, and perceived service quality in golf courses. *Journal of Sport Management, 26*(2), 143–158.
4. Podsakoff, P. M., MacKenzie, S. B., Paine, J. B., & Bachrach, D. G. (2000). Organizational citizenship behaviours: A critical review of the theoretical and empirical literature and suggestions for future research. *Journal of Management, 26*, 513–563.
5. Vigoda-Gadot, E. (2007). Redrawing the boundaries of OCB? An empirical examination of compulsory extra-role behavior in the workplace. *Journal of business and psychology, 21*(3), 377–405.
6. Smith, N. L., Barnhill, C., & Sung, H. (2020). Effects of Employees' Extra-Role Behaviors on Organizational Performance: An Assessment of Minor League Baseball Team Front Offices. *Journal of Global Sport Management, 1–18.*
7. Love, A., & Kim, S. (2019). Organizational citizenship behavior in sport: a perspective from athletes. *Journal of Sport Management, 33*(1), 25–36.
8. Wolfe, R., Wright, P. M., & Smart, D. L. (2006). Radical HRM innovation and competitive advantage: The Moneyball story. *Human Resource Management, 45*(1), 111–145.
9. Smith, N.L. & Green, B.C. (2020). Examining the Factors Influencing Organizational Creativity in Professional Sport Organizations. *Sport Management Review.* https://doi.org/10.1016/j.smr.2020.02.003.
10. Rubera, G., & Kirca, A. H. (2012). Firm innovativeness and its performance outcomes: A meta-analytic review and theoretical integration. *Journal of Marketing, 76*(3), 130–147.
11. Smith, N. L., Barnhill, C., & Sung, H. (2020). Effects of Employees' Extra-Role Behaviors on Organizational Performance: An Assessment of Minor League Baseball Team Front Offices. Journal of Global Sport Management, 1–18.
12. Amabile, T. M., Conti, R., Coon, H., Lazenby, J., & Herron, M. (1996). Assessing the work environment for creativity. *Academy of Management Journal, 39*(5), 1154–1184.
13. Troilo, M., Bouchet, A., Urban, T. L., & Sutton, W. A. (2016). Perception, reality, and the adoption of business analytics: Evidence from North American professional sport organizations. *Omega, 59*, 72–83.
14. Ratten, V. (2014). Future research directions for collective entrepreneurship in developing countries: a small and medium-sized enterprise perspective. *International Journal of Entrepreneurship and Small Business, 22*(2), 266–274.
15. Amabile, T. M., & Pratt, M. G. (2016). The dynamic componential model of creativity and innovation in organizations: Making progress, making meaning. *Research in organizational behavior, 36*, 157–183.
16. Perry-Smith, J. E., & Shalley, C. E. (2003). The social side of creativity: A static and dynamic social network perspective. *Academy of management review, 28*(1), 89–106.

17. Chang, S., Jia, L., Takeuchi, R., & Cai, Y. (2014). Do high-commitment work systems affect creativity? A multilevel combinational approach to employee creativity. *Journal of Applied Psychology, 99*(4), 665.

18. Amabile, T. M., & Pratt, M. G. (2016). The dynamic componential model of creativity and innovation in organizations: Making progress, making meaning. *Research in organizational behavior, 36*, 157–183.

19. Wolfe, R., Wright, P. M., & Smart, D. L. (2006). Radical HRM innovation and competitive advantage: The Moneyball story. *Human Resource Management, 45*(1), 111–145.

20. oche, R. (2016). Promoting women's soccer through social media: how the US federation used Twitter for the 2011 World Cup. *Soccer & Society, 17*(1), 90–108.

21. Amabile, T., & Kramer, S. (2011). *The progress principle: Using small wins to ignite joy, engagement, and creativity at work.* Harvard Business Press.

22. Zhang, X., & Bartol, K. M. (2010). Linking empowering leadership and employee creativity: The influence of psychological empowerment, intrinsic motivation, and creative process engagement. *Academy of management journal, 53*(1), 107–128.

23. Kellison, T. B., & Hong, S. (2015). The adoption and diffusion of pro-environmental stadium design. *European Sport Management Quarterly, 15*(2), 249–269.

24. Smith, N.L. & Green, B.C. (2020). Examining the Factors Influencing Organizational Creativity in Professional Sport Organizations. *Sport Management Review.* https://doi.org/10.1016/j.smr.2020.02.003.

25. To, M. L., Herman, H. M., & Ashkanasy, N. M. (2015). A multilevel model of transformational leadership, affect, and creative process behavior in work teams. *The leadership quarterly, 26*(4), 543–556.

26. Winand, M., & Anagnostopoulos, C. (2017). Get ready to innovate! Staff's disposition to implement service innovation in non-profit sport organisations. *International Journal of Sport Policy and Politics, 9*(4), 579–595.

27. Matthew, C. T. (2009). Leader creativity as a predictor of leading change in organizations. *Journal of Applied Social Psychology, 39*(1), 1–41.

28. Hoeber, L., & Hoeber, O. (2012). Determinants of an innovation process: A case study of technological innovation in a community sport organization. *Journal of sport management, 26*(3), 213–223.

29. Desbordes, M. (2002). Empirical analysis of the innovation phenomena in the sports equipment industry. *Technology Analysis & Strategic Management, 14*(4), 481–498.

30. Hoeber, L., Doherty, A., Hoeber, O., & Wolfe, R. (2015). The nature of innovation in community sport organizations. *European Sport Management Quarterly, 15*(5), 518–534.

31. Greenhalgh, G., Dwyer, B., & Biggio, B. (2014). There's an App for That: The Development of an NFL Team Mobile Application. *Journal of Applied Sport Management, 6*(4); Hoeber, L., Doherty, A., Hoeber, O., & Wolfe, R. (2015). The nature of innovation in community sport organizations. *European Sport Management Quarterly, 15*(5), 518–534; Winand, M., & Anagnostopoulos, C. (2017). Get ready to innovate! Staff's disposition to implement service innovation in non-profit sport organisations. *International Journal of Sport Policy and Politics, 9*(4), 579–595.

32. Barnhill, C. R., & Smith, N. L. (2019). Psychological contract fulfilment and innovative work behaviours of employees in sport-based SBEs: the mediating role of organisational citizenship. *International Journal of Sport Management and Marketing, 19*(1–2), 106–128.

33. Ratten, V. (2014). Future research directions for collective entrepreneurship in developing countries: a small and medium-sized enterprise perspective. *International Journal of Entrepreneurship and Small Business, 22*(2), 266–274.

34. Rader, B.G. (2008) *Baseball: A history of America's game.* University of Illinois Press.

35. Svensson, P. G., & Seifried, C. S. (2017). Navigating plurality in hybrid organizing: The case of sport for development and peace entrepreneurs. *Journal of Sport Management, 31*(2), 176–190.

36. Barnhill, C. R., & Smith, N. L. (2019). Psychological contract fulfilment and innovative work behaviours of employees in sport-based SBEs: the mediating role of organisational citizenship. *International Journal of Sport Management and Marketing, 19*(1–2), 106–128.

37. Amabile, T. M., & Pratt, M. G. (2016). The dynamic componential model of creativity and innovation in organizations: Making progress, making meaning. *Research in organizational behavior, 36*, 157–183.

38. Barnhill, C. R., & Smith, N. L. (2019). Psychological contract fulfilment and innovative work behaviours of employees in sport-based SBEs: the mediating role of organisational citizenship. *International Journal of Sport Management and Marketing, 19*(1–2), 106–128.

39. de Jonge, J., Spoor, E., Sonnentag, S., Dormann, C., & van den Tooren, M. (2012). "Take a break?!" Off-job recovery, job demands, and job resources as predictors of health, active learning, and creativity. *European Journal of Work and Organizational Psychology, 21*(3), 321–348.

40. Cai, D. J., Mednick, S. A., Harrison, E. M., Kanady, J. C., & Mednick, S. C. (2009). REM, not incubation, improves creativity by priming associative networks. *Proceedings of the National Academy of Sciences, 106*(25), 10,130–10,134.

41. Yu, C. P. S., & Hsieh, H. (2020). Beyond restorative benefits: Evaluating the effect of forest therapy on creativity. *Urban Forestry & Urban Greening.*

In between the organizational level and the individual level are workgroups and teams. Each workgroup and team is unique, even within one organization. This unit will examine the important elements of workgroups and the different types of work teams employed by sport organizations. Then we will discuss how to build creative and innovative work teams, as well as engage in the innovation process. We'll also discuss conflict and negotiation, and understand the role of politics and power in work teams. Finally, we'll learn about how leadership plays a role in these workgroups. Understanding how these workgroups are formed, interact, create, negotiate, conflict, and are lead can help any manager in the sports industry seeking to build a successful organization or workgroup.

> **Learning Objectives** After reading this chapter, students should be able to:

- Recognize the difference between informal groups, formal groups, and teams.
- Determine which types of teams are most appropriate for a project.
- Outline the factors that influence team success.
- Understand the dangers of groupthink.

Dennette Thornton: Director of Group Sales and Stadium Tours, Arthur M. Blank Sports and Entertainment
To listen to the interview <click here>

Reopening Estadio Cuauhtémoc Heliot was thrilled with his new assignment. It had been over a year since CF Puebla had wel-comed spectators into Estadio Cuauhtémoc for a match. Now that Covid-19 restrictions have been lifted, the club would be able to welcome spectators back when it opened its season in two months. The opening match would be a friendly against Argentinian club River Plate. Heliot missed the vibrant atmosphere of match day with 50,000 spectators in attendance. Now, he was in charge of making sure that Estadio Cuauhtémoc was ready to (1) welcome back spectators, (2) host a pre-match festival outside the venue, and (3) host a post-match concert on the pitch. As excited as he was, this was a huge undertaking. Heliot knew he would need a team. Whom would he ask to be a part of it?

If you were in Heliot's shoes, how would you form your team? Would you choose people you work well with, or would you prefer people based on expertise? Would your team be solely dedicated to this project, or would people contribute to the team while also completing their other duties? Would your team be limited to organizational members, or would you bring in outsiders? These decisions can be difficult for even more experienced managers, but they also have a significant effect on whether the team will be successful.

Supplementary Information The online version of this chapter (https://doi.org/10.1007/978-3-030-67612-4_14) contains supplementary material, which is available to authorized users.

Sport organizations rely on teamwork, both on and off the field. As a sport manager, you will be asked to be a member of many groups and teams. You will also be tasked with developing and managing teams. This chapter will focus on group and team dynamics. Topics that will be discussed include differences between groups and teams, the formation of group and team norms, and factors that influence team success.

▶ **Groups** Two or more people who influence one another through social interaction.

▶ **Teams** Groups working within the larger organization, with defined membership and assigned roles requiring interdependency, to conduct tasks in line with the organizational mission.

14.1   Defining Work Groups and Teams

The terms "groups" and "teams" are often used interchangeably. I'm sure your professor has likely done so in this course, but within organizational behavior, groups and teams are very different. Groups are simply two or more people who influence one another through social interaction.[1] Teams are groups working within the larger organization, with defined membership and assigned roles requiring interdependency, to conduct tasks in line with the organizational mission.[2] Teams can further be distinguished from groups in that teams' actions affect stakeholders within and outside of the organization. Both groups and teams can have significant impacts on organizations. Let's begin by exploring the types of groups that may form within an organization.

▶ **Formal Groups** Groups that are formally recognized by the organization but do not have a defined organizational function.

14.1.1 Formal Groups

Formal groups are groups that are formally recognized by the organization but do not have a defined organizational function. You may belong to several formal groups on your campus, for example, a sport management majors club or a club sports team. These groups are recognized by your institution and may receive funding, but they do not directly contribute to the university's mission. In the workplace, formal groups often form around hobbies. For example, organizations often support book clubs, jogging clubs, and many other activities enjoyed by employees. These clubs provide comradery that contributes to relationship building. For employees who are lower on the organizational chart, formal groups offer opportunities to gain social capital by providing chances to interact with more powerful employees.[3] Formal groups can also develop feelings of attachment to the organization, which can spur engagement.

▶ **Affinity Groups** Groups that are organized around a shared identity like race, gender, sexual orientation, age, and mental health.

Formal groups can also exist to support employees. Affinity groups, also known as employee resource groups, are generally organized around a shared identity like race, gender, sexual orientation, age, and mental health. These groups provide a safe space or refuge for employees belonging to underrepresented populations to speak freely about their experiences and find belonging amongst others who have shared experiences. Employees have multiple social identities tied to their career, employer, society, and personal lives. Affinity groups can help employees find meaningful links between their identities but also discuss conflict.[4]

▶ **Mentoring Groups** Groups that offer less experienced employees opportunities to interact with and gain advice from more experienced and more powerful employees.

Mentoring groups offer less experienced employees opportunities to interact with and gain advice from more experienced and more powerful employees.[5] Affinity groups and mentoring groups are generally recognized by organizations making them formal groups. They can also have significant positive impacts on the organization, but to be effective, their primary focus must be on employee well-being and development.

▷ **Informal Groups** Groups are not sanctioned or provided support from the organization.

14.1.2 Informal Groups

Unlike formal groups, informal groups are not sanctioned or provided support from the organization. However, they often serve many of the same functions as formal groups. Informal groups often form when employees share a common interest and are seeking social connections. Common examples of informal groups include lunch clubs, Bible studies, bowling teams, and many other activities in which employees may enjoy with each other. Since informal groups are not sanctioned by the organization, they can include outside members. For example, executives from several Major League Baseball (MLB) organizations belong to a running club. The club formed during the Covid-19 pandemic as a way to build camaraderie and enjoy friendly competition.[6] There are many, now formal groups, such as Women in Sports and Events (WISE), that began as informal groups.

Benefits to membership in an informal group are generally positive for employees. Potential benefits include socialization, mentorship, satisfaction, and development of social capital.[7] However, these benefits are less likely to be attributed to the organization by the employee. Informal groups can also have negative outcomes. If members are disgruntled, their unhappiness can spread throughout the informal group. If certain employees or groups of employees are left out or excluded from informal groups, it can lead to feelings of resentment and isolation. Specifically, informal groups can be used to isolate and discriminate against women, people of color, and lesbian, bisexual, gay, transgender, and queer (LBGTQ) individuals by denying them access to social capital.[8] Thus, organizations need to be aware of informal groups forming in their organization and industry.

Many of you will join alumni groups when you graduate from your institution. In part, this allows you to maintain elements of your former social identity as you move into massive changes in your life. Similarly, group membership, be it with informal or formal groups, often becomes a critical element of an individual's workplace identity to the point where people often try to maintain affiliation with groups after their relationship with the organization ends. Work teams can also become part of one's social identity, but more so for the recognition membership brings within the organization.

14.2   Work Teams

As the previous section noted, workgroups are important elements of an organization. As their primary objectives, they allow employees to share information, create relationships, forge a social identity, and generate social capital. Teams can also provide these benefits, but their primary objective is to benefit the organization's mission. Suppose Heliot, from the opening of the chapter, formed an organizationally sponsored kickball team that played in the local recreational league after work (a formal group). In that case, the team could be successful even if it never won a game. The kickball team's purpose would be to have fun, relax, and get to know coworkers. Heliot's stadium preparation team may also enjoy working together and building relationships between members; however, if the stadium is not prepared for the opening match, it would be viewed as a failure. The team's only prescribed goal was for the stadium to be ready.

Teams exist to accomplish a task, and their performance is measured as a collective. In other words, the team members are only considered successful if the team is successful. Although teams may share many characteristics of groups, members are chosen because they provide a complementary skill or knowledge set that will positively impact team performance.[9] Team members generally have assigned roles. Accountability occurs at both the individual and collective levels.[10] Members may be removed from the team if they do not contribute to team success. In this section, we'll explore various elements of teams, beginning with different types of teams.

14.3 Types of Teams

Teams can be formed to accomplish a variety of tasks that meet the organization's needs. Teams can be formed to make decisions, influence policy, influence change, develop new products and services, or even alter public perception of the organization. Teams may be permanent or temporary, but each should be created deliberately to accomplish the ascribed task the team is assigned. Let's discuss common types of teams.

14.3.1 Departmental Teams

We often don't think of our department as a team. In fact, departmental teams are one of the most common types of teams in sport organizations. Departmental teams consist of employees within a unit of the organization's structure to accomplish specific elements of the organization's operational needs. Members of departmental teams have assigned roles that exist within the department's own bureaucratic hierarchy. However, the bureaucratic functions of the department may be quite different from the rest of the organization.[11] For example, an organization's marketing department may have a very flat structure with informal communication channels, all the while functioning within a larger, more formal firm. Departmental teams are common in sport organizations. US Volleyball has four departmental teams that oversee various operational functions and six departmental teams related to the function of various national teams. The Calgary Stampeders of the Canadian Football League (CFL) has nine departmental teams that contribute to its business operations and six departmental teams on its football operations side (see Table 14.1).

Table 14.1 Calgary Stampeders departmental teams

Business operations teams	Football operations teams
Communications	Coaching
Digital media	Player personnel
Marketing	Scouting
Sponsorship sales	Medical
Ticket sales	Equipment
Fan services	Video operations
Event operations	
Stampeders foundation	
Retail operations	

14.3.2 Functional Teams

Functional teams consist of multi-skilled members from interrelated functional areas that oversee the ongoing function of the organization. We can sub-categorize function teams based on their organizational function. Production teams produce tangible products. These teams are common in manufacturing segments of the sports industry. If you were to visit the Wilson Sporting Goods factory in Ada, Ohio, you would see one of their production teams making "The Duke," the official ball of the National Football League (NFL).[12] Service teams build relationships with customers over multiple transactions. The Nashville Predators have several service teams that build relationships with various types of customers, including sponsors, premium seat holders, and season ticket holders.[13] Management teams are made up of upper-level managers who coordinate multiple departments. Many college athletic departments have three management teams: an internal operations team that coordinates operational departments, an external operations team that coordinates departments who interact with external stakeholders, and a senior executive team that coordinates the internal and external operations teams. Project teams are temporary teams that oversee a specific project, such as the development of a product or running of an event. For example, a city recreation department may develop a project team to handle a tennis facility's renovations. Likewise, a WNBA team may convene a project team to redesign their mascot. Many municipal sports councils form project teams to bid on hosting sporting events. If the bid is successful, another project team can be created to plan and run the event.

14.3.3 Self-Managed Teams

Self-managed teams are very similar to functional teams, but they function autonomously from the organization.[14] Intercollegiate athletic teams can be considered self-managed teams. Even though they are part of larger organizations (i.e., athletic departments and educational institutions), intercollegiate athletic teams are generally allowed to function independently with little oversight from other administrators. Self-managed teams can also provide more experienced or more creative employees the freedom to explore innovative solutions to issues.[15]

14.3.4 Advisory Teams

Advisory teams are formed to advise the organization on various issues that have the potential to impact the firm.[16] Potential issues in sport could include changes in technology, policy, or broader societal issues related to diversity and inclusion or gender issues. For example, in 2019, the National Hockey League (NHL) and the NHL Players' Association created an advisory committee focused on creating opportunities for women in hockey.[17] The Australian Football League (AFL) and the AFL Players Associations each formed indigenous advisory boards in efforts to improve relations between the league and indigenous peoples.[18] Both advisory teams include members of the indigenous communities.

14.3.5 Problem-Solving Teams

Often called taskforces, problem-solving teams are short-term, cross-functional teams formed to address an immediate concern.[19] For example, many sports leagues worldwide started task forces to determine how to deal with the Covid-19 pandemic. The NCAA has multiple taskforces to address concerns in college athletics, including

taskforces on the mental health of athletes and on gender equity.[20] In 2016, UEFA formed a task force to determine Kosovo's eligibility for World Cup qualifiers, despite the fact that some UEFA members didn't recognize the country's independence.[21] Like many of the other team types discussed, problem-solving teams often include experts from outside the organization.

14.3.6 Skunkworks

Skunkworks teams are extremely independent teams designed to foster innovation within an organization.[22] These teams are often located in different buildings or even different cities from the rest of the organization, specifically to foster their independence. Nike's Sport Research Lab and Innovation Kitchen is located in Beaverton, Oregon, with the rest of Nike's headquarters, but it is isolated from the rest of the campus. One of the research lab's most famous creations was the AirJordan sneaker, but it is responsible for developing many of Nike's high-performance products used by its sponsored athletes.[23] Before Nike divested out of the golf segment, it operated "The Oven" in Fort Worth, Texas, which focused on designing high-performance golf equipment. Skunkworks are often found in larger organizations that desire to harness the entrepreneurial spirit of a startup. Some scholars have argued that small businesses with limited resources, such as most sport organizations, could benefit most from skunkworks teams.[24] In mimetic industries like sport, innovative outcomes provide important advantages.

14.3.7 Virtual Teams

Virtual teams are simply teams that meet in a virtual environment instead of face to face.[25] Virtual teams offer the advantage of not being tied to a location, thus allowing members from various locations to be members. Sport organizations have been less reliant on virtual teams than organizations in other industries, but the Covid-19 pandemic demanded their use. It remains to be seen if virtual teams become more prominent in sports following the pandemic. Some sport employees enjoyed the work-life balance afforded by virtual work. Others complained of fatigue and the lack of inspiration they derived from human interaction.

14.4   Factors Influencing Team (and Group) Success

Numerous models outlining critical elements of team success have been put forth by academics and professionals. Robbins and Judge[26] put forth a model that essentially summarizes what we know about creating effective teams. You can see the model in Fig. 14.1. Before we discuss the elements of the model, it is critical to note a few important caveats. (1) Every team is different. They have different functions, sizes, and structures. The model can be used as a guide to create

a successful team, but organizations must be flexible. Not all of the elements will work. (2) Not every situation demands the creation of a team. Organizations need to look at their goals and what needs to be done to reach their goals. In some cases, teamwork is necessary. In other situations, teamwork may hinder organizational efforts. Teams should only be created when they can outperform the work of independent employees.

14.4.1 Context

Contextual factors are related organizational environment in which the team operates. In other words, does the organization support the team? There are four contextual factors in the model: adequate resources, leadership and structure, a climate of trust, and an evaluation and reward system.

Context
- Adequate resources
- Leadership and structure
- Climate of trust
- Evaluation and reward systems

Composition
- Abilities of members
- Personality
- Role allocation
- Diversity
- Team size
- Flexibility of members
- Member preferences

Work Design
- Autonomy
- Skill variety
- Task identity
- Task significance

Process
- Common purpose
- Specific goals
- Team efficacy
- Conflict levels
- Social loafing

Fig. 14.1 Team effectiveness model[27]

14.4.1.1   Adequate Resources

Of all the factors influencing team success, access to adequate resources may be the most important element in team success. All teams, regardless of their level of autonomy, rely on their parent organization for resource support. Resources that influence team success include access to information, time to function, financial support, access to proper equipment, administrative assistance, and proper staffing. Additionally, teams need political support throughout the organization and emotional support from leadership. Without proper resource support, teams will flounder regardless of how well the members function together.

14.4.1.2   Leadership and Structure

We can think of teams as smaller sub-organizations functioning within a broader organizational context. In order to be successful, team members must ensure that all members are contributing as needed to the team workload. Teams must also determine meeting schedules and deadlines, determine how decisions are made, how to resolve conflict, and what processes are needed to complete the team's tasks. Often, the organization will contribute to the team's initial structure by selecting key members and delegating roles. However, most successful teams will eventually develop at least basic autonomy levels over team-based decisions, including roles and decision-making processes around a shared, team-level vision of success.[28]

14.4.1.3   Climate of Trust

In many ways, team members take on a level of risk when they join. Evaluations of their performance are now at the team level instead of based on their individual performance. In other words, if the team fails, each member will likely be held to some level of responsibility regardless of their personal performance. Successful teams need high levels of trust between members bonded around their shared responsibilities. Think about team projects in your classes. Not only do you need to do your part, but you must also trust others to do their work at a high level for the team to earn a high grade. When teams do not develop

trust, members must exert time and energy monitoring their colleagues. This detracts from the original purpose of team formation. In contrast, teams with high trust levels are more likely to seek innovative solutions because information flows more freely, and members are less inhibited in sharing ideas.[29]

14.4.1.4   Evaluation and Reward System

As already noted, teams are judged more on overall performance, not individual performance. At the team level, determining how to hold others accountable is essential in building trust and accountability. Rewards are almost always preferable to punitive measures. The organization can help by clearly outlining what is expected of the team and outlining rewards for the team's success.[30] It is important to remember that in many cases, team members will be completing team-related duties in addition to their normal in-role duties. The organization can facilitate team-level efforts by clearly outlining financial and non-financial incentives for team success.

14.4.2   Composition

Composition factors relate to consideration around team member selection. Some questions that the organization should consider are: How big should the team be? What skills are needed for the team to be successful? What are the personalities of the team members? What types of diversity are needed?[31] This section explores composition factors in Robbins and Judge's model.[32]

14.4.2.1   Abilities of Members

Tom Brady is one of the most successful quarterbacks in NFL history. With his teammates, he has won six championships. Now imagine a team full of Tom Brady's. They would likely not win a game. Tom Brady has an amazing skill set as a quarterback, but most of those skills would not transfer to other positions on the field.

Similarly, an event team needs members with knowledge in facilities, event planning, marketing, sponsorship, finance, and sales. Trying to plan an event with people who only have a sponsorship background would be a disaster. Effective teams synergize the knowledge, skills, and abilities of individual members to accomplish tasks that are beyond the scope of an individual. And, while most teams need members with necessary technical skills (i.e., ability to build a budget or advertising campaign), successful teams also need members who possess problem-solving skills, decision-making skills, and interpersonal skills to integrate technical contributions into a collective effort.[33]

14.4.2.2   Personality

In addition to complementary skill sets, team members need to have compatible personalities. Most effective teams have higher levels of extraversion, conscientiousness, agreeableness, openness, and emotional intelligence.[34] The exact mix of personality traits needed may depend on the type of team and its overall goals. A skunkworks team is going to require members to be more open to ideas. A team confronting a difficult challenge will need the stability provided by emotional intelligence. One important finding from the research is that variability in personality traits between team members often leads to poor performance.[35] In other words, a team with some highly agreeable members and some less agreeable members will likely struggle to meet its goals.

14.4.2.3   Role Allocation

In most team types, members have assigned roles. This allows members to understand how they contribute to the team's success. A critical component of team selection is placing members in roles that fit their abilities. Imagine if Tom Brady was playing offensive line instead of quarterback or if Messi was moved to keeper. It just wouldn't work. However, managers also need to be aware of the members' desire to have a specified role. Imagine your favorite sport to play. What is your least favorite position? How does your effort change when you are in a role you do not enjoy, even if you have the required abilities? Assigning team members to roles that they do not want to have

can cause burnout. It can also cause rifts in teamwork if one member is less motivated. As a manager, it may be best to choose someone who is slightly less talented by excited for the opportunity to contribute.

14.4.2.4   Diversity

In 2017, University of Missouri Athletics featured a social media campaign titled, "More than a Student-Athlete." The campaign intended to showcase the non-sport aspirations of its athletes. Verbiage next to photos of White athletes highlighted their career aspirations, while the verbiage next to Black athletes focused on their racial identity. The campaign was criticized because it gave the impression that Black student-athletes were just Black, while White student-athletes had other ambitions. A major criticism leveled at Mizzou was that none of the team members who designed or approved the campaign were people of color. Unfortunately, there are many similarities both in sport and in other industries. See SJ Magazine's 2017 panel titled "Women in Business: A man's point of view" as a similar example.[36]

Diversity on teams has a significant impact on team success.[37] Homogeneous teams tend to view issues from similar perspectives,[38] whereas heterogeneous teams, those composed of people with different perspectives and backgrounds, explore issues from multiple viewpoints.[39] Diverse teams are more likely to avoid mistakes like racist advertising campaigns, sexist discussion panels, and failing to consider qualified job candidates. More importantly, diverse teams are more likely to outperform homogeneous teams across a wide range of functions.

Chapter 3 noted that diversity encompasses many elements, including age, gender, race, nationality, sexual orientation, personality, education, experience, expertise, and disabilities. Diverse groups are more likely to engage in cognitive conflict (see Chap. 16), which stems idea generation, creativity, innovative behaviors, and problem-solving. Diversity has been found to benefit every type of team and is vital for certain team types like advisory teams, problem-solving teams, and skunkworks.

14.4.2.5 Team Size

Organizations must give careful thought to team size. Teams should be no bigger than needed to accomplish the necessary task. Larger teams are more susceptible to role ambiguity, communication issues, and time issues, to name a few. According to several scholars and practitioners, teams should never have more than ten members.[40]

14.4.2.6 Flexibility of Team Members

Teams can be much more adaptable to change than the larger organization. Further, teams often need to be adaptable due to the nature of their tasks. If team members are flexible, both in their abilities and willingness to adapt, teams can adjust faster than the organization as a whole.[41] Without flexibility among members, teams may need to recruit new members or remove members who no longer fit the team's mission.

14.4.2.7 Member Preferences

It has already been discussed within several factors on this list, but it is extremely important that chosen members want to be a part of the team in their assigned role. Many employees do not want to be a part of a team. Selecting an individual who does not want to take part in a team's work will damage that individual's workplace attitudes and likely lower team morale.

14.4.3 Work Design

Work design factors relate directly to the purposes of the team's existence. Teams should exist because they are needed to accomplish a task that falls outside of the organization's general functions. Thus, they will also need to function somewhat independently from the organization's prevailing operating norms.

14.4.3.1 Autonomy

By definition, self-managed teams and skunkworks must function with near-total autonomy from the rest of the organization. However, all teams need some level of autonomy to develop their own processes and norms. Even departmental teams and functional teams need enough autonomy to develop efficient processes, roles, and norms.[42]

14.4.3.2 Skill Variety

In many instances, team members will be engaging in tasks that are outside of their normal job functions. Team members report being motivated by opportunities to showcase skillsets that they do not normally use in their regular organizational roles, as well as opportunities to learn new skill sets.[43] Skill variety encourages engagement, leading to a host of positive outcomes for the individual, team, and organization. That said, too much task variety can lead to stress if the employee feels that they are being asked to do too much. It can also damage team effectiveness if employees are asked to engage in skills that fall outside of their abilities.

14.4.3.3 Task Identity

If you talk to someone on a work team, there is a good chance they will bring it up in a conversation about their work. They state something like, "I really enjoy my job. I work in community relations, but I am also part of the youth development team." Membership on a team can add to an employee's work-based and career-based social identity. For many employees, just being asked to be a part of a team is a tremendous sign of recognition. Organizations can use this to build motivation of members, increasing team effectiveness. Social capital also comes with the new identity as employees gain access to people in other segments of the organization and with more political power.[44]

14.4.3.4 Task Significance

Similar to task identity, task significance can have influence workplace attitudes and motivation of members. Task significance relates to the importance of the task to the organization. More important tasks carry greater task significance.

14.4.4 Process

The final factors of team effectiveness are process factors. These factors relate to member behaviors. Teams work when members find ways to harness their collective efforts to achieve a common goal. When teams are dysfunctional, the collective effort can detract from what members could accomplish working independently.

14.4.4.1 Common Purpose
Teams must have a common purpose around which their mission, goals, and tasks are built. Although the organization provides the initial task around which the team is built, team members build the common purpose by discussing and agreeing on not only what it will take to accomplish the task but also what successful accomplishment looks like. The common purpose belongs to the team as a collective as well as each individual member. The common purpose provides direction, allows members to understand how their role contributes to team success, and motivates members to work together.[45]

14.4.4.2 Specific Goals
Based on the common purpose, successful teams develop specific goals. Just with organizational goals, team goals need to be measurable and achievable, but also challenging. The team members agree upon the goals that move the team closer to the common purpose. Achieving goals moves the team closer to achieving the common purpose and also builds confidence among members.[46]

14.4.4.3 Team Efficacy
Speaking of confidence, teams build a belief that they can succeed. This belief is known as team efficacy. Organizational and team leaders can help build efficacy by providing necessary resources, including training for team members so that they feel confident in taking on new tasks. In addition, as team success builds efficacy, leaders should celebrate initial triumphs. Meeting initial goals helps members believe they can meet more challenging goals ahead.[47]

14.4.4.4 Conflict Levels
It is commonly assumed that effective teams avoid conflict. Actually, effective teams harness conflict to spur creativity and innovation.[48] As noted in Chap. 16, conflict that is task-focused stimulates discussion and critical assessment of

ideas.[49] Because teams are often working on novel problems, task conflict spurs members to contemplate their best options for developing a solution. Task conflict also helps avoid groupthink, one of the most detrimental behaviors for teams. However, managing conflict is difficult. Team leaders must encourage task conflict while avoiding having conflict become personal between members. Relational conflict pulls energy away from team goals and damages trust among members.[50]

14.4.4.5 Social Loafing
Social loafing is an undesirable behavior among team members where an employee essentially hides out on the team to avoid their normal roles or because they lose motivation to achieve the common purpose. Social loafing detracts from a team's efficiency because another member has to cover for the loafer. In some cases, social loafing occurs when a team member's role cannot be tied to the common purpose.[51] It is best to make sure that employees chosen to be on the team are selected because they will be productive members who contribute to the team and that all team member's roles are necessary. Creating a team culture where members are held accountable via reward and evaluation systems can reduce loafing.

14.5 Team Norms

Team norms are the underlying agreement among group members for how the group will function. Norms are formed during the initial stages of team development. At the initial outset, team members find themselves with newfound freedom but also a void regarding what behaviors are expected. So, team members discuss with each other how they think the team and team members should behave. In essence, they create a culture based on what the members decide it will be through mutual agreement.[52] Norms can govern any number of team behaviors, including formality, communication channels, and decision-making methods. As norms are communicated, they are adopted or altered per the will of the team.[53]

Clearly defined team norms have many bene-fits. Norms ensure predictive behaviors among team members. This allows members to feel comfortable knowing how others will behave and how they should behave within the group. Building on that idea, norms help teams avoid interpersonal conflict that often arises when members have differences in agreement over behaviors. Next, norms help members understand the common purpose of the team, helping mem-bers form an identity.[54] Finally, norms help teams become more effective in working toward their goals. Norms can be informal or formal; how-ever, teams that are most effective adopt formal norms. Often successful teams use their initial meetings to discuss norms and codify them through negotiation. Thus, later meetings can be conducted in an atmosphere where behavior expectations are known, and team members can focus on working together to achieve goals.[55]

14.6   Groupthink and Crisis of Agreement

Teams allow organizations to take advantage of collective intelligence. In other words, teams can take advantage of their individual members' expertise and creativity to address complex issues. However, under certain circumstances, teams reach agreement without seeking alterna-tive solutions. This is known as dysfunction in decision-making. When this occurs, teams fail to reach their potential and may become less effi-cient than the members working independently.[56]

▶ **Groupthink** A phenomenon that occurs in highly cohesive groups when pressures to make any decision begin to outweigh the importance of making the best decision.

14.6.1 Groupthink

One possible cause of dysfunction in decision-making is groupthink. Groupthink occurs in highly cohesive groups when the pressure to

make any decision begins to outweigh the impor-tance of making the best decision.[57] When this happens, groups rely less on their mental abili-ties, instead opting for the simplest plausible solution even if significant flaws are foreseeable. Groupthink most often occurs when team mem-bers develop a myopic belief in the team's effi-cacy. They believe that the team is so good at what it does, that the team can do no wrong. This allows team members to rationalize flaws in the decision to discount negative outcomes and place pressure on any voices of reason to fall in line. Because of the pressure to fall in line, team mem-bers with concerns self-censor and project unwavering agreement. This creates the illusion of unanimity in support of the decision.[58]

Groupthink has been blamed for numerous strategic political and military disasters such as the Bay of Pigs Invasion and Watergate.[59] One notable example from sport was a decision by the MLB Umpires Association to have all umpires resign in mass as part of a negotiation tactic dur-ing a dispute with the league over pay and perfor-mance evaluations. The umpire's association believed this tactic would force MLB to meet their demands because games couldn't be played without umpires to officiate. Unfortunately for the umpire's association, MLB began accepting resignations and hiring new umpires. According to reports, the umpires believed so strongly that the tactic would work; they never considered that MLB would accept their resignations.[60]

There are several ways teams can avoid the dangers of groupthink:[61]

1. Encourage task-based conflict.
2. Assign members to serve as objective evalua-tors of decisions.
3. Team leaders should maintain impartiality during the decision-making process.
4. Seek outside counsel.
5. Once consensus is reached, allow team mem-bers to voice concerns.

▶ **Crisis of Agreement** A phenomenon that occurs when other team members' acceptance is the most important factor driving decision-making.

14.6.2 Crisis of Agreement: The Abilene Paradox

Crises of agreement, also known as the Abilene Paradox, occurs when other team members' acceptance is the most crucial factor driving decision-making.[62] Unlike with groupthink, in which there is a general belief that the team is making the best decision, team members experiencing a crisis of agreement are aware that a bad decision is being made. In this instance, team members simply want to be accepted as one of the teams and, as such, wish to appear agreeable to what others are proposing. The name Abilene Paradox comes from a parable in which four people depart on a road trip, each knowing individually that the trip will be miserable, all because each believes they are the only one who doesn't want to go. It's not until after the trip that when each member is complaining the collective realization that no one actually wanted to go on the road trip. Had anyone voiced their concerns, the doomed road trip would have been avoided.[63] In the work world, a crisis of conflict could result in many unfavorable outcomes, such as a hiring team making a flawed selection because no members want to voice their concerns. Teams can avoid crises of conflict by setting individual-level goals to keep members motivated and focused on excellence. Leaders need to be mindful of the atmosphere during team meetings. If members seem unmotivated and/or overly agreeable, leaders should take action to refocus the team on outcome importance.

14.7 Stages of Team Development

Most international soccer teams engage in a series of training and friendly matches to prepare for their upcoming competition. The idea is to work out players' roles and develop team strategies. Similarly, work teams need to develop before they reach their potential. When building a team, it is essential to understand that the members will not become a cohesive unit the moment the team is formed. Teams evolve through stages. This means that many of the success factors discussed throughout this chapter will take time to form, and leaders will have to nurture their development. The most widely accepted model of team development is the five-stage model.[64]

14.7.1 Stage 1: Forming

During the forming stage, team members are selected and introduced to one another. At the individual level, team members are generally honored to be chosen and excited about contributing to the team's success. However, they may also be nervous about being able to contribute. The team will begin exploring its own culture, but the team will mainly defer decision-making to a leader or even outside authority. The team's focus should be on developing cohesion and worry less about task accomplishment during this stage of development.

14.7.2 Stage 2: Storming

As the team moves from the early excitement of the forming stage toward understanding the task and developing processes, the common purpose and goals are set. The storming stage is often described as one of conflict. Team members jockey for roles and influence. Some members who do not agree with their assigned roles or norms will demonstrate anger and frustration. At this stage, the team will have experienced little task-related success, so that some members may doubt the team's efficacy. Team leaders must be diligent in encouraging task-based conflict while eliminating relational conflict. During this stage, team norms begin developing, and the team should arrive at its common purpose. Teams that have a dysfunctional make-up may not move beyond the storming stage.

14.7.3 Stage 3: Norming

The initial norms developed during the storming stage are refined and adapted. Team members accept the team as part of their identity and understand their role in achieving the common purpose. Team members are also more trusting and comfortable around each other. At this stage, the team will have a distinguishable culture from the larger organization and may even develop its own language and jokes. However, the team is now task-focused, and conflict is productive. At the norming stage, the team will begin real productivity toward the assigned task, and goal accomplishment will start occurring more frequently.

14.7.4 Stage 4: Performing

Team members have strong feelings of team efficacy at this point. Members feel like they function well together and can accomplish the greatness they laid out in their common purpose. Goals are met frequently, and team success is celebrated. For many teams, they will achieve the task that has been assigned toward the end of the performing stage. Many members feel a great sense of personal and professional accomplishment when the common purpose is achieved.

14.7.5 Stage 5: Adjournment

Once the team has delivered on its assigned tasks, some teams will be assigned new tasks by the organization and will move back to one of the earlier stages. Other teams, despite their success, will no longer be useful to the organization and be adjourned. This can be a trying time for team members whose feelings of accomplishment will be mixed with a degree of sadness or loss. It can be hard for team members to move back into their regular tasks, which can now be less rewarding. The organization needs to be aware of these feelings and recognize members for their contributions.

14.8 Summary

Groups and teams are incredibly vital to the functioning of sport organizations. When a sport organization identifies the need for a team, it must then determine the type of tasks the team will complete, who will be on the team, and the level of autonomy needed for the team to be successful. The team members then determine their goals, norms, and their own processes to complete the tasks assigned by the organization. When successful, teams can accomplish far more than members could on their own. Organizations can help teams to be successful by providing resources, supporting team development, but allowing the team to be independent throughout the process.

Notes

1. Forsythe, D. R. (1999). *Group Dynamics*. Wadsworth.
2. Hitt, M.A., Miller, C.C., Colella, A., Triana, M. (2017). *Organizational Behavior* (5th ed.). Wiley.
3. Oh, H., Chung, M. H., & Labianca, G. (2004). Group social capital and group effectiveness: The role of informal socializing ties. *Academy of management journal, 47*(6), 860–875.
4. Colgan, F. & McKearney, A. (2012), Visibility and voice in organisations: lesbian, gay, bisexual and transgendered employee networks. *Equality, Diversity and Inclusion: An International Journal, 31*(4). 359–378; Dennissen, M., Benschop, Y., & van den Brink, M. (2019). Diversity networks: networking for equality?. *British Journal of Management, 30*(4), 966–980.
5. Carvin, B. N. (2011). The hows and whys of group mentoring. *Industrial and Commercial Training, 43*(1), 49–52.
6. Brown, T. (2020. April 13). Running club: Quarantined baseball executives find a new competition, camaraderie. *Yahoo Sports*. Retrieved from https://sports.yahoo.com/running-club-coronavirus-quarantined-mlb-baseball-executives-find-a-new-competition-camaraderie-142819731.html.
7. McShane, S., & Von Glinow, M. (2021). *Organizational Behavior: Emerging Knowledge. Global Reality* (9th ed.). McGraw Hill; Oh, H., Chung, M. H., & Labianca, G. (2004). Group social capital and group effectiveness: The role of informal socializing ties. *Academy of management journal, 47*(6), 860–875.
8. Scott, K. L., & Thau, S. (2013). Theory and research on social exclusion in work groups. 65–73. In Dewall, C.N. (Ed.). *The Oxford handbook of social exclusion*, Oxford University Press.
9. Dyer Jr, W. G., Dyer, J. H., & Dyer, W. G. (2013). *Team building: Proven strategies for improving team performance*. John Wiley & Sons.
10. Hitt, M.A., Miller, C.C., Colella, A., Triana, M. (2017). *Organizational Behavior* (5th ed.). Wiley.
11. Witziers, B., Sleegers, P., & Imants, J. (1999). Departments as teams: Functioning, variations and alternatives. *School Leadership & Management, 19*(3), 293–304.

12. Wilson (n.d.). *Handmade in the USA: Ada, Ohio* Retrieved from: https://www.wilson.com/en-us/explore/football/ada-ohio-factory.
13. Nashville Predators (n.d.). *Nashville Predators Staff Listing*. Retrieved from https://www.nhl.com/predators/team/staff-listing.
14. McShane, S., & Von Glinow, M. (2021). *Organizational Behavior: Emerging Knowledge. Global Reality* (9th ed.). McGraw Hill.
15. den Hartog, S. C., Runge, J. M., Reindl, G., & Lang, J. W. (2020). Linking personality trait variance in self-managed teams to team innovation. *Small Group Research, 51*(2), 265–295.
16. McShane, S., & Von Glinow, M. (2021). *Organizational Behavior: Emerging Knowledge. Global Reality* (9th ed.). McGraw Hill.
17. NHL (2020, September 3). NHL announces initiatives to combat racism, accelerate inclusion efforts. *NHL.com* Retrieved from https://www.nhl.com/news/nhl-announces-initiatives-to-combat-racism-accelerate-inclusion-efforts/c-318873398.
18. AFL Players (2016). *Many Stories, One Goal: Supporting Indigenous Footballers*. Australian Football League Players Association. Retrieved from http://www.aflplayers.com.au/wp-content/uploads/2014/03/BestPracticeGuidelines_2016_Final_p.pdf.
19. McShane, S., & Von Glinow, M. (2021). *Organizational Behavior: Emerging Knowledge. Global Reality* (9th ed.). McGraw Hill.
20. NCAA (n.d.). NCAA Committees. Retrieved from http://www.ncaa.org/governance/committees.
21. Associated Press (2016, May 18). UEFA asks task force to place Kosovo in World Cup qualifying group. *SportsNet*. Retrieved from https://www.sportsnet.ca/soccer/uefa-asks-task-force-place-kosovo-world-cup-qualifying-group/.
22. Larsson, A. (2019). The seven dimensions of skunk works: A new approach and what makes it unique. *Journal of Research in Marketing and Entrepreneurship, 21*(1), 37–54. https://doi.org/10.1108/JRME-09-2017-0038; McShane, S., & Von Glinow, M. (2021). *Organizational Behavior: Emerging Knowledge. Global Reality* (9th ed.). McGraw Hill.
23. Nisen, M. (2013, February 19). 17 of the most mysterious corporate labs. *Business Insider*. Retrieved from https://www.businessinsider.com/coolest-skunk-works-2013-2.
24. Larsson, A. (2019). The seven dimensions of skunk works: A new approach and what makes it unique. *Journal of Research in Marketing and Entrepreneurship, 21*(1), 37–54. https://doi.org/10.1108/JRME-09-2017-0038.
25. Mittleman, D. & Briggs, R.O. (1999). Communicating technologies for traditional and virtual teams. In Sunderstrom E. et al. (Eds.). *Supporting Work Team Effectiveness*. 246–270.
26. Robbins, S.P., & Judge, T.A. (2019). *Organizational Behavior* (18th ed.). Pearson.
27. Robbins, S.P., & Judge, T.A. (2019). *Organizational Behavior* (18th ed.). Pearson.
28. Dyer Jr, W. G., Dyer, J. H., & Dyer, W. G. (2013). *Team building: Proven strategies for improving team performance*. John Wiley & Sons; Hitt, M.A., Miller, C.C., Colella, A., Triana, M. (2017). *Organizational Behavior* (5th ed.). Wiley; McShane, S., & Von Glinow, M. (2021). *Organizational Behavior: Emerging Knowledge. Global Reality* (9th ed.). McGraw Hill; Robbins, S.P., & Judge, T.A. (2019). *Organizational Behavior* (18th ed.). Pearson.
29. Costa, A. C. (2003). Work team trust and effectiveness, *32*(5), 605–622; Costa, A. C., Fulmer, C. A., & Anderson, N. R. (2018). Trust in work teams: An integrative review, multilevel model, and future directions. *Journal of Organizational Behavior, 39*(2), 169–184.
30. Cacioppe, R. (1999). Using team–individual reward and recognition strategies to drive organizational success. *Leadership & Organization Development Journal, 20*(6), 322–331; DeMatteo, J. S., Eby, L. T., & Sundstrom, E. (1998). Team-based rewards: Current empirical evidence. *Research in organizational behavior, 20*, 141–183; Sarin, S., & Mahajan, V. (2001). The effect of reward structures on the performance of cross-functional product development teams. *Journal of marketing, 65*(2), 35–53.
31. Dyer Jr, W. G., Dyer, J. H., & Dyer, W. G. (2013). *Team building: Proven strategies for improving team performance*. John Wiley & Sons; Hitt, M.A., Miller, C.C., Colella, A., Triana, M. (2017). *Organizational Behavior* (5th ed.). Wiley; McShane, S., & Von Glinow, M. (2021). *Organizational Behavior: Emerging Knowledge. Global Reality* (9th ed.). McGraw Hill; Robbins, S.P., & Judge, T.A. (2019). *Organizational Behavior* (18th ed.). Pearson.
32. Robbins, S.P., & Judge, T.A. (2019). *Organizational Behavior* (18th ed.). Pearson.
33. Mathieu, J. E., Tannenbaum, S. I., Donsbach, J. S., & Alliger, G. M. (2014). A review and integration of team composition models: Moving toward a dynamic and temporal framework. *Journal of Management, 40*(1), 130–160; Stevens, M. J., & Campion, M. A. (1999). Staffing work teams: Development and validation of a selection test for teamwork settings. *Journal of Management, 25*(2), 207–228.
34. Barrick, M. R., Stewart, G. L., Neubert, M. J., & Mount, M. K. (1998). Relating member ability and personality to work-team processes and team effectiveness. *Journal of applied psychology, 83*(3), 377; Kichuk, S. L., & Wiesner, W. H. (1997). The big five personality factors and team performance: implications for selecting successful product design teams. *Journal of Engineering and Technology management, 14*(3–4), 195–221; Neuman, G. A., Wagner, S. H., & Christiansen, N. D. (1999). The relationship between work-team personality composition and the job performance of teams. *Group & Organization Management, 24*(1), 28–45.

35. Mohammed, S., & Angell, L. C. (2003). Personality heterogeneity in teams: Which differences make a difference for team performance?. *Small group research, 34*(6), 651–677; Prewett, M. S., Brown, M. I., Goswami, A., & Christiansen, N. D. (2018). Effects of team personality composition on member performance: A multilevel perspective. *Group & Organization Management, 43*(2), 316–348.
36. Fiorillo, V. (2017, October 24). Here's how not to host a women's empowerment event. *PhillyMag.com* Retrieved from https://www.phillymag.com/news/2017/10/24/south-jersey-magazine-womens-empowerment/.
37. Lauring, J., & Villeseche, F. (2019). The Performance of Gender Diverse Teams: What Is the Relation between Diversity Attitudes and Degree of Diversity? *European Management Review, 2*, 243. https://doi.org/10.1111/emre.12164.
38. LePine, J. A., Hollenbeck, J. R., Ilgen, D. R., Colquitt, J. A., & Ellis, A. (2002). Gender composition, situational strength, and team decision-making accuracy: A criterion decomposition approach. *Organizational Behavior and Human Decision Processes, 88*(1), 445–475.
39. Herring, C., 2009, "Does diversity pay? Race, gender, and the business case for diversity". *American Sociological Review, 74*: 208–224; Stahl, G. K., Maznevski, M. L., Voigt, A., & Jonsen, K. (2010). Unraveling the effects of cultural diversity in teams: A meta-analysis of research on multicultural work groups. *Journal of international business studies, 41*(4), 690–709.
40. Robbins, S.P., & Judge, T.A. (2019). *Organizational Behavior* (18th ed.). Pearson.
41. Georganta, E., Kugler, K. G., Reif, J. A. M., & Brodbeck, F. C. (2020). Diving deep into team adaptation: How does it really unfold over time? *Group Dynamics: Theory, Research, and Practice.* https://doi.org/10.1037/gdn0000133.supp. (Supplemental).
42. Cordery, J. L., Morrison, D., Wright, B. M., & Wall, T. D. (2010). The impact of autonomy and task uncertainty on team performance: A longitudinal field study. *Journal of organizational behavior, 31*(2–3), 240–258.
43. Wu, C.-H., & Wang, Z. (2015). How transformational leadership shapes team proactivity: The mediating role of positive affective tone and the moderating role of team task variety. *Group Dynamics: Theory, Research, and Practice, 19*(3), 137–151.
44. Ellemers, N., Sleebos, E., Stam, D., & de Gilder, D. (2013). Feeling included and valued: How perceived respect affects positive team identity and willingness to invest in the team. *British Journal of Management, 24*(1), 21–37; Mitchell, R., Boyle, B., Parker, V., Giles, M., Chiang, V., & Joyce, P. (2015). Managing inclusiveness and diversity in teams: How leader inclusiveness affects performance through status and team identity. *Human Resource Management, 54*(2), 217–239.
45. Kleingeld, A., van Mierlo, H., & Arends, L. (2011). The effect of goal setting on group performance: A meta-analysis. *Journal of Applied Psychology, 96*(6), 1289–1304.
46. Kleingeld, A., van Mierlo, H., & Arends, L. (2011). The effect of goal setting on group performance: A meta-analysis. *Journal of Applied Psychology, 96*(6), 1289–1304.
47. Gully, S. M., Incalcaterra, K. A., Joshi, A., & Beaubien, J. M. (2002). A meta-analysis of team-efficacy, potency, and performance: interdependence and level of analysis as moderators of observed relationships. *Journal of applied psychology, 87*(5), 819.
48. Bradley, B. H., Klotz, A. C., Postlethwaite, B. E., & Brown, K. G. (2013). Ready to rumble: How team personality composition and task conflict interact to improve performance. *Journal of Applied Psychology, 98*(2), 385; Bradley, B. H., Postlethwaite, B. E., Klotz, A. C., Hamdani, M. R., & Brown, K. G. (2012). Reaping the benefits of task conflict in teams: The critical role of team psychological safety climate. *Journal of Applied Psychology, 97*(1), 151.
49. Bradley, B. H., Klotz, A. C., Postlethwaite, B. E., & Brown, K. G. (2013). Ready to rumble: How team personality composition and task conflict interact to improve performance. *Journal of Applied Psychology, 98*(2), 385; Bradley, B. H., Postlethwaite, B. E., Klotz, A. C., Hamdani, M. R., & Brown, K. G. (2012). Reaping the benefits of task conflict in teams: The critical role of team psychological safety climate. *Journal of Applied Psychology, 97*(1), 151.
50. Dyer Jr, W. G., Dyer, J. H., & Dyer, W. G. (2013). *Team building: Proven strategies for improving team performance.* John Wiley & Sons; Hitt, M.A., Miller, C.C., Colella, A., Triana, M. (2017). *Organizational Behavior* (5th ed.). Wiley.
51. Robbins, S.P., & Judge, T.A. (2019). Organizational Behavior (18th ed.). Pearson; Rutte, C. G. (2003). Social loafing in teams. *International handbook of organizational teamwork and cooperative working*, 361–378.
52. Levi, D., & Askay, D. A. (2021). *Group Dynamics for Teams* (6th ed.). Sage.
53. Hitt, M.A., Miller, C.C., Colella, A., Triana, M. (2017). *Organizational Behavior* (5th ed.). Wiley; Levi, D., & Askay, D. A. (2021). *Group Dynamics for Teams*. Sage; McShane, S., & Von Glinow, M. (2021). *Organizational Behavior: Emerging Knowledge. Global Reality* (9th ed.). McGraw Hill.
54. Griffin, B. (2015). Collective norms of engagement link to individual engagement. *Journal of Managerial Psychology, 30*(7), 847–860; Levi, D., & Askay, D. A. (2021). *Group Dynamics for Teams* (6th ed.). Sage.
55. Levi, D., & Askay, D. A. (2021). Group Dynamics for Teams (6th ed.). Sage.
56. Lunenburg, F. C. (2010). Group decision making: The potential for groupthink. *International Journal of Management, Business, and Administration, 13*(1), 1–6.
57. Janis, I. L. (1982). *Groupthink.* Boston: Houghton; Lunenburg, F. C. (2010). Group decision making: The potential for groupthink. *International Journal of Management, Business, and Administration, 13*(1), 1–6.
58. Kim, Y. (2016). A comparative study of the "Abilene Paradox" and "groupthink." *Public Administration Quarterly, 25*(2), 168–189; Lunenburg, F. C. (2010). Group decision making: The potential for group-

think. *International Journal of Management, Business, and Administration, 13*(1), 1–6; McCauley, C. (1989). The nature of social influence in groupthink: Compliance and internalization. *Journal of Personality and Social Psychology, 57*(2), 250–260. https://doi.org/10.1037/0022-3514.57.2.250.

59. Kim, Y. (2016). A comparative study of the "Abiliene Paradox" and "groupthink." *Public Administration Quarterly, 25*(2), 168–189; Lunenburg, F. C. (2010). Group decision making: The potential for groupthink. International *Journal of Management, Business, and Administration, 13*(1), 1–6; McCauley, C. (1989). The nature of social influence in groupthink: Compliance and internalization. *Journal of Personality and Social Psychology, 57*(2), 250–260. https://doi.org/10.1037/0022-3514.57.2.250; Taras, D. G. (1991). Breaking the silence: Differentiating crises of agreement. *Public Administration Quarterly, 14*(4), 401–418.

60. Koerber, C. P., & Neck, C. P. (2003). Groupthink and sports: An application of Whyte's model. *International Journal of Contemporary Hospitality Management, 15*(1), 20–28. https://doi.org/10.1108/09596110310458954.

61. Lunenburg, F. C. (2010). Group decision making: The potential for groupthink. *International Journal of Management, Business, and Administration, 13*(1), 1–6.

62. Taras, D. G. (1991). Breaking the silence: Differentiating crises of agreement. *Public Administration Quarterly, 14*(4), 401–418.

63. Harvey, J. B. (1988). The Abilene Paradox: The management of agreement. *Organizational Dynamics, 17*(1), 17–43. https://doi.org/10.1016/0090-2616(88)90028-9.

64. Tuckman, B. W. (2001). Developmental sequence in small groups. *Group Facilitation*, (3), 66–81.

> **Learning Objectives** After reading this chapter, students will be able to:

- Identify what aspects of the workplace create innovative team in sports
- Define creativity and innovation in the sports industry
- Apply the innovation process to the sports industry context

Alyse LaHue: General Manager, Sky Blue FC

To listen to the interview <click here>

15.1 Creativity and Innovation in Teams

Creativity and innovation are often attributed to an individual. Think about the famous sports example of Bill Veeck. Stories are often told about him and his creative ideas to promote baseball games. However, he did not implement his ideas independently, nor did he likely come up with all of the credited innovations. He was inspired by others, and he had assistance in the successful execution of these new ideas. Therefore, it is important to understand how work teams or groups influence creativity and innovation. These teams can be multipliers, suppressors, or supporters of individual creativity, depending on a number of factors we'll discuss in this chapter. If done well, groups can multiply the effects of individual creativity, not just become the sum of the individual creative effort in the group.[1]

Depending on the structure of an organization, it may not be clear what constitutes a work team. Consider a work team as a group of individuals who regularly work together to achieve collective goals or perform tasks.[2] There are many factors to think about when building a creative or innovation-focused work team, some more leader-driven and others more employee-driven. In a previous chapter, we discussed how an individual could be creative and engage in creative behaviors. Those are a key part of having an innovative organization, but now we will discuss how teams and workgroups can be creative.

When building a creative or innovative team, the elements to consider are the leader of the group, work environment, interactions within and external to the group, and resource elements such as time and rewards. As discussed in the previous chapter, workgroups are essentially two or more

Supplementary Information The online version of this chapter (https://doi.org/10.1007/978-3-030-67612-4_15) contains supplementary material, which is available to authorized users.

members organized around an activity or interest. Work teams are groups that have an assigned task that aids the organization. Both groups and teams develop roles, including leaders who play key roles in shaping the tone, environment, and processes of the group. The second important element is the innovative work environment, which consists of four aspects: participative safety, vision, task orientation, and support for innovation. The third point of consideration for any team is interaction with new people and new ideas. By incorporating new perspectives into the team, opportunities for creative ideas increase. Different lived experiences allow new ideas to come about through different ways of thinking about the problems or new solutions the current group members may have never thought of (see the concept of task conflict in Chaps. 14 and 16). Alternatively, seeking out advice and thoughts outside the team can also increase innovation in a team. The fourth and final element of an innovative team is resource-related, both time and rewards. While these four encompassing elements cannot guarantee a successfully innovative organization, innovation is unlikely to happen without these building blocks.

15.2 Supporting Creativity and Innovation

Table 15.1 outlines eight key aspects of organizational support for creativity and innovation in its workgroups and teams.

15.2.1 Leader-Member Exchange

A traditional view of work assumes leaders exchanged wages for labor. Employees do what the leaders wanted them to do for pay. However,

Table 15.1 Key aspects of supporting creativity and innovation

Leader-member exchange	Participative safety
Vision and goal clarity	Support for innovation
Task orientation	Diversity and inclusion
Social interaction	Time and rewards

this simplistic view hinders creativity because of its focus on transactional relationships.[3] The relationship between leaders and work team members can play a crucial role in improving employee creativity. When leaders build environments similar to the ones we'll describe next, they build trust with employees. That trust can lead to employees being more willing to take risks to address organizational problems. This, in turn, increases the likelihood of producing creative solutions or products. This relationship also goes the other way. When leaders have high-quality exchanges with their team members, they become more confident in the employees. That confidence means the leaders are more willing to provide resources and autonomy to support their employees' creativity.[4] Conversely, when those exchanges are of low quality, employees will be less likely to go beyond their prescribed responsibilities to come up with new and useful ideas.

▶ **Participative Safety** Participative safety is the idea that employees need to feel safe sharing new ideas in their workplace.

15.2.2 Participative Safety

Participative safety is the idea that employees need to feel safe sharing new ideas in their workplace. The more comfortable someone is sharing new ideas with their work team, the more likely someone will develop an incredibly useful idea. Of course, not all ideas are that good, at least initially. Many ideas need further refinement to reach their full potential and provide a competitive advantage for the organization. Other times, the technology has not yet been created to make implementation possible, or the cost outweighs the benefits.

However, by allowing people to share ideas and feel comfortable doing so, the team members increase the likelihood of finding those genuinely innovative or creative ideas. Creative environment of participative safety involves two elements—time to share and safety within the group. Building in time is pretty self-explanatory. Team members need time to workout and share their ideas in an environment free of other distractions. Feelings of safety is a little more challenging. Think about any group dynamic. Someone raises their hand, a brave move to begin with, and they share an idea or pose a question. Other group members immediately roll their eyes or scoff at the proposal. What a mood killer! Employees would be significantly less likely to raise their hand or share an idea in the future. As we mentioned in Chap. 13, idea generation is not about assessing feasibility or applicability yet, it's about coming up with the ideas themselves.

15.2.3 Vision and Goal Clarity

Even when people may feel comfortable sharing ideas, those ideas will only be useful if they are directed at helping the organization. As discussed in Chap. 14, workgroups and teams differ in their purposes. Workgroups can be focused on any number of objectives, including but not limited to organizational outcomes (i.e., mentoring groups are focused on employee development; a bowling team may only be focused on camaraderie). On the other hand, teams are created for the specific purpose of addressing an issue related to organizational success. Leaders initially set the direction of the group or team, but eventually, successful groups and teams develop shared goals around a common purpose (see Chap. 14). As we discussed in the last chapter, vision and goals provide direction for group and team members. Maintaining direction toward the team's purpose (i.e., achieving goals) is the primary indicator of team success. Thus, having a clear purpose and detailed goals that are well understood by members is essential, especially when it comes to idea generation. If creativity efforts and innovative behaviors are not directed at group or team goals, members can lose focus. It is much more difficult to come up with new ideas for any and everything related to that sport organization than it is to address a specific problem.

An example of this can be seen in any classic brainstorming session. Imagine sitting in a conference room and being asked for your ideas on increasing attendance? You could generate ideas, but the question is so broad that it would be difficult for the group to find an effective direction. No, imagine if the question was, how can we attract students from the nearby colleges to attend. The group now has more focus, so there will be more debate, generating beneficial task conflict.

A clear purpose and goals are only effective if the group and team members buy-in.[5] Why does that matter? Creating innovative ideas or implementing them can be challenging. Doing new things requires motivation, and not many people would be motivated to do hard things in service to a goal or vision they don't value (see Chaps. 9 and 12). Similarly, if a goal is unattainable, members who want their innovative ideas to be implemented successfully end up feeling overwhelmed and frustrated. Once again, team-developed purposes and goals provide utility in developing ideas.

15.2.4 Support for Innovation

Support for innovation is more complicated than merely saying, "we support innovation" to the team members. Yes, a verbal affirmation can be a signaler of support, but creating a work environment supportive of innovation is more than that. When team members are open to new ideas from colleagues themselves, time is provided for employees to be creative, and policies or procedures are built around innovation encouragement, support for innovation becomes apparent. When employees perceive that support, they are more likely to try out new ideas, engage in the creative process, and seek problems that need to be addressed.[6] Support through access to professional development and time to engage in passion projects are policies supporting autonomy and leveraging the intrinsic motivation of their employees. Researchers have already found this support for innovation, and change in the sports industry has made organizations more innovative.[7]

15.2.5 Task Orientation

Motivation in the workplace can be difficult at times, particularly for pushing past the easy solutions or feeling overwhelmed by the problems facing a work team in the sports industry. Engaging in the creative process as a team is helped substantially by the level of effort individuals put into their actions and behaviors. That orientation toward the tasks of a team also increases feedback and cooperation.[8] While intrinsic motivation increases individual creativity (see Chaps. 12 and 13), having the group oriented toward the task at hand provides a shared focus. For example, if one portion of an National Basketball Association (NBA) sales team is focused on selling as many tickets as they can, but another portion of the team is focused on creating excellent customer experiences (so they can retain customers), these team factions will not cooperate as cohesively on decisions or solutions to problems. Likewise, suppose there are different levels of motivation for coming up with creative or innovative ideas. In that case, some group members will not provide as much feedback or cooperate with teammates as much. Those less motivated will also be more likely to be satisfied with whatever the easiest solution is to a problem, rather than something creative or innovative. It is that shared concern for the goals and vision that helps groups overcome resistance within the group or organization. These four elements of a work environment: participative safety, shared vision, support for innovation, and task orientation are the building blocks of creating an innovative team, but there are other aspects to consider as well.

15.2.6 Diversity and Inclusion

A theme that runs throughout this book and particularly the final unit is that homogeneous organizations and teams are far less efficient at generating new ideas and are much more likely to fall victim to groupthink. If everyone in a group approaches issues from the same perspective, the solutions proposed will fall within a much narrower range than those offered in a more diverse group. Additionally, people with different perspectives or life experiences can also see problems not previously noticed, reframe a problem through a different paradigm, or by bringing in new expertise about potential solutions. Researchers in sport management have looked at this exact issue and found that an increase in diversity does improve the perception of a creative work environment.[9]

As Chap. 3 discussed, diversity alone is not enough. Inclusion is the other part of the paradigm that allows a diverse workforce to function at its true potential.[10] Going back to that concept of participative safety, when people feel like they can bring their perspective, feedback, or idea into a meeting or to a colleague/supervisor, then the whole group is more likely to be innovative. Therefore, inclusion is just as important as diversity when it comes to being an innovative team.

15.2.7 Social Interaction

The research indicates the relationship between innovation and team cohesion is an inverted-U shape. Meaning that too little team cohesion and creativity and innovation is limited, but with too much cohesion, the team suffers the same problem. Work teams with intense cohesion lack creativity because they never go outside their group to learn new things or interact with others. On the other hand, if a work team has no cohesiveness, there will be too much conflict within the group to focus on the work team's goals and how creative ideas can achieve those goals (see Chap. 16).[11] Social interaction remains a useful way to discover new ideas or processes, particularly if the team members are only loosely connected. As a manager, getting the team to spend time learning from, talking to, interacting with people who are not in their work team or immediate group of friends/family is vital to becoming more creative.[12] Opportunities for social interaction beyond one's immediate connections can arise at conferences, job shadowing, working in different geographic locations or industry sectors, non-sport community work, and so on. While there are many sport-specific conferences available to those in the sports industry, team members may also want to branch out and learn from non-sport-industry individuals. At first, the topics or ideas may not seem relevant to the sports industry, but seeking out new avenues of information can improve the skill of juxtaposing ideas. Not comfortable at first, by practicing bringing two disparate ideas together to create something new, employees will become more innovative over time. Not as ideal as social interaction, even reading articles from unique sources can increase the likelihood of new ideas. For example, while *Forbes SportsMoney* can help a practitioner understand the sports industry better, reading something like *Inc.* can help them see potential opportunities beyond what the current sports industry is doing. Therefore, to become a more innovative team, encourage colleagues or employees to seek different perspectives and create balanced team cohesion.

15.2.8 Time

As with social interaction, time allocation for building creativity in a work team is a balance. Sport is fortunate in that there are pretty strict deadlines for a number of reasons, however, one limitation is its restricting effect on creativity. The Olympics or World Cup finals have never been delayed because the organizers weren't ready (note, the 2020 Olympics was delayed however, due to the Covid-19 pandemic). This differs from product or app launches, which more readily see delays due to production issues. Strict adherence to deadlines means employees may rush through the creative process or look for the easiest solution to any problem that presents itself. We can see that examples of this in the sports industries attempt to engage Generation Z. While understanding and engaging Generation Z's sport fandom is incredibly complicated in its relation to technology, youth participation, shifting values, the economy, and social interaction, among other potential intersectional layers, sport marketers have generally been tempted to reach for easier solutions such as adding an esports team or giving away more food at a sporting event. These may or

may not be effective solutions, but they don't address the more complicated generational shifts in consumer taste for sport.

Providing time for practicing engagement in the creative process can help individuals and teams push through easy-to-see solutions to potentially novel solutions. Employees also need time away from work to process everything they've learned. Allowing time for sleep, physical activity, or spending time in nature is critical.[13] In balance to providing that time to engage in the creative process is also creating time constraints. Again, balance is the key to innovation. Time constraints can motivate employees to work harder on a problem or develop new synapses in the brain while practicing divergent thinking. Teams in sport organizations need to balance their time constraints and opportunities, particularly with those who work on a seasonal schedule, such as in professional or youth sports. While during a season or a game, it may not be wise to address complex problems for the organization that aren't urgent. Using off-season wisely can provide the necessary time for coming up with innovative solutions or new products.

15.2.9 Rewards

Another aspect to consider when building an innovative work environment is rewards and punitive measures. Punitive measures are punishments, such as verbal warnings or termination from the position. Rewards can be a wide variety of things, including verbal affirmation, financial bonuses, prizes, extra paid time-off, promotions, or awards. There are differences between rewarding production, outcome, or process. If a team leader wants to reward people for producing things regardless of their quality, they should reward the quantity of production. Think about the creativity stage of innovation, when the focus remains on coming up with new ideas. In that case, rewards should focus on the number of ideas generated, not on successful implementation. In sport, rewarding return customer engagement for ticket sales staff would encourage developing relationships with clients.

Suppose a leader is concerned about the outcome and its success in achieving an organizational or team goal. In that case, they want to reward the quality or effective implementation of an idea. If the concern is regarding the team's engagement in the creative process, then rewarding effort is more important than the outcome. Rewarding only the outcome could deter a team from digging deeper to find more complex yet genuinely innovative solutions. One example in the sports industry indicated that offering a prize for innovation and invention helped develop new products.[14] Reward systems can be complicated and result in a number of unintended consequences. Therefore, make sure to think through what behaviors are actually being encouraged through the reward system rather than what is hoped to be the result.

15.3   Innovation Types

Many different types of innovation can benefit an organization. This section explores product and process innovation in sport.

15.3.1 Innovation as a Product

The invention of T-20 rather than test matches in cricket was an innovative product, first played in 2003. Traditional cricket matches are called test matches, and they are played over a multi-day period. T-20 is a cricket game structured in such a way that the game is played in two to three hours. This allowed for a cricket match to be enjoyed by fans with the inability to watch a multi-day event and to engage the casual fan who may only want to watch a sport for a few hours. Cricket's rise in popularity over the past decade is attributed to this product innovation.[15]

A new product does not always mean an innovative product. Suppose the new product does not help the organization achieve its goals or vision. In that case, it is merely new, not innovative. Think about the prevalence of alternative jerseys in American college football. Home and away jerseys that maintain contrasting colors with the

opposing team made logical sense as a progression of the codification of the sport. However, in the 1990s, thanks to their close relationship with Oregon-based sporting goods company Nike, the University of Oregon created a third jersey style/color. For the University of Oregon, it was an innovative idea that complimented their brand and organizational goals of being first adopters. Oregon football enjoyed a new brand image and which allowed them to attract better players. However, there lacks any evidence that the same practice helps the much smaller Football Championship Subdivision (FCS) (second-tier of Division I football) programs, yet a large number of college football programs utilize the practice. Later in this chapter, we'll discuss how the tendency to copy and paste the other organizations in a given industry is different from adopting innovative ideas. There are many different types of innovative products in the sports industry, not just new games or extra jerseys. Innovations can range from new products for the game itself, fan experience, participant experience, technology, or facilities. Innovation can also be found in the processes and systems of an organization.

15.3.2 Innovation as a Process

Products are easy to identify. Signboards, luxury box suites, on-field analytic assessments, mobile tickets, or replica jerseys are all innovative products that we've seen in the sports industry. Innovation can also come as a process in the organization. For example, customer service processes can change to improve the team flow, such as who takes the calls or how the customer service team processes those requests. Interestingly, in the sports industry, new sectors that are growing rapidly, such as cycling and snowboarding, tend to implement more product innovations, whereas more established and declining sectors, such as yachting and skiing, tend to focus on process innovations.[16] There may be more hesitation in implementing product innovations when an established sport organization has a great deal of nostalgia and institutional knowledge built up around the product itself. When looking at process innovations in a team, try to visualize all the different processes put into place for that team or within the organization. Sometimes, employees find that some processes were created for a specific purpose that is now no longer needed, yet remains a part of the organization. Analyzing systems and processes can provide an opportunity for replacing semi-functional processes with innovative ones.

15.4 Innovation in Organizations

Building a creative and innovative team is the first step toward becoming a more innovative organization; however, not the last step. As theorized by Damanpour and Schneider, the process of innovation within an organization involves three stages at multiple levels.[17] These three phases are the idea initiation, idea adoption decision, and idea implementation phases. After the idea is presented to the organization, the organization must decide if they want to adopt the idea. After the team or organization has adopted the idea, then the implementation of the idea begins.

Each of these phases is important, and they are also all affected by multiple levels: individual, group, organizational, and environmental levels. Individuals play a role in this process for an organization by bringing in new ideas, creating a creative work environment, allocating resources, and encouraging those resistant to innovation adoption and implementation. This can come at the team level or the organizational level, depending on the idea. It is not unusual to have a very innovative team within a traditional organization. However, that situation could limit the extent to which innovative ideas are adopted or implemented by the whole organization. In sport, the external environment also has a profound effect. For some sport organizations, this is due to the role sport plays in society, and for others, it is due to their league structure. For example, the NFL office was the instigating force for NFL teams to adopt a mobile app technology that would increase fan connectivity.[18] That external force was very influential in the adoption decision-making process for NFL franchises.

15.4.1 Creativity as the Beginning Steps

Innovation encompasses creativity but also includes the implementation of any creative idea. Creative ideas are defined as both new and useful to the organization. These creative ideas then need to be considered by the organization and implemented effectively. Creative ideas aren't much use to an organization without the successful adoption decision and effective implementation, but often overlooked is the other opposite problem. When organizations don't start with creative ideas and simply look to adopt new ideas to embrace new ideas, they can run into issues of mimetic isomorphism. A simplified way to think about this concept is that organizations will copy and paste each other's ideas more and more as time goes on so that soon every organization in a particular sector looks very similar.

Think about the adoption of electronic signboards in venues. For many sport organizations, this could provide exponential commercial value; however, they also come at a significant cost, so they are only useful if implemented effectively. Adopting to keep up with others in the same sector can be dangerous for sport organizations. For example, hundreds of college athletic programs, seeking the riches of athletic programs like the University of Texas, have adopted many ideas that have only left these smaller programs entirely reliant on student fees to prop up their athletic budget. This behavior is so common among athletic departments that it is widely known as the "arms race" by industry practitioners and academics. Therefore, engaging in the creative process to come up with context-specific creative ideas for a sport organization can be a much more effective use of resources. This ensures an idea adoption decision is built on a new and useful idea.

▷ **Innovation Champion** An innovation champion is someone who doggedly pursues the successful adoption and implementation of a particular innovation, whether it be a process or product innovation.

15.4.2 Innovation Champion

Something much of the sport management literature has found to be key for innovation in a sport organization is an innovation champion.[19] An innovation champion is someone who doggedly pursues the successful adoption and implementation of a particular innovation, whether it be a process or product innovation. Innovation champions can be incredibly helpful in the innovation process for an organization in several ways. First, this person is someone who clearly believes in the innovation. If you have read *Moneyball*, Billy Beane is not the innovator. He was desperate to try anything to improve his team's prospects despite the Oakland Athletics' smaller budget. When he learned of the concept of sabermetrics, he jumped at the option to solve his major issue. It was Assistant General Manager, Paul DePodesta's ideas that Beane was championing.[20]

The innovation champion is motivated to push through any obstacles. Innovation adoption and implementation can be challenging, and even the best ideas can get lost in bureaucratic red tape, resistant colleagues, and lack of resources.[21] Championing an innovation through the entire process can involve a lot of time and effort. Thus, a motivated innovation champion provides those essential resources. The innovation champion doesn't always have to be in a position of power, such as the General Manager, although that can make it easier for organizational buy-in. However, a strong sales pitch, a clear understanding of who has decision-making power, and how an innovation can benefit the organization can allow anyone in an organization to become a successful innovation champion.

15.5   Summary

Whether in sales, coaching, communications, operations, or another aspect of the sports industry, building a creative and innovative work team is possible. Remember, an innovative work environment's key elements include participative safety, clear vision, support for innovation, and task orientation. Other factors to think about include time, rewards, innovation champions, diversity and inclusion, and social interactions. Finally, keep in mind that innovation can be a part of a group or team as a tangible product and a new or improved process. Innovation and creativity will only increase in importance for the sports industry as generational tastes shift, technology changes more rapidly, and competition within the sports industry increases.

Discussion Questions

1. Identify an innovation from the sports industry. Why do you think it was innovative? How did it bring a competitive advantage to the organization?
2. Discuss what makes you feel safe to participate. How do you feel supported by others in your new ideas?
3. Find one new source of information that is unrelated to the sports industry. Read an article or listen to a podcast episode and write down two to three things you think relate back to or would be useful in the sports industry.

Notes

1. Taggar, S. (2002). Individual creativity and group ability to utilize individual creative resources: A multilevel model. *Academy of management Journal, 45*(2), 315–330.
2. Cirella, S., & Shani, A. B. (2012). Collective Creativity by Design: Learning from an Italian Fashion Design Company. *Irish Journal of Management, 32*(1).
3. Carnevale, J. B., Huang, L., Crede, M., Harms, P., & Uhl-Bien, M. (2017). Leading to stimulate employees' ideas: A quantitative review of leader–member exchange, employee voice, creativity, and innovative behavior. *Applied Psychology, 66*(4), 517–552.
4. Zhao, H., Kessel, M., & Kratzer, J. (2014). Supervisor-subordinate relationship, differentiation, and employee creativity: A self-categorization perspective. *The Journal of Creative Behavior, 48*(3), 165–184.
5. Anderson, N. R., & West, M. A. (1998). Measuring climate for work group innovation: development and validation of the team climate inventory. Journal of Organizational Behavior: *The International Journal*

of Industrial, Occupational and Organizational Psychology and Behavior, 19(3), 235–258.

6. Clegg, C., Unsworth, K., Epitropaki, O., & Parker, G. (2002). Implicating trust in the innovation process. *Journal of Occupational and Organizational Psychology, 75*(4), 409–422.

7. Winand, M., Vos, S., Zintz, T., & Scheerder, J. (2013). Determinants of service innovation: A typology of sports federations. *International Journal of Sport Management and Marketing, 13*(1–2), 55–73.

8. Somech, A., & Drach-Zahavy, A. (2013). Translating team creativity to innovation implementation: The role of team composition and climate for innovation. *Journal of Management, 39*(3), 684–708.

9. Cunningham, G. B., & Melton, E. N. (2011). The benefits of sexual orientation diversity in sport organizations. *Journal of Homosexuality, 58*(5), 647–663.

10. Perry-Smith, J. E. (2006). Social yet creative: The role of social relationships in facilitating individual creativity. *Academy of Management Journal, 49*(1), 85–101.

11. King, N., and Anderson, N. (1990). Innovation in Working Groups. In M. A. West and J. L. Farr (eds.), *Innovation and Creativity at Work*. New York: Wiley.

12. Perry-Smith, J. E. (2006). Social yet creative: The role of social relationships in facilitating individual creativity. *Academy of Management Journal, 49*(1), 85–101.

13. Stickgold, R., & Walker, M. (2004). To sleep, perchance to gain creative insight?. *Trends in Cognitive Sciences, 8*(5), 191–192.

14. Yuan, B., Liu, C., KAO, K., & HSU, Y. (2009). Entrepreneurship and innovation process in the health industry in Taiwan. *European Business Review,21*(5): 453–471.

15. The Economist (2016, Mar). The Economist Explains: Why Twenty20 cricket is so successful. *The Economist*. Retrieved from https://www.economist.com/the-economist-explains/2016/03/13/why-twenty20-cricket-is-so-successful.

16. Desbordes, M. (2002). Empirical analysis of the innovation phenomena in the sports equipment industry. *Technology Analysis & Strategic Management, 14*(4), 481–498.

17. Damanpour, F., & Schneider, M. (2006). Phases of the adoption of innovation in organizations: effects of environment, organization and top managers. *British journal of Management, 17*(3), 215–236.

18. Greenhalgh, G., Dwyer, B., & Biggio, B. (2014). There's an App for That: The Development of an NFL Team Mobile Application. *Journal of Applied Sport Management, 6*(4), 51–73.

19. Hoeber, L., & Hoeber, O. (2012). Determinants of an innovation process: A case study of technological innovation in a community sport organization. *Journal of Sport Management, 26*(3), 213–223.

20. Lewis, M. (2003). *Moneyball: The Art of Winning an Unfair Game*. W.W. Norton & Company.

21. Flanders, S., Smith, N., Jones, C., & Greene, A. (2020). Examining the Innovation Process of a Graduate Apprenticeship Program for Sport Organizations. *Sports Innovation Journal, 1*, 106–119.

▶ **Learning Objectives** After reading this chapter, students should be able to:

- Differentiate between forms of functional and dysfunctional conflict.
- Identify strategies to manage conflict.
- Identify strategies to manage negotiation.

Rahman Anjorin: Player Manager, National Football League Players' Association; Founder and Lead Consultant, Deed Firm
To listen to the interview <click here>

Rugby in the United States The sport of rugby is well established throughout the world, with countries having developed hierarchies that include youth development,

_____

Supplementary Information The online version of this chapter (https://doi.org/10.1007/978-3-030-67612-4_16) contains supplementary material, which is available to authorized users.

club, national, and professional systems. In the United States, there is strong evidence that the sport has significant growth potential.[1] The United States has a growing club system and emerging opportunities for high-school and collegiate athletes. However, without a youth system to teach children about the game and develop talent, the scholastic and club systems are starved for qualified players. At the same time, the United States National Team (USA Rugby) and professional systems are foundering. USA Rugby filed for bankruptcy in 2020, and several professional leagues have been created and folded over the last decade.[2] This has left one executive to suggest that the US rugby pyramid resembles a Christmas tree without a base or top.[3]

Conflict among stakeholders is commonly cited as the main reason for rugby's failures in the United States. The leadership of the four different prospective professional leagues (Major League Rugby, PRO Rugby, Super 7's, and Guinness 14) have different perspectives on how to create a professional rugby league. In a country with an abundance of rugby players and fans, this would not be a problem. There may not be enough talent or fans in the

United States to support one professional league fully. It could be proposed that the league leaders pool their ideas to find innovative solutions to their problems. Instead, conflict between the leaders likely ensures that none of the leagues will be successful. Further adding to the conflict, many premier amateur rugby clubs have decried the possibilities of professional rugby because they will lose access to top-level talent.[4]

16.1   The Nature of Conflict

Conflict and the failure to manage it can tear apart sport organizations. Managers often squash disagreements between employees out of fear that conflict will pull employees' focus away from organizational goals. Yet, most organizational behaviorists argue that conflict is also necessary for organizational success.[5] Conflict occurs when one party perceives that their ideas or interests are being opposed or negatively affected by another party.[6] This chapter will discuss how conflict can be managed and harnessed to positively impact creativity and innovation, leading to positive organizational outcomes. We will begin by discussing the nature of conflict before distinguishing the benefits and consequences of different conflict types.

▶ **Conflict** When one party perceives that their ideas or interests are being opposed or negatively affected by another party.

▶ **Traditional View of Conflict** All conflict is detrimental because it pulls energy away from the organizational mission.

As mentioned in the previous paragraph, many organizations attempt to avoid conflict. In fact, until relatively recently, avoiding all types of conflict was seen as good practice.[7] The traditional view of conflict teaches that any type of conflict within an organization is bad. It pulls

energy away from accomplishing the organizational mission, damages cohesiveness among employees, and signals to outsiders that the organization is dysfunctional.[8] Indeed, we can all probably think of a time when a disagreement between friends or peers spiraled out of control.

Under the traditional view, managers who allowed conflict to flourish are seen as ineffective. The prevailing notion was that conflict was caused by poor communication and out of control politics within a vacuum caused by ineffective leadership. The case study highlighted what can happen when leadership is lacking. Instead of stepping in and coordinating efforts between stakeholders, USA Rugby allowed disagreements and power grabs to become the norm. All of this despite the fact that the stakeholders essentially shared common goals. Yet, would eliminating conflict and forcing compromise to be the answer to the unique challenges facing rugby in the United States? Can you think of a time when an organization that you belonged to settled on an unsatisfactory outcome in an effort to prevent hurting the feelings of members? How did that make you feel?

▶ **Human Relations View of Conflict** Conflict is human nature and, therefore, unavoidable.

A second view of conflict that became popular in the mid-twentieth century was the human relations view of conflict, also known as the optimal conflict perspective. The human relations view acknowledged that conflict was human nature and, therefore, unavoidable. Instead of avoiding conflict, the human relations view argued that managers should try to harness conflict but keep it at a moderate level. When conflict is too low, organizations stagnate through underproductive agreement. When conflict is too high, organizations underperform because of constant disagreement. However, at optimal levels, conflict spurs constructive discussion leading to improved alternatives being put forth from the collective. At optimal levels, conflict actually improves cohesion as everyone feels valued and is motivated through the team effort.[9]

▷ **Interactionist View of Conflict** Conflict should be encouraged when it can remain respectful, peaceful, and cooperative.

▷ **Functional Conflict** Conflict that is beneficial to organizational outcomes.

▷ **Dysfunctional Conflict** Conflict that pulls energy away from organizational objectives.

Modern organizational behaviorists have moved on from the human relations view to the interactionist view of conflict, which states that conflict is not inevitable, but it should be encouraged when it can remain respectful, peaceful, and cooperative. The interactionist view argues that organizations need functional conflict to spur change, creativity, and innovation, as well as to avoid stagnation and apathy among employees.[10] Thus, organizations should actively encourage functional forms of conflict. On the other hand, organizations need to eliminate dysfunctional forms of conflict which hinder performance through non-productive disagreement. To that end, scholars have explored four distinct types of conflict that arise in organizations.

▷ **Task Conflict** Perceptions of disagreements among group members about the content of their work decisions.

16.1.1 Task Conflict

Task conflict is defined as perceptions of disagreements among group members about the content of their work decisions.[11] Many youth sports associations with the mission to grow their game locally face challenges with task conflict. For example, imagine a youth lacrosse league in your hometown. Is it best to push resources to increase recreational participation, thus exposing more people to the game? Or, is it best to push resources toward elite club teams whose success could attract newcomers to the game? Both strategies hold potential for success, but most youth sports associations have limited resources to allocate and therefore cannot do both. Thus, task

conflict could arise between members who feel passionately about one of the strategies. Organizational members agree on the mission but disagree on the goals that will lead to mission attainment.

Moderate levels of task conflict are very beneficial for sport organizations. When organizational members engage in productive dialogue dissecting competing views of how to achieve organizational objectives, creative solutions are more likely to be found (see Chaps. 13 and 15). Moderate task conflict is correlated with better organizational decision-making and performance.[12] However, low and high levels of task conflict can have negative impacts.[13] Low task conflict is a possible sign that workers are not being challenged or are apathetic toward the organization's objectives. Low task conflict is also associated with decision-making problems such as groupthink and crises of agreement. At the other end of the spectrum, high task conflict pulls effort from organizational objectives and focuses on the conflict itself. The various parties involved in the conflict refuse to acknowledge any weaknesses in their ideas or strengths in alternative ideas presented; thus, the decision-making process is paralyzed.

Process Conflict

16.1.2 Process Conflict

Process conflict regards how the work is to be completed.[14] In other words, what process should the team or organization use to accomplish its task? Low levels of task conflict can be productive for an organization.[15] For example, students running a scholarship golf tournament may discuss what jobs need to be completed and which roles each member will have. During the discussion, process conflict would be exemplified by students debating each other's role qualifications and providing advice on how to complete certain jobs. This innocent level of debate can ensure team members are placed in optimal roles. Suppose process conflict arises to moderate or high levels. In that case, organizational production will slow significantly as team members fight over who should complete each job and bicker over how others complete their tasks.

▶ **Relationship Conflict** A dysfunctional form of conflict where organizational members' disagreements are based on personal differences.

16.1.3 Relationship Conflict

Relationship conflict is a dysfunctional form of conflict where organizational members' disagreements are based on personal differences.[16] Employees fight not to improve organizational outcomes, but because of their own goals, values, or personalities. Relationship conflict is harmful at any level because it immediately pulls employees away from organizational tasks.[17] Imagine being in a meeting where instead of ideas being critiqued on merit, idea presenters were insulted by meeting attendees?

16.1.4 Intercultural Conflict

With organizations slowly embracing the importance of diversity, more scholars are exploring the impact of intercultural conflict. Intercultural conflict occurs when employees share different perspectives based on their own cultural backgrounds. Intercultural conflict can be task- or relationship-based. Task-based intercultural conflict can improve organizational decision-making and creativity as members bring different perspectives based on their cultural experiences.[18] For example, an NBA team trying to increase fandom within the local Latinx community could benefit greatly from cultural knowledge shared by Latinx employees. However, for task-based intercultural conflict to be productive, organizational members must be respectful and genuinely interested in learning about cultural differences among employees. Relationship-based intercultural conflict is immensely destructive and should never be tolerated within an organization.[19]

16.2   What Creates Conflict?

Understanding that certain types of conflict can be productive at optimal levels, managers need to be keenly aware of factors that encourage both functional and dysfunctional conflict. By understanding the structural and contextual factors that influence conflict, organizations can eliminate potential relationship conflict and monitor factors that encourage functional forms of conflict.

16.2.1 Structural Factors

Structural factors are those that relate to the organization itself, such as task interdependence or resource allocation.[20] Structural factors can be directly monitored and altered to discourage dysfunctional conflict while encouraging functional conflict types.

16.2.1.1   Specialization and Differentiation

For larger organizations or those with diverse functions and offerings, specialization of departments and employee functions are necessary to maintain operational efficiency. The result is organizational units and employees that are differentiated from one another. For example, Adidas is a multinational company that produces equipment and apparel for a wide variety of sports, including soccer, cricket, gymnastics, basketball, and tennis, to name just a few. Thus, it is quite understandable, if not likely, that employees focused on creating high-performance apparel for the Indian Premier League would have different perspectives than employees marketing lacrosse apparel in the United States.

Specialization and differentiation are common in many segments of the sports industry. In the NCAA, most athletic departments have separate departments dedicated to the organization's academic and commercial functions. Many professional soccer clubs have both men's and women's teams and developmental and club teams with employees dedicated to each. Sport organizations can tap into specialized employees' diverse perspectives to generate task conflict toward complex organizational issues. However, for smaller organizations, differentiating and specialization may not be possible. Minor League Baseball franchises lack the necessary resources to hire specialists. Thus, many employees take on generalist roles, contributing to multiple organizational functions. This lack of specialization limits their ability to generate task conflict based on differentiation of employees for smaller organizations.

16.2.1.2   Interdependence

Interdependence relates to the degree to which various employees or departments must depend on one another for success. High degrees of interdependence increase opportunities for every type of conflict. Priority point systems used by college athletic departments to reward their most loyal donors create a scenario where ticket offices and fundraising offices are highly interdependent. Ticket offices must deliver ticket buying opportunities to customers that are commensurate with donation levels. At the same time, fundraisers are dependent on the ticket office for both leads and operational support of their fundraising efforts. Task conflict can arise when the two offices work together to overcome challenges. However, if either office feels the other is dictating how work is to be done, process conflict can arise. Worse, disagreements can easily lead to relationship conflict if exchanges become personal.

16.2.1.3   Resource Allocation

As has been discussed throughout the textbook, the nature of the sports industry means that most organizations operate with minimal resources. Allocation of resources can become contentious. When one segment of an organization receives what it perceives to be less than its share of resources compared to others, it can signal to employees within the affected department that they are less important than others within the organization. Managers can use resource allocation activities, such as budget development, as an opportunity to generate task conflict by allowing affected departments and employees to voice opinions and provide input. To keep conflict at optimal levels, managers need to open clear communication channels and provide transparency in the process.

16.2.1.4   Communication Channels

Open communication channels, clear messaging, and broad access to information provide opportunities for critical debate of ideas. In smaller organizations, or in organizations with flatter bureaucratic structures, direct communication opportunities are more plentiful than in larger, more vertical organizations. Modern communication techniques have opened up more channels than once existed, but organizations should work to open up channels to individuals or departments in conflict. If open channels are not available or information is not transparent, misunderstandings between parties are more likely. As Chap. 5 discusses, messages are dependent on perception. Therefore, any communication methods that increase opportunities for misunderstandings, such as the use of third parties, can also increase dysfunctional conflict. Poor communication can also increase dysfunctional conflict. The Pac 12 and Big Ten Conferences both canceled their 2020 football seasons over concerns related to Covid-19. The Big Ten received substantial criticism from stakeholders, while the Pac 12 was subject to very little criticism despite similar reasons given by leaders of both conferences. However, the Pac 12 was widely praised for being transparent and clear in its communication. On the other hand, the Big Ten Conference struggled to communicate with stakeholders to second-guess its decision.[21] See Chap. 5 for further discussion of the communication process.

16.2.1.5   Workspace Configuration

Related to communication, workspace configuration can influence conflict by increasing or decreasing opportunities for interaction. The physical proximity of workspaces affects opportunities for informal interaction. More interaction can increase collaboration and functional conflict as employees share ideas and work through misunderstandings. Thus, organizations often try to place offices of employees who need to interact frequently nearer to each other. In some instances, organizations have moved to open workspace concepts. Open workspaces are literally open in that walls are removed, and employees share an open area instead of working in offices.

Interestingly, open workspaces have been shown to inhibit interaction and increase relationship conflict.[22] Without a special boundary, personal issues are magnified and can become the focus of a relationship.

Communication quality also suffers when parties are separated physically. Simple issues, like having offices on different floors or in different buildings, limits face-to-face communication and increase the uses of less clear methods, such as texts or messenger applications. If time-zones separate collaborators, communication is more likely to be conducted asynchronously. Thus, time delays, such as via email. Misunderstandings that can be cleared up within minutes when workspaces are near can take hours to be addressed when workspaces are separated by time-zone differences.

16.2.1.6   Decision-Making Hierarchy

Decision-making hierarchies created by organizational structures alter power dynamics. Task conflict can be inhibited when lower-tiered employees feel that those in power will not be receptive to their ideas or criticisms of ideas generated by others. At the same time, task conflict can be increased when employees feel like those in charge are micromanaging their work processes. Organizations can encourage functional conflict types by decentralizing decision-making authority. Although power dynamics will still exist, a decentralized process allows for greater input authority from employees lower on organizational charts.

16.2.1.7   Policies

Finally, organizational policies can influence perceptions of organizational values. If policies signal to an employee that their idea is likely to be received positively, the idea is more likely to be shared. Similarly, employees may hold back ideas that they feel will go against organizational standards. Although there can be substantial benefits from having clear policies, those policies should not inhibit meaningful discussion and criticism of the organization. In particular, policies can interfere with the benefits of intercultural conflict.

16.2.2   Addressing Structural Factors

Managing conflict requires vigilance and emotional intelligence by management. Not only do managers need to be aware of conflict levels, they also need to understand how conflict is affecting the emotions and behaviors of those involved. If a manager senses that conflict is becoming dysfunctional, several strategies can be employed to limit the influence of structural factors.[23]

- **Emphasize organizational goals:** Conflict is much more likely to be functional when the focus is on accomplishing a task. Thus, managers should redirect any negative conflict by refocusing the parties on the task at hand.[24]
- **Improve communication:** There is substantial evidence that employees are less likely to engage in dysfunctional conflict when they feel the organization is being transparent and that their concerns are being acknowledged. Therefore, improving communication between parties is one of the most important functional conflict drivers and one of the best inhibitors of dysfunctional conflict.
- **Reduce differentiation:** Differentiation and specialization are often necessary. Yet, in circumstances where the organization has become too compartmentalized, differentiation and specialization can make an organization less efficient while creating unnecessary conflict.
- **Reduce interdependence:** Similarly, as organizations evolve, departments that were once highly dependent may become less dependent. When this occurs, the organization should address processes and policies that create unnatural dependencies.
- **Resource allocation:** Resources are scarce. It is not always possible to increase resources. However, struggles for resources are a primary factor in conflict escalation. Transparency regarding resource allocation has been shown to limit dysfunctional conflict.

16.2.3   Contextual Factors

Contextual factors are those related to the individuals involved in conflict or to the situation in which the conflict occurs.[25] Contextual factors are mainly out of an organization's control but can significantly influence conflict levels.

16.2.3.1   Individual Expectations

Employees often have differing career expectations. Career-driven individuals can be highly motivated toward task success, leading to optimal task conflict if they are paired with similarly motivated individuals. However, expectations can also lead to dysfunctional conflict. Suppose an individual with high expectations allows their personal motivations to interfere with organizational or team goals. In that case, it can create resentment from others. This is especially true if one person tries to take credit for collaboratory success. At the other end of the spectrum, employees with low expectations may not engage, creating low task conflict levels.

16.2.3.2   Competition

Although conflict is necessary to drive ideas forward, ideas must be resolved to evolve into plans and actions. In functional conflict, the parties exchange ideas all involved are willing to move toward the best solution regardless of whose ideas win out. When winning the competition of ideas becomes the goal of one or more of the involved parties, conflict cannot be resolved optimally. Instead, parties become steadfast in their position leading to more conflict.[26] Examples of toxic idea competition can be seen throughout the sports industry. Work stoppages are prime examples. MLB has not had a work stoppage since a players' strike disrupted the 1994 and 1995 seasons. During that strike, the players' association and the owners became so focused on winning the conflict that neither side was willing to acknowledge the other's issues, leading to the prolonged work stoppage. Analysis by sports economists found that both parties would have been better off had the players and owners found solutions to their disagreements before the strike.[27] In fact, both sides have acknowledged the 1994–1995 strike as the primary reason that MLB has not had a work stoppage since.

16.2.3.3   Perceptions

As discussed in Chap. 10, perceptions are an individual's cognition of reality. Perceptions can significantly impact conflict in two ways. First, perceptions influence how we receive and process information. When one party perceives a message from another party differently from the intended message, it can create unintended conflict. For example, imagine what would happen if you told an employee that they were doing a great job, but they mistook your tone as sarcastic.

The second way that perceptions affect conflict comes from the opinions that we hold of others. If we perceive someone to be trustworthy, we are more likely to believe them than someone we perceived to be dishonest. If we perceive someone to be highly competent, we will give more weight to their ideas than the ideas of someone we believe to be less capable. If we perceive a person to be likable, we are more likely to seek agreement on conflict than we would if we disliked them.

16.2.3.4   Personality and Values

Personality can influence whether a person is more willing to engage in conflict. In particular, people with more aggressive and competitive personality types are more likely to seek out and engage in conflict. Similarly, some people and cultures value conflict more than others.[28]

16.2.3.5   History

As noted in Chap. 10, past experience provides a framework against which current experiences can be interpreted. While we may not know what the future holds, we better understand our past and what the outcomes were in similar situations. Our history can affect conflict in two unique ways. First, history as it relates to outcomes from similar situations. Individuals who are experienced working with functional conflict will be more comfortable and ready to engage as appropriate. Individuals who have not experienced conflict or experienced dysfunctional conflict often try to avoid conflict when it arises.[29]

The second way that history can influence conflict relates to past interactions with the people involved. People who have a history of engaging in functional conflict to create productive outcomes feel comfortable repeating the process. However, people who have had negative experiences working together are more likely to avoid conflict altogether or engage in relationship conflict depending on past experiences.[30]

16.2.4 Addressing Contextual Factors

Contextual factors can be more challenging to manage. Although it is tempting to want to eliminate all forms of conflict caused by contextual factors, that would be a mistake as the conflict can be functional. In this section, we will discuss managerial strategies for encouraging functional contextual-based conflict, as well as strategies to mitigate dysfunctional conflict caused by contextual factors. To begin, we will identify possible outcomes of contextual-based conflict.

16.2.4.1 Potential Outcomes of Contextual-Based Conflict

Conflict must always reach some sort of resolution. When individuals or groups engage in conflict, there are four types of outcomes that can occur. Please note that versions of the model outlined below date to the 1960s and have been adapted many times over the years.[31] Some scholars argue that the win-win, win-lose outcomes described below have been overused and oversimplified in the 60 years since their introduction.[32] We present these tactics as general guidelines. As a manager, you must be aware that strategies vary from one situation to the next.

- **Lose-Lose:** A lose-lose outcome occurs when none of the involved parties gains what they initially desired. Lose-lose outcomes are common when parties dig in, and winning the conflict takes priority over achieving a mutual goal. The Philadelphia Phillies and their 1997 first-round draft selection, J.D. Drew engaged in a famous lose-lose conflict following his

selection. Before the draft, Drew made it clear that he did not want to play for the Phillies and that he would sign for no less than $10 million. The Phillies had no intention to pay Drew that amount and drafted him despite his declaration that he would not sign. True to his word, Drew did not sign but with no recourse to play for another team due to MLB rules, he signed to play in the independent Northern League for far less than the Phillies had offered. In the end, the Phillies wasted a high-level draft pick on a player who did not want to sign with the organization, and Drew wasted a year of his career playing in a low-level minor league. When he eventually signed with an MLB club, it was for far less than $10 million.[33]

- **Win-Lose:** Win-lose outcomes occur when one party gains their desired outcome at the expense of the other party. Win-lose outcomes are common when there is a significant power disparity between the conflicting parties. Several recent examples of win-lose outcomes are available in sport. In 2020, MLB refused to extend its existing partnership with Minor League Baseball, unless all of its demands were met. Minor League Baseball, which operates with subsidies from MLB, had no choice but to relent to remain in business. As a result of the one-sided negotiations, more than 40 Minor League clubs lost their affiliations.[34] Another example comes from a dispute between US Soccer and the US Women's National Soccer Team (USWNT). US Soccer's refusal to negotiate with the USWNT fairly resulted in a lawsuit and substantial bad press for the organization.[35] This ongoing dispute has a chance to become a lose-lose if the USWNT loses the lawsuit.

- **Win-Win:** Win-win outcomes occur when both parties receive the benefits initially sought in the conflict. For Omni Hotels, which was looking to generate unique customer experiences, partnerships with the Atlanta Braves and Dallas Cowboys are viewed as a win-win for all parties. For Omni, the partnerships allowed the hotel chain to offer one of a kind experience by providing resort-type experiences within a major sports facility's confines. Omni can also build loyalty among team fans by being the official hotel for two high-profile North American sport franchises. For the Cowboys and Braves, the partnership provided anchors for major for live, work, play real estate projects, as well as guaranteed revenues from the evenly split partnerships.[36] Win-win outcomes are often very good for the organization as long as the parties involved pursue organizational objectives.

- **Compromise:** A compromise outcome where both parties give up something desired but also gain something in the exchange. Compromise is thought by some to be a path to less desirable outcomes like crises of agreement or low levels of engagement from the involved parties. This can most certainly be true. Following several high-profile incidents of domestic abuse perpetrated by players and fans, many leagues around the world formed working groups to address the issue. Unfortunately, the focus of most of the working groups was to mitigate the impact of negative publicity, not instigating real change. Thus, most of these committees arrived at compromises that failed to address the actual causes of domestic violence in sport.

- That does not mean that all compromise results in less desirable outcomes. Often, compromise results from shedding inferior initial ideas in exchange for better ideas generated by the group. Many successful sponsorship activations have been the result of compromises. For example, the Winston Cup, the title of NASCAR's top level of competition from 1971 through 2003, resulted from a compromise between tobacco producer R.J. Reynolds and NASCAR driver Junior Johnson. Negotiations initially began over sponsoring Junior Johnson's race team but evolved into a series-wide sponsorship that benefitted the sport and company far beyond what a single car sponsorship could have.[37] Most conflicts result in compromise outcomes.

16.2.5 Managerial Responses to Contextual-Based Conflict

When addressing contextual-based conflict, the manager needs to first identify which type of outcome is desired by the organization as well as which outcome the parties are heading toward. Using this knowledge, managers can adapt their approach to maintaining functional conflict. Common approaches listed next are consistent with Dual Concern Theory[38] and have been supported via robust academic study.[39]

16.2.5.1   Problem-Solving
When a win-win outcome is possible, a problem-solving approach can remove barriers to success. Problem-solving involves removing barriers, facilitating information exchanges, providing resources, and encouraging the involved parties to seek an innovative or optimal solution to the issues faced. A problem-solving approach may also be needed when a group with win-win potential is seeking a less desirable compromise outcome.

16.2.5.2   Conflict Avoidance
When the conflicting parties are heading toward a lose-lose outcome, a conflict avoidance strategy can be adopted. In conflict avoidance, the manager eliminates the conflict by removing the parties involved from the situation. For example, removing individual members or even disbanding teams that have become too dysfunctional to be successful. A conflict avoidance strategy is often needed once conflict has become relationship-based and cannot be redirected back to a task-based focus. Thus, continuing the conflict is going to be counterproductive to the organization. It is important to note that a conflict avoidance strategy does not mean ignoring conflict or simply hoping it will go away. Dysfunctional conflicts rarely disappear without further mitigation. Instead, conflict avoidance within this context, refers to the removal of the dysfunctional parties so that the remaining group or a new group can focus on the task while the dysfunctional parties work to mitigate their conflict separately.

16.2.5.3　Forcing

A forcing approach should be taken when the conflict is heading toward a win-lose outcome, where stakes are high, time is of the essence, and the organization has a vested interest in one party's ideas winning out. For example, many sport organizations with Native American imagery are reconsidering logos that are racist or offensive. In a work team with charges to rebrand the organization and remove offensive imagery, it is not in the organization's interest to retain or seek a compromise that maintains racist images. A forcing approach would be necessary if conflict arose over an effort to retain offensive imagery instead of seeking to remove it. Managers should only use forcing approaches when essential, as it is likely to damage the organization's relationship with the losers in the conflict.

16.2.5.4　Yielding

Yielding is another approach that can be considered during a win-lose conflict. In a yielding approach, a manager encourages the conflicting parties to adopt the solution that has the most support among the group. A yielding approach can be adapted when the stakes are low and the organization is indifferent about the task's outcome. A yielding approach may also be necessary when the organization is in conflict with a more powerful organization. For example, Minor League Baseball adopted a yielding approach with MLB in an effort to survive the conflict and hopefully find favor in future conflicts.

16.2.5.5　Compromising

In an instance where a compromise outcome is the focus of the conflicting parties but also beneficial to the group, managers can adopt a compromising approach. In this scenario, the manager would look for ways to facilitate compromise. A compromising approach may also be necessary for a scenario where the parties are heading toward a win-lose outcome, but a compromise is best for the organization. The adoption of a compromising approach often requires managers to serve as an arbitrator to facilitate negotiation between parties.

▶ **Negotiation** When two or more interdependent parties work to resolve conflicting goals.

▶ **Arbitrator** A person that serves as a facilitator in the negotiation process.

16.3　Negotiation

Negotiation transpires when two or more interdependent parties work to resolve conflicting goals.[40] An arbitrator serves as a facilitator in the negotiation process. Managers often serve as arbitrators but may also serve as a negotiator when their workgroup or team is in conflict with another organizational unit or when representing the organization against other stakeholders.

In a negotiation, each party is faced with a continuum of potential outcomes that range from most desirable to least desirable. Illustrated in Fig. 16.1,[41] each party in the negotiation begins with a target point. The target point represents the point in the negotiation where a party receives all of its desires. The resistance point represents the worst acceptable outcome of the negotiation. As you can see in the figure, most of what each party wants is past the other party's resistance point. However, there is a range where the continuums of both parties overlap. This is the potential settlement range. The potential settlement range is where both parties can gain enough to be satisfied with the negotiation outcome. As an arbitrator, your goal is to focus both parties on this area.[42]

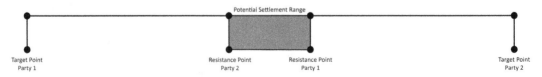

Fig. 16.1 Negotiation range

16.3.1 Managing the Negotiation

Helping parties in conflict find mutual ground requires preparation from managers. Imagine being in conflict with a group member, and your professor tells you to just work it out. If you could work it out, you wouldn't be seeking counsel. To take on an arbitrator role, managers must first gather information about the conflict. Critical information includes learning about the nature of the conflict, understanding the conflicting parties' personalities and histories, and learning about the organizational needs for the outcome. Gathering this and other critical information will allow a manager to form a strategy for handling the negotiation.[43]

Next, the manager needs to create ground rules for the negotiation. Establish who will represent the parties in the negotiation. If the conflict is between work teams and organizational units, gathering whole teams will bog down the negotiation. Instead, allow each party to identify who will represent their interests. Provide the parties time to meet with their teams and develop their cases but establish the focus of the negotiation. Negotiating complex conflicts with many issues is difficult. By limiting the focus of negotiations, you can redirect the parties to solve one problem at a time.[44]

We then want to facilitate the sharing of information between the parties. Facilitation can begin by allowing each party to state their initial positions, which will likely be at their target points. As an arbiter, you can help the process by identifying initial areas of common ground. You can also allow parties to question each other and seek clarification and find out why the other party wants what they are asking for. Throughout, it is imperative that questioning remains information-seeking and not confrontational. The arbiter can help by redirecting back to the common goal and easing each party toward the settlement range. When problems arise, your role will be to problem-solve, helping the parties work past hurdles that are in the way of a deal.[45]

At the conclusion of the negotiation, managers have one more duty to formalize the agreement. Negotiations can be stressful. Reaching an agreement can be a moment of relief, but also a moment of euphoria. It is common for one or both parties to forget or perceive details differently after an agreement is made. You can help by putting the agreement in writing via email or document and sharing it with the negotiators immediately following negotiations. If one of the parties disputes what is in writing, bring everyone back to discuss.

16.4 Summary

As this chapter has shown, nobody looks forward to conflict, but some forms of conflict are very beneficial. Without conflict, organizations would not move forward. Managers play a critical role in maintaining functional conflict while eliminating dysfunctional conflict. Anytime conflict moves toward relationship-based arguments, managers need to redirect the involved parties. Depending on the conflict's scenario, managers have many different strategies that can be deployed.

Discussion Questions

1. Discuss a time when your team was involved in a task-based conflict. What strategies did the team employ to solve the conflict? Did the team reach an optimal solution?
2. Think about a project group that you've been involved with. What were the structural and contextual causes of conflict within the group?
3. Find an example of a win-win outcome in sports. Why do you believe the parties arrived at a win-win outcome compared to potential compromise or win-lose outcomes?
4. Discuss a time when you were involved in a negotiation. What negotiation strategies did you employ?

Notes

1. Morley, G., Thomas, A. (2017, March). US rugby is on the rise—should the NFL be worried? *CNN* Retrieved from https://www.cnn.com/2017/03/16/sport/rise-of-american-rugby-ebner-serevi-wooching/index.html.
2. USA Rugby (2020, March). *USA Rugby files Chapter 11; Agrees to support for continuation of reorganiza-*

tion. Retrieved from https://www.usa.rugby/2020/03/usa-rugby-files-chapter-11-agrees-to-support-for-continuation-of-reorganization/.

3. McLeod, C. M., & Nite, C. (2019). Human Capital Ecosystem Construction in an Emerging Rugby Market. *Journal of Sport Management, 33*(4), 261–274. https://doi.org/10.1123/jsm.2018-0265.

4. McLeod, C. M., & Nite, C. (2019). Human Capital Ecosystem Construction in an Emerging Rugby Market. *Journal of Sport Management, 33*(4), 261–274. https://doi.org/10.1123/jsm.2018-0265.

5. Robbins, S.P. (1978). "Conflict management" and "conflict resolution" are not synonymous terms. *California Management Review, 21*(2), 67–75.

6. McShane, S., & Von Glinow, M. (2021). *Organizational Behavior: Emerging Knowledge. Global Reality* (9th ed.). McGraw Hill.

7. Balasubramanian, S., & Bhardwaj, P. (2004). When not all conflict is bad: Manufacturing-marketing conflict and strategic incentive design. *Management Science, 50*(4), 489–502.

8. Robbins, S.P., & Judge, T.A. (2019). *Organizational Behavior* (18th ed.). Pearson.

9. Follett, M.P. (1942). Constructive conflict. In Metcalf, H.C., and Urwick, L. (eds.). *Dynamic administration: The collected Papers of Mary Parker Follett.* Harper and Brothers. 30–37.

10. Robbins, S.P. (1978). "Conflict management" and "conflict resolution" are not synonymous terms. *California Management Review, 21*(2), 67–75; Robbins, S.P., & Judge, T.A. (2019). *Organizational Behavior* (18th ed.). Pearson.

11. Jehn, K. (1995). A multimethod examination of the benefits and detriments of intragroup conflict. *Administrative Science Quarterly, 40*, 256–282.

12. Todorova, G., Brake, M. R. W., & Weingart, L. R. (2020). Work design and task conflict in interdisciplinary groups. *International Journal of Conflict Management, 31*(4), 623–646. https://doi.org/10.1108/IJCMA-08-2019-0139.

13. De Dreu, C. K. (2006). When too little or too much hurts: Evidence for a curvilinear relationship between task conflict and innovation in teams. *Journal of management, 32*(1), 83–107.

14. Jehn, K. A. (1997). A qualitative analysis of conflict types and dimensions in organizational groups. *Administrative science quarterly, 42*(3), 530–557.

15. Jehn, K. A., & Mannix, E. A. (2001). The dynamic nature of conflict: A longitudinal study of intragroup conflict and group performance. *Academy of management journal, 44*(2), 238–251.

16. Jehn, K. A. (1997). A qualitative analysis of conflict types and dimensions in organizational groups. *Administrative science quarterly, 42*(3), 530–557.

17. Jehn, K. A., & Mannix, E. A. (2001). The dynamic nature of conflict: A longitudinal study of intragroup conflict and group performance. *Academy of management journal, 44*(2), 238–251.

18. Chua, R., & Jin, M. (2020). Across the Great Divides: Gender Dynamics Influence How Intercultural Conflict Helps or Hurts Creative Collaboration. *Academy of Management Journal, 63*(3), 903–934.

19. Chua, R., & Jin, M. (2020). Across the Great Divides: Gender Dynamics Influence How Intercultural Conflict Helps or Hurts Creative Collaboration. *Academy of Management Journal, 63*(3), 903–934.

20. Robbins, S. P. (1974). *Managing organizational conflict.* Englewood Cliffs, NJ: Prentice-Hall.

21. Briggs, D. (2020, August 20). Here's where the Big Ten completely blew it. *Toledo Blade.* Retrieved from https://www.toledoblade.com/sports/college/2020/08/20/briggs-Here-s-where-the-Big-Ten-blew-it/stories/20200820144.

22. Bernstein, E. S., & Turban, S. (2018). The impact of the 'open' workspace on human collaboration. *Philosophical Transactions of the Royal Society B,* 373. https://doi.org/10.1098/rstb.2017.0239.

23. McShane, S., & Von Glinow, M. (2021). *Organizational Behavior: Emerging Knowledge. Global Reality* (9th ed.). McGraw Hill.

24. Sherif, M. (1958). Superordinate goals in the reduction of intergroup conflict. *American journal of Sociology, 63*(4), 349–356.

25. March, J. G., and H. A. Simon. (1958). *Organizations.* Wiley.

26. Alper, S., Tjosvold, D., & Law, K. S. (2000). Conflict management, efficacy, and performance in organizational teams. *Personnel psychology, 53*(3), 625–642.

27. Staudohar, P. D. (2003). Why no baseball work stoppage? *Journal of Sports Economics, 4*(4), 362–366. https://doi.org/10.1177/1527002503257390.

28. Augsberger, D.W. (1992). *Conflict mediation across cultures: Pathways and patterns.* Westminster.

29. Amason, A. C., & Mooney, A. C. (1999). The effects of past performance on top management team conflict in strategic decision making. *International Journal of Conflict Management, 10*(4); Peterson, R. S., & Behfar, K. J. (2003). The dynamic relationship between performance feedback, trust, and conflict in groups: A longitudinal study. *Organizational behavior and human decision processes, 92*(1–2), 102–112.

30. Amason, A. C., & Mooney, A. C. (1999). The effects of past performance on top management team conflict in strategic decision making. *International Journal of Conflict Management, 10*(4); Greer, L. L., Jehn, K. A., & Mannix, E. A. (2008). Conflict transformation: A longitudinal investigation of the relationships between different types of intragroup conflict and the moderating role of conflict resolution. *Small group research, 39*(3), 278–302.

31. Pondy, L. R. (1967). Organizational conflict: Concept and models. *Administrative Science Quarterly, 12,* 296–320; Walton, R. E. (1969). *Interpersonal peacemaking: Confrontations and third party consultations.* Reading, MA: Addison-Wesley.

32. McNary, L. D. (2003). The term "win-win" in conflict management: A classic case of misuse and overuse. *The Journal of Business Communication, 40*(2), 144–159.

33. Zolecki, T. (2018, May 30). Drew's Draft tactics drew ire of Phillies, fans. *MLB.com* retrieved from https://www.mlb.com/news/phillies-drafted-but-did-not-sign-j-d-drew-c278287718.

34. ESPN Staff (2020, September 3). Why MLB's minor leagues as you know them will end Sept. 30. *ESPN.com*, Retrieved from https://www.espn.com/mlb/story/_/id/29795127/why-mlb-minor-leagues-know-end-sept-30.

35. ESPN Staff (2020, June 3). USWNT lawsuit versus U.S. Soccer explained: Defining the pay gaps, what's at stake for both sides. *ESPN.com*. Retrieved from https://www.espn.com/soccer/united-states-usaw/story/4071258/uswnt-lawsuit-versus-us-soccer-explained-defining-the-pay-gapswhats-at-stake-for-both-sides.

36. Eisen, D. (2015, June 10). Omni finds sweet spot in sports partnerships. *Hotel Management*. Retrieved from https://www.hotelmanagement.net/development/omni-finds-sweet-spot-sports-partnerships.

37. Johnson, J. (2011, March 24). I didn't get my sponsor, but NASCAR got a new era. *Motorsports Unplugged*. Retrieved from https://motorsportsunplugged.com/i-didnt-get-my-sponsor-but-nascar-got-a-new-era/.

38. Dubrin, A.J. (2010) *Leadership: Research Findings, Practice, and Skills* (6th ed.). Cengage; Pruitt D.G., & Rubin J. (1986). *Social Conflict: Escalation, Stalemate and Settlement*. Random House: New York.

39. De Dreu, C.K.W., Evers, A., Beersma, B., Kluwer, E.S. and Nauta, A. (2001). A theory-based measure of conflict management strategies in the workplace. *Journal of Organizational Behavior, 22*: 645–668. https://doi.org/10.1002/job.107; De Dreu, C. K., Weingart, L. R., & Kwon, S. (2000). Influence of social motives on integrative negotiation: a meta-analytic review and test of two theories. *Journal of personality and social psychology, 78*(5), 889–905; Dubrin, A.J. (2010) *Leadership: Research Findings, Practice, and Skills* (6th ed.). Cengage.

40. Hitt, M.A., Miller, C.C., Colella, A., Triana, M. (2017). *Organizational Behavior* (5th ed.). Wiley.

41. Robbins, S.P., & Judge, T.A. (2019). *Organizational Behavior* (18th ed.). Pearson.

42. McShane, S., & Von Glinow, M. (2021). *Organizational Behavior: Emerging Knowledge. Global Reality* (9th ed.). McGraw Hill.; Robbins, S.P., & Judge, T.A. (2019). *Organizational Behavior* (18th ed.). Pearson.

43. Robbins, S.P., & Judge, T.A. (2019). *Organizational Behavior* (18th ed.). Pearson.; Thompson, L.L. (1991). Information exchange in negotiation. *Journal of Experimental Social Psychology*. 161–179.

44. Robbins, S.P., & Judge, T.A. (2019). *Organizational Behavior* (18th ed.). Pearson.

45. Thompson, L.L. (1991). Information exchange in negotiation. *Journal of Experimental Social Psychology*. 161–179.

Power and Politics in Sport Organizations

> **Learning Objectives** After reading this chapter, students should be able to

- Describe the various sources of power in sport organizations;
- Understand how resource acquisition can influence one's power in a sport organization;
- Gather a deep understanding of organizational politics as they exist in sport organizations;
- Explain the components of political skill and their influence in sport organizations.

Matthew Althoff: Director of Equipment Operations, University of Virginia
  To listen to the interview <click here>

Supplementary Information The online version of this chapter (https://doi.org/10.1007/978-3-030-67612-4_17) contains supplementary material, which is available to authorized users.

17.1 Sources of Power and Influence in Organizations

Sport organizations are positioned in an environment that is grounded in the belief that the "coach is always right" and the players are to do as told by their coaches. Given these circumstances, sport organizations are likely to have a "top-down" mentality for their organizational hierarchies. Those at the top of the organization would seemingly have the most power, while those at the bottom would have the least. This could be an oversimplification of sport organizations, but a consistent flow of research has been dedicated to the study of coaches and other leaders (e.g., Athletics Directors and Front Office officials). Regardless, there are important reasons to improve your understanding of why and how the ideas of power and politics permeate throughout sport organizations. This chapter is dedicated to both power and politics and will cover general business perspectives as well as how both concepts are utilized within the sports industry.

> **Power** One's influence over organizational outcomes.

> **Legitimate Power** Power that is formally granted to an organizational member.

> **Authority** The ability to make decisions on behalf of the organization.

17.1.1 Legitimate Power

We will start with the concept of power, which is generally viewed as one's influence over organizational outcomes.[1] From there, power can be split into various perspectives, such as legitimate power, which is power that is formally granted to an organizational member, such as a supervisor. This type of power can be viewed as an authority that is bestowed upon the individual to make decisions and coordinate the path for an organization.[2] Those with authority can use their power to offer benefits or rewards to works and threaten punishment for not reaching objectives and meeting standards. Reflecting upon your previous work experiences, you have surely seen such processes play out with past supervisors either offering a bonus or a Saturday off from work or perhaps warning of consequences for not coming to work on time. Whether or not your career path is meant to enter the sports industry, you will experience the impact of formal power and authority in the modern workplace. A supervisor with immense power and decision-making ability is a "fact of life" in most organizations in or out of the sports industry.

▶ **Expert Power** Power that arises from unique skills or capacities that hold incredible value for the organization.

17.1.2 Expert Power

There is another, more informal, type of power that also exists. Sometimes, individuals in organizations hold unique skills or capacities that hold incredible value for the organization. In such cases, an individual with this kind of knowledge or talent is thought to have expert power.[3] Those who have expert power may be located at any position within an organizational hierarchy. In the realm of sport, we can see this concept clearly in that certain players are so valuable to a team's performance that the team simply cannot function properly without them. This is also true in sport organizations. Some

employees have working knowledge of how the football field should be maintained, how the conference will interpret NCAA compliance regulations, or an efficient manner to maneuver through a yearly equipment audit. These examples reflect fundamental business circumstances that demonstrate the value—and power—of individuals who know how to confront such challenges. Yet, power in sport organizations can take on new meaning and importance when considering participants' welfare. The sports industry is plagued with stories of overuse injuries among youth participants. More specifically, the power of coaches in regard to the concussion epidemic in football has also been called into question.[4] As such, it is important to have an even better understanding of where power comes from and how it is generated.

17.2 Resource Acquisition

Chapter 1 discussed the role of resource dependency theory and the processes organizations use to gather resources.[5] This concept is related to power as it directly relates to the acquisition of resources—tangible and intangible. Tangible resources are usually typified in the form of financial resources (i.e., money) or physical buildings and capacities. Intangible resources do not exist in a physical capacity; instead, they exist in forms such as intelligence, social connections, and psychological abilities. Another way to look at the concept of resources is the idea of "capital." Essentially, capital is another word for resources in that having significant or adequate financial capital equates to having enough money to accomplish one's objectives. From an intangible capital perspective, intellectual capital (i.e., superior intelligence), social capital (i.e., influential social connections), or psychological capital (i.e., meaningful cognitive strengths) are all valuable forms of capital or resources for sport organizations. An important concept to take away is that capital (and power) comes in many forms, not just money.

17.2.1 Power and Resource Acquisition

Another critical concept is that resource acquisition and the ability to do so is a form of power. To better understand this concept, we will turn to the work of Hickson, Hinings, Lee, Schneck, and Pennings,[6] who explained that the degree of power held by departments within organizations are predicted based on three concepts that are related to their resources: coping with uncertainty, the uniqueness of the department's skills, and the impact of uncertainty on the organization. In other words, those individuals with power in organizations are likely to hold central and unique skillsets and are able to contend with the uncertainty that is relevant to their organizational environment. Furthermore, power is often bestowed to those within the organization who bring in external (usually financial) resources.[7] This example is seen keenly in sport. Look no further than the power held by professional athletes. When a superstar athlete desires a change within an organization, they are likely to see that change happen (e.g., coaching change or a trade). An even clearer example lies in college sport where coaches are paid hefty salaries, and athletes are not considered employees but instead receive financial support for their education along with some of the cost of living expenses. However, a segment of coaches receive millions of dollars. Why could this be? Well, their salaries are a reflection of their power, or more so their university's belief of their ability to bring in resources. Keep in mind, a university (or any business) will only pay a salary if they believe there will be a return on investment. Consequently, college coaches have enormous power within athletics departments.[8]

Another example of power within sport is the concussion epidemic that has fundamentally changed the way sports are played and managed. Our growing understanding of the dangers of concussions has illuminated the power of coaches. Take, for example, a situation in the early 2010s where collegiate football coaches were firing athletic trainers for not permitting concussed student-athletes to return to the field, and in other cases changing the formal reporting structure so athletic trainers reported to the coach as opposed to medical doctors.[9] In a follow-up study, Oja and Bass[10] explored the power dynamics between collegiate football coaches and equipment managers. Equipment managers in the study revealed that they felt adequately supported by their coaches in terms of fitting helmets. While this was not a universal experience, it was surmised that equipment managers retained some degree of power because they were protecting the organization's resources, in this case, the student-athletes. In sum, sport organizations value the degree to which employees can gather and preserve financial resources and reward power and authority to those who can do so.

17.2.2 Resources and Legitimacy

Another form of resource acquisition was also introduced in Chap. 1—legitimacy and the processes sport organizations undertake to achieve it.[11] As you will recall, legitimacy is the "generalized perception or assumption that the actions of an entity are desirable, proper, or appropriate within some socially constructed system of norms, values, beliefs, and definitions" (p. 574).[12] This perspective is not focused on accumulating financial resources as much as gathering influence based on perceived legitimacy. Specific sport organizations hold significant power and influence throughout the industry. Consider why this might be. Could it be a result of the organization or the organization's leader having a significant degree of influence because they are viewed as a trusted voice? This concept extends beyond organizations and to various leagues and conferences. Many soccer leagues and clubs will look to the top-tier European soccer leagues to guide their decision-making. By doing so, they will increase their perception of being a legitimate organization. Importantly, the organizations that appear to be legitimate will gather increasing power and influence. Put another way, it is difficult for sport organizations or leagues to gain power and influence when they do things differently than established and successful organizations. This is not to say that individuals and organizations should not strive to create their own original path to success.[13] However, the point is that gaining power and influence is often achieved by ascribing to the norms of the given sector of the sports industry.

An interesting perspective arises when considering resources and legitimacy as sources of power and influence. Why do employees follow the directions of their supervisors? Is it because of the amount of resources they bring to the organization, or is it due to the acknowledged power they hold because of the position's legitimacy? The answer is likely both. From a practical standpoint, subordinates follow their superiors' directives because failing to do could result in detrimental effects on their job—even potentially being terminated. However, supervisors are given authority, and actual power, to make decisions on the organization's behalf because of the resources they are believed to bring into the organization. Then, organizations bestow a title that implies legitimacy upon the supervisor, which allows them to make such decisions. In this way, both resource acquisition and legitimacy are likely to play a role in the degree of power one holds within an organizational setting.

17.2.3 Episodic Power

Yet another depiction of organizational power utilizes a dichotomy of systemic and episodic power to explain how power is distributed throughout an organization.[14] Episodic power is characterized by strategic behaviors designed to benefit the actor (i.e., the person taking action) and considered a traditional view of management studies. The focus is on those employees with the most influence within an organization.[15] The systemic form of power uses an alternative perspective of power being dispersed throughout the organization, which is accomplished through the organization's daily practices.[16] Another way to look at this dichotomy is that power can be condensed within certain positions or individuals

(i.e., episodic) or diffused throughout the organization within various groups and departments (i.e., systemic).

Importantly, episodic and systemic forms of power can assist in the understanding of organizational politics, which is the next topic in this chapter.[17] Organizational politics, broadly the actions taken to gather power, are shaped by power disbursement in organizations. Power can be densely compacted at the top of organizational hierarchies (i.e., vertical), and it can also be spread out within the organizational hierarchy (i.e., horizontal). The density of power is likely determined by factors that we have just discussed: the need for resources and what form of power density would reflect a legitimate organizational hierarchy. Regardless of the dispersion of power within an organization, it is important for sport managers to understand where power is located and the degree of power that various members hold. In sport organizations, coaches traditionally have immense power, but, in some cases, super star athletes have even more power than coaches. In Oja and Bass's[18] study, it was found that coaches had more power than athletics directors, even though the athletics directors were considered coaches' formal supervisors. This finding was described as an informal power hierarchy that can exist in college athletics departments. Although this study is just one example, it seems that sport organizations could have unique power structures, which means that sport employees' understanding of their organization's power structure is even more important.

17.3 Organizational Politics

Politics within organizations is not what you are likely to expect when you hear the word "politics" on a media platform. While much attention has been given to the governmental version of politics, this section is dedicated to exploring how politics within sport organizations affect members and the manner by which they attempt to meet organizational goals. In a very broad sense, organizational politics is a function of power that individuals will use as they jockey for positioning to be more influential. As a demonstration of the connection to power, Lawrence et al. described politics as "the dynamics of power in organizations" (p. 180).[19] As such, politics and power are entwined as organizational politics describes how individuals attempt to gain power within organizations.

▶ **Organizational Politics** A social influence process in which behavior is strategically designed to maximize short-term or long-term self-interest, which is either consistent with or at the expense of others' interest.

▶ **Assertive Behavior** When an individual takes the initiative to gain an advantage.

▶ **Defensive Behavior** Reactionary behavior that occurs when an individual is faced with a threat.

▶ **Tactical Behavior** Behavior that is geared toward specific and short-term purposes.

▶ **Strategic Behavior** Ambiguous behaviors focused on long-term endeavors.

A contemporary scholar who has significantly expanded the study of organizational politics is Gerald Ferris, who developed and expanded various models of organizational politics and their influence within organizations. Organizational politics are viewed as "a social influence process in which behavior is strategically designed to maximize short-term or long-term self-interest, which is either consistent with or at the expense of others' interest" (p. 145).[20] Organizational politics has been divided into two forms: assertive-defensive and tactical-strategic.[21] As described by Ferris et al.,[22] assertive behavior is when an individual takes the initiative to gain an advantage. On the other hand, defensive behavior is reactionary and occurs when an individual is faced with a threat. Tactical behavior is geared toward specific and short-term purposes. Strategic behaviors are done for long-term endeavors and are more ambiguous. These forms of behavior help us to understand the actions that people can take to gain or retain their influence in sport organizations.

Keeping in mind that organizational politics describes deliberate attempts by individuals (although this is not limited to individuals, as departments and organizations also take part in organizational politics) to gain, expand, and protect their influence within organizations, in a sport organization, an employee could use all four of the previously mentioned behaviors to attain their goals and/or improve their degree of influence. From an assertive behavior perspective, a sport employee could volunteer to take on the tasks of an employee who has left for a position at a different organization. By doing so, the employee could position themselves for promotion by demonstrating a commitment to the organization, and if the former employee was at a higher position in the organizational hierarchy, they could show they are capable of handling the demands of the job. Utilizing a defensive behavioral reaction to a surprising event such as a shipment of equipment not arriving in time for the start of a season, a sport employee could offer excuses and apologies to try and hold off blame and punishment. In a sense, a defensive reaction is meant to distract and avoid the loss of influence or positioning. Tactical behaviors that a sport employee might use to gain influence would be smaller maneuvers or initiatives such as getting to know coworkers or taking credit for a successful marketing campaign. Lastly, strategic behaviors are meant to enhance long-term qualities such as expertise and status, and a sport employee could do so by seeking opportunities to learn and develop their skills, or more specifically, gaining a skill set that they know will position themselves to advance within the organization. These are just a few examples of how a sport employee could improve their power or influence within their organization.

17.3.1 Behavior Engagement

So, when do individuals engage in political behaviors? According to Ferris et al.,[23] political behaviors are more likely when (a) employees are able to reflect upon their status and available options, (b) there is a lack of rigid rules or constraint in social interactions, (c) opportunities (and threats) exist to use political behaviors, (d) belief of success in political efforts, (e) the circumstances and potential outcomes are important, and (f) when an employee recognizes others partaking in political behaviors, especially when successful. A few important takeaways from this list: There needs to be a correct setting for political behaviors to occur. This requirement includes the employee's internal beliefs and an appropriate environment that supports and welcomes political behaviors. First, let's look at those internal perspectives. Employees need to believe that their efforts will result in the successful attainment of influence or other goals, and those outcomes need to be important to the sport employee in order to put forth the effort to engage in political behaviors. Political behaviors are risky as they are usually not interpreted kindly,[24] and doing so can bring about negative consequences. They also take considerable time and effort to achieve long-term goals and aspirations (notwithstanding the tactical behaviors, as they usually build upon each other for a higher purpose).

Now let's inspect the organizational setting aspect. An essential element of politics in organizations is the recognition of a "playing field." That is, organizations are fundamentally political, and there is a "game" being played in most organizations (sport and non-sport) as employees seek to enhance their positioning within the organizational hierarchy.[25] Sport employees who recognize this "game" and understand it are likely to have a sense of control over the process, which could lead to favorable outcomes. As such, organizational politics can be viewed as either a threat or an opportunity depending on how well one understands the political game.[26] For sport employees who feel inclined to play the game of organizational politics would need to evaluate the likelihood of success after deciphering who the powerbrokers are in an organization, as well as their own ability to carve a path to their goals.

How would one go about either determining their ability or developing skills to excel in organizations that allow political behaviors to exist? A construct that is borne of organizational politics and demonstrates whom individuals can influence others in order to achieve their goals is known as political skill. Treadway et al.[27] described the connection (and separation) between organizational politics and political skill as "understanding what political behaviors to demonstrate (i.e., organizational politics) and the skills to effectively execute them successfully (i.e., political skill)" (p. 1609). Although individuals can use political skill in their own pursuits, it can also be viewed from a leadership perspective. Our leadership chapter follows this one, but, as you read through the content, regarding political skill and then the various leadership strategies, consider the ways that political skill can impact how a leader may interact with their subordinates. To add to the construct's complexity, political skill has four components that entail different aspects of influence that need to be reviewed individually to fully understand the concept.

▶ **Political Skill** The ability to effectively understand others at work and to use such knowledge to influence others to act in ways that enhance one's personal and/or organizational objectives.

17.4 Political Skill

Success in one's career is undoubtedly influenced by concepts such as hard work and tenacity, but being savvy, influential, and understanding the political landscape of organizations is also thought to contribute to one's potential.[28] Political skill has been described as "a fundamental building block for success" (p. 118).[29] Defined, political skill is "the ability to effectively understand others at work, and to use such knowledge to influence others to act in ways that enhance one's personal and/or organizational objectives" (p. 311).[30] Then, political skill is a reflection of the concepts of savviness and being influential. More so, political skill is a description of "how" one is influential[31] and the resulting adjustment of one's behavior in order to influence (or control) coworkers and subordinates.[32] Those who have a high degree of political skill are able to demonstrate a shrewdness to adjust their behavior when needed in order to influence or control others.[33] A key feature of politically skilled individuals is the ability to convey confidence and seem sincere while providing solutions or advice, which has the effect of masking any internal motives they may have. In other words, those who are politically skilled are able to influence others to act or behave in a way that helps the influencer and/or the organization. To be clear, this means that those who have political skill could use their savviness to influence others for selfish reasons (but not always, as there can be benevolent intentions!), but a central feature of political skill is that the individual who is being influenced does not realize this is occurring.[34] Although not a perfect analogy, one way to view political skill is a "Jedi mind trick," as political skill is a learned activity and not a form of brainwashing.

▶ **Social Astuteness** The awareness of individuals concerning not only other individuals but of social engagements in general.

17.4.1 Social Astuteness

As alluded to, political skill has been conceptualized to include four components: social astuteness, interpersonal influence, networking ability, and apparent sincerity. These dimensions describe specific aspects or tools that a politically skilled individual would have. The first aspect, social astuteness, as described by Ferris et al.,[35] is the awareness of individuals concerning not only other individuals but of social engagements in general. Those who have high degrees of social astuteness are able to accurately diagnose others' behavior and intentions, as well as having great self-awareness. In short, such individuals can effectively interact with others because they can

understand the views of others and control their own reactions to present an appropriate response to others. Another way to look at social astuteness is being able to identify with others, which can then lead to applying influence to obtain one's objective.[36] A sport manager with social astuteness would be able to recognize that a subordinate or coworker is highly appreciative (or susceptible) to praise. By taking opportunities to offer support and compliments, they could gain influence to convince them to work with a ticket software program that will greatly favor the socially astute individual.

▶ **Interpersonal Influence** A subtle and convincing personal style that exerts a powerful influence on those around them.

17.4.2 Interpersonal Influence

The second dimension, interpersonal influence, describes how such individuals have "a subtle and convincing personal style that exerts a powerful influence on those around them" (p. 129).[37] Those with interpersonal influence can adapt and act appropriately to achieve a desired response with the use of flexibility in their responses.[38] Put another way, politically skilled individuals use an attractive and appealing personal style or communication strategy that can be adapted to different settings to influence others.[39] An employee with interpersonal influence would be able to use an appealing communication style which includes the ability to adjust their message and posture to solicit influence over others by fitting their communication to be appropriate in a given context. In a sport setting, a sport manager with interpersonal influence would be able to use the right tone when speaking to a participant or coach after a competition and would be able to adjust their tone based on the outcome of the competition in a way that would be received as supportive by the participant or coach.

▶ **Networking Ability** The capacity to cultivate a diverse set of contacts and relationships.

17.4.3 Networking Ability

The third dimension, networking ability, represents the capacity to cultivate a diverse set of contacts and relationships.[40] The development of these networks of relationships is forged to become close to those who hold valuable resources, which can then be utilized to gain influence. Put another way, politically skilled individuals are able to gain friendships and professional relationships with those who hold considerable power and influence themselves, and due to that friendship, they are able to tap into the resources of their powerful friends.[41] Another function of networking ability is the capability to exchange information, which in turn supports the development of friendship.[42] This concept is not unlike "social capital" or the value of one's relationships with others. A common phrase that can describe this political skill dimension could be "it's not what you know; it's whom you know." Relationships are essential to any employee (and are a basic human need), as they help support and encourage individuals during both difficult and cheerful times. However, one with high political skill would selectively and purposely choose who they align themselves with in order to maximize their influence within an organization. For sport employees, this would likely involve befriending those near or at the top of the organizational hierarchy. Doing so could provide access to privileged information or even protection in the face of layoffs. Another strategy for a sport employee could be to connect with those who are long-time employees or who have access to the inner workings of the organization to bolster their knowledge of other employees' organizational culture and perspectives.

▶ **Apparent Sincerity** Appearing to have a genuine interest that shields any ulterior motives that an influencer may or may not have.

17.4.4 Apparent Sincerity

The final dimension, apparent sincerity, is a crucial consideration as it portends a genuine interest and shields any ulterior motives that an influencer may

or may not have. As part of this aspect of political skill, such an individual would "appear to others as possessing high levels of integrity, authenticity, sincerity, and genuineness. They are, or appear to be, honest, open, and forthright" (p. 129).[43] Ferris et al.[44] also added that being sincere is likely to determine whether or not influence will be gained or rejected. Suppose an individual is perceived to be attempting to gain influence or control (i.e., ulterior motive), in that case, they will likely be rebuffed.[45] Apparent sincerity represents trustworthiness and a genuine concern for others. One way to describe someone who does not have high levels of apparent sincerity is "fake." We have all likely encountered people who we could tell were being nice to us for a certain reason, or we knew they had other intentions. When we recognize this, we immediately put our guard up and view such an individual as distrustful. As you can see, for one to gain influence (or control), it is absolutely essential that they are perceived as authentic and sincere in their offers to help. Within the sports industry, fundraising is a department where apparent sincerity is critical. Fundraisers, especially in the American college sports industry, will solicit donations of boosters and alumni. This often involves courting donors by taking them out to dinner, golf outings, and generally being friendly. However, the reason the fundraiser is taking such actions is that it is literally their job to ask for donations (of course, many employees in development/fundraising genuinely enjoy their jobs and getting to know donors), but if the potential donor starts to believe the relationship is strictly based on securing a donation, then the relationship is likely to fall apart. Consequently, those in fundraising departments (although this is certainly not limited to just fundraising) need to have high levels of apparent sincerity to acquire donations from boosters.

17.4.5 Political Skill Examples in Sport

The concept of political skill has been around for quite some time, but scholars have just recently applied the theory within the sports industry. Most of the studies have viewed political skill as a leadership quality, specifically pertaining to coaches. One of the first studies involving sport and political skill examined the impact of football coaches' recruiting ability (i.e., political skill) and head coaches' performance on recruiting effectiveness.[46] The study found that football coaches' political skill did improve their ability to recruit talented student-athletes. A similar study found that head coaches' political skill positively impacted recruiting class quality, satisfaction with the recruiting class, and their performance in recruiting.[47] This study demonstrated the impact of coaches' political skill on objective and subjective measures of recruiting ability. In another study, assistant coaches were asked about their head coaches' political skill and its influence on their reputation and effectiveness. The results revealed that political skill influenced head coaches' reputation, which in turn improved their team and leadership effectiveness.[48] Lastly, as a leadership quality, political skill has been theorized to positively impact sport employees' psychological capital, specifically the HERO model,[49] which was discussed in Chap. 1. While coaches' political skill seemingly has the potential to have positive outcomes, there are plenty of possibilities for individuals who are not coaches or organizational leaders to use political skill to create their own positive outcomes.

One last note on political skill. The concept of political skill, much like sport, is a neutral entity and can be used for positive or negative purposes, but its outcomes depend on the intentions of the person at hand. That is, an individual who possesses a high degree of political skill could use their abilities for selfish desires (e.g., promotions or preventing others from advancement), or they could use them to foster personal development in others by helping coworkers connect within their own vast professional networks or providing meaningful feedback. Also, political skill, which certainly comes easier to some than others, is a skill, meaning that it can be learned, developed, and honed. For those of you who are reading this chapter and are excited about political skill possibilities, we implore you to use these skills for only positive outcomes!

17.5 Summary

In this chapter, we examined both power and politics and applied both concepts to the sports industry. Power comes in many forms and can be cultivated through personal skills as well as following legitimate practices of an organizational environment. Organizational politics is a function of how power is distributed within organizations. Within the concept of organizational politics is the perspective of political skill, which can be developed by both employees and leaders to attain personal and professional goals. As we discussed, the sports industry contains dense areas of power (i.e., coaches and some administrators), but an improved understanding of both power and politics can help aspiring sport employees to better navigate their future organizational environments.

Discussion Questions

1. What are the various sources of power in a sport organization?
2. How does resource acquisition influence one's power in a sport organization?
3. What are organizational politics, and how can they impact a sport organization?
4. How can political skill elevate one's career prospects?

Notes

1. Bowditch, J. L., Buono, A. F., & Stewart, M. M. (2008). *A primer on organizational behavior*. Hoboken, NJ: John Wiley & Sons, Inc.
2. Bowditch, J. L., Buono, A. F., & Stewart, M. M. (2008). *A primer on organizational behavior*. Hoboken, NJ: John Wiley & Sons, Inc.
3. Bowditch, J. L., Buono, A. F., & Stewart, M. M. (2008). *A primer on organizational behavior*. Hoboken, NJ: John Wiley & Sons, Inc.
4. Wolverton, B. (2013, September 2). Coach makes the call: Athletic trainers who butt heads with coaches over concussion treatment take career hits. *The Chronicle of Higher Education*. Retrieved from http://chronicle.com/article/Trainers-Butt-Heads-With/141333/
5. Pfeffer, J., & Salancik, G. R. (2003). *The external control of organizations: A resource dependence perspective*. Stanford, CA: Stanford University Press.

6. Hickson, D. J., Hinings, C. R., Lee, C. A., Schneck, R. E., & Pennings, J. M. (1971). A strategic contingencies' theory of intraorganizational power, *Administrative Science Quarterly, 16*(2), 216–229.

7. Salancik, G. R., & Pfeffer, J. (1974). The bases and use of power in organizational decision making: The case of a university. *Administrative Science Quarterly, 19*(4), 453–473.

8. Knoppers, A., Meyer, B. B., Ewing, M., & Forrest, L. (1990). Dimensions of power: A question of sport or gender? *Sociology of Sport Journal, 7*(4), 369–377.

9. Wolverton, B. (2013, September 2). Coach makes the call: Athletic trainers who butt heads with coaches over concussion treatment take career hits. *The Chronicle of Higher Education.* Retrieved from http://chronicle.com/article/Trainers-Butt-Heads-With/141333/

10. Oja, B. D., & Bass, J. R. (2016). Safety or style? An examination of the role of football equipment personnel. *Journal of Applied Sport Management, 8*(1), 29–54.

11. Suchman, M. C. (1995). Managing legitimacy: Strategic and institutional approaches. *Academy of Management Journal, 20*(3), 571–610.

12. Suchman, M. C. (1995). Managing legitimacy: Strategic and institutional approaches. *Academy of Management Journal, 20*(3), 571–610.

13. Grant, A. (2016). *Originals: How non-conformists move the world.* New York, NY: Penguin Books.

14. Clegg, S. (1989). *Frameworks of power.* London, UK: Sage; Hardy, C., & Clegg, S. R. (1996). Some dare to call it power. In S. R. Clegg, C. Hardy, & W. R. Nord (Eds.), *Handbook of organization studies* (pp. 622–641), London, UK: Sage; Lawrence, T. B., Mauws, M. K., Dyck, B., Kleysen, R. F. (2005). The politics of organizational learning: Integrating power into the 4I framework. *The Academy of Management Review, 30*(1), 180–191 Lawrence, T. B., Winn, M., & Jennings, P. D. (2001). The temporal dynamics of institutionalization. *Academy of Management Review, 26*, 257–272.

15. Lawrence, T. B., Mauws, M. K., Dyck, B., Kleysen, R. F. (2005). The politics of organizational learning: Integrating power into the 4I framework. *The Academy of Management Review, 30*(1), 180–191.

16. Clegg, S. (1989). *Frameworks of power.* London, UK: Sage; Lawrence, T. B., Mauws, M. K., Dyck, B., Kleysen, R. F. (2005). The politics of organizational learning: Integrating power into the 4I framework. *The Academy of Management Review, 30*(1), 180–191.

17. Lawrence, T. B., Mauws, M. K., Dyck, B., Kleysen, R. F. (2005). The politics of organizational learning: Integrating power into the 4I framework. *The Academy of Management Review, 30*(1), 180–191.

18. Oja, B. D., & Bass, J. R. (2016). Safety or style? An examination of the role of football equipment personnel. *Journal of Applied Sport Management, 8*(1), 29–54.

19. Lawrence, T. B., Mauws, M. K., Dyck, B., Kleysen, R. F. (2005). The politics of organizational learning: Integrating power into the 4I framework. *The Academy of Management Review, 30*(1), 180–191.

20. Ferris, G. R., Russ, G. S., & Fandt, P. M. (1989). Politics in organizations. In R. A. Giacalone & P. Rosenfeld (Eds.), *Impression management in the organization* (pp. 143–170). Hillsdale, NJ: Lawrence Erlbaum Associates.

21. Tedeschi, J. T., & Melburg, V. (1984). Impression management and influence in the organization. In S. B. Bacharach & E. J. Lawler (Eds.), *Research in the sociology of organizations* (Vol. 3, pp. 31–58). Greenwich, CT: JAI Press.

22. Ferris, G. R., Russ, G. S., & Fandt, P. M. (1989). Politics in organizations. In R. A. Giacalone & P. Rosenfeld (Eds.), *Impression management in the organization* (pp. 143–170). Hillsdale, NJ: Lawrence Erlbaum Associates.

23. Ferris, G. R., Russ, G. S., & Fandt, P. M. (1989). Politics in organizations. In R. A. Giacalone & P. Rosenfeld (Eds.), *Impression management in the organization* (pp. 143–170). Hillsdale, NJ: Lawrence Erlbaum Associates.

24. Ferris, G. R., Russ, G. S., & Fandt, P. M. (1989). Politics in organizations. In R. A. Giacalone & P. Rosenfeld (Eds.), *Impression management in the organization* (pp. 143–170). Hillsdale, NJ: Lawrence Erlbaum Associates.

25. Mintzberg, H. (1985). The organization as a political arena. *Journal of Management Studies, 22*, 133–154.

26. Ferris, G. R., Russ, G. S., & Fandt, P. M. (1989). Politics in organizations. In R. A. Giacalone & P. Rosenfeld (Eds.), *Impression management in the organization* (pp. 143–170). Hillsdale, NJ: Lawrence Erlbaum Associates.

27. Treadway, D. C., Adams, G., Hanes, T. J., Perrewé, P. L., Magnusen, M. J., & Ferris, G. R. (2014). The roles of recruiter political skill and performance resource leveraging in NCAA football recruitment effectiveness. *Journal of Management, 40*(6), 1607–1626.

28. Ferris, G. R., Russ, G. S., & Fandt, P. M. (1989). Politics in organizations. In R. A. Giacalone & P. Rosenfeld (Eds.), Impression management in the organization (pp. 143–170). Hillsdale, NJ: Lawrence Erlbaum Associates; Pfeffer, J. (1981). *Power in organizations.* Boston: Pitman.

29. Perrewé, P. L., Ferris, G. R., Stoner, J. S., & Brouer, R. L. The positive role of political skill in organizations. In D. Nelson, & C. L. Cooper (Eds.). *Positive Organizational Behavior* (pp. 117–128). Thousand Oaks, CA: Sage.

30. Ahearn, K. K., Ferris, G. R., Hochwarter, W. A., Douglas, C., & Ammeter, A. P. (2004). Leader political skill and team performance. *Journal of Management, 30*(3), 309–327.

31. Ferris, G. R., Treadway, D. C., Perrewé, P. L., Brouer, R. L., Douglas, C., & Lux, S. (2007). Political skill in organizations. *Journal of Management, 33*(3), 290–320.

32. Ferris, G. R., Treadway, D. C., Kolodinsky, R. W., Hochwarter, W. A., Kacmar, C. J., Douglas, C., & Frink, D. D. (2005). Development and validation of the political skill inventory. *Journal of Management, 31*(1), 126–152.

33. Ferris, G. R., Treadway, D. C., Kolodinsky, R. W., Hochwarter, W. A., Kacmar, C. J., Douglas, C., & Frink, D. D. (2005). Development and validation of

the political skill inventory. *Journal of Management*, *31*(1), 126–152.

34. Ferris, G. R., Treadway, D. C., Kolodinsky, R. W., Hochwarter, W. A., Kacmar, C. J., Douglas, C., & Frink, D. D. (2005). Development and validation of the political skill inventory. *Journal of Management*, *31*(1), 126–152.

35. Ferris, G. R., Treadway, D. C., Kolodinsky, R. W., Hochwarter, W. A., Kacmar, C. J., Douglas, C., & Frink, D. D. (2005). Development and validation of the political skill inventory. *Journal of Management*, *31*(1), 126–152.

36. Pfeffer, J. (1992). *Managing with power: Politics and influence in organizations*. Boston, MA: Harvard Business School Press.

37. Ferris, G. R., Treadway, D. C., Kolodinsky, R. W., Hochwarter, W. A., Kacmar, C. J., Douglas, C., & Frink, D. D. (2005). Development and validation of the political skill inventory. *Journal of Management*, *31*(1), 126–152.

38. Ahearn, K. K., Ferris, G. R., Hochwarter, W. A., Douglas, C., & Ammeter, A. P. (2004). Leader political skill and team performance. *Journal of Management*, *30*(3), 309–327.

39. Ferris, G. R., Treadway, D. C., Kolodinsky, R. W., Hochwarter, W. A., Kacmar, C. J., Douglas, C., & Frink, D. D. (2005). Development and validation of the political skill inventory. *Journal of Management*, *31*(1), 126–152.

40. Ferris, G. R., Treadway, D. C., Kolodinsky, R. W., Hochwarter, W. A., Kacmar, C. J., Douglas, C., & Frink, D. D. (2005). Development and validation of the political skill inventory. *Journal of Management*, *31*(1), 126–152.

41. Ferris, G. R., Treadway, D. C., Kolodinsky, R. W., Hochwarter, W. A., Kacmar, C. J., Douglas, C., & Frink, D. D. (2005). Development and validation of the political skill inventory. *Journal of Management*, 31(1), 126–152; Pfeffer, J. (1992). *Managing with power: Politics and influence in organizations*. Boston, MA: Harvard Business School Press.

42. Ferris, G. R., Treadway, D. C., Brouer, R. L., & Munyon, T. P. (2012). Political skill in the organizational sciences. In G. R. Ferris & D. C. Treadway (Eds.), *Politics in organizations: Theory and research considerations*, (pp. 487–528). New York, NY: Routledge.

43. Ferris, G. R., Treadway, D. C., Kolodinsky, R. W., Hochwarter, W. A., Kacmar, C. J., Douglas, C., & Frink, D. D. (2005). Development and validation of the political skill inventory. *Journal of Management*, *31*(1), 126–152.

44. Ferris, G. R., Treadway, D. C., Kolodinsky, R. W., Hochwarter, W. A., Kacmar, C. J., Douglas, C., & Frink, D. D. (2005). Development and validation of the political skill inventory. *Journal of Management*, *31*(1), 126–152.

45. Jones, E. E. (1990). *Interpersonal perception*. New York, NY: Freeman.

46. Treadway, D. C., Adams, G., Hanes, T. J., Perrewé, P. L., Magnusen, M. J., & Ferris, G. R. (2014). The roles of recruiter political skill and performance resource leveraging in NCAA football recruitment effectiveness. *Journal of Management, 40*(6), 1607–1626.

47. Magnusen, M. J., Kim, Y. K., & Perrewe, P. L. (2014). Gaining a competitive edge when recruiting student-athletes: The role of political skill. *International Journal of Sports Science and Coaching, 9*(6), 1291–1310.

48. Kim, M., Wells, J. E., & Kim, A. C. H. (2016). What are they saying about your head coach? The relationship among political skill, reputation, and effectiveness. *Journal of Applied Sport Management, 8*(3), 48–67.

49. Kim, M., Perrewé, P. L., Kim, Y. K., & Kim, A. C. H. (2017). Psychological capital in sport organizations: Hope, Efficacy, Resilience, and Optimism among Employees in Sport (HEROES). *European Sport Management Quarterly, 17*(5), 659–680.

> **Learning Objectives** After reading this chapter, students should be able to

- Identify behaviors of leaders;
- Differentiate between various leadership theories;
- Determine leadership styles that suit their abilities.

Chad Kimmel: Assistant Athletic Director for Development, University of Wisconsin

To listen to the interview <click here>

It's Your Turn Joanna had never thought of herself as a leader. Throughout college, she was a good student and had many friends. She was the Treasurer of the Sport

Management Club and active in other organizations, but Joanna never felt like the person that others looked to for inspiration. Joanna never sought leadership roles. She didn't feel comfortable making decisions that affected others, and she definitely didn't think she could lead others. Upon graduation, Joanna took the Events Coordinator position with the Regina Sports Council. Joanna's role was perfect. She loved planning events, but she was able to stay behind the scenes. Her boss, the Director of Events, took on all of the leadership responsibilities—especially with volunteers during events.

Arriving at work this morning, Joanna had a note on her door. It was from her boss Anthony asking her to come to his office. "Joanna, please sit down. I have some news," Anthony began. "I just accepted a position with Sport Canada. Friday will be my last day."

"Congratulations!" Replied Joanna. "I am so happy for you!" Joanna really was happy for Anthony, but she was also worried. The Regina Sports Festival was in three weeks. It's a huge multiple-day festival with events spread throughout Regina. Joanna had spent most of her year planning it. "I wish you weren't leaving so soon,"

Supplementary Information The online version of this chapter (https://doi.org/10.1007/978-3-030-67612-4_18) contains supplementary material, which is available to authorized users.

Joanna continued. "The Sports Festival is in a few weeks. There are so many people to coordinate. I doubt your replacement will be ready for that challenge. You will be hard to replace."

"I think my replacement is more than prepared," Anthony said with a grin. "I spoke with the Board, and it was unanimous, you are the new Director of Events. Congratulations!"

Joanna was thrilled that her hard work had been recognized. She was also terrified. She had spent her life avoiding leadership positions. Now, she was in charge.

18.1   Leadership

The sports industry is characterized by its dynamic nature. Many sports industry professionals will tell you one of the aspects they love most about their job is that no two days are the same. There is always a new challenge for sport organizations to face. Never were those sentiments more accurate than in 2020. A global pandemic rendered business models that relied on full stadiums obsolete while also making some sports unsafe to play. At the same time, protests over racial injustice spread throughout the United States and much of Europe, placing pressure on sport organizations to become engaged and reexamine their own cultures. Throughout this upheaval, some long-time sport organization leaders found their influence waning, while other sport organization members found themselves thrust into leadership roles without warning.

▶ **Leadership** Persuading, motivating, and empowering others to contribute to the success of their organization.

Leadership can be defined as persuading, motivating, and empowering others to contribute to the success of their organization.[1] There are many different leadership theories. Some theories argue that leadership ability is based on traits that are inherent to the individual, while others contend that anyone can become a leader. Some theories make the case that leaders can be influential in any situation, while others state that leadership is situational or even a function of those that are being led. In this chapter, we will explore a number of leadership theories, beginning with the trait theories that were popular in the early to mid-twentieth century and building toward modern theories like servant leadership, which have gained a foothold in the modern sports industry. We will begin by understanding what roles a leader plays in an organizational setting.

18.2   Roles of Leaders

What is the difference between leaders and managers? Aren't all managers leaders? Management involves controlling employees' behaviors to accomplish a goal. This seems close to the definition of leadership. But, whereas management's ability to affect behavior derives from power and control, leaders influence behavior through inspiration.[2] We could say that people follow managers because they have to, but they follow leaders because they are moved to. Leadership is one of the functions of effective management, along with planning, organizing, and controlling. On a football team, the head coach and quarterback can be considered upper-managers and middle-managers, respectively. Through their roles, they plan, organize, and control the movements of the other players on the team. Players who do not follow their directions may be removed from the field or face punishment. These powers are granted through their role, just like a sales manager can fire an employee who does not make the required number of cold calls during the week. Players who are just going through the prescribed movements because they have to are not likely to be effective, and the team is unlikely to reach its goals. Players who are inspired through leadership are more likely to stay after practice working on their assignments or help their teammates. They will be enthused about their role, and the team is more likely to perform better. Thus, an effective manager should rely on leadership instead of power to influence employees.

Because leadership doesn't require power, anyone in the organization can emerge as a leader as long as management provides that opportunity. In the football example above, the quarterback may emerge as a leader through their role, but other players could also become team leaders through their ability to inspire their teammates. Similarly, a call center colleague may have a unique ability to encourage others in the office to meet or exceed organizational goals. Thus, we could say that all managers should be leaders, but not all leaders are managers.

18.2.1 Leadership Behavior

As we will see throughout this chapter, leaders can exhibit many different behaviors. Nevertheless, there is an agreement in the literature that most leaders exhibit some combination of behaviors. Klapfl and Kruja[3] call this list of behaviors the Leadership Behavior Menu (Table 18.1). A leader does not have to demonstrate all of the attributes of the Leader Behavior Menu to be effective. In certain circumstances, leaders may exhibit only one of these behaviors and still be effective. Next, let's look at different theories on leadership. We'll begin with the trait theories, which contend that people become leaders because they have certain traits, qualities, or characteristics that non-leaders do not possess.

▶ **Trait Theories** Based on the notion that effective leaders have certain inherent traits that allow them to influence others.

18.3 Trait Theories of Leadership

The trait theories of leadership grew from early twentieth-century scholars' beliefs that effective leaders were born with inherent traits that made it easier for them to influence others. In other words, some people are natural-born leaders, and others are not. Intuitively, this concept makes

Table 18.1 Leadership behavior menu

Leadership behavior	
Value proposition	Leaders effectively articulate the value of meeting the organization's vision. The value proposition provides employees with a sense of what future performance should look like or produce.
Ethical values	Leaders demonstrate integrity and commitment to all concerned organizational constituencies.
Execution skills	Leaders have the ability to translate vision into actionable plans which are carried out by organizational members.
Innovation and creativity	Leaders generate unique ideas and solutions to meet organizational goals.
Communication	Leaders can clearly articulate their message to followers in a manner that is easily understood. Leaders also actively listen to constituents to gauge comprehension, gain perspective, and understand concerns.
Enabling skills	Leaders enable by using their position to acquire resources and provide opportunities for constituents to grow. Enabling often involves delegating authority to others.
Team building	Leaders have the ability to influence a group to collaborate around common objectives. Effective leaders identify the unique attributes of team members and organize tasks to take advantage of group members' strengths.
Confront adversity	Leaders are often confronted with complex problems. Effective leaders monitor and plan for potential problems. If problems arise, leaders seek solutions even under less than desirable conditions.
Tenacity	Leaders demonstrate persistence to see plans and actions through completion.
Culture building	Leaders positively influence the team and organizational culture.

sense. You likely know someone who seems like a natural leader. People just seem drawn to this person. It is easy to believe that some people were born to influence and lead others.

Unfortunately for researchers, the trait theories were difficult to study. If something is inherent, like an "it factor," how can these traits be studied? Scholars studied thousands of traits, ranging from physical appearance, various abilities, and personality characteristics.[4] Instead of using a systematic approach and building off prior research, many trait theory studies introduced new traits; thus, comparisons could not be made between studies. Inconsistent definitions of traits created scenarios where one study identified a particular trait as extremely important, but others indicated that the very same trait was a non-factor. Situational factors created further inconsistency.[5] For example, a person may be very effective at rallying a community to support building local athletic fields, but struggle to keep volunteers to maintain the field once they are built. Lastly, researchers found that the results of trait theory studies are greatly influenced by whether the traits are self-identified or observed. Studies that use observation are more accurate.[6]

The problems associated with trait theory research, along with the notion traits were something hereditary, caused trait theories to fall out of favor among scholars, but remain popular among practitioners. Advancement of the Big Five Personality trait model along with acknowledgments of the shortcoming of previous research revived trait theory studies in the 1990s. The Big Five model states that effective leaders are more likely to demonstrate extroversion, agreeableness, conscientiousness, emotional stability, and openness to experience.[7] Among these traits, extroversion, conscientiousness, and openness are consistent indicators of leadership emergence and leader effectiveness when accounting for situational factors. However, agreeableness and emotional stability appear to have little effect on one's leadership ability.

Another major change that has made trait theories of leadership more relevant is the abandonment of the notion that traits are inborn. Although some people may be inherently more extroverted or open to new experiences, people can adapt to be more extroverted or open. Other traits that impact leader effectiveness have also emerged.

Kirkpatrick and Locke[8] identified the following traits as indicators of effective leaders.

- *Drive*: The level of ambition, persistence, and initiative demonstrated by an individual. Some argue that drive is an indicator of extroversion,[9] but drive has also been found to impact leaders' abilities to develop a clear vision and see it through implementation.
- *Leader Motivation*: A person's desire to be in a position of leadership. Some people may want to lead because they desire to be responsible for and inspire others to achieve a goal (socialized power motive). Others may want to be in a position of leadership to have power over others (see Chap. 17).[10] Socialized power motives are more strongly associated with leader effectiveness.
- *Honesty and Integrity*: This trait is tied to ethical behavior, as discussed earlier in the chapter.
- *Self-Confidence*: People who are assured of their abilities are more likely to maintain poise and learn from mistakes. They are also less likely to second guess or doubt their decisions.
- *Cognitive Ability*: The ability to process and understand complex and changing situations.
- *Industry Knowledge*: A deep understanding of the organization's mission and the environment in which the business functions. Leaders with strong industry knowledge can anticipate potential problems and solutions before others.

A final trait that has gained increased attention from both academics and practitioners is emotional intelligence. Emotional intelligence, as discussed in Chap. 11, is a person's ability to recognize their own emotions and the emotions of others. Goleman[11] identified five components of emotional intelligence.

- *Self-Awareness*: The ability to recognize and understand your own emotions, feelings, and motivations and how they affect others in the organization. People with high self-awareness are generally more confident but also able to accept criticism and acknowledge shortcomings.

- *Self-Regulation*: The ability to recognize and control disruptive impulses, feelings, and behaviors. People who self-regulate are known to think before speaking, take in all information, and are open to change. In a study by Yeow and Martin,[12] managers with better self-regulation were considered to be better leaders by their employees. Their teams were also more effective than teams lead by managers who were rated to have low self-regulation.
- *Intrinsic Motivation*: As noted throughout this book, leaders who are more intrinsically motivated push through obstacles. Followers believe that the passion demonstrated by highly motivated leaders can be contagious.
- *Empathy*: The most recognizable component of emotional intelligence, empathy, is the ability to recognize and fully consider others' feelings and how they are impacted by decisions. Empathy has been strongly tied to employee retention. Employees who work for empathetic leaders often describe them as compassionate and understanding. People with high degrees of empathy are also more likely to be sensitive to the experiences of marginalized groups.
- *Social Skill*: The ability to build and maintain rapport with individuals. Leaders who possess social skills have the ability to build teams by finding common ground with members. They can also garner support for ideas through persuasiveness, which can be effective during times of change or uncertainty.

It is evident that the traits explored in the trait theories can lead to managerial behaviors that are beneficial to the organization. After all, a smart box office manager, who understands the product is open to change, and is motivated by the challenge is better than the alternative. On the other hand, a deviant employee who possesses many of these traits could greatly damage the organization through their influence on others. As we move forward in this chapter, hopefully, it is clear that leadership theories already discussed influenced new theories. You should also notice that

the theories overlap. Thus more than one may explain a leader's influence. More importantly, as we move away from the idea that leaders are born, you will hopefully see that anyone can be a leader by harnessing their own attributes. Next, we will discuss the behavioral theories of leadership.

▶ **Behavioral Theories** Leaders are effective because their actions influence others.

18.4 Behavioral Theories

Taking their cue from the trait theories' initial failures, the behavioral theories were a repudiation in many ways. The behavior theories of leadership are based on the idea that leaders are effective because of their actions, not because of inerrant traits or abilities. When the behavioral theories were proposed, this was a major concept. They acknowledged that someone could be trained to be a leader. Also, they grew from that great rivalry: the University of Michigan versus Ohio State University! For soccer fans, imagine if Real Madrid and FC Barcelona were universities that also played soccer. As an alumnus of Ohio State, I like to think a real competition existed between the Ohio State researchers (Stogdill and Fleishman) and the Michigan scholars (Likert, Katz, and Kahn). Alas, no evidence of competition exists. Let's begin by analyzing The Ohio State University's contribution.

18.4.1 The Ohio State Studies

The Ohio State studies[13] sought to identify dimensions of managerial behavior that impacted leader effectiveness. Beginning with thousands of potential dimensions, two behavior dimensions were identified: initiating structure and consideration. Initiating structure is a leadership style where interpersonal relationships and roles are clearly defined as they relate to espoused goals. This includes behaviors to organize workgroups, task assignments, and communication patterns, as well as behaviors to implement policies, performance standards, work designs, and deadlines. Leaders who exhibit many of the initiating structure behaviors might be considered micro-managers by employees. Depending on the setting, this could hurt team performance. For example, in an organization focused on creative design and innovation, initiating structure behaviors could hinder organizational goals. On the other hand, leaders overseeing NCAA compliance for an athletics department may need to exhibit initiating structure behaviors to ensure policies are followed.

Consideration behaviors are characterized by actions that demonstrate mutual trust, kindness, caring, friendship, and respect for others personally and professionally. An athletic director inviting an intern to a meeting and asking them for an opinion is an example of consideration. Followers state that these behaviors made them feel valued, creating a sense of satisfaction with their role and status on the team.

While it may appear that consideration and initiating behaviors are opposites of each other, research has demonstrated that leaders can exhibit both behaviors at the same time.[14] In other words, a leader can look over employees' work, provide honest evaluations, and also demonstrate that they care about the individual's contribution to the team's success. Further, both styles have been linked to positive views of leadership when accounting for situational factors.

18.4.2 The Michigan Studies

Similar to the Ohio State studies, the University of Michigan studies also sought to identify behaviors of effective leaders.[15] Like the Ohio State studies, the Michigan studies identified two behavior dimensions, but these dimensions existed on a continuum. In other words, the more of one behavior a leader exhibited, the less they could exhibit the other behavior dimension. At one end of the continuum, job-centered behaviors emphasize tasks and processes needed to accomplish a goal. Job-centered behaviors are very similar to the initiating structure behaviors found by the Ohio State. Similarly, employee-centered

behaviors are comparable to consideration behaviors. Thus, the real difference between the two sets of studies was Michigan's theory that the behaviors exhibited a degree of mutual exclusivity.

18.4.3 The Managerial Grid

Blake and Mouton[16] recognized that people could exhibit different degrees of behaviors, as well as exhibit different behaviors simultaneously. Building on the aforementioned behavioral theories, they developed the Managerial Grid, which rates leader behaviors on two behavioral continuums: concern for people and concern for production. Behaviors are rated on scales (1 = low concern to 9 = high concern). The Managerial Grid (Fig. 18.1) is often used by organizations to rate leader performance. A 9,9 leadership style is considered optimal, while a 1,1 is considered the worst possible leadership style.

▶ **Contingency Perspective** Leader effectiveness is dependent on situational factors within the leaders' environment.

18.5 The Contingency Perspective of Leadership

Think about a moment in your life where you felt completely confident in taking control. Maybe it was the people you were around—your classmates, teammates, friends? Perhaps it was something about the situation itself that made you think, "I've got this?" Maybe it was something else that you cannot explain, but you just felt very confident in your ability to be a leader at that moment? Now, flip this notion around, is there a moment in your life when you felt like you were the worst person in the world to lead? That you were in over your head? That you did not have what it takes for your group to succeed?

If we are honest with ourselves, we have to acknowledge that the situation matters when it comes to leadership. The sports industry is full

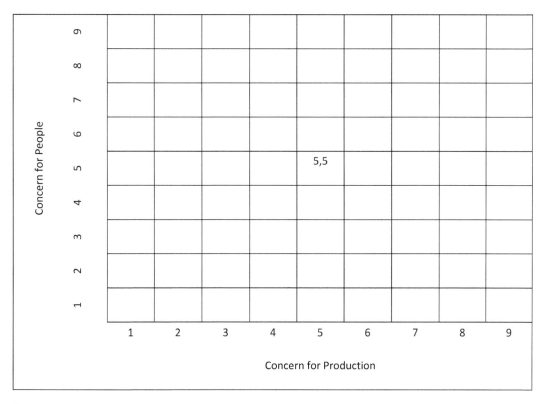

Fig. 18.1   The managerial grid. (Blake, R. R., & Mouton, J. S. (1982). A comparative analysis of situationalism and 9,9 management by principle. *Organizational Dynamics, 10*(4), 20–43)

of famous examples where a person had tremendous success in a leadership role at one organization but struggled elsewhere. Bill Belichick has been Head Coach and Director of Football Operations for the NFL's New England Patriots since 2000. In his time with the Patriots, the organization has won a record six Super Bowls and appeared in the league's championship game nine times. Few coaches in any sport have enjoyed that level of success. Obviously, Belichick is a tremendous leader. However, in his only prior head coaching opportunity, Belichick coached the Cleveland Browns for five years and recorded only one season with a winning record. Belichick has acknowledged that he changed his leadership approach between his time with the Browns and Patriots; however, many situational factors allowed his leadership to flourish in New England.

The contingency perspective of leadership posits that certain leadership styles will work well in favorable situations but will be ineffective in others. This is in strong contrast to the trait theories and a more substantial acknowledgment of the role that situation factors have compared to the behavioral theories. There are many different contingency perspective theories. From an applied perspective, the theories are very detailed but problematic. It is very difficult to match leaders to situations, especially in sport where the environment changes rapidly. It is also extremely challenging for leaders to change their styles to meet situations. Thus, practitioners in most industries recognize contingency theories but find them nearly impossible to adopt in practice. In this section, we'll limit our discussion to Path-Goal Theory, which is probably the most widely recognized of the contingency perspectives. Other perspectives that you might find interesting to explore include Fiedler's Model and Situational Leadership Theory.

18.5.1 Path-Goal Theory

Path-Goal Theory outlines four unique leadership styles, each of which it contends is effective given specific situational factors and employee characteristics (Fig. 18.2). When a leadership style is matched to the employee and situation, employees will be motivated to achieve organizational goals. In essence, the leader's behaviors clear obstacles from the employee's path to the goal. A mismatch will result in a more unsatisfactory outcome. Let's begin by discussing leader behaviors.

18.5.1.1   Leader Behaviors

Directive leaders provide psychological structure for employees by clearly outlining task completion procedures, goals for completion, and performance standards. Employees who lack experience or skills related to the task will appreciate directive leaders, as will those who feel the need for security from their leader.[17] For example, a person volunteering at a track meet for the first time will likely appreciate a leader who provides lots of directions and guidance. Similarly, more experienced and skilled volunteers may appreciate directive leaders

when tasks are complex. During the Covid-19 pandemic, conference commissioners and athletic directors were frustrated by the NCAA's lack of directive regarding whether fall sports should be played. This led to some questioning the leadership capabilities of NCAA executives.

Supportive leadership is similar to the employee-centered styles outlined earlier in the chapter. Supportive leaders provide psychological reassurance to employees through their actions. Supportive leaders are empathetic, friendly, and approachable. This leadership style is effective when the team lacks cohesion, lacks structure, or when outcomes cannot be clarified. Supportive leadership is also important when employees desire growth.[18]

Participative Leaders encourage employee involvement in decision-making. This style can be particularly useful when employees are highly skilled and experienced. Imagine taking over as the President of a city sports tourism commission that already hosts several highly successful annual events. Your charge is to develop another event that accentuates the commission's current offerings. It would be a mistake not to take advantage of the commission's

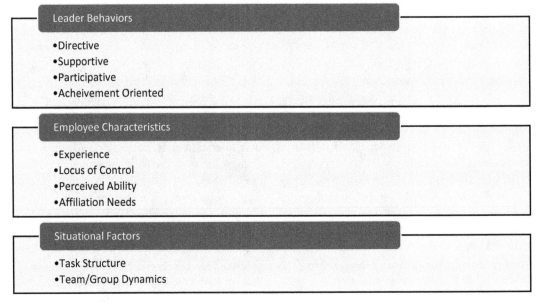

Fig. 18.2 Path-goal theory

employees' expertise when creating a new event. In fact, they may feel undervalued and resentful if you make decisions without their input. By including existing employees in the decision-making process, participative leaders build trust, demonstrate respect, and increase the chances that employees will buy-in to new ideas.[19]

Achievement-oriented leadership is another approach that can be successful with highly experienced and highly skilled employees. Achievement-oriented leaders engage in behaviors to push their employees to their highest levels of performance. They set challenging goals and push employees to demonstrate improvement. At the same time, the leader demonstrates confidence in the employees' abilities and provides support. This approach can work well with a team that has become bored or complacent.[20]

18.6 Inspirational Leadership

Hopefully, you are beginning to see the overlap among these theories. From the trait theories, to the behavioral theories, to the contingency theories, each identifies characteristics of the leader and tries to relate how those characteristics interact with the individual and factors of the situation. Increasingly, concepts of emotional intelligence are being identified as critical to effective leadership. Many of the theories to this point have also alluded to the importance of goal setting, but, for the most part, have focused on short-term motivation or task completion, that is, reaching the goal. For the remainder of this chapter, we will discuss leadership styles that are less focused on the task at hand and more focused on broader perspectives. The next two styles that we discuss fall under the category of inspirational leadership. Inspirational leaders have higher goals or vision that provides broader meaning to the tasks at hand. The focus is not necessarily on accomplishing the organization's goals. Inspirational leaders seek to meet the various needs of the employee.[21] Let's begin by looking at charismatic leadership.

18.6.1 Charismatic Leadership

Charisma is an often intangible quality that others attribute based on perceptions of unique power, purpose, or resolve.[22] Charismatic leaders use their charisma to persuade others to follow a vision. Martin Luther King Jr. is a tremendous example of a charismatic leader. He used his charisma to persuade Americans, particularly white Americans, to see and believe in a vision of the United States that differed from the vision they had been taught to accept.[23] Muhammad Ali is an example of a charismatic leader in sport. He too used his charisma and platform as a world champion boxer to push for social change around the world. More recently, Megan Rapinoe has used her position on the US Women's National Soccer team to advocate for social change. Mark Cuban, owner of the NBA's Dallas Mavericks, is also considered by many to be a charismatic leader because of his influence on league policy as well as on issues beyond sports.

Charisma influences followers on three different dimensions. When a charismatic leader grabs followers' attention because of their appearance, cadence in their speech, or other socially desirable traits, they are using referent power. Expert power is the ability to influence because of the specialized knowledge that one holds (see Chap. 17). Innovators are often considered to have expert power because they hold the knowledge that others want to acquire. The final dimension is the power to influence job involvement. Charismatic leaders are able people excited about their work. Charismatic leaders exercise their power via a four-step process to influence followers.[24]

1. Charismatic leaders set a vision that links the organization's present with its future. Unlike the leadership styles discussed earlier in the chapter, where the leader sets clear goals, charismatic leaders often leave them vague. For example, a new soccer club president may begin their tenure with many speeches discussing championships in the organization's future. The idea is to get organizational members to believe championships are possible.

Specific tasks and goals can be filled in once people have bought into the idea.

2. Charismatic leaders communicate high expectations but also portray confidence that their followers can meet lofty standards. They create belief among their followers that together, greatness can be achieved.
3. Charismatic leaders change the organizational culture through their own behaviors. The leader acts as an example for others to follow.
4. The charismatic leader engages in emotion-inducing behaviors to stir conviction in their followers. Often, these behaviors may fly against norms. Examples can include using personal stories to create a relational connection with followers, or creating rousing videos that are part pep talk. Some charismatic leaders engage in risk-taking behaviors to demonstrate their conviction to their followers.

18.6.1.1 Dangers of Charismatic Leadership

Because of the power attributed to charismatic leaders by their followers, it is easy for unethical individuals to use their charisma for nefarious purposes.[25] Many dictators rose to power through movements where they used charisma to influence citizens. In sport, sexual abuse scandals in USA Gymnastics and Penn State University football can partially be attributed to charismatic leadership influencing organizational members to cover up criminal behavior. Charismatic leaders fall into one of two categories. Socialized charismatic leaders use their power to benefit others. Followers are empowered to make ethical, responsible decisions, and the values and vision set forth meet high ethical standards. Followers are free to reject behaviors that fall below standards, even if that behavior is from the leader themselves. On the other hand, personalized charismatic leaders exert their power to serve their own interests primarily. They exercise little to no constraint over their powers and often expect obedience from followers. In sport, personalized charismatic behaviors have resulted in the exploitation of athletes, fraudulent financial behaviors, and cheating scandals, to name a few of the negative outcomes.

18.6.2 Transformational Leadership

Transformational leaders seek to create positive change by influencing followers to move beyond their own self-interests toward the betterment of the group, organization, or society.[26] Both within and outside of the sports industry, transformational leaders can be effective at turning around struggling organizations. Transformational leaders are also common and effective at leading non-profits. Let's look at how transformational leaders influence employees using two examples from the sports industry. Billy Beane is the Executive Vice President of the Oakland Athletics. He is credited with revolutionizing how MLB clubs use data analytics to evaluate player performance. His story was popularized in the bestselling book *Moneyball*[27] which was also made into a motion picture. Carolyn McKenzie is the founder of Soccer in the Streets, a non-profit sport development organization that uses soccer to teach life-skills and enrich lives of underserved communities in Atlanta, Georgia, as well as other cities in the United States.

18.6.2.1 Raise Awareness

Transformational leaders first influence followers by raising their awareness of the importance and benefits of achieving the vision, along with guidance for how it could be achieved.[28] For Beane, he had to alert others within the Oakland Athletics organization of the clubs' financial constraints that would prohibit their ability to compete in MLB using commonly accepted practices. He also provided a path forward by laying out a plan where the Athletics used analytics to adopt unique game strategies and player evaluation techniques to overcome their limited resources.

McKenzie believed Soccer in the Streets could create educational pathways for youth in inner cities by bringing the program to the neighborhoods where the children she wanted help lived. She understood traveling outside of their troubled neighborhoods was a barrier for the youth she wanted to serve. To accomplish her vision, McKenzie had to raise awareness of several constituencies. First, she had to convince community leaders that there was value in investing in neighborhoods with high poverty, crime, and drug abuse rates. McKenzie set up multiple pilot events that brought financial supporters and volunteers into the community to see the impact soccer could have. At the same time, she had to convince community residents that soccer could lead to opportunities for their children. Soccer was not a popular sport in the communities she was trying to serve. To raise the residents' awareness, she developed a program that allowed parents and children to learn about soccer while also showcasing academic achievement opportunities. In doing so, she allowed parents to envision the impact soccer could have on their children.[29]

18.6.2.2   Look Beyond Self-Interest

Next, transformational leaders help followers look beyond their self-interest by assisting them to see the big picture. Often, change asks some followers to sacrifice for the greater good.[30] The transformational leader has to help members see how the sacrifice will be worth it in the end. McKenzie had to help city leaders, business leaders, and volunteers see how their time and financial investments would impact Atlanta as a whole.[31] Beane had to convince players, coaches, and scouts to adopt tactics that were not financially rewarded by other clubs in MLB.[32]

18.6.2.3   Search for Self-Fulfillment

Transformational leaders must help followers search for self-fulfillment.[33] Asking others to look at their actions through a different prism can lower satisfaction among employees. After all, they likely had a different view of success before the leader began pursuing transformational change. It is up to the leader to help the follower to see how accomplishing the vision will lead to satisfaction. Beane used two tactics to help others find self-fulfillment. At the group level, he shared a vision of team success that would not be possible without transformation. Beane also provided vital team members important roles in the transformation so that they could see the tangible outcomes of their sacrifice.[34] On the other hand, McKenzie centered stakeholders' focus on the success of the youth that Soccer in the Streets

served. Thus, her constituents could find satisfaction in the program's success.[35]

18.6.2.4   Overcome Resistance to Change

One obstacle all leaders must overcome is resistance to change. Humans are creatures of habit; therefore, even beneficial change is uncomfortable. Transformational leaders must help followers see the need for change.[36] Often, transformational leaders create emotional appeals to overcome resistance. McKenzie is known for her passion. She literally flew around the country, pitching her ideas in one-on-one settings. However, McKenzie also had a background in public relations, which she used to get press coverage for Soccer in the Streets. She openly states that she used the "hype" around the 1994 World Cup to promote the organization.[37] Beane, who is more reserved, used a combination of one-on-one and group interactions to build acceptance of the need for change.

18.6.2.5   Sense of Urgency

Next, transformational leaders must create a sense of urgency in their champions.[38] Throughout the process, champions of the leader's vision will emerge. These champions, often other managers, will become front-line leaders in plan implementation. Often these champions are tasked with generating buy-in from resistant organizational members. A sense of urgency centered on an event or opportunity helps these champions in their task. For McKenzie, the 1994 World Cup was a critical moment because soccer was never more visible in the United States and in the communities she was looking to serve. McKenzie used the World Cup to create a national board that championed Soccer in the Streets around the nation.[39] Beane used the 2002 baseball season to create a sense of urgency. The team had lost a number of important players to teams who had larger budgets than the Athletics during the preceding off-season and were not expected to be competitive in 2002. This provided a window for the Athletics to prove that their new plan could be effective. The Athletics ultimately ended up winning their division in 2002.[40]

18.6.2.6 Adopt an Attitude of Greatness

Transformational leaders adopt an attitude that greatness is achievable and ask all of their followers to seek it.[41] This includes getting others to see greatness in themselves. Beane used the negative projections of the Athletics' prospects for success and the pride that most high-performance athletes have to achieve this idea. Other MLB teams had released many of the players that Beane signed to contracts. Beane let them know he saw greatness in their abilities. McKenzie's focus is on opportunities for greatness in the communities served by Soccer in the Streets. She has created a vision where these communities can rise above the cynical view that others hold of them. Her ultimate goal is for youth who participate in Soccer in the Streets to become leaders themselves.[42] McKenzie retired from Soccer in the Streets, but her vision was carried on by others in the organization.[43]

18.6.2.7 Future Perspective

Transformations cannot be successful unless they are maintained. For a transformational organization, this means adopting broad-based adaptable future perspectives.[44] Soccer in the Streets used its programs to develop leaders that continue to identify needs in the communities it serves. In 2016, Soccer in the Streets launched a new initiative called the Soccer Station program designed to address the lack of green spaces in inner cities, while at the same time providing innovative solutions to the transportation barriers that were identified at the program's outset. As worldwide civil unrest in 2020 placed a spotlight on racial injustice, McKenzie stated, "As we are living in an uncertain time right now, I want the Soccer in the Streets community to know that we are all in this together. Along with the Black Lives Matter movement, it was like what we had back then with drug and crime prevention. Soccer in the Streets now has an opportunity to use the climate of racial division to offer hope to the inner cities."[45]

For Beane and the Oakland Athletics, the transformation has been a continuous process. As clubs with more financial resources saw the Athletics success, they adopted the Athletics methods. In order to maintain their competitive advantage, Beane and his champions continuously refine and tweak their processes. Without this commitment to transformation, the Athletics success would have been short-lived.

18.6.2.8 Build Trust

In order for transformational leaders to be successful, they must build trust.[46] Whether, in the case of Beane, it is asking people who have spent their entire careers in the industry to rethink how goals are achieved, or, in the case of McKenzie, it was asking people to believe in communities that have been written off by most of society, trust is a critical component of success. Neither could have achieved success without others believing in them and their visions. Transformational leaders build trust by providing a voice to their followers, being empathetic to followers' experiences, accepting risks, and empowering others to become leaders.[47]

18.6.2.9 Concentrate Resources

Finally, transformational leaders concentrate resources on areas that need the most change.[48] Following a period in which Soccer in the Streets expanded nationally, the organization refocused its resources back on Atlanta, where it was founded and could make the most impact. As the organization states on its own website,[49] "Over the next decade, the organization refocused its efforts on Atlanta and on creating year-round, innovative programs. In spite of limited resources, Soccer in the Streets continued to serve thousands of kids throughout the metro Atlanta area in schools, parks, and community centers."

18.6.2.10 Outcomes of Transformational Leadership

Transformational leadership shares many of its components with other leadership theories discussed in this chapter, including charismatic leadership. Transformational leadership differs in its focus on building leaders from followers. As seen in the Soccer in the Streets example, McKenzie's vision was carried on after her retirement from the organization. Many of Billy Beane's assistants went on to become leaders of other MLB clubs. Transformational leadership encourages followers to question established ideas, including those of the leader themselves. Compared to other leadership styles, transformational leadership has been shown to effectively improve employees' career satisfaction while having positive impacts on organizational performance.[50] Followers of transformational leaders often hold a very positive view of their leadership teams.[51]

▷ **Moral Leadership** Ability to inspire by providing a virtuous example, guided by higher principles and overarching unselfishness in their actions.

18.7 Moral Leadership

We conclude this chapter by exploring moral leadership concepts. Moral leadership is defined by the leader's ability to provide a virtuous example, guided by higher principles and overarching unselfishness in their actions.[52] Although leaders and organizations can experience success without moral guidance, these organizations also miss out on true optimal performance because their lack of moral standards may push away stakeholders or scandals damage reputations. The International Olympic Committee has seen its reputation hurt by corruption from its leaders and also by its unethical practices regarding sustainability. This has made it harder for the organization to find host sites for future Olympiads. The NCAA has faced constant calls for reform and leadership change due to its treatment of student-athletes. On the other hand, Branch Rickey was able to change the fortunes of the Brooklyn Dodgers when he broke ranks with other MLB owners and began signing Black baseball players to his team. And, the WNBA has seen its fandom grow among groups who appreciate the league's position on social issues.

Because of the impact sport has on society, sports organizations' calls for ethical behavior have been growing.[53] Moral leadership is a critical principle of the positive organizational behavior movement.[54] This section looks at the three major moral leadership theories: authentic leadership, ethical leadership, and servant leadership. As Fig. 18.3 illustrates, all of the moral leadership styles aim to influence moral and ethical behavior by their followers and organizations but are different in their approach. We'll begin by exploring the concept of authentic leadership.

18.7.1 Authentic Leadership

Authentic leadership is the least studied of the moral leadership theories. In many ways, it mirrors transformational leadership.[55] Authentic leaders are also guided by long-term vision and seek to transform their followers into leaders. However, authentic leaders rely less on emotional appeals and individualized relationships, and more on self-awareness and transparency. Authentic leadership emphasizes four characteristics. The first and perhaps the most important characteristic is self-awareness. In other words, authentic leaders spend time getting to know themselves. What are their strengths and weaknesses? What are their beliefs? How do their actions affect others? How do others see them? Why do they want to be a leader? To develop self-awareness, it is important to be honest with yourself and value feedback, even when it is unflattering. Once a person develops self-awareness, they often become more confident because they know their abilities. People with high self-awareness are more consistent in their actions because actions become intentional. Self-awareness also aids in connecting with others because consistent actions develop trust.[56]

The second characteristic of Authentic leadership is an internalized moral perspective. Authentic leaders are guided by their values, and they are highly aware of what is important to their lives. Based on their values, authentic leaders set principles for how they intend to lead others. It is these principles that guide their actions. Along those same lines, authentic leaders set

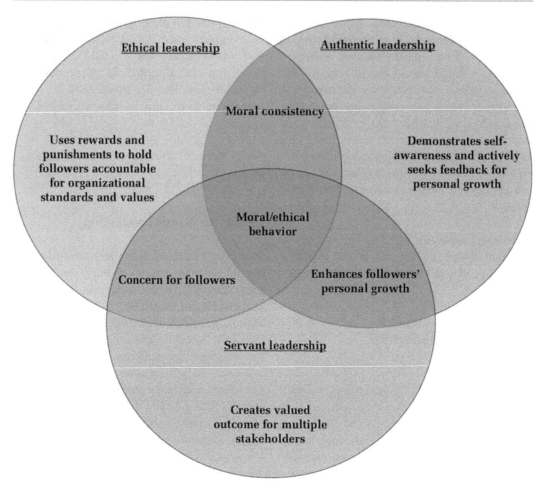

Fig. 18.3 Moral leadership approaches. (Lemoine, G. J., Hartnell, C. A., & Leroy, H. (2019). Taking Stock of Moral Approaches to Leadership: An Integrative Review of Ethical, Authentic, and Servant Leadership. *Academy of Management Annals, 13*, 148–187, https://doi.org/10.5465/annals.2016.0121)

ethical boundaries that limit actions they are willing to take.[57]

The third characteristic of authentic leadership is the unbiased processing of information. As we have seen in Chap. 5, bias influences how people seek and perceive information. To be authentic, people must become aware of their biases and try to interpret information from a neutral perspective. To accomplish this difficult task, authentic leaders must continuously search for information. Authentic leaders often seek feedback from others, including those with different perspectives than their own. In a similar vein, the fourth characteristic relational authenticity relies on the leader's ability to develop open

and honest relationships with both followers and mentors. Authentic leaders are effective because they are viewed as role models by those they lead, but they are also viewed as approachable. Employees working for authentic leaders are often very comfortable sharing their opinions, even when it differs from that of the leader. These elements of authentic leadership are strongly associated with trustworthiness.[58]

18.7.2 Ethical Leadership

Ethical leadership is defined as demonstrating normatively appropriate behavior in one's own life as well as in interpersonal relationships, as well as the promotion of such conduct to followers via communication, reinforcement, and decision-making.[59] The concept of ethical leadership is similar to both authentic leadership, which we just discussed, and servant leadership, which we will discuss next. However, there are critical differences between all three leadership concepts. Authentic leaders rely on ethical consideration when making decisions, but they do not encourage normative conformity. In fact, authentic leaders encourage a questioning attitude, whereas ethical leaders encourage conformity to ethical standards. Ethical leaders may discipline followers who fail to meet espoused standards, making the theory more transactional in nature. Servant leaders also consider moral dilemmas, but, in contrast to ethical leaders, focus on creating rewarding outcomes for followers.[60]

There are two dimensions to ethical leadership: being a moral person and being a moral manager. The moral person dimension concerns an individual's behavior in their personal lives. Moral persons are fair and principled when making decisions and have a deep concern for the society as a whole. Moral managers want their organization and the people within it to maintain high moral standards. They are proactive in their approach and actively attempt to influence the actions of others. Further, moral behavior is a central point of their leadership agenda. Moral managers communicate the importance of values and morality, and vigorously hold others accountable.[61]

One major concern with ethical leadership is that morals are influenced by religious beliefs and societal norms. Ethical leadership, more so than other moral leadership types, pushes for conformity in moral standards.[62] This creates the potential for conflict within an organization based on different perspectives regarding values and morality. For example, a leader who feels all organizational members should stand for the national anthem out of respect for the military may find themselves at odds with organizational members who believe kneeling is a valid form of protest against police brutality. A college coach who ends every practice with prayer may create

conflict with those who have a different belief system than his or her own.

Understanding one's own moral orientation can help avoid conflict. Using world religions and philosophical paradigms, scholars established four moral orientations that can affect ethical leaders' principles and intern their behaviors. Ethical leaders with a humane orientation see others as humans deserving of dignity and respect. By adopting a humane orientation, an ethical leader will be more accepting of others' views and seek to find common ground with those who have a different worldview than their own.[63]

A second orientation is the justice orientation. Ethical leaders with a justice orientation try to avoid discriminating by always seeking fairness and consistency in outcomes. A justice orientation can lead to leaders who are perceived as fair, equitable, and trustworthy by followers.[64] However, justice-oriented leaders must be aware of their biases, which can influence their views of fairness. Justice-oriented leaders must also be aware of situational factors that can affect followers' perceptions of fairness. These can include outside factors like historical and structural prejudices that affect followers' personal and professional lives.

Responsibility and sustainability-oriented ethical leaders hold a broader perspective regarding how their decisions and organizational actions impact their communities. Personal interaction is viewed through the lens of how they affect the long-term health of the community.[65] For example, an ethical leader with a responsibility and sustainability orientation may be more apt to reward employees for developing a zero-waste initiative for an external event than for addressing other moral issues in the office.

The final orientation is the moderation orientation that describes ethical leaders who balance their personal beliefs with organizational objectives and stakeholder desires. A moderation orientation can be extremely effective when leaders can identify which organizational actions to tolerate and which actions to push against.[66] For example, a leader may personally believe that politics should not be discussed in the workplace but be okay with a Black Lives Matter sign being added to the playing surface. At the same time, they would reject an employee who says, "Why can't we have a White Pride Night?" because of the racist messaging.

If an ethical leader with a moderation orientation cannot identify which behaviors deserve tolerance and which do not, they can be subject to a number of negative outcomes. Moral relativism can lead to the leader tolerating immoral behavior because it is good for the organization. For example, many in the Houston Astros organization personally disagreed with the team's uses of sign stealing and other illegal tactics to win baseball games, but did not speak out because "the team was just trying to win games" and the behavior "didn't hurt anyone" or "really effect the outcomes of games." Many leaders have hired or tolerate employees with bigoted beliefs because "they are very effective at their jobs." Further, research has demonstrated that ethical leaders with moderation orientations are in significant danger of developing narcissistic tendencies because of their beliefs that they can manage distinctions between tolerable and intolerable behaviors.[67]

Despite its shortcomings, ethical leadership can be effective as long as leaders maintain self-awareness and cultural awareness. Ethical leadership has been shown to increase employees' commitment, improve individual and organizational performance, and influence employees to engage in organizational citizenship behaviors.[68] Ethical leadership is also relatively under-researched compared to other leadership styles, meaning that we will continue to learn more about its effectiveness.

18.7.3 Servant Leadership

Servant leaders are guided by an unwavering commitment to serve others. In an organizational setting, this includes serving colleagues as well as those who you are in charge of, as well as customers, stakeholders, and community members.[69] Power and influence, which are strong motivators for many leaders, are not strong motivators for

servant leaders. Power and influence are acquired by followers' perceptions of the servant leader as a role model to emulate. Servant leadership is characterized by several important components.[70]

- *Place Service Before Self-Interest*: The primary motivation of a servant leader is to help others. In order to help others, the leader takes interest in others and attempts to satisfy their needs. To the servant leader, serving others is a moral obligation, even if the leader's actions are outside of the organization's goals.
- *Developing Other People*: The servant leader empowers others to become leaders through mentoring, coaching, and sharing decision-making roles. Servant leaders are very transparent and share information so that others can make informed decisions that are then supported by the leader. These behaviors are designed to instill self-confidence and feelings of empowerment in others.
- *Active Listening*: Servant leaders are active listeners. They want to know and understand the challenges faced by others. They want to know others' personal and career goals so that they can help the follower achieve their desires.
- *Humility*: Servant leaders understand their own limitations as well as the benefits of allowing others to demonstrate their expertise. When credit comes for accomplishment, servant leaders ensure that others are awarded recognition for their contributions. The servant leader is also quick to highlight the impact others have had on his or her success.
- *Build Trust*: For servant leadership to be successful, the leader must build trust with followers. Servant leaders are honest in their assessment of others but are generous in their offers to assist. They welcome two-way feedback and value criticism.
- *Focus on What Can Be Accomplished*: Despite their idealistic nature, servant leaders understand that neither they nor their organization can accomplish everything. Instead, servant leaders focus on the most pressing needs

before them. Sometimes this focus means that other goals are ignored.

- *Empathy*: Servant leaders demonstrate great empathy for the lives of those they lead. It is not uncommon for a servant leader to encourage an employee to focus on a personal need even if it interferes with their work.
- *Acceptance*: Servant leaders accept others for who they are.
- *Stewardship*: While servant leaders are quick to defer credit, they are also willing to put the responsibility for success on their own shoulders. This alleviates pressure from others.

Servant leaders are sometimes criticized for appearing passive or uninterested in their own success. Yet, true servant leaders have to be supremely driven and proactive to manage the strenuous undertaking that comes with placing others before yourself. While many may seek to be servant leaders, it is an incredibly difficult leadership style that many cannot live up to. However, many benefits come from effective servant leadership. In addition to positive outcomes like committed and satisfied employees, employees are also often motivated to go above and beyond their positional roles (organizational citizenship) and demonstrate innovative behaviors.[71]

18.7.3.1 Servant Leadership in Sport

Despite the challenges faced with implementing servant leadership, its potential to be an effective paradigm in sport has been recognized. Many sport organizations contain elements of service within their missions. Sport for development and peace-based organizations are built around the concept of servant leadership. This has led to calls for organizations within this segment of the sports industry to adopt servant leadership principles throughout their leadership teams.[72] Sport management scholars have also opined that servant leadership has great potential to improve ethical climates in sport organization offices[73] and to improve ethical issues in coaching.[74]

18.8 Summary

Leadership is a tricky issue to discuss. It is incredibly important, but even experts disagree on what it takes to be a great leader. It is true that some people have natural gifts that help them influence others, but, as you can see, there are many ways leaders can have a positive impact on others. Hopefully, as you read this chapter, you learned some ways that you can be a leader. The moral leadership theories, especially authentic leadership and servant leadership, provide examples of how one can be a leader by being true to oneself. Moving forward, expect more sport organizations to adopt servant leadership principles that are in line with their organizational missions.

Discussion Questions

1. Can you name someone in your life that you think of as a leader? What makes them a leader? Which theory(ies) match their leadership style?
2. Being honest with yourself, where do you fall on the Managerial Grid? What do you think about that assessment?
3. Which of the leadership theories do you find most useful for your journey? Why?
4. Select a segment of the sports industry that you think could be improved through servant leadership. Explain your answer.

Notes

1. House, R., Javidan, M., & Dorfman, P. (2001). Project GLOBE: An introduction. *Applied Psychology, 50*(4), 489–505.
2. Nayer, V. (2013, August 2). Three differences between managers and leaders. *Harvard Business Review*. Retrieved from https://hbr.org/2013/08/tests-of-a-leadership-transiti.
3. Krapfl, J. E., & Kruja, B. (2015). Leadership and Culture. *Journal of Organizational Behavior Management, 35*(1–2), 28–43. https://doi.org/10.1080/01608061.2015.1031431.
4. Jago, A. G. (1982). Leadership: Perspectives in theory and research. *Management Science, 28*(3), 315–336.
5. Hitt, M. A., Miller, C. C., Colella, A., Triana, M. (2017). *Organizational Behavior* (5th ed.). Wiley.

6. Colbert, A. E., Judge, T. A., Choi, D., & Wang, G. (2012). Assessing the trait theory of leadership using self and observer ratings of personality: The mediating role of contributions to group success. *The Leadership Quarterly, 23*(4), 670–685.

7. McCrae, R. R., & Costa, P. T. (1997). Personality trait structure as a human universal. *American Psychologist, 52*(5), 509–516.

8. Kirkpatric, S. A., & Locke, E. A. (1991). Leadership: Do traits matter? *Academy of Management Executive, 5*(2), 48–60.

9. Robbins, S. P., & Judge, T. A. (2019). *Organizational Behavior* (18th ed.). Pearson.

10. Hitt, M. A., Miller, C. C., Colella, A., & Triana, M. (2017). *Organizational Behavior* (5th ed.). Wiley.

11. Goleman, D. (2006). *Emotional intelligence.* Bantam.

12. Yeow, J., & Martin, R. (2013). The role of self-regulation in developing leaders: A longitudinal field experiment. *The Leadership Quarterly, 24*(5), 625–637.

13. Stogdill, R. M., & Coons, A. E. (1957). *Leader behavior: Its description and measurement.*

14. Hitt, M. A., Miller, C. C., Colella, A., & Triana, M. (2017). *Organizational Behavior* (5th ed.). Wiley; Robbins, S. P., & Judge, T. A. (2019). *Organizational Behavior* (18th ed.). Pearson.

15. Likert, R. (1950). *The Leadership Studies at the University of Michigan.* Michigan, United States: University of Michigan.

16. Blake, R. R., & Mouton, J. S. (1982). A comparative analysis of situationalism and 9,9 management by principle. *Organizational Dynamics, 10*(4), 20–43.

17. Dubrin, A. J. (2010). *Leadership: Research Findings, Practice, and Skills* (6th ed.). Cengage; Robbins, S. P., & Judge, T. A. (2019). *Organizational Behavior* (18th ed.). Pearson.

18. Dubrin, A. J. (2010). *Leadership: Research Findings, Practice, and Skills* (6th ed.). Cengage; Robbins, S. P., & Judge, T. A. (2019). *Organizational Behavior* (18th ed.). Pearson.

19. Dubrin, A. J. (2010). *Leadership: Research Findings, Practice, and Skills* (6th ed.). Cengage; Robbins, S. P., & Judge, T. A. (2019). *Organizational Behavior* (18th ed.). Pearson.

20. Dubrin, A. J. (2010). *Leadership: Research Findings, Practice, and Skills* (6th ed.). Cengage; Robbins, S. P., & Judge, T. A. (2019). *Organizational Behavior* (18th ed.). Pearson.

21. Salas-Vallina, A., Simone, C., & Fernández-Guerrero, R. (2020). The human side of leadership: Inspirational leadership effects on follower characteristics and happiness at work (HAW). *Journal of Business Research, 107*, 162–171.

22. Dubrin, A. J. (2010). *Leadership: Research Findings, Practice, and Skills* (6th ed.). Cengage; Robbins, S. P., & Judge, T. A. (2019). *Organizational Behavior* (18th ed.). Pearson.

23. Robbins, S. P., & Judge, T. A. (2019). Organizational Behavior (18th ed.). Pearson.

24. Shamir, B., House, R. J., & Arthur, M. B. (1993). The motivational effects of charismatic leadership: A self-concept based theory. *Organization Science, 4*(4), 577–594.

25. Robbins, S. P., & Judge, T. A. (2019). Organizational Behavior (18th ed.). Pearson.

26. Dubrin, A. J. (2010). *Leadership: Research Findings, Practice, and Skills* (6th ed.). Cengage.

27. Lewis, M. (2003). *Moneyball: The Art of Winning an Unfair Game.* W.W. Norton & Company.

28. Dubrin, A. J. (2010). *Leadership: Research Findings, Practice, and Skills* (6th ed.). Cengage.

29. Soccer in the Streets (n.d.). *The Success of Soccer in the Streets: Q&A with Founder Carolyn McKenzie.* Retrieved from https://www.soccerstreets.org/history.

30. Dubrin, A. J. (2010). *Leadership: Research Findings, Practice, and Skills* (6th ed.). Cengage.

31. Soccer in the Streets (n.d.). *The Success of Soccer in the Streets: Q&A with Founder Carolyn McKenzie.* Retrieved from https://www.soccerstreets.org/history.

32. Lewis, M. (2003). *Moneyball: The Art of Winning an Unfair Game.* W.W. Norton & Company.

33. Burns, J. M. (1978). *Leadership, Harper and Row.* New York, NY; Dubrin, A. J. (2010) *Leadership: Research Findings, Practice, and Skills* (6th ed.). Cengage.

34. Lewis, M. (2003). *Moneyball: The Art of Winning an Unfair Game.* W.W. Norton & Company.

35. Soccer in the Streets (n.d.). *The Success of Soccer in the Streets: Q&A with Founder Carolyn McKenzie.* Retrieved from https://www.soccerstreets.org/history.

36. Dubrin, A. J. (2010). *Leadership: Research Findings, Practice, and Skills* (6th ed.). Cengage; Tichy, N. M., & Devanna, M. A. (1990), *The Transformational Leader,* Wiley, New York, NY.

37. Soccer in the Streets (n.d.). *The Success of Soccer in the Streets: Q&A with Founder Carolyn McKenzie.* Retrieved from https://www.soccerstreets.org/history.

38. Tichy, N. M., & Devanna, M. A. (1990), *The Transformational Leader,* Wiley, New York, NY.

39. Soccer in the Streets (n.d.). *The Success of Soccer in the Streets: Q&A with Founder Carolyn McKenzie.* Retrieved from https://www.soccerstreets.org/history.

40. Lewis, M. (2003). *Moneyball: The Art of Winning an Unfair Game.* W.W. Norton & Company.

41. Dubrin, A. J. (2010). *Leadership: Research Findings, Practice, and Skills* (6th ed.). Cengage.

42. Soccer in the Streets (n.d.). *The Success of Soccer in the Streets: Q&A with Founder Carolyn McKenzie.* Retrieved from https://www.soccerstreets.org/history.

43. Bevington, R., & Saliby, S. (2019, June 9). Soccer in the streets celebrates 30 years of youth development in Atlanta. *Georgia Public Broadcasting.* Retrieved from https://www.gpb.org/news/2019/06/09/soccer-in-the-streets-celebrates-30-years-of-youth-development-in-atlanta.

44. Dubrin, A. J. (2010). *Leadership: Research Findings, Practice, and Skills* (6th ed.). Cengage.

45. Soccer in the Streets (n.d.). The Success of Soccer in the Streets: Q&A with Founder Carolyn McKenzie. Retrieved from https://www.soccerstreets.org/history.

46. Dubrin, A. J. (2010). *Leadership: Research Findings, Practice, and Skills* (6th ed.). Cengage.
47. Tichy, N. M., & Devanna, M. A. (1990), *The Transformational Leader,* Wiley, New York, NY.
48. Dubrin, A. J. (2010). *Leadership: Research Findings, Practice, and Skills* (6th ed.). Cengage.
49. Soccer in the Streets (n.d.). The Success of Soccer in the Streets: Q&A with Founder Carolyn McKenzie. Retrieved from https://www.soccerstreets.org/history.
50. Burton, L. J., & Peachey, J. W. (2009). Transactional or transformational? Leadership preferences of Division III athletic administrators. *Journal of Intercollegiate Sport, 2,* 245–259; Kim, S., Magnusen, M. J., Andrew, D. P. S., & Stoll, J. (2012). Are transformational leaders a double-edged sword? Impact of transformational leadership on sport employee commitment and job satisfaction. *International Journal of Sports Science & Coaching, 7*(4), 661–676.
51. Burton, L. J., & Peachey, J. W. (2009). Transactional or transformational? Leadership preferences of Division III athletic administrators. *Journal of Intercollegiate Sport, 2,* 245–259.
52. Gini, A. (1997). Moral leadership: An overview. *Journal of Business Ethics, 16*(3), 323–330. https://doi.org/10.1023/A:1017959915472.
53. Burton, L., & Welty Peachey, J. (2013). The call for servant leadership in intercollegiate athletics. *Quest, 65*(3), 354–371. https://doi.org/10.1080/00336297.2013.791870.
54. Nelson, D. L. & Cooper, C. L. (Eds.) (2007). *Positive organizational behavior.* London: SAGE Publications Ltd. https://doi.org/10.4135/9781446212752.
55. Sidani, Y. F., & Rowe, W. G. (2018). A reconceptualization of authentic leadership: Leader legitimation via follower-centered assessment of the moral dimension. *The Leadership Quarterly, 29,* 623–636.
56. AOM Insights (2019). Why moral leadership matters. *Academy of Management Insights* Retrieved from https://journals.aom.org/doi/epub/10.5465/annals.2016.0121.summary; George, B., & Sims, P. (2007). *True* North. Wiley; Lemoine, G. J., Hartnell, C. A., & Leroy, H. (2019). Taking Stock of Moral Approaches to Leadership: An Integrative Review of Ethical, Authentic, and Servant Leadership. *Academy of Management Annals, 13,* 148–187, https://doi.org/10.5465/annals.2016.0121.
57. AOM Insights (2019). Why moral leadership matters. *Academy of Management Insights* Retrieved from https://journals.aom.org/doi/epub/10.5465/annals.2016.0121.summary; George, B., & Sims, P. (2007) *True* North. Wiley; Lemoine, G. J., Hartnell, C. A., & Leroy, H. (2019). Taking Stock of Moral Approaches to Leadership: An Integrative Review of Ethical, Authentic, and Servant Leadership. *Academy of Management Annals, 13,* 148–187, https://doi.org/10.5465/annals.2016.0121.
58. AOM Insights (2019). Why moral leadership matters. *Academy of Management Insights* Retrieved from https://journals.aom.org/doi/epub/10.5465/annals.2016.0121.summary; George, B., & Sims, P. (2007). *True* North. Wiley; Lemoine, G. J., Hartnell, C. A., & Leroy, H. (2019). Taking Stock of Moral Approaches to Leadership: An Integrative Review of Ethical, Authentic, and Servant Leadership. *Academy of Management Annals, 13,* 148–187, https://doi.org/10.5465/annals.2016.0121.
59. Brown, M. E., Treviño, L. K., & Harrison, D. A. (2005). Ethical leadership: A social learning perspective for construct development and testing. *Organizational Behavior and Human Decision Processes, 97,* 117–134.
60. AOM Insights (2019). Why moral leadership matters. *Academy of Management Insights* Retrieved from https://journals.aom.org/doi/epub/10.5465/annals.2016.0121.summary; George, B., & Sims, P. (2007). *True* North. Wiley; Lemoine, G. J., Hartnell, C. A., & Leroy, H. (2019). Taking Stock of Moral Approaches to Leadership: An Integrative Review of Ethical, Authentic, and Servant Leadership. *Academy of Management Annals, 13,* 148–187, https://doi.org/10.5465/annals.2016.0121.
61. Brown, M. E., Treviño, L. K., & Harrison, D. A. 2005. Ethical leadership: A social learning perspective for construct development and testing. *Organizational Behavior and Human Decision Processes, 97,* 117–134.
62. Brown, M. E., & Treviño, L. K. (2006). Ethical leadership: A review and future directions. Leadership Quarterly, 17(6), 595–616. https://doi.org/10.1016/j.leaqua.2006.10.004; Eisenbeiss, S. A. (2012). Re-thinking ethical leadership: An interdisciplinary integrative approach. *Leadership Quarterly, 23*(5), 791–808. https://doi.org/10.1016/j.leaqua.2012.03.001.
63. Eisenbeiss, S. A. (2012). Re-thinking ethical leadership: An interdisciplinary integrative approach. *Leadership Quarterly, 23*(5), 791–808.
64. Xu, A. J., Loi, R., & Ngo, H.-Y. (2016). Ethical Leadership Behavior and Employee Justice Perceptions: The Mediating Role of Trust in Organization. *Journal of Business Ethics, 134*(3): 493–504.
65. Wart, M. Van. (2014). Contemporary varieties of ethical leadership in organizations. *International Journal of Business Administration, 5*(5), 27–45. https://doi.org/10.5430/ijba.v5n5p27.
66. Wart, M. Van. (2014). Contemporary varieties of ethical leadership in organizations. *International Journal of Business Administration, 5*(5), 27–45. https://doi.org/10.5430/ijba.v5n5p27.
67. Eisenbeiss, S. A. (2012). Re-thinking ethical leadership: An interdisciplinary integrative approach. *Leadership Quarterly, 23*(5), 791–808. https://doi.org/10.1016/j.leaqua.2012.03.001.
68. Brown, M. E., & Treviño, L. K. (2006). Ethical leadership: A review and future directions. *Leadership Quarterly, 17*(6), 595–616. https://doi.org/10.1016/j.leaqua.2006.10.004; Lemoine, G. J., Hartnell, C. A.,

& Leroy, H. (2019). Taking stock of moral approaches to leadership: An integrative review of ethical, authentic, and servant leadership. *Academy of Management Annals, 13*(1), 148–187. https://doi.org/10.5465/annals.2016.0121.

69. AOM Insights (2019). Why moral leadership matters. *Academy of Management Insights* Retrieved from https://journals.aom.org/doi/epub/10.5465/annals.2016.0121.summary; George, B., & Sims, P. (2007). *True* North. Wiley; Lemoine, G. J., Hartnell, C. A., & Leroy, H. (2019). Taking Stock of Moral Approaches to Leadership: An Integrative Review of Ethical, Authentic, and Servant Leadership. *Academy of Management Annals, 13*, 148–187, https://doi.org/10.5465/annals.2016.0121.

70. Van Dierendonck, D., & Nuijten, I. (2011). The servant leadership survey: Development and validation of a multidimensional measure. *Journal of business and psychology, 26*(3), 249–267.

71. AOM Insights (2019). Why moral leadership matters. *Academy of Management Insights* Retrieved from https://journals.aom.org/doi/epub/10.5465/annals.2016.0121.summary; George, B., & Sims, P. (2007). *True* North. Wiley; Lemoine, G. J., Hartnell, C. A., & Leroy, H. (2019). Taking Stock of Moral

Approaches to Leadership: An Integrative Review of Ethical, Authentic, and Servant Leadership. *Academy of Management Annals, 13*, 148–187, https://doi.org/10.5465/annals.2016.0121.

72. Welty Peachey, J., & Burton, L. (2017). Servant leadership in sport for development and peace: A way forward. *Quest, 69*(1), 125–139.

73. Burton, L., & Welty Peachey, J. (2013). The call for servant leadership in intercollegiate athletics. *Quest, 65*(3), 354–371; Burton, L. J., Peachey, J. W., & Wells, J. E. (2017). The role of servant leadership in developing an ethical climate in sport organizations. *Journal of Sport Management, 31*(3), 229–240; Lee, Y. H. (2019). Emotional intelligence, servant leadership, and development goal orientation in athletic directors. *Sport Management Review, 22*(3), 395–406.

74. Hammermeister, J., Burton, D., Pickering, M., Chase, M., Westre, K., & Baldwin, N. (2008). Servant-leadership in sport: A concept whose time has arrived. *The International Journal of Servant-Leadership, 4*(1), 185–215; Rieke, M., Hammermeister, J., & Chase, M. (2008). Servant leadership in sport: A new paradigm for effective coach behavior. *International Journal of Sports Science & Coaching, 3*(2), 227–239.

Index[1]

---

[1]Note: Page numbers followed by 'n' refer to notes.

Printed in the USA
CPSIA information can be obtained
at www.ICGtesting.com
CBHW082141230724
12043CB00012B/648